W9-CRO-156

The Little
Book of
Big Ethical
Questions

Also by Susan Liautaud

The Power of Ethics

The Little
Book of
Big Ethical
Questions

Susan Liautaud

**SIMON &
SCHUSTER**

London · New York · Sydney · Toronto · New Delhi

First published in the United States by Simon & Schuster, Inc., 2022
First published in Great Britain by Simon & Schuster UK Ltd, 2022

Copyright © Susan Liautaud, 2022

The right of Susan Liautaud to be identified as the author
of this work has been asserted in accordance with the
Copyright, Designs and Patents Act, 1988.

1 3 5 7 9 10 8 6 4 2

Simon & Schuster UK Ltd
1st Floor
222 Gray's Inn Road
London WC1X 8HB

www.simonandschuster.co.uk
www.simonandschuster.com.au
www.simonandschuster.co.in

Simon & Schuster Australia, Sydney
Simon & Schuster India, New Delhi

The author and publishers have made all reasonable efforts
to contact copyright-holders for permission, and apologise
for any omissions or errors in the form of credits given.
Corrections may be made to future printings.

A CIP catalogue record for this book
is available from the British Library

Hardback ISBN: 978-1-4711-8863-3
eBook ISBN: 978-1-4711-8865-7

Interior design by Paul Dippolito

Printed in the UK by CPI Group (UK) Ltd, Croydon, CR0 4YY

To Luca, Olivia, Parker, Alexa, Cristo, and Bernard: This is for you.

And for all of you who try hard to make ethical choices and engage in thoughtful conversation: my deepest admiration and hope that this book will support you and give you the courage to create your best stories.

Contents

CHAPTER 2: POLITICS, COMMUNITY, AND CULTURE

Contents · xi

CHAPTER 3: WORK

CHAPTER 4: TECHNOLOGY

CHAPTER 5: CONSUMER CHOICES

CHAPTER 6: HEALTH

The Little
Book of
Big Ethical
Questions

Introduction:
Ethics for Everyone

I was at a casual outdoor dinner with family and friends when someone pointed to the Impossible Burger on the menu. We all realized that despite seeing it advertised everywhere, we had no idea what was in it (soy and potatoes, with a plant-based molecule called heme for taste, created by Stanford University biochemist and Impossible Foods founder Patrick O. Brown), the true health benefits (good for a low-cholesterol or weight loss diet?), the cost (about the same as the beef burger on this menu), or environmental impact (all positive or unexpected negatives?).

How often do we find ourselves assessing the ethical stakes of day-to-day questions, from health to the environment to the economy—frequently without the information we need?

As we caught up on life and the news, and shared a taste of the Impossible Burger and some good wine, our discussion wandered from whether we were comfortable buying from a company with a track record of treating its employees poorly to the Netflix film about the college cheating scandal—*Operation Varsity Blues*—to one friend's employer now requiring Covid-19 vaccinations to return to the office . . . then back to the intensely personal . . .

questions about aging parents and a sibling's partner's secrets. The conversation was spirited and fun . . . yet thoughtful and great learning.

We confront choices every day involving ethical challenges that we don't know enough about—choices that affect our health, families and friends, work, technology, and our impact on the world. Sometimes we're alone in grappling with a question. Often these dilemmas lead to conversations with others.

The Little Book of Big Ethical Questions will guide you when you're on your own, as well as spur conversations in the company of others. Scenario by scenario the book will show you (and whomever you're talking to) how to consider your decisions even when you are confused, lack information, or feel intimidated by a complicated or cutting-edge tech issue. You don't need to be an expert: in fact, that's the point. I don't need to understand how an internal combustion engine works to know that I don't want a twelve-year-old obtaining a driver's license. I don't have to be conversant with code to worry about the potential mental health and addictive consequences of social media.

Some of the questions in the pages that follow are personal, involving family, friends, health, spirituality, emotions, or ambitions. Can we be friends with someone whose political views diverge strongly from our own? Should you take away the car keys from an elderly parent? Do you tell your best friend that their spouse is having an affair? Others are workplace dilemmas—challenges with colleagues and bosses, career choices. Should employers be able to consider a candidate's social media posts when recruiting? Should unconscious bias training be required annually? Still others relate to clarifying our opinions about the news and the world around us. Should voting be mandatory? Should we hire robots to care for the elderly? And then there are those occasions when we're called on to offer advice—considering our own views, while helping others to make the decisions they feel are best for them. The bottom line is ethics touch every aspect of our lives and our relationships. In one way or another, every decision we make matters.

My goal in this book is to *democratize ethics*: to make ethics accessible to people from all backgrounds and all walks of life; to help you experience how much power you have to make a difference in your own life and in the world around you.

The Questions

The pages that follow set out more than seventy questions to share and debate with friends, family, and colleagues—over dinner, on a Zoom call, while waiting for a train or a meeting to start, during a workout, on a walk—or to ponder on your own. All look to strengthen your *connection* with others, including those whose views differ from your own. All spur us to refine our understanding of ourselves.

Each question is paired with an exploration that includes practical points, guidance about how to prioritize what matters most, and hopeful paths forward while steering clear of blame, shame, fear, and guilt. Although organized by topic, the questions can be read in any order. The learning and insights I try to tease out in each question apply to many of the others.

Some of the questions require deeper thought. Others model "ethics on the fly"—decisions made quickly when you don't have much time, or don't need more information.

My hope is that, question by question, you will pick up themes and tips that will guide you with respect to *any* dilemma you face in your life or see on the news. You will also consider different perspectives on the issues explored that will help you shape how you view, and engage with, the world.

Some questions may seem deceptively simple at first glance. The explorations are designed to challenge the instinctive knee-jerk answer that skips over critical nuance and consequence.

I don't claim to have all the answers. In fact, often there isn't one right answer. I invite you to be my ethics sparring partner. Together we'll grapple with the issues and discover the best answers and reasoning *for you*. The questions in the book give us permission to err—while holding ourselves and others to a higher standard.

A Few Conversation Guidelines

- Don't look at these as "yes or no" questions. Look instead for the *opportunities and risks* of a decision.

- Start with *facts*. There is no such thing as alternative facts—with ethics or anything else.

- Watch for *assumptions* such as best guesses, gut instinct, relying on unverified social media posts, or confusing gossip with reliable data.

- Consider your decision from the perspective of the person most adversely affected by it. *What would it be like to be them?* Then imagine that person is you.

- Keep an *open mind*. Ethical solutions can lurk in unexpected places. And we all have *conscious and unconscious bias*.

- *Eliminate the word "perfect"* from your vocabulary. Surprisingly, striving for perfection can be a driver of unethical behavior and lead to toxic blaming, shaming, and guilt. We all err from time to time. My hand goes up first.

Sometimes we think that in grappling with ethical questions, our good character is enough. It's not: *ethics happen when character meets situations.* Whatever our character may be, we're only as ethical as our last decision.

So as you turn the pages of *The Little Book of Big Ethical Questions*, enjoy. Ponder. Share. Listen. Debate. Challenge. Trust . . . and test . . . yourself, with your friends and family, as well as in chance encounters. One conundrum at a time.

Chapter 1

Family and Friends

Could you be friends with someone whose political views differ from your own?

In the lead-up to the June 2016 Brexit vote in the United Kingdom about whether or not the United Kingdom should exit the European Union, family relationships and friendships began to show signs of stress. For some, the Brexit vote cut to the core of their—and their nation's—identity and autonomy. For others, economics, trade, the future of the younger generation, education, national security, and more were at stake. Additionally, the mix of views suffered from distorted information, fueling racism and anti-immigrant sentiments. Still, I found it difficult to believe that families were not speaking to one another, or worse, over a political matter.

Fast-forward to the highly contentious November 2020 U.S. presidential election. Many supporters of candidate Biden felt that under then President Trump we had lost our American integrity and global reputation—both the "soul of the nation" and the very foundations of democracy. Many supporters of President Trump claimed, like

Brexiteers, that American identity and "greatness" were at stake. Relationships among friends, colleagues, and family members across the country were fraying under the keenly felt strain of political polarization.

Exploration

This question probes the ethical foundations of friendship. When relationships collide with some of the most contentious issues in modern society, topics that at first might have seemed abstract rapidly become personal.

Friendship doesn't require friends to agree with each other on everything. Presumably, you didn't become friends with someone solely because of their political perspective. Friendships result in a fundamental human connection that can far outlast our political views, which can change or become outdated over time.

Moreover, expressing political views and voting constitute free speech, a pillar of democracy. Friendships (and society) are strengthened by both the exchange of ideas and engagement with people with whom we disagree— even vehemently. Information silos are one of the most powerful spreaders of unethical behavior. Doris Kearns Goodwin's award-winning biography of Abraham Lincoln, *Team of Rivals*, reminds us that our most ethical selves can emerge from intentionally engaging with those challenging our views, just as President Lincoln established a cabinet of rivals. Do we want our friendships to be judged based on how well our political views align? Or do we want to share our life experiences with humility, open-mindedness, and vulnerability? The latter option allows our friends to point out where they think we'd benefit from thinking again (even if we dig in our heels before doing so).

Recently, I must admit that this general view has challenged me more than at any other time in my life, because disregarding truth has become normal in politics. Increasingly, votes on political issues are seen as so important and defining that voting has become a choice between two sides: politics versus relationships. The distance between who we are and who our friends are, and who or what they voted for, has narrowed.

How do we reconcile our friendship with sometimes extreme politics? I believe we owe friends honesty about our own views, and the respect to not shame or condemn theirs except in extraordinary circumstances. As a practical matter, many people strike a balance with a friend whom they disagree with on a particular subject: they just don't talk about certain issues and focus instead on the many points they have in common. This is also a good approach for work, where others may feel uncomfortable engaging in discussions about politics.

There are limits, however. Because of my principles, I might part ways with a friend who goes so far as to support inciting violence or harming others. Lying about the results of a democratically held election is a close second, because if the person is willing to lie about such an important proven fact I might wonder in what other areas they ignore the truth in favor of the results they prefer.

Should you take away the car keys from an elderly parent whose driving may be unsafe?

A close friend was worried about her elderly father driving. His driving skills and attention to the road had diminished over the years. She raised her concerns with him repeatedly, but he refused to consider giving up driving. His ability to drive gave him a sense of independence that was important to him.

One day, my friend knew her father was going to the doctor for an appointment and decided to force his hand. She called the police to stop him (keenly aware that his driving would be erratic), and they arrived just as he was pulling out of the driveway. They administered a test, which he failed, so they took away his driver's license. He was unhappy, but it ultimately solved the problem.

Exploration

This question boils down to a potential conflict among key principles: safety, respect, and autonomy. Is it more important for the individual and the public to be safe, or for an individual to have the freedom and autonomy to do as they please? Other principles can be applied as well: courage, responsibility, truth, and compassionate nonjudgment. To navigate this balancing act, consider the *potential consequences* to the other stakeholders. If you don't take the keys away, are there outcomes you couldn't live with? Consider injury to your parents, and impact on anyone else on the road—not to mention *their* parents, children, and loved ones—and how you and your parents would feel if someone was badly injured.

One challenge this question spotlights is informed consent. In this case, you have all the information you need, so the "informed" part of informed consent isn't an issue. But obtaining consent—asking a parent to give up freedom, and accept the reality of age-related concerns—is challenging. For many, it's the first time an adult child may have to look after or "parent" their parents. Remind your parents of the risks and responsibilities, so they understand what is at stake. Be as specific as possible—a baby carriage being pushed across the street, a cyclist edging into the road, a jogger who crosses an intersection quickly . . . Ask them to consider how they would feel if they harmed someone else.

Even well-intentioned choices (postponing the discussion) can spread unethical behavior and breed a tolerance or normalization of potentially harmful behavior. Skewed incentives (our parent's desire to remain independent, and our desire to avoid a difficult, emotional conversation) are one force that fuels this contagion. But it is possible to create positive contagion as well, starting with having conversations with your parents or relatives about when it is the right time to stop driving . . . and hoping that others follow your good practice.

If possible, seek alternatives and blended solutions. Elderly adults can maintain autonomy by using a rideshare service, a taxi service, or public transportation. Or, if they have the resources, your parent could pay someone to drive them on a regular basis to the stores they want to patronize, a friend's house, or a religious service. A parent may also have friends who are safe drivers who can assist. Finally, you can call on the authorities as a neutral arbiter where it might help—for example, taking them for a voluntary driver's license renewal test that you're concerned they would fail.

Even easing into a difficult decision is better than doing nothing. Perhaps they will agree to no longer drive at night, or on the highway, or during rush hour. We might be under the impression that if we don't attempt to take away the car keys of an elderly parent who is no longer safe behind the wheel, we haven't made a decision. But of course, not making a decision is *also* a decision. We have decided not to intervene and leave open the possibility that they could get into a serious accident, injuring themselves—or innocent others.

Are you ethically obligated to help a neighbor?

A friend of someone I know—I'll call her Monica—lives next to an elderly woman in the Pacific Northwest. The elderly woman doesn't have much of a local support system, so one day she asked Monica for a favor. That favor has morphed into Monica driving her to doctor appointments, picking up her prescriptions, and checking in on her during the Covid-19 pandemic. Monica was torn between how much she should support her, versus how that physical support impacts the safety of her own family and children. She helped her neighbor set up a cell phone, calls her regularly, and stops in when she can.

Attempting to balance helping her neighbor with her own needs and responsibilities as a mother is a challenge. But Monica knows she would feel terrible if something happened to her neighbor because she hadn't been able to lend a hand. And she is trying to navigate whether the fact that someone lives close by matters to the ethics of our decisions—how we define "neighbor" in a Zoom-connected world.

Various books of the Hebrew and Christian bibles, from Leviticus to Galatians, from Matthew to Mark, proclaim

"Love thy neighbor as thyself." Buddhism highlights compassion and our connection to each other. The Fourteenth Dalai Lama says, "The more we care for the happiness of others, the greater our own sense of well-being becomes."

Exploration

Whatever the circumstances of your neighbor in need, in considering the question, start with an ethics triage, as if you were in an emergency room. Are the consequences of not helping a neighbor important and irreparable—such as a person falling gravely ill, or a young child being left unattended? Are you *able* to help—physically, practically, financially? For meeting many needs, living next door likely puts you in a unique position.

If you do decide to help set limits at the start: be specific about what you can and cannot do (feed the dog for three days, pick up prescriptions for the next month, or bring dinner several times, rather than "help out for a while" or "shop for food until a family member arrives from out of state"). Doing so sets expectations and establishes boundaries. If you prioritize kindness, compassion, and generosity, helping your neighbor may help reinforce the kind of person you want to be.

Nonetheless, we are not required to put ourselves at risk of harm, such as entering the home of someone with an infectious disease or stepping in to stop physical violence.

When you have fulfilled your offer to help, communicate that clearly. You are not obligated to continue. Sometimes the most effective help you can offer is to assist your neighbor in finding more sustainable alternatives—from home delivery services or maintenance providers to at-home care or other friends or family members. Or calling the authorities in the case of domestic violence.

I believe that we should try to contribute to the common good, particularly when we have the time, expertise, and resources to do so. There is an expectation that neighbors take care of one another. But no one has the resources to help everyone all of the time. And there's no right way to define what a "neighbor" is or how to contribute. The person living next door may be a relative stranger, while a friend across town (or even at the other end of a Zoom call) is more of a real neighbor than those across the street. Additionally, you may be better able to offer a particular kind of help other than the requested task. In situations like this, we can proactively propose alternative help that we *can* provide.

I avoid considering why and how someone ended up in difficulty: once someone is in need, whether because of an accident, a health problem, or an unfortunate circumstance, the cause is less important than a forward-looking view of consequences of their situation and the provision, or not, of help. We are all susceptible of ethical mishaps. Keeping someone safe from contagious illnesses can prevent the spread in the wider community. Helping a neighbor can spur others to do the same, causing our actions to ripple outward and inspire others.

Are you ethically bound to pay for your uninsured sibling's medical care for a serious illness or accident?

David was taken aback. His older sister, whom he hadn't spoken to much in recent years apart from birthdays and holidays, had called to let him know that she had been diagnosed with breast cancer. Her oncologist wanted to schedule surgery, to be followed by extensive treatment. But what threw David even more was that his sister confided that she didn't have health insurance. A single mother with two teenage sons, she worked as a freelance publicist and didn't have much in the way of savings or retirement funds. Nonetheless, she took her kids on expensive vacations for many years. When pressed, she would tell David she was only fifty, and that she had plenty of years left.

Without health insurance, David realized that her medical bills would be more than she could handle. And she had no one else to turn to. Her marriage had ended acrimoniously, and their parents were no longer alive. When his sister talked about putting off the surgery for a few months, he felt an obligation to help out. David and his husband didn't have a lot, but he knew he could tap into his retirement account. Thinking about it made him angry, though. He and his husband had always been so frugal with their expenses, savings, and mortgage—and his sister hadn't been as responsible.

Exploration

The key issues here are your relationship with the individual (how close you are—or not), kinship (however you define family, not limited to biological relationships), how deserving you feel someone is of help, and your own financial situation.

Health care in the U.S. is a complicated mix of private employer-sponsored plans and government programs. According to the U.S. Census Bureau, in 2019 55.4 percent of Americans get their health care coverage through their jobs. Senior citizens who are sixty-five and over are covered through the federal Medicare program while those with low incomes receive help from federal Medicaid programs. Still others buy subsidized health care through the Affordable Care Act (Obamacare) marketplaces. But it's a patchwork system, and ultimately not everyone has, or can afford, health care—the Census Bureau reports that 26.1 million people did not have health insurance in 2019. In other developed countries such as the United Kingdom, obtaining lifesaving medical care is not left up to the individual. As of 1948, virtually every citizen in the U.K. is covered by the National Health

Service, which offers comprehensive health care through the government.

We are under no obligation to underwrite another's health care, whether a family member or not. We are not ethically responsible to make up for an inadequate health care system, or to do harm to ourselves in the name of helping others. Only you can assess your capacity and your desire to help. Every situation is unique, and this decision also requires considering how our resources and needs may change over time.

If you're unsure of your answer, there are a few other questions that can help. Is the illness so serious or severe that expensive treatment is the only option? Does it matter to you if your sibling could have obtained medical insurance but did not? Or led an unhealthy lifestyle? Or could have saved money but instead splurged on luxuries? If you do decide to help financially, clarify limits on your generosity up front—the amount and whether this is an outright gift or a loan.

If you'd like to help, but are financially unable, there are other avenues to explore. Perhaps your sibling can secure a loan or other family members can help share the financial burden. You may be able to help research other sources of aid, provide assistance navigating the health care system, or offer support in other ways, like driving them to appointments or delivering groceries. But it's a personal choice, and only you can know what is right for you.

Should you read your child's or teenager's diary or journal?

Years ago, I saw a story in the news about a well-meaning mother who regularly read her fifteen-year-old's diary. She thought it would offer insight into why their conversations were so fraught with anger. Similarly, a friend of mine secretly reads her son's diary because she is concerned about his "extremely erratic behavior." She shares the contents with her therapist, but no one else. Her justification is that she has tried unsuccessfully to discuss her concerns with him. She has never read the diaries of her other children. Nonetheless, she worries that she is modeling disrespect and betrayal—and if she is discovered, won't be forgiven. But then she pushes the thought away, sighing, "Teenagers don't have perspective."

Anne Frank's diary, published as *The Diary of a Young Girl*, is one of my favorite books of all time. It chronicles a young Jewish girl and her family, hiding in the attic of another Dutch family in Amsterdam for several years, trying to escape the Holocaust. Published posthumously—Anne Frank died in the Bergen-Belsen concentration camp in

1945—her diary is said to be the most widely read nonfiction book in the world other than the Bible. It reveals the fears, hopes, infatuations, and inner life of a young girl caught up in the horror of Nazi Europe. And it reminds us that diaries act not only as literary records of our thoughts, but also as tools for navigating life.

Exploration

I'm not a mental health professional or parenting guru (I'm a highly imperfect mother of five young adults), and every situation is unique. But this question often triggers guilt and defensiveness, and in my view there's little productive place in ethics for either. In the midst of day-to-day parenting, we often lose perspective. Ethics can help us reason through the emotion and shift 20/20 hindsight to problem-solving foresight.

A child's diary is a private sanctuary, whether online or on paper, whether it is conveyed in words, drawings, or photographs. A diary serves as a healthy outlet to express one's deepest emotions, dreams, and ideals. Let's be clear. Reading a child's diary without their knowledge or permission is dishonest, disrespectful, and a violation of privacy. It undermines trust, as does any form of dishonesty. It's possible that if your actions are discovered you could push your child or teenager to withhold even more, which could have lasting effects on your relationship with them.

But ethical questions are rarely "yes or no," "black or

white" dilemmas. I like to ask the question: *When—and under what circumstances—should we act?* When might you compromise honesty due to concern for your child's well-being? How do other principles like privacy, safety, respect, and truth factor into your decision? What is the result you're trying to reach? Imagine looking back on your decision a month, a year, five years down the line, and ask yourself: Will my justifications still make sense once more time has passed? To me, the most compelling reasons to read a child's diary without permission are health and safety—of the child and others.

One way to look at this is to consider other instances where privacy and confidentiality are involved. At one extreme, medical professionals are permitted to violate doctor-patient confidentiality if they believe someone's life is at stake. Contracts may not be airtight: society is less and less tolerant of enforcing nondisclosure agreements signed by victims of sexual misconduct, because they allow perpetrators to continue with impunity. On the other hand, a parent's mere curiosity is not justification to compromise honesty or respect; as my research assistant says, there's a "difference between concerned and nosy." Intrusive or controlling parenting is not an excuse for dishonesty.

Consider other alternatives first—speaking to your child about your concerns, or perhaps getting professional advice to determine whether the red flags you are seeing are as serious as you think. Ask yourself if there are other ways you might discern whether your child's safety is at risk. If you do decide it is necessary to read their diary, only share the contents with confidentiality-bound professionals who can help guide you.

Children often don't have perspective on how serious their situation is—or the type of help that might be available.

Would you give someone who has wronged you several times another chance?

Perhaps your mother continually breaks confidences with you by telling other family members about your problems. Or your supervisor consistently takes credit for work you have done. Or your teenage daughter lies about things she did, or didn't do, like claiming she was at the library while she was really at a party drinking.

The closer the individuals are to us (a spouse, child, relative, or close friend as opposed to an occasional friend or professional colleague), the more we have to lose emotionally, socially, and sometimes materially when there's a breach of trust. We may feel ethically responsible for attempting to maintain the relationship, or continuing to support the other person—but what's our obligation?

Exploration

We've all been there: someone lied to us, cheated on us, betrayed a confidence, or has been consistently irresponsible or unreliable. We may have the old proverb "fool me once, shame on you; fool me twice, shame on me" lingering in the back of our minds. How would we approach repairing the relationship—and should we?

In order to recover from ethics transgressions—reconcile a past wrong inflicted on you in this case—the other person needs to tell you the full truth, take responsibility for their actions, and assure you that the behavior will not be repeated. Establishing their trustworthiness is the foundation for future connection. Start by asking whether you have the information you need to consider the ethics of the decision. You need to know what the *other person* knew. Did they know that their behavior was ethically wrong? Should they have? If you have talked with them after previous missteps, they had all the information they needed to make an ethical choice—and they chose not to. What might have been a mistake the first time becomes intentional when it is repeated—especially the third or fourth time. Is there reason to believe their behavior will change in the future?

Then consider the danger of impunity. If you continue to tolerate unwanted behavior, you remove incentives to improve, and you may become part of the problem as an enabler.

Perhaps you decide to continue to engage with them, but only in limited ways—for example, in a work environment (where you may not have much of a choice), you might continue to be respectful and act professionally, but no longer treat them as a trusted colleague or friend.

There are times when gut-wrenching decisions about our most important relationships are at stake—leaving a cheating spouse when you have children and no place to go. Or choosing to let an adult child stand on their own after repeated incidents of dishonesty or misconduct.

What if someone is struggling with health issues—can we make the argument that "they can't help it"? For example, people suffering from addiction are battling a tragically difficult disease. We might call on our compassion more than we would in the case of hurtful behavior from someone who is well. The same goes for someone struggling with mental health issues. But that doesn't mean that we have to live with these individuals or continue to support them in everything. In cases like these, we can set boundaries on the relationship.

Conversely, physical or verbal abuse, dangerous behavior involving weapons, dealing or using illegal drugs, and drunk driving—these are all deal breakers, in my view. In such cases, other considerations such as safety override everything else.

Finally, there is often confusion between forgiveness and ethical recovery. Many wise people say that forgiveness is for the forgiver. It's about moving on; it's not about changing the other person's behavior. However, ethics recovery requires the other person to change: telling the truth, taking responsibility, and committing to different future behavior. Second (or third) chances cannot take place without their agreeing to all three.

Are you obligated to give all your children equal shares of your estate?

conic French rock star Johnny Hallyday (known as the French Elvis) passed away in 2017, having left his two biological adult children out of his will—in violation of French law. After a sordid media battle between the children and Hallyday's wife at the time of his death, the adult children prevailed in court and were awarded part of his estate.

Most families do not have their succession play out in court or the media, but we do face questions of how to distribute our worldly belongings. How do ethics matter when deciding what children with different sized families—or no children at all—should receive? What if one child is wealthy, while another is struggling to pay the rent? What if one has a bigger family or costly medical needs? Should personal preference be a factor?

Exploration

The question is highly personal, cultural, and, in some cases, even religious. I clarify a few ethics threads, but in most cases, there is no right or wrong answer here. We don't owe anyone our possessions (or our attention, time, letters of recommendation, loans, friendship, love, organs)—in life or in death.

There is an important distinction between equal (the same share to each) and equitable (fair and impartial). In some cases, equal may not seem fair and fair may not seem impartial. You will need to decide what principles are important to you, and how you can apply them.

Let's consider the question of inheritance on a spectrum.

At one extreme, in France, the Napoleonic Code, introduced in 1804, limits one's freedom on bequeathing assets, except for property held abroad: everything from apartments to bank accounts to favorite handbags is divided up among children in accordance with legally mandated percentages tied to the number of children, as the court decided in the case of Johnny Hallyday.

At the other extreme, there are ethical wills, which harken back to centuries-old Jewish and Muslim tradition, but today are used by people of all faiths. They pass on ethical principles and priorities from one generation to the next. You might leave your commitment to humility and compassion to child A, your love of people and volunteering to child B. They are fascinating add-ons to formal wills, although they don't determine distribution of material possessions.

Between these extremes, most of us decide for ourselves how to divide our material possessions.

You can't predict how your children and others will respond, but you can start with two pillars: responsibility and transparency. Responsibility: Do you have children that you are still legally responsible for (or feel responsible for)—perhaps one is battling an illness or has special needs, or is caring for children with special needs? Transparency: consider telling your adult children of your estate plans so you can manage their expectations, and that any questions or conflicts can surface while you are still alive.

You may also consider what has been given already. In the case of children who assumed the role of caregiver to you, potentially forgoing income, perhaps now is the time to pay them back in kind. Additionally, it may be helpful to consider what you've given your various children during their lifetimes: education, loans, weddings.

Ethics do not offer a one-size-fits-all answer, nor do they guarantee family harmony. Conversations around money and family are often fraught with emotion. But starting with responsibility and transparency helps distill the ethics stakes in your situation and can offer a foundation for your conversations. And of course we have the right to change our decision over time.

Would you use direct-to-consumer genetic testing kits?

You hear a friend has purchased a 23andMe kit. You're intrigued and would like to find out more about your family's ancestry. You don't fully understand what you will learn from the kit, but you're also curious about your health and genetic history.

Many of us have seen the direct-to-consumer (DTC) genetic testing kits advertised in media ranging from Oprah's Favorite Things to *People* magazine. And it's easy to do: order the kit, spit into a vial, and send it to the company. Then wait to discover the results. Teenagers think of it as a great gift idea, and parents are using it with their children. Technically, AncestryDNA and 23andMe require users to be eighteen years of age, but parents can do the tests "on behalf of . . . those for whom [they] have legal authority." According to *MIT Technology Review*, the total number of people in the databases of 23andMe, AncestryDNA, and several smaller companies grew to more than 26 million people by the beginning of 2019.

After checking, you see that among the range of

information you might uncover using 23andMe are insights about your health (an increased risk of certain diseases), ancestry (origins and relationship to "groups of people . . . across the globe"), and family (paternity, such as your biological father not being who you thought he was). These kits can provide important opportunities if used thoughtfully.

Exploration

The central question is whether there are irreparable consequences or *potential* consequences to consumers learning the information they may obtain from DTC genetic testing kits. Autonomy (the right to know and the right *not to know*), privacy, health, and safety are all at stake here. Perhaps the most critical: *you cannot un-know information once you have learned it.*

Ordinarily, information concerning your health and the health of your family would be kept confidential. But here, as 23andMe warns on its website, "genetic information that you share with [others] may be used against your interests," and their privacy policies can change at any point. If insurance companies access this data, or require you to provide it, they could decide not to cover you or raise the cost of insurance.

Then there's the unpredictability of how you will react—for example, if you discover you have the gene for a serious disease such as cancer. In the case of teenagers or children, processing the implications of health information could bring confusion and distress. In my view, children under eighteen should not be made responsible for decisions about sharing or not sharing genetic information that could affect others.

DTC kits can dismantle one of the long-standing pillars of ethics—informed consent. As adults we consent for ourselves. With teenagers, parents consent for them. This deprives them of the right to decide for themselves when they are older. They may learn something at a young age that, when they're an adult, they wouldn't have chosen to know. Or vice versa. Worse, in some situations, using DTC kits could lead to exposing others who have no opportunity to consent (a spouse who learns they are not the child's parent, siblings learning of a genetic disease, even family members of criminals caught using DTC kit results uploaded on various sites).

In medically prescribed genetic testing, the patient would have a professional walk them through the decision— the reasons for the test, the scope of information required, and the risks and benefits of possible outcomes. Likely, the tests would be limited to those necessary to the medical matter at hand. DTC kit technology eliminates the professional filter between you and potentially life-altering knowledge.

Our ethical responsibility is even greater when there is no driving imperative to do DTC genetic testing and there are alternatives. Doctors can recommend and supervise targeted (and possibly more accurate) tests for specific health concerns. The American Society of Human Genetics encourages parents to defer predictive testing for children for adult-onset diseases until adulthood, or "the child is an older adolescent who can participate in decision-making in a relatively mature manner."

If you're planning to send in your DNA, or the DNA of your child, read the fine print and detailed disclosure they provide and then pause to reflect on its implications. And remember, whatever a company's terms of service, they can change. Better yet, seek a professional opinion *before* you use the kit rather than waiting until after you have obtained the results.

Would you tell your friend information about their fiancé you think they should know before getting married?

Your best friend is engaged to be married. You want to be thrilled, but although you've met your friend's fiancé a number of times, something about them makes you feel uneasy, as if they are hiding something or acting in a way that doesn't seem entirely honest. But you keep it to yourself because, after all, it's just a feeling.

But then you stumble upon a more specific concern—a transgression, a lie—that confirms your worst fears. And you're pretty sure your friend knows nothing about it. Perhaps you discovered that the person cheated on your friend. Or lied about their financial situation. You're not sure if you owe it to your friend to tell them. The thought of bringing this new information to your friend, and possibly ruining their happiness, is terrifying. But what if you don't tell your friend, and he or she discovers it later once they are married?

Exploration

First, separate the ethics question from your opinion about your friend's partner. You may need to act if your friend (or someone else) is at risk of harm, or if you know of behavior on the part of their fiancé that violates their core values such as abuse, a hidden addiction, history of lies, or mistreatment of others. A general dislike or feeling that your friend's intended is "just not good enough" is not an ethics matter.

At the same time, you can use ethics to guide what you view as your responsibility as a friend. In relationships, for me these considerations may include honesty, compassion, transparency, and loyalty.

Ask yourself, *Why do I feel compelled to tell them?* Is it out of concern for their well-being? Is it so that your friend has all the information needed to make the right decision for them? The more precise you can be about the issue, and the clearer you are about your goals, the easier it will be to share your concerns, and for your friend to be able to hear them. And the more you'll stay in your ethics lane.

Check first that your information is accurate. You can approach the fiancé, asking them to clarify the situation and giving them the opportunity to tell your friend first. If that doesn't seem possible, tell your friend how you came across this information (that's part of transparency). Any time we are a bystander, there's a risk that we may not know the full story and could cause unintended harm.

Focus only on the concern—not condemning the other

person. Avoid gossip. Share information privately with your friend to give them space to react without others present. Again, you're not trying to suggest the right decision for your friend—only to give them the information they need to make sure they make the right decision for themselves, and for you to fulfill your obligations as a friend.

Consider also whether you are willing to live with the consequences of telling your friend (or not). Of course, your friend could be extremely upset, whatever you decide. Some might not want to risk a friendship by telling their friend upsetting news. But what if your friend finds out, years later, that you knew and didn't tell them? They may feel betrayed by your lack of transparency.

Most importantly, consider your friend's point of view: What would your friend want to know, based on the history of your friendship? When your friend responds, listen to what they tell you—not what you want or expect to hear. Remember, this is not about you. The fact that life, and our decisions, don't have perfect outcomes doesn't mean we aren't doing our best ethically.

What are the differences between a white lie and a serious ethical transgression?

Recently, during the Q&A after a talk I gave, a member of the audience who was in the process of selling her house asked whether she was ethically obligated to tell her real estate agent and the buyer about any negative experiences she had had with the house. Another audience member asked me whether it was okay to embellish her accomplishments on a dating website. A third audience member asked about lying to the police about why she had been speeding.

Exploration

These kinds of questions essentially ask when and under what circumstances distorting the truth is acceptable—if ever.

To me, truth is a nonnegotiable foundation for ethical decision making. Without truth, we violate ethical commitments like honesty, integrity, empathy, and transparency. We lack the accurate information we need to consider who will be affected by our decisions and how. There is no such thing as alternative facts when it comes to ethics.

There is a pattern in the examples above: we're consciously acting out of self-interest to get someone to *make a choice that we don't think they would make if they knew the truth*. We want someone to purchase our house, go out on a date with us, or give us a pass on a speeding ticket. In other words, getting someone else to agree to what we want based on *distorted truth.* We can contrast that with the white lies we sometimes tell to avoid hurting others' feelings—"You haven't aged a day!" or "I love that dress." In these cases the other person is not using our information to make a choice. Put differently, we are expressing an opinion, not stating (or misstating) a fact.

All of these stories spotlight the danger of contagion of falsity, whether by commission or omission. The danger is that compromised truth can become a habit. It becomes normalized and, over time, we up the ante, confusing self-interest with a legitimate rationale.

You don't owe the purchaser of your house disclosure of every detail. But regardless of the law, you do owe them honesty about issues significant enough to affect their decision to purchase the house at the price you set. Most real estate sales are contingent upon the house passing an inspection by a professional and your representations of the house. If the buyer discovered a major flaw post-closing, you could be held liable under the contract. You might also ask yourself, aside from what is legal, is this something *I* would want to know if I were in the buyer's position?

We all know people frequently distort the truth on dating apps. Chipping a few years off your age or lying about your interests are intended to get a foot in the door. These lies are intentional, to influence the other person's choice. The people who do it know they are not being truthful and those lies often come out later. Acknowledging and apologizing for a falsehood is a lot harder than telling the truth the first time, because it not only reveals the lie, it also shows that you are someone who isn't completely trustworthy. A person may think: *What else might this person lie about?*

It goes without saying that lying to a police officer or other official is unwise. Moreover, it also says that you are prepared to violate two of our culture's most fundamental principles: truth and safety. Driving above the speed limit is a mistake that many of us make—an ethics failure (whether or not intentional) because it puts us and others at risk. But lies are an *intentional* failure of ethics.

Would you violate your teenager's confidence if not doing so might lead to harm?

Perhaps your teenager confided in you about a friend who has been using and selling drugs—swearing you to absolute secrecy. Or you found some pills in your teenager's possession that had been given by a friend to increase concentration for upcoming exams.

You know that if you break a promise, your teenager's trust could be undermined, as well as their willingness to share future information. It can also set in motion other dangerous behaviors (including lying or hiding the truth). On the other hand, if you don't speak up, harmful behavior could continue unchecked. Innocent people could be hurt.

Exploration

Dilemmas that pit confidentiality against other ethics guideposts, such as safety and responsibility, happen all too often.

Explain to your child in clear terms that you feel you must break confidentiality *in this particular case* and *why*. By asking permission, you transform your request from a broken promise into a situation-specific exemption from your promise. In contrast, if you lie about or hide your intentions, your actions are a violation of the confidentiality you promised.

Consider whether there are more options (i.e., beyond tell or don't tell). For example, urge your child to convince their friend to come clean or stop the behavior. (This works better for adults, as it may burden your child with a lot of responsibility.) Or you can obtain your child's agreement to share some, but not all, of the information. Explain exactly what you would share with surgical precision: the least amount of information to the fewest number of people, with a very specific goal in mind.

If your child refuses to give permission, you might talk to the parents of the other child, keeping the conversation general, or consult a doctor or counselor for further advice. ("Many students are trying this new drug X, and nobody knows where it's coming from.") In the end, you may feel you have to violate your child's confidentiality, but you will have been honest and transparent.

Before acting, assess the credibility of the information you have: the source, the level of detail, and the quality (an eyewitness account versus gossip). Be sure it's a serious matter, like one involving illegal drugs, driving under the influence, or cheating that could result in expulsion. Weigh the immediate and longer-term consequences, including others who may potentially be affected by the situation: a friend, an innocent victim of drugs or a car accident, and the other person's family. If you know of potential harm and say nothing, you bear some responsibility if it transpires. Do whatever you can to eliminate any risk of harm to your child, such as forbidding your child to get in a car with a friend who drinks and drives. Finally, encourage them to consult with medical, legal, and mental health providers and religious advisors whose confidentiality obligations are both legally binding and based on professional ethics.

If you decide to tell the child's family, remember that they may not welcome the information. You cannot control the other person's response—only your own. Put yourself in their shoes: How would you feel if someone told *you* this? On the other hand, how would you feel looking back on your decision after the worst had already happened? Or how would you feel if someone else knew of a serious issue with your child and didn't tell you?

We are being asked here to consider more than just whether it is our story to tell. We are being asked whether it is a story we can afford *not* to tell.

Would you call the police on a friend you fear might drive under the influence of alcohol?

I have a dear friend whose spouse regularly drinks too much in social settings—at parties, at restaurants on some occasions, at sporting events. Yet despite the fact he's had too much to drink to drive safely, he will get behind the wheel of his car to drive home, claiming he is only traveling "locally." Which is true, but "locally" refers to a big city with complex traffic patterns and varied speed limits—and ignores the fact that he shouldn't be behind the wheel of a car anywhere in his condition. If he is with his wife, she will drive. But sometimes he is on his own.

Here are a few chilling statistics for perspective: it's illegal to drive with a blood alcohol level of .08 g/dL or higher in every state in the U.S. (except Utah, where the limit is .05 g/dL). That is roughly equal to three drinks for most people, depending on their weight and the amount of time that has transpired. In 2019, according to the

National Highway Traffic Safety Administration, 10,142 people in the U.S. died in a drunk-driving accident—one person every fifty-two minutes. In 2019, 28 percent of all fatal car accidents in the U.S. involved a driver who had been drinking.

Exploration

This question appears to pit ethical principles against each other—safety of the driver and innocent people versus the loyalty and confidentiality of our friendship. Let's start with what I call 20/20 foresight. Catapult yourself into the future: looking back on your decision in a month, a year, five years, how would you feel if someone was injured because you didn't try to stop your friend? Would you feel differently if nothing happened? Assuming our sources are reliable, or we've witnessed our friend's behavior for ourselves, we have all the information we need to make an ethical decision. If you lose a loved one to a drunk driver, you don't care whether it was the driver's first offense or a habitual pattern of abuse.

First, I would do everything that I could to change the situation directly, from telling my friend unequivocally not to drive, to reaching out to a partner to come and pick them up, to persuading my friend to wait for a few hours at least until they are sober enough to drive.

If your friend is about to get behind the wheel, and others fail to act, you may need to involve the authorities. Alerting the police about the drunk driving of a friend could result in your friend being arrested. While this could cost you the friendship, the consequences of not doing so could be far worse. And loyalty in my view does require trying to prevent a friend from making a life-altering mistake.

The more difficult situation involves a chronic drinker. You're not always there to intervene. Speak to your friend— maybe they're not aware of how much they are drinking. Failing that, speak to family members or a partner. The point here is to urge them to seek a lasting solution to protect their own safety and the safety of others—not to preach, criticize, or shame. Police generally do not engage in these situations because there is not an imminent criminal act.

People struggling with addiction are battling a disease. Compassion and humility are in order, but we don't owe them blind loyalty, such that we enable them to do harm.

We should ask how we might allow for earlier, confidential, safety-focused ways to report fears of someone *about* to drive under the influence—perhaps resulting in a warning with no permanent consequences unless there are multiple offenses. I don't have a perfect solution. But I have seen repeatedly how official but non-threatening options for reporting potential wrongdoing can increase willingness to seek help and offer a life- or career-saving wake-up call.

In the end we can't control what our friends do. And

let's circle back to the idea that safety and loyalty might conflict here: if we do feel compelled to call the police, hopefully our friend will realize that our principles in fact align. Their safety and their best long-term interests are both expressions of our loyalty.

Would you pay, or allow teachers to pay, your children to study or read books?

You discover that the parents of one of your ten-year-old's classmates pay him $20 for every A he earns. Another family incentivizes their child by giving money for every completed homework assignment. A third uses the stick rather than the proverbial carrot—they won't let their child play sports or have play dates unless she achieves certain grades. The high school English teacher of your older child, to bring up the lower-performing end of the class, is rewarding students by giving them $5 for every grade improvement. (You have no idea whether the lower-performing students come from more difficult or less privileged home environments. Nor do you know if the teacher receives a bonus or other benefits for class grades.) These are a mix of real situations I saw as a parent.

Exploration

Are the efforts described above legitimate strategies to incentivize students or simple bribery? Cheating? Mundane parenting tactics like threatening to take the phone away if they use inappropriate language, or offering TV time in exchange for extra household chores? Is something being sold that shouldn't be sold? If so, what?

The *Oxford Advanced Learner's Dictionary* defines cheating as "act[ing] in a dishonest way in order to gain an advantage." Cheating violates principles like honesty, fairness, and equity, and is unacceptable. But most parents I have met over the years are not trying to obtain an unfair advantage—they simply want to incentivize learning. Education is not an even playing field, with or without parental inducements.

Next, is something for sale that shouldn't be sold, like friendship, kidneys, or sex, as Harvard University professor and political philosopher Michael Sandel intriguingly asks in a lecture he gave at the Oxford Union. If you think education is for sale here, bear in mind that we sell education all the time—through university fees, private nursery schools, property taxes for public schools, or paying for ballet lessons and math camps. Is there much difference between paying your child $5 per book read and hiring private tutors and coaches?

In my view, we're not buying or selling education, but rather motivation and effort. The child doesn't lose the underlying good—education. On the contrary, they gain it. One clear guideline in my view: We *shouldn't* pay for ethical conduct like telling the truth, showing respect, and being honest and compassionate. *Ethics are not for sale*. Doing well in school, however, is not an ethical principle. Many morally upstanding people do not excel in the classroom, the way I fail miserably at many sports. And they might do better—and learn better—with incentives. Still, Sandel makes a critical point that markets, and the economics underpinning choice, should not function independently of morality.

One of the students in Sandel's audience argued that if the payment incentivizes the child to read more, it is a small price to pay to jump-start a lifetime of learning. Others argue that children will miss the joy of discovering reading for themselves. Perhaps most importantly, reading is a fundamental life skill regardless of parental ambitions or enjoyment—and an indicator of the egregious inequality in our society. Considering the benefits of reading young, the harm of parents using financial transactions to encourage creating those benefits may seem small.

Teachers have to balance motivation, discipline, incentives, and a love for learning. There is no way to be truly fair about choosing which students to pay as teachers can never know the full story of what's going on at home. Because of that, I don't support teachers giving students money for anything. That said, I very much admire teachers and sympathize with the challenge of being attentive to their students' diverse learning needs.

Would you tell—or want to be told—about an affair?

Some years ago I was at a casual dinner with a group of friends, and the question arose as to what we would do if we found out that a close friend's spouse was having an affair. Would we tell our friend? A few in the group said they would. They also would want to know if their own spouse was having an affair and would end the marriage immediately. One friend whose husband traveled constantly on business answered, "I wouldn't want to know. As long as he comes home on Friday night, I want my life, my children's lives, and our home life protected. If someone tells me, I'd have to respond—and maybe be judged if I don't throw him out or act the way others think I should." She felt that even if others knew, as long as she didn't know, she wasn't responsible for having to face painful life decisions. Still others, while not condoning affairs, wrestled with whether they would tell and wondered if they would want to be told. One wanted to be told, but didn't care if her spouse was having an affair.

Exploration

To start, let's clarify whose ethics we are talking about. Our own principles don't apply to other people's relationships. People are free to manage their relationships with their own ethics. Individuals decide their principles and make practical compromises all the time—whether putting up with an affair, sacrificing emotional intimacy, or doing a disproportionate share of the housework.

So let's stay focused on our own ethics. How do *our* principles—and how they play out in our friendship—relate to whether or not we tell? My answer rests on one mantra-like question: *Is it your story to tell?* And a corollary: Your friend *cannot un-know* information once you tell them.

The first step is to make sure we have the information we need to make an ethical choice. Are you sure that what you think is true is true? Unless one of the parties having the affair told you (ideally, both of them told you), you may not know as much as you think. Even if you do have reliable firsthand information, no one can know what is going on in someone else's marriage. Maybe your friend already knows and is trying to work it out quietly, or is suffering with the knowledge but is not ready to share.

More important, it's not your information, your truth, or your story to tell. It's theirs. You won't be the one living with the consequences. So I try my best to be careful about making choices that affect the people who will be living with them. If your friendship is based on honesty, transparency, and loyalty, you may feel that you need to share this.

Fair enough—again assuming you have thought through the caveats. Perhaps try testing the water a bit; ask your friend whether everything is okay at home.

I almost always ask how we would feel in the shoes of the person most adversely affected by our decision—a query that calls up our empathy, compassion, and humility. Whether or not you would want to know is irrelevant; what matters is what you believe your friend would want. Even if you think you know or heard your friend's views in a theoretical dinner discussion, when we are living through an ethical conundrum ourselves, we may not be so sure. For example, I wouldn't assume that my friend's dinner commentary a while ago would reflect their wishes if their spouse was cheating today.

In most cases, there is no driving imperative to reveal information here. You are not a bystander to someone who is in danger, as would be the case, for example, if you were witnessing imminent danger like physical abuse. Asking whether it's your story to tell applies to so many areas of life. Seemingly harmless information can become significantly more perilous when shared. If you share it, you assume some responsibility for the consequences of that sharing.

Would you return the
extra change?

I had the privilege of interviewing Rob Chesnut, former chief ethics officer of Airbnb. I started by asking him where he got his true north . . . his own set of ethical principles that have guided him personally and throughout his successful legal and ethics career. Without hesitation, he praised his mother. He recalled an experience as a young child. He and his mother were leaving the supermarket when his mother discovered the cashier had mistakenly given her some extra change. She turned around, with her son in tow, and went back inside to return the money. Today, this act may seem quaint, but it stuck with me as an example of how one small act can set an example for a lifetime of ethical behavior.

As I was preparing for the interview, I read a graduation speech given by retired Navy four-star Admiral William H. McRaven, then the chancellor of the University of Texas. McRaven had been the commander of the U.S. Special Operations Command who oversaw the Navy SEALs' successful raid that killed Osama bin Laden. His commencement speech became the anchoring story in a subsequent bestselling book, *Make Your Bed*. Admiral McRaven advised that making your bed "will encourage you to do another task and another and another. By the end of the day, that one task completed will have turned into many tasks completed. Making your bed will also reinforce the fact that little things in life matter. If you can't do the little things right, you'll never be able to do the big things right."

"If you want to change the world," McRaven advised, "start off by making your bed. . . ."

Exploration

This question asks us to consider when, whether, and why little things matter. It asks us to press pause and think about our day-to-day decisions, what I consider our "ethics housekeeping." It probes how we draw lines: What's worth worrying about?

Rob Chesnut's childhood story describes one of those rare "yes or no" moments. We shouldn't leave with money that doesn't belong to us. It doesn't depend on the situation. But we often rationalize our actions away—"It's too small an amount to be worth the effort to go back inside to return it" or "It doesn't matter to the store or even the cashier." But like many seemingly mundane ethical moments, the lessons are far-reaching.

Small transgressions can be cumulative. They become habits. And the thinking can spread to other areas. Just as shoddy bed making can lead to leaving more important things undone, leaving with money that isn't yours can lead to seemingly minor ethical missteps, such as exaggerating your contribution to the team's report or lying to a friend about why you declined an invitation. On the positive side, finding a wallet and making the effort to return it, or tipping generously when warranted, spreads good habits.

Our principles define us. They tell the world who we are, how we will behave in a given situation, and what we would hope for from others. We don't get to cherry-pick principles based on convenience. And we don't get free passes. Honesty and integrity are just as valid at the supermarket, and with respect to small amounts, as they are with our family, friends, and work colleagues and bigger transgressions.

In the case presented at the beginning of the question, there is no need for additional information. We have money that isn't ours, and we know to whom it belongs.

Finally, while this dilemma may seem to be mostly about you (and possibly the cashier who made the mistake), not so fast. We affect many others over time when we start to negotiate with ourselves in compromising our ethics ("just this once"), instead of sweating the small stuff. Whether it is the cashier, a colleague we disrespect, a partner that we subtly bully, or that friend who is upset about a social media post, our choices always affect others.

Small things matter even when the frequency or the seriousness of the offense are not at issue. As Admiral

McRaven says, and Rob Chesnut's mother modeled, it's about training our ethics muscles and our minds. It's about being honest with ourselves so that we see clearly that there are indeed lines to be drawn. It is about establishing an ethics baseline and building an ethics reflex, so that we can do the big things right. It's about making our ethics bed.

Chapter 2

Politics, Community, and Culture

Should we prosecute someone who steals food during a crisis?

A student once described to me witnessing a young teenager grab a bag of chips from a New York subway vendor and run off without paying. He could have reported the incident to the police or the vendor . . . or walked away and forgotten the matter. Instead, he paid for the chips. He didn't know whether this grab-and-run was a one-off in response to a dare, a pattern of minor theft, or the desperate act of a starving youth. So my student responded with compassion and generosity—and deft creativity.

Now let's up the ante—examining widespread food theft during a crisis. On August 29, 2005, Hurricane Katrina tore through coastal Louisiana, breaching the levees around New Orleans. Hundreds of thousands of people were evacuated; about 25,000 of those left behind fled to the Superdome. Approximately 80 percent of New Orleans was underwater. There was almost no food, shelter, or potable water. Almost 2,000 lives were lost as a result of engineering flaws and ineffective governmental oversight.

With $108 billion in damages, it was at the time one of the costliest hurricanes in U.S. history.

In the days that followed the media reported that "looters floated garbage cans filled with clothing and jewelry down the street" or stole drinks, chips, and diapers from a Walgreens drugstore. Citizens who never would have imagined themselves stealing were driven to take food out of necessity.

Police responses were inconsistent. Some police stood guard to allow stealing for necessities; other looters were arrested—a jail was constructed of chain-link cages in the main New Orleans train station.

Exploration

This story cuts to the core of our humanity. Watching the news, I felt overwhelming sympathy for the victims of Katrina. I also felt a foreboding that a major disaster could cause such damage to our infrastructure, shatter the lives of so many citizens, and result in further inequality in the aftermath. I found myself thinking, What would I have done if *my* children were desperate for food or water? What would happen if the most well-intended members of the National Guard and my local police were unable to protect us? For me, the primary principles in a crisis like this are human safety and well-being—but tightly tethered to dignity, independence, and compassion.

The two principles of safety and well-being are hard to argue with even if breaking the law is the trade-off. We can pay back stolen goods or broken windows (and sometimes shop owners can collect insurance or government support). But we can't walk back the consequences of not having enough money to pay for health care, hospitalization, shelter, or food. Who among us wouldn't consider grabbing food we couldn't pay for if our child was starving? Who among us wouldn't be grateful for someone looking the other way in a time of crisis?

In stark contrast, looting is unethical, whatever is going on in the streets, and whether the perpetrator is in a gang, a mother of six, a protester, or a police officer.

Clear principles can help us combat *arbitrariness* that can occur in times of crisis—one of the most dangerous drivers of the spread of unethical behavior (whether the unfair distribution of ventilators during the Covid-19 crisis or ignoring the poorest neighborhoods post-Katrina). Arbitrariness conveys the message that there is no clear link between our efforts and our impact—so why bother to try? Arbitrariness on the part of even highly skilled and well-meaning authorities also matters, such as instances of some New Orleans police enforcing the law while some overlooked it.

The people who looted or committed violent acts out of pent-up anger against the authorities hurt fellow citizens who had nothing to do with the inequality of the disaster response, or decades of poverty. (In my view the disproportionately negative impact of this disaster on poorer communities is not random: it's the toxic mix of systemic and institutionalized racism and inequality.)

Whatever your view on prosecuting first-time offenders,

consider how we, as individuals and as a society, can ethically respond to such crises with principles, and to avoid arbitrariness.

No one should have to choose between stealing food and going hungry. My fallback position is that when theft of food and necessities for survival is the only option, we should show respect and compassion and redouble our efforts to contribute to healing.

Do we have a responsibility to speak up if we're in a conversation where racist comments are made?

magine that you are at an after-hours business event with other people from your industry, and while circulating around the room over drinks and hors d'oeuvres someone makes a racist remark. You are not part of the conversation; you are a bystander. You don't know the individual well, but you recognize what company they work for. You are wondering if you have an obligation to speak up—or if you even want to speak up. This has happened to you before with complete strangers, like when striking up a casual conversation with the person in front of you while waiting in line to buy a coffee. What would you do?

Exploration

Racism plagues our society. I attempt to approach questions relating to discrimination, inequality, and injustice with a hefty dose of humility, as well as gratitude for my many teachers. I include friends, colleagues, and students who have modeled thoughtfulness and sensitivity, as well as the insights of writers such as James Baldwin, Maya Angelou, Ta-Nehisi Coates, Toni Morrison, Claudia Rankine, and Ibram X. Kendi.

Racism is never acceptable. However, confronting racism asks us to consider when and under what circumstances we speak up. If we say nothing, we are complicit. Passively standing by results in impunity (the person getting away with racist comments, or worse, assuming their views and language are acceptable, or at least tolerated). Impunity is one of the most dangerous drivers of the spread of unethical behavior because it sends the message to observers that they, too, can get away with the unacceptable attitudes and language. We are never really a bystander to racism. By hearing the language, we become a participant. We are not responsible for the other person's behavior, but we are responsible for our response to it.

First, ask *why* you should (or shouldn't) speak up in a specific situation. The goal should be to stop racist rhetoric and the misguided ideas that underpin them, rather than bringing attention to yourself or stirring up trouble.

Next, ask *how* you can best speak up. Are you explaining, with humility and respect, why the words make you uncomfortable and why you feel we can't tolerate racism in any guise? Or do you attempt to call the person out, embarrassing them and upping the ante? There are many ways to speak up effectively. In all circumstances, it starts with listening well, paying attention, and aligning your words with these goals. You can speak up at the time, and also have a private conversation later, write a thoughtful text or email, or even send the person an article or book that has helped you along your own journey. If you encounter racism at work, I strongly advise reporting it to Human Resources, your boss, a confidential hotline, or Ombuds services.

I tell my students that they should never miss an opportunity to shout out someone else's positive contributions to human dignity, but decline every opportunity to call out someone else's error or weakness. To me, racism is a clear exception. *Call it out.* But offer the benefit of the doubt; share your point of view rather than casting shame and blame; learn along with the person you are correcting. Gratuitous criticism and "gotcha" retorts make *you* the ethics problem, rather than the other person's racist behavior or words.

Some people don't speak up out of understandable concern of saying the wrong thing or initiating a confrontation. Sometimes, the offender is in a position of power and we fear retaliation. Other times, we freeze and lose the moment to shock, outrage, or inaction. But in the words of bestselling author Ibram X. Kendi, the director of the Center for Antiracist Research at Boston University, we are either actively antiracist, or racist; there's no such thing as neutrality. We must be active participants in combating racism in all its forms.

Should voting be mandatory?

Compulsory or mandatory voting is a system in which eligible citizens are legally required to register and vote, and may suffer penalties, sanctions, or fines if they fail to do so.

More than twenty countries have mandatory voting requirements, including Argentina, Australia, Belgium, Costa Rica, and Mexico—although violations are not always enforced. Before Australia passed mandatory voting for national elections in 1924, only 47 percent of registered voters participated in the national election. Over 91 percent of registered voters voted in Australia's 2019 federal election.

Historically, voter turnout in U.S. general elections has been low. In the 2016 presidential election, only 55 percent of eligible voters cast a ballot. (In 2020, voting was the highest it's been in a century, with an estimated 66.8 percent of voters voting.) In addition, voting is often disincentivized, depending on the laws of the individual states that set the voting rules, and many voters experience disenfranchisement. In 2021, Georgia passed a slew of laws that many argue discourage voting by minorities, requiring photo IDs, encouraging or discouraging voting by mail, and limiting the number and location of polling places, which leads to long lines. Florida and Texas have passed similar voting laws. Add to this mix the overwhelming challenge of verifying the accuracy of the information the public receives, including fake news on social media, microtargeted advertising, and potential influence by foreign agents.

Exploration

I believe that with the right to vote—an immense privilege—also comes great responsibility. Our vote, or decision not to vote, impacts the outcomes of elections, and speaks not only to how we view ethics, but positively or negatively affects ethics in the political sphere.

Advocates of mandatory voting focus on our collective civic duty, similar to paying taxes or obeying the speed limit. Some experts argue that it sends a message to the public that everyone's voice is valued and could stimulate more engagement in the issues of the day. In the short term, mandatory voting might do away with the potential misuse of voter ID requirements, or the politically motivated distribution of polling locations or ballot boxes to limit access. If *everyone* is required to vote, disenfranchisement becomes harder to accomplish.

Critics, on the other hand, argue that mandatory voting diminishes individual freedom, including the decision *not* to use one's voice. Inaction is also a form of action, and citizens may choose to use their voice by *not* speaking. Some critics also argue that forcing citizens to vote could lead to box ticking—citizens voting without informing themselves about the candidates and issues—or even the deliberate manipulation of the vote. Some are skeptical that an effective system can be put in place that doesn't exacerbate inequality through penalties that fall most heavily on those with the fewest resources.

Ultimately, the most important question is whether mandatory voting protects or undermines democracy.

To get our bearings, consider other constitutionally entrenched rights, such as freedom of speech and freedom to assemble, which allow us, but do not force us, to speak or assemble peacefully.

Also, ask whether the decision *not to vote* harms others. The potential consequences for others are fundamental to laws about drunk driving, wearing seatbelts, and smoking in public places (jail time, losing a driver's license, fines). Does abstaining from voting harm others? If so, what sanctions would be appropriate to spur compliance and mitigate that harm?

Instead of falling back on a "yes or no" answer, we should consider blended solutions and alternatives. With or without mandatory voting, we should ensure that every citizen has not just the right, but the *opportunity* to vote. We should make registration and voting easier. We should create incentives to vote: time off work, offering a tax credit or voucher for those who vote, and improving communication about the candidates and issues. We should develop technology to assure tamper-proof ways to vote by smartphone. We could also strengthen warnings of the dangers of not voting—the "smoking kills" version for civic responsibility.

We should only consider adopting compulsory voting if we can't find another way to overcome low voter turnout and barriers to voting that don't effectively take choice away from citizens. And there should be exemptions to the requirement where appropriate, such as religious exemptions.

With or without mandatory voting, every vote matters. The I VOTED stickers are a hopeful sign that many of us are proud to vote, and to let others know that we did. Would we have the same impetus to wear a sticker that said, essentially, THEY MADE ME VOTE?

Should we give money directly to those who are experiencing homelessness?

Every time I walk by the local Peet's Coffee shop in my northern California town, a homeless man outside extends a cup as a way of asking for money. We exchange greetings and smiles, and I often do drop some money for breakfast into his cup. I see him so often that he recognizes me. One block over, the local boutique grocery store prominently displays a sandwich board pleading with customers not to give to individuals asking for money, but rather to donate to nonprofit organizations set up to support those in need.

If you live in a major metropolitan area, it's likely that you frequently encounter someone experiencing homelessness (although homelessness is not by any means confined to large cities). In *The 2020 Annual Homeless Assessment Report to Congress*, the U.S. Department of Housing and Urban Development reported that 580,000 people experienced homelessness on any given night in the U.S.

Exploration

This is what I refer to as an "ethics on the fly" question—one we can answer with the limited information we already have at hand. I don't think anyone wants to live on the street, sleeping all night in the cold or begging for change to buy food. Most of us don't know what it's like to sleep on a sidewalk or subway grate for days, weeks, or months, never knowing where our next meal is coming from, living a life of fear, stigma, and sheer physical discomfort. As someone close to me once said, you don't know what poverty is like until you're going through it, with no clear path of escape. In addressing this question, I would lead with compassion, dignity, autonomy, generosity, and respect.

People end up experiencing homelessness and hunger for many reasons that have nothing to do with unethical behavior or criminal intent. One recipient of assistance from a nonprofit I worked for, a father with a successful job and loving family, was walking his young daughter to school one day when a taxicab hit and killed her. He subsequently experienced mental illness and drug addiction, ultimately losing his job and his ability to support himself. According to a 2021 study in high-income countries, approximately three quarters of the people experiencing homelessness also experience a mental health disorder.

When I do choose to give, I offer cash rather than food. It's not my job to second-guess what the person might do with the money I give them. To me, giving them the dignity to make their own choices is the least I can offer. I also give them information, when it's appropriate and they are interested, about other services—a food bank, shelter, nonprofit, or mental health organization—that can provide additional aid. You may feel differently, and wish to ensure that your generosity is being spent on food rather than alcohol, cigarettes, or drugs.

We don't owe any particular person or organization our generosity. But we can lift our gaze and contribute in whatever way makes the most sense to us (whether giving our time, money, used clothing, a smile, or an offer to babysit while someone goes to a job interview). We can also support organizations that aid those experiencing homelessness, and fight to change the system that allows people to go hungry, without shelter, and without basic medical care in one of the wealthiest countries in the world.

What are the key ethical considerations behind museums returning artifacts to the countries of origin?

In 1897, James Phillips, a British government official, went to visit the ruler of the Kingdom of Benin, in what is now Nigeria. When Phillips and most of his party were killed, the British government sent in 1,200 troops who ransacked the palace in retaliation, taking troves of valuable items. Over the decades, at least 3,000 of the Benin Bronzes (as they became known)—artifacts from the thirteenth to the seventeenth centuries—were dispersed throughout the world to museums and private collections. Almost 1,000 sculptures are on display and in storage in the vaults of the British Museum. The governments of both Nigeria and Benin City have sought to have the artifacts returned, but museums are unclear as to whom the art should be returned, or where it would be housed—a planned museum in Benin City is an empty lot today.

French president Emmanuel Macron promised that France would return twenty-six of the stolen artifacts (a small percentage of the works requested by the government of Benin). In 2021, the Netherlands announced it would begin "returning cultural heritage objects to their country of origin." "There is no place in the Dutch State collection for cultural heritage objects that were acquired by theft," said Ingrid van Engelshoven, the Netherlands' minister of education, culture, and science. And the Metropolitan Museum of Art has had to reassess the provenance of many pieces in its collection, including an artifact known as Nedjemankh and His Gilded Coffin, which the Met returned to Egypt in 2019.

Exploration

The starting point for this question is for both the museums and the countries of origin to work together to protect irreplaceable historic objects—whatever the national origin or current political context. Preservation is paramount in determining location, transporting, display, and storage—including whether objects are susceptible to theft or terrorism. Independent experts and home country experts should review museums' claims that objects cannot be safely transported or maintained in their home country.

Countries able to contribute to the protection of artifacts should do so, regardless of the rightful ownership or the location of the artifacts. (Private donors support such efforts outside their own countries as with the restoration of Venice.)

In terms of legal ownership, I believe robust peer-reviewed scholarship and outside expertise (ideally a diverse international group) should determine provenance and inform rightful ownership. Museums, plus governments and the public, must confront the range of possible broken links in the chain—theft during colonial rule, wartime looting, illegally purchased pieces hidden away in private collections, and more.

The accessibility of art and artifacts is another thorny factor, since cultural heritage should be accessible to all. Some argue that in major metropolitan cities like New York, London, Paris, and Madrid, more people will see them. That may be true, but if the art originated in West Africa, it is not likely that many West African citizens would see it. Covid-19 travel restrictions—not to mention violence from terrorism and political unrest—complicate equitable access. Many artifacts can travel on loan, unlike ancient architecture sites such as the Taj Mahal in India, the pyramids of Egypt, or the Great Wall of China. And technology can bring us closer. Google Arts & Culture and many other online sources offer online tours, education, and interaction.

So how do museum administrators navigate these potentially conflicting ethical principles? Let's first separate the question of ownership from location. Museums regularly house and display collections that they have on loan. Loans of artwork can be renewed indefinitely. Conceding that Greece owns the Elgin Marbles in the British Museum or that present-day Nigeria owns the Benin Bronzes does not necessarily mean that rightful ownership cannot be recognized while allowing them to remain *on loan* to a European or American museum.

Second, we should heed the global call to decolonialize,

to free our countries from colonial attitudes. Holding on to another country's property is a form of colonization—and failure to stand up to past moral failings. We should take responsibility for restoring justice, without jeopardizing any artifacts. Hopefully France's and the Netherlands' commitment to returning stolen artwork will prove contagious.

Museums all over the world depend on revenue from collections and donors, as well as on government support. And local and national governments depend on artifacts for tourism revenue. While a museum's finances shouldn't be central to the decision, I want to be realistic. Organizations should integrate ethics into their budgets. Museums and governments that borrow, lend, or claim to own artifacts should heed the research and ethical concerns and manage the financial consequences accordingly.

How should we engage with the works of artists, writers, producers, and actors who commit sexual misconduct?

In the two-part 2019 HBO documentary *Leaving Neverland*, two men describe being invited to pop star Michael Jackson's Neverland Ranch as young boys and allege that while they were there Jackson showed them pornographic images and molested them. Jackson's album *Thriller* is one of the bestselling albums of all time.

Despite allegations against him, and although he was indicted in 2003 on ten criminal counts, including child molestation, Michael Jackson was never convicted. Hollywood producer Harvey Weinstein was convicted of sexual assault and rape and sentenced to twenty-three years in prison in March 2020. And R & B musician R. Kelly was convicted of nine counts that included eight violations of the Mann Act against sexual trafficking in September 2021. The allegations prompted long-overdue conversations about how we should engage with the work of artists accused of such behavior.

Exploration

Sexual misconduct of all kinds is abhorrent and unaccept-able. When famous artists are perpetrators, how we react individually and as a society reflects on *our own* ethics.

With the question of whether and under what circum-stances we would seek to restrict or ban someone's artistic legacy, it is important to identify the stakeholders. In the cases of Michael Jackson and R. Kelly, the stakeholders include all of us who listen to their music on Spotify, Apple Music, and other streaming services; the directors of their shows and videos; and those involved in their tours and beyond. With Harvey Weinstein, the stakeholders include all of us who have watched his films over the decades, as well as innocent artists and contributors to the creation of those films.

If we choose to urge theaters and streaming services like Netflix and Amazon Prime Video to no longer show or carry or stream the work of these artists, we should keep in mind that banning artistic material negates the work and contributions of many other artists and contributors who did nothing wrong. Such bans would also distort the artistic canon and deprive future audiences of enjoying the art and understanding the full sweep of art history.

For these reasons, without in any way tolerating their despicable behavior, I lean toward protecting the art that Michael Jackson, Harvey Weinstein, and R. Kelly created. Eradicating an individual's oeuvre does little to discourage other predators. It also does not penalize those around them who tolerated their behavior and did not step forward. Most importantly, it does not repair the trauma and suffering that survivors experience.

Then the question becomes, what *should* we do, knowing that nothing can make up for the survivors' unspeakable suffering? Each of us must probe whether our own response is consistent with our principles. We can decide individually whether and how we want to engage with the art of those who have committed sexual misconduct. As a society, we can fight to ensure that the artists (or their estate) lose rights to future profits, as well as any copyrights they hold. The distributors of Harvey Weinstein's films could add a note to the beginning of his films that he was convicted of felony sex crimes, and that the participants in the creation of the film do not condone such behavior. While an imperfect solution, by removing financial gain, reminding everyone of the specifics of the horrific behavior, and providing an educational opportunity, I believe we show respect for art, music, history, cinema, and the many stakeholders involved in creating that art, while putting it in its factual context.

These very small steps toward showing respect for the survivors might at least assure them that their truth will not be covered up or forgotten. And truth would also be the essential first step if a perpetrator seeks to take responsibility for their despicable acts and commit to change.

Should there be age limits for U.S. presidential candidates?

At age seventy-eight, former U.S. vice president Joe Biden was the oldest person to be sworn in as president of the United States. His opponent, President Donald Trump, was seventy-four at the time of his reelection campaign. For perspective, the youngest U.S. president was John F. Kennedy, who was forty-three on inauguration day; President Emmanuel Macron of France, at age thirty-nine upon taking office, is the youngest French president in history; and New Zealand prime minister Jacinda Ardern became the world's youngest leader at thirty-seven. U.S. presidential candidates must be natural-born citizens, at least thirty-five years of age, and have been a resident for fourteen years, as spelled out in the Constitution. In the U.S., it is left for the voters to determine if a candidate or political leader is fit to be elected to office. Unfortunately, voters may not know a great deal about the health of those seeking the presidency. Neither the Democratic frontrunners nor President Trump released full health records in 2020, although many released some medical documents and letters from their physicians testifying to their overall health.

This question could apply just as easily to U.S. senators, members of the House of Representatives, and the Supreme Court. Most recently, legendary Supreme Court justice Ruth Bader Ginsburg passed away at eighty-seven having served for decades through multiple illnesses.

Exploration

Two questions target the ethics of presidential age limits. First, the information we need: do age limits help assure us that the president is fit to act on behalf of the nation in accordance with an individual voter's—and our nation's—ideals? Some argue that with age comes greater wisdom. Others believe that older presidents in their eighth decade and beyond might not have the physical stamina and mental acuity to handle highly complex, life-and-death decisions.

Second, do age limits violate our nation's principles? To some, imposing a maximum age limit on candidates would thwart democracy and violate free speech, as voters would be prevented from electing the candidate they prefer. Generalizing about the impact of age on an individual's physical stamina and mental acuity could be inaccurate and discriminatory.

For perspective, let's consider a few other professions that include an age limit when there is a responsibility for human life or significant social impact. At one hospital I advise, mandatory retirement for surgeons is usually set at age sixty-eight, while the age for non-surgical doctors requiring less dexterity is seventy. Under the Age Discrimination in Employment Act of

1967, companies are permitted to impose mandatory retirement for executives in high policy positions at age sixty-five. The mandatory retirement age for commercial airline pilots is sixty-five. The mandatory retirement age for military personnel under the rank of general or admiral is sixty-two.

The president is the ultimate decision maker in terms of responsibility for both human life (most notably as commander in chief of the U.S. Armed Forces) and global policy. The election of the president affects a vast stakeholder group, including citizens of other countries who have no say in our elections. The president has the potential to impact virtually every person in the world—as a model of ethics or a spreader of unethical behavior—today and for generations to come. The president helps to influence national policies, the advancement of technology (autonomous weapon systems, nuclear weapons, space exploration), the climate, geopolitical stability, national security, and infrastructure. However, in contrast to some of the professions just mentioned, the president's position, while emotionally and physically demanding, does not require high levels of physical dexterity or strength. He is also advised by experts and a senior cabinet and is held accountable by checks and balances from the two other branches of government.

In the end, I support our freedom to choose the right person with the right policies and ethics rather than the right age. But it's not "yes or no." We shouldn't prohibit candidates from running for office on the basis of a number, but the information related to each candidate is necessary to assess their leadership capacity and avoid discriminatory generalizations regardless of the number.

Should political candidates and initiatives be allowed to accept donations and support from outside the districts, cities, and states in which they're on the ballot?

Crucial runoff elections for Georgia's two U.S. Senate seats were held on January 5, 2021: between Democratic contender Jon Ossoff and Republican incumbent David Perdue and between Democratic challenger Rev. Raphael Warnock and Republican incumbent Kelly Loeffler. The outcome would determine which party would control the U.S. Senate. The race between Ossoff and Perdue would be the most expensive Senate election in American history; between the primaries, general election, and runoff election, the two candidates spent nearly $470 million. The race between Warnock and Loeffler was the second most expensive in history.

According to FiveThirtyEight (the award-winning website owned by ABC News that analyzes polls based on their accuracy, demographics, and voting patterns), 96 percent of the money Democrats raised through their ActBlue online site came from out-of-state donors. And 92 percent of the money raised by Republicans on the WinRed conservative online site was from non-Georgia residents.

Exploration

The issue of Georgia's Senate elections highlights the ethics opportunities and risks when people and organizations outside of a state fund a significant portion of a state's political campaigns.

Current law often permits individuals, political parties, political action committees (or PACs, organizations that raise money to support or defeat political candidates), and other organizations to contribute to candidates outside of the state they live in or are headquartered in. There is a strong argument in favor in the case of federal elected representatives. The president and Congress enact legislation that affects Americans throughout the country—from civil rights and voting rights to health care and infrastructure. In Georgia's case, the Democrats had to win both seats to have enough votes to be able to hold the majority in the Senate.

When the offices are not national, the argument is often less convincing. It's hard to argue for out-of-state money when it comes to governors and state-level legislators and referendums. Why should citizens outside of a district have a say in who represents the people of that district? Politicians in one state may object to money from another state influencing the outcome of their elections and distorting local fundraising efforts.

However, an argument can also be made that state-specific laws often serve as models for bills and legislation in other states. The passage of voter suppression laws in Georgia has encouraged politicians in other states to propose and pass similar legislation. Florida passed a "stand your ground" law in 2005, justifying the use of deadly force when a person believes they are in serious danger, and versions of this self-defense law have since been adopted in numerous states.

What about corporate donations? In 2010, the Supreme Court in the *Citizens United v. FEC* ruling allowed corporations to spend unlimited amounts of money on campaign ads as long as the money is not given directly to a specific candidate or party. This can give corporations outsize influence in elections, which can overwhelm individual voices and contributions. A key argument was that campaign donations constitute free speech.

In my view, we all should pay close attention to Supreme Court justice John Paul Stevens's ninety-page dissent in the case, in which he argues that the law should distinguish between funding from individual constituents and corporations. Justice Stevens emphasized that corporate campaign funds may exert "undue influence on an office-holder's judgment" and "can generate the impression that corporations dominate our democracy." He added that corporations "have no consciences, no beliefs, no feelings, no thoughts . . . They are not themselves members of 'We the People' by whom and for whom our Constitution was established."

Justice Stevens believed that the laws should distinguish between funding from individual constituents and contributions from corporations and out-of-state donors, and argued for an amendment to the Constitution "to create a level playing field." Even if we don't go as far as prohibiting out-of-state donors, Justice Stevens's proposed exclusion of corporate donations might be a helpful middle ground to making sure that the voices of individual citizens are heard, no matter where they live.

Should college basketball athletes be paid?

In a recent case, *National Collegiate Athletic Association v. Alston*, the Supreme Court unanimously ruled that the National Collegiate Athletic Association, or NCAA, must allow payment of "education-related benefits" (graduate or vocational tuition, internships, and so forth) to college athletes. The Court declined to rule on other forms of compensation, such as salary or payment for image and likeness. The Court disagreed with the NCAA's argument that allowing such payments would blur the lines between amateur and professional sports or would result in a slippery slope to abuse (like giving athletes sports cars under the guise of needing transportation).

The Supreme Court called the NCAA, the organization that governs college sports, a "massive business," citing examples such as its broadcast contract for March Madness for approximately $1.1 billion per year, and the fact that the president of the NCAA earns approximately $4 million per year. For context, universities with the top-rated teams earn millions of dollars a year from student athletes' unpaid performances on the court largely benefiting athletic departments, coaches, and university administrations. The total revenues from college athletics departments in 2019 was \$18.9 billion according to the NCAA.

With practices, games, training, and travel, for basketball players at NCAA Division I universities, their sport is a full-time job—not just in season but throughout the year. Teams can spend fifty hours a week training. Often college basketball players are at the peak of their athletic marketability and could potentially earn huge salaries if they played professionally.

On the other hand, universities offer full scholarships to attract top talent, and players are given a national platform and the kind of media attention that can result in lucrative offers from professional teams after graduation. Moreover, the majority of college athletic departments lose money—on average, \$16 million a year, reports the *Wall Street Journal*.

Exploration

Those who argue against paying students point out that student athletes are enrolled full-time as students and not as employees of the university. Many basketball players are on scholarship (which is a form of compensation) from their university already. (NCAA rules permit Division I schools to offer thirteen full scholarships to players in the men's basketball program, and fifteen full scholarships to athletes in the women's program.)

Moreover, paying athletes raises questions of fairness and institutional priorities. Students involved in nonathletic extracurricular activities (like serious musical groups or writing for the college newspaper) do not get paid, so why should players on the basketball team be paid? Why shouldn't the financial resources be used in ways that benefit more students? Paying only student athletes in revenue-generating sports like football and basketball, but not those in other sports, would increase inequality in college athletics.

In addition to their education, student athletes are provided with expensive training facilities, experienced coaching, media exposure, and an environment in which they can develop their skills. Athletes hoping to turn professional can enter the NBA draft if they are nineteen and are a season removed from high school, or they can seek work opportunities outside of sports.

Those in favor of paying players argue that athletes in revenue-generating sports like football and basketball are being exploited as cheap labor. For many, college athletics is their best avenue out of their circumstances. College basketball players generate—through ticket sales, television licensing rights, merchandise sales, and corporate sponsorships—significant income for their schools, without sharing in any of the profits. And during their time in college athletics, they risk serious injury that could prematurely end their athletic careers. While many aspire to play professionally after college, the NCAA estimates that in 2019 only 1.2 percent of men's basketball players will make the NBA.

I often urge us to break out of "yes or no" binary decisions. Recent legal changes seem to strike a fair balance.

Twenty-six states, as of 2021, have passed laws allowing college athletes to receive compensation for their names, images, or likenesses, and several additional states passed similar laws slated to go into effect in the next few years. The NCAA announced that it was embracing a temporary set of rules allowing student athletes to receive compensation for their names, images, or likenesses, beginning July 1, 2021. But watch this space. In the Supreme Court's ruling against the NCAA in June 2021, Justice Brett Kavanaugh indicated the court might be interested in going further in a future case. Other states may have more to say.

Should we remove books from bookstores, libraries, internet sales, and reading lists because they are no longer seen as politically correct or culturally acceptable?

Generations of Americans grew up reading Dr. Seuss's *How the Grinch Stole Christmas!*, *Green Eggs and Ham*, and *The Cat in the Hat*. His inventive wordplay and clever rhymes have been an essential part of childhood and have been instrumental in teaching children to read.

On March 2, 2021, Dr. Seuss Enterprises (the company that controls Dr. Seuss's estate) announced that, after consulting with experts and educators, they had decided to stop publishing six of Seuss's books because of their "hurtful and wrong" portrayals of people from other cultures. None were among his bestselling books. Among the six were *And to Think That I Saw It on Mulberry Street* (first published in 1937) and *If I Ran the Zoo* (first published in 1950), both of which display verbal and visual racial stereotypes.

The decision sparked an enormous controversy with Americans across the political spectrum, some who saw this as a positive corrective for racist and xenophobic children's literature, and others who saw the decision as yet another example of what had become known as "cancel culture," in which aspects of our culture are removed, ostracized, or called out as toxic because they don't reflect evolving social attitudes.

In August 2021, I encountered a vivid reminder of this kind of censorship at my weekly outing to my favorite California bookstore, Kepler's Books & Magazines. An unmistakable sign—BANNED BOOKS—was displayed on a table at the entrance to the open-air tent they had set up. It was the bookstore's way of reminding us of the dangers of censorship. The titles, all fiction, were classics of literature, including works by two authors who had won the Nobel Prize in Literature: J. D. Salinger's *The Catcher in the Rye*, Nobel laureate Toni Morrison's *The Bluest Eye*, Aldous Huxley's *Brave New World*, George Orwell's *1984*, Nobel laureate John Steinbeck's *Of Mice and Men*, Harper Lee's *To Kill a Mockingbird*, Maurice Sendak's *Where the Wild Things Are*, and most recently, J. K. Rowling's Harry Potter books.

I picked up copies of all the books I hadn't yet read and went inside.

Exploration

This question forces us to face a key ethical point: Who gets to determine and enforce the ethics of reading material?

Let's clarify at the outset that the decision to stop publishing several books by Dr. Seuss was taken voluntarily by the rights holder itself, rather than by another organization, publisher, school board, retailer, or individual. Accordingly, this is not what is commonly referred to as "cancellation" by another person or organization.

First, there is a compelling argument that children's books should be held to a higher standard than books for adults, because kids don't have the tools to read books critically. Authors of famous children's books have revised their books over concerns about racist content in the past. When it was first published in 1964, *Charlie and the Chocolate Factory* depicted the Oompa-Loompa factory workers as pygmies from Africa. Facing accusations of racism by the NAACP and others, author Roald Dahl reimagined them in a revised 1973 version of the book as fantasy creatures from Loompaland.

Those opposed to removing books that don't meet contemporary standards argue that banning books from curriculums, libraries, and retailers can be a slippery slope. Ten years ago, new editions of Mark Twain's *The Adventures of Huckleberry Finn* had many of the book's racial slurs removed. Nonetheless, in 2019 two New Jersey state lawmakers issued a resolution to remove *Huckleberry Finn* from state schools entirely. This leads us to important questions: How do we avoid trampling on artistic freedom? Are fictional characters depicting racism helpful to show the damage and consequences of racism? Why would we ban earlier works when contemporary works also contain racist, homophobic, and other unacceptable characters? Does erasing this literary history destroy the foundation for learning from past mistakes, and making and monitoring progress?

The question of who gets to make the decision on which books are banned or made unavailable to the public takes on a new dimension in a technological world. After the Dr. Seuss rights holder's decision, eBay immediately delisted the six books from its site. *New York Times* op-ed columnist Ross Douthat wrote that "in a cultural landscape dominated by a few big companies . . . you don't need state censorship for books to swiftly vanish."

Literature is rife with racism, and even well-meaning teachers and parents don't always recognize it. But we should not rely on authors, rights holders, publishers, and distributors of books alone to arbitrate the acceptability of literature in society. The real progress in understanding the complex relationship among fiction, persistent racism, and the need for systemic change to eradicate racism can only come with broader education and our individual commitment to learn to recognize our own responsibility.

Is it ethically acceptable to alter your date of birth so that you appear younger (or older) than you are?

In 2018, a sixty-nine-year-old Dutchman named Emile Ratelband petitioned a Netherlands court to have the date on his birth certificate changed from March 11, 1949, to March 11, 1969. He claimed that his doctor told him he had the body of a man in his early forties, and that he feels forty-nine. "Why can't I decide my own age?" Ratelband argued. Ratelband's view: the law should be changed to permit individuals to determine their own biological age, in the same way we can change our name and gender. The court disagreed. There are a number of rights and duties related to age, the court pointed out, such as the right to vote and the duty to attend school. Granting the request would cause "all kinds of legal problems," in the view of the court, effectively erasing twenty years of life events.

Exploration

The answer here rests on the single most important force driving ethics: truth. It is the foundation of our society. Truth is based on facts, not beliefs, feelings, or opinions. Compromised truth is *the* most virulent driver of the spread of unethical behavior; it undergirds every other driver of contagion—from arrogance to fake news to efforts to skirt legal compliance.

Age is a verifiable fact. Our date of birth is recorded in formal government records. There are plenty of reasons that people might like to claim to be older or younger, like making themselves appear younger and potentially more appealing on a dating website or feeling that they can better compete against younger candidates in a job market that often prioritizes youth. Some young people want to appear older to purchase alcohol or get into age-restricted bars and clubs. A member of my family, now deceased, lied about her age for decades because as a young woman she seemed destined for spinsterhood, too old to find a husband in her mind (at age twenty-five at the time).

This is not a whimsical question. Chronological facts such as age are the scaffolding for society: rights and privileges such as marriage, civil partnerships, divorce, citizenship, voter registration, driver's licenses, Medicare, Social Security, immigration forms, and an array of official documents all hinge on chronological accuracy. It is also the foundation for social contracts. We can only consent to certain acts such as medical procedures and sexual relationships when above the legally permitted age to do so. And important matters from medical diagnoses to the ability to perform functions safely at work may depend on our age.

We are not entitled to our own truth—to distorting facts in life or on the internet—despite what we encounter on social media. We *are* entitled to our opinions. If someone asks whether we like their dress, our response is an opinion, not a fact—we can keep it to ourselves if we don't like it, or we can compassionately find something positive to say. Ethical decision making hinges on keeping the difference between fact and opinion squarely in mind.

Should athletes be penalized for using legal marijuana?

On June 28, 2021, Sha'Carri Richardson, the American sprinter who won the women's 100-meter race at the U.S. Olympic Team Trials in track and field in Oregon, accepted a suspension of one month after testing positive for marijuana. The suspension voided her victory at the Olympic trials, meaning that she would not be able to compete in Tokyo in July in the 100-meter race (her signature event), even though she was one of the athletes expected to be a star at the Olympics. Although U.S. Track & Field (USTAF)—the national governing body for the sport in the U.S.—had full discretion to give her a slot in the 4x100-meter relay, which was scheduled for after expiration of the thirty-day punitive period, they declined to do so.

Richardson apologized to fans, family, sponsors, and the media. "Don't judge me, because I am human . . . I just happen to run a little faster." A week before the trials, Richardson, who was raised by her grandmother, learned that her biological mother had died, and she said that she fell into an emotional panic, and used the marijuana to calm her emotions. Marijuana is legal in Oregon.

Nicholas Thompson, CEO of the *Atlantic* magazine

and former editor in chief of *Wired*, in discussing Richardson's case said, "Pretty convinced that marijuana is not a 'performance enhancing' drug for a sprinter. Please let Sha'Carri Richardson run in Tokyo." The *Washington Post* editorial board called on USTAF to lobby the World Anti-Doping Agency to change the rules "rather than lend legitimacy to poor policy" by excluding Richardson from the 4x100-meter relay.

Exploration

Where do we draw the line in crafting rules about legal, occasional, and recreational use of marijuana in athletic competitions?

Marijuana is on the list of substances prohibited by the World Anti-Doping Agency, or WADA, and the U.S. Olympic & Paralympic Committee follows its rules. The list, which is extensive, is updated each year. The reason for the ban is that WADA believes marijuana can enhance performance, it poses a health risk to athletes, and its use violates the "spirit of the sport" (including the idea that the "role model of athletes in modern society is intrinsically incompatible with use or abuse of cannabis"). Other banned substances include anabolic androgenic steroids, growth hormones, diuretics, stimulants, and erythropoietins, all of which can enhance performance. However, marijuana is only banned the day before a competition, and a small amount of THC, the main psychoactive substance, will not cause a positive test. The minimum penalty for a positive test, which Richardson received, is a one-month suspension.

Attempts to enhance athletic performance by using banned substances is clearly cheating. But legal recreational use of marijuana is not a performance enhancement, according to the *Journal of Sports Medicine and Physical Fitness* and other experts. In the wake of Richardson's suspension, the *New York Times* reported "an overview of the research concludes that marijuana hinders performance by reducing stamina and peak performance." In 2019, Major League Baseball removed marijuana from its banned substances list effective Spring Training of 2020.

We should also consider the use of substances that are permitted, like alcohol—potentially dangerous to both health and the role model objective, if abused. Some studies suggest that caffeine may enhance athletic endurance. Perhaps because caffeine is contained in so many beverages and products, from coffee, tea, and soda to protein bars, attempting to ban it would be virtually impossible. (To be clear, I'm not arguing that all products containing caffeine should be banned—just that we need perspective.)

By Richardson's own acknowledgment, she knew the rules. We often live by guidelines and ethical standards to be part of a community—for example, a university, a competition, or a workplace—that are more restrictive than the generally applicable laws and rules. Effective international guidelines can spread positive standards and behaviors and raise our ethics along with our athletics.

Richardson should not have done what she did. But she was a role model here in two important respects. She showed us that there is no place for blame and shame in ethics—deploying her world-class athlete status and celebrity to remind us that we all make mistakes instead of offering excuses. And she took responsibility and made a plan to move forward: the very definition of ethical resilience.

WADA and the U.S. Olympic & Paralympic Committee are rightfully committed to eradicating dangerous, performance-enhancing substances. But in my view the issue of banning legal marijuana use is ripe for reconsideration.

Is voting—or deciding not to vote—an ethics choice?

I received an email from BallotTrax Notifications in the fall of 2020: "Your ballot for the 2020 General Election was received and will be counted. Thank you for voting!" The verification of my vote was particularly important to me for a presidential election—it recorded one of the most ethically important decisions that I can make.

In these challenging times, voting—and considering a candidate's ethics in our decisions—can seem daunting. I have several friends who admitted to me before the 2020 U.S. presidential election that they planned to sit it out. They were reacting to the deluge of claims, facts and fake news, and the extreme partisanship. There were many other factors at play as well—wait times, the potential to become infected by Covid-19, and the very real constraints embedded in our voting infrastructure that disenfranchise voters, such as gerrymandering, manipulation of the location of official voting ballot boxes, and challenges to online voting. Particularly in combination, these challenges understandably made voting feel, for some, overwhelming and not worth the effort.

Exploration

The election of a political leader—whether at the federal, state, or local level—is a game-changing opportunity to vote our consciences.

Abstaining from voting diminishes our influence on matters such as national security, domestic policy, individual rights, privacy, Supreme Court appointments, and immigration. We forfeit our voices on cutting-edge, ethically critical issues such as internet safety, gun rights, gene editing, global warming, and artificial intelligence that will shape society for decades to come. And because we have the power to choose—whether or not we use it—we have responsibility; refraining from voting does not absolve us of ethical responsibility for the results of elections.

I work with a four-word framework for ethical decision making that can help guide us through this question: *principles*, *information*, *stakeholders*, and *consequences*.

First, your principles signal to the world who you are, how you act, and how you expect others to behave. Do the candidates' stated principles align with yours?

Second, evaluate the available information. Ask whether the candidates' actions—their behaviors, policies, voting records, and positions on specific issues—align with their stated principles and promises. Conversely, ask whether the candidate exhibits drivers of the spread of unethical behavior: greed, bullying, failure to listen, abuse of power, a demand for loyalty over a diversity of views, arrogance, and manipulation of social media. Most importantly, ask whether the candidate values truth. Compromising truth is, in my view, the greatest global systemic risk of our time, because it infiltrates and catalyzes every other action and behavior.

If you strongly agree with the candidate's policies (or you're a single-issue voter) but find their behavior abhorrent, ask yourself: Would I tolerate this same behavior from a friend? How would I feel if the CEO of my company or my direct boss acted this way?

Finally, think about stakeholders and consequences. Some would argue that your individual vote doesn't matter. But fewer than a combined total of 80,000 votes in the states of Michigan, Wisconsin, and Pennsylvania would have swung the presidential election to Hillary Clinton in 2016. Al Gore lost to George W. Bush in 2000 in the decisive state of Florida by 537 votes out of over 6 million cast. More recently, in the two elections in Georgia for the U.S. Senate, the two Democratic candidates, in a traditionally Republican state, won runoff elections, by about 55,000 votes in the case of Jon Ossoff, and about 93,000 votes in the case of Raphael Warnock, giving Democrats control of the Senate. So not only did these elections affect people on a state level, but also the national level and beyond our borders.

The consequence of abstaining from voting is that we are giving up our power to determine who leads us and the ethics of our leadership today and in the future. One of the candidates is going to be elected. We don't get to choose "none of the above." If all eligible voters vote, and consciously factor in the ethics of the candidates into our decisions, imagine how we would raise the collective ethical standards of the leaders we elect.

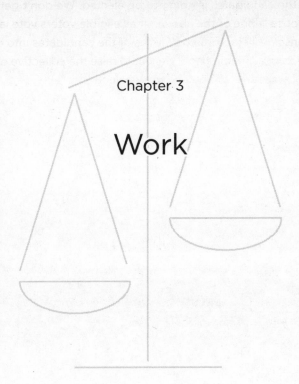

Chapter 3

Work

What is appropriate behavior in a "business social" setting?

The 2018 *Financial Times* headline read: "Men Only: Inside the charity fundraiser where hostesses are put on show." The story that followed described the exclusive Presidents Club Charity Dinner, an annual "secretive black-tie" event at one of London's most prestigious hotel ballrooms, that hired 130 hostesses wearing revealing black outfits and underwear. The charity donated money to the world-renowned Great Ormond Street Hospital for Children, bringing together business colleagues, clients, the political elite, and wealthy donors, in what was supposed to be a social evening. The *Financial Times* reported that "At an after-party many hostesses—some of them students earning extra cash—were groped, sexually harassed and propositioned."

Another example: At a company conference in Texas, which included corporate clients, managers, and employees, the days were full, but the evenings were free. A mid-level female manager casually suggested that her team—all men—go out for drinks at a local strip club.

Exploration

Most work social situations don't make newspaper headlines or involve political leaders. But events that mix business with leisure (and often alcohol) can frequently go awry ethically. And taking a wrong step can alter career trajectories and reputations.

Social gatherings are an important part of work, whether catching up at the coffee machine, formal company events like a holiday party, inviting colleagues to charity events, or more informal smaller group activities. There's nothing unethical about colleagues having a drink or participating in a sporting activity after work. But over the years, I have seen a disproportionate number of high-performing, thoughtful people tainting their reputations in these mixed social settings.

The ethical boundaries between work and our personal lives are not complicated. To understand expectations for behavior at an event described as "business social," just eliminate the word "social" in your mind, and you'll have your guide. Ditto any social situation with colleagues. This includes going out for meals, or an evening out when traveling for work. Conferences are not ethics-free zones—even after hours and off-site. And this applies to all aspects of behavior, from attire and alcohol consumption to topics of conversation. Employees can be made to feel uncomfortable or pressured to participate in various activities, particularly if invited by a manager or boss. Nonetheless we are each responsible for our behavior, whether or not a manager invited us.

Headlines about misconduct at Uber, the Presidents Club event, and beyond have effectively put organizations on notice that wherever misbehavior happens (even online) the world no longer tolerates a culture of "it's not that serious." Let's be clear: there is no corporate "culture" that should tolerate inappropriate language or behavior in the office, online, or around gatherings of company stakeholders outside of the office. And in the end, corporate culture reflects individual decisions.

Every CEO and chief legal, ethics, or compliance officer I know has seen the destructive fallout of drinking too much. People say and do things they never otherwise would. Rob Chesnut, former chief ethics officer of Airbnb, described what he called Rob's Rule to me: two drinks. That's his maximum, to have a nice time and remain in control. Your own rule may be different. But as Rob says, the point is to have a rule in place before you start socializing. The worst time to negotiate that kind of stop limit with yourself is while you're at a party.

A lot of reported misbehavior occurs at after-parties. Here again, there is no problem with colleagues going off as a group to a bar or a restaurant after the formal event. But in a business setting, drop the word "after"; behave as if the original business event is continuing. The ethics haven't changed, whether the partners are there or not.

Overstepping boundaries or outright misconduct is not limited to a particular gender or level of seniority. Companies are responsible for clarifying policies and consequences. But it bears repeating that each of us is responsible for our actions.

Should your employer have a say in what you post on your private social media?

A key member of the senior management team of a company posted anti–Black Lives Matter movement comments on her private social media account. Offended by the posts, a group of employees wanted the CEO to fire the executive.

In practice, the individual involved was one of the company's strongest proponents of diversity and inclusion and ran a highly diverse team. She took issue with the politics of a splinter group within the movement, not with the importance of fighting racism. The CEO asked the executive to take down the social media posting and apologize. The executive refused, citing her freedom to post on private social media as long as the posts are in accordance with the law and the social media company's terms of service.

Exploration

People chatting about the inner workings of a company or current events used to be called watercooler gossip. The audience reach was limited and the banter by and large reasonably acceptable.

Today, millions share their personal lives and political views on multiple social media and communications platforms, from Facebook and Twitter to Instagram, Slack, and LinkedIn. Furthermore, companies depend on social media to reach customers and promote products. With some companies, the platform *is* their business model. Drawing a line between work life and private life can pit free speech against a company's right to uphold its ethical principles—and protect its reputation.

Four guides apply in all situations.

First, inciting violence, hate speech, bullying, and harassment is off limits (and also not permitted under the terms of service of most social media apps).

Second, you may not have control over where content ends up. Anything you post could be forwarded to employers, clients, the media, and beyond. When in doubt, err on the side of professionalism.

With company communications, there are some clear "no" situations. Company electronic signature lines (with titles and work contact details), email addresses, stationery, websites, and logos are for company business only. You are acting as a representative of the company. What would you think if colleagues were to advocate for causes or products you or others don't support using company communications?

Private social media is a more challenging dilemma. For example, sexually graphic material or offensive jokes are often within the normal bounds of free speech, but not likely acceptable to an employer. What you do outside of work also reflects who you are as a person, as well as your judgment. Ask yourself if you are potentially making others feel uncomfortable, or even undermining trust—and how private your social media groups are. In the above scenario, the executive could have communicated privately her specific concerns about the behaviors and statements of individuals within the Black Lives Matter movement, while recognizing the movement's important anti-racist work and affirming her commitment to fighting racism at and outside of work. Senior leaders are more visible and have a greater responsibility to a wide range of stakeholders.

Third, the fact that we work from home is not a license to mix the personal with our professional responsibilities. The shift to working remotely due to Covid-19 and new technologies may further smudge the lines. And the boundaries may differ depending on the type of organization you work for (a tech start-up versus a governmental department).

Finally, in some countries, social media can put others in danger. Employees in one situation I researched knew that posting commentary critical of the government was likely to incite a serious response from the police such as arrest. The posting could have been potentially dangerous, whether or not it would have been considered protected speech elsewhere.

Ask yourself whether your post is worth the various risks.

What would you do when others take credit for your work?

As a very junior lawyer, I was working on a huge international deal with a senior associate who was trying to make partner. I spent days preparing over eighty documents for a deal closing. On the morning of the closing, I overheard one of the firm's senior partners complimenting the senior associate I was working with on what he referred to as the "superb organization." She thanked him, slipping in that she had worked through the night, even though I was the one who had stayed up all night to organize the documents.

Exploration

Taking credit when you do not deserve it tramples on ethical principles many of us share: honesty, integrity, collegiality, accountability, generosity, and, most importantly, truth. These principles apply regardless of seniority, or the situation.

Taking credit for other people's work is all too common. For example, the husband of a friend who has a skewed view of his contributions to the evening's dinner, or a colleague accepting a boss's compliment for a report that was largely produced by an outside advisor. Even if these situations seem small, each requires us to tackle the *spread* of unethical behavior, not just the behavior itself. Silence can allow falsity to fester and become the norm. And if we allow truth to be compromised, other threats to ethics will breed as well: competition, jealousy, greed, pressure, fear.

We usually don't need a lot of information to make an ethical decision in scenarios like these. But it's worth considering frequency (whether this is a first offense or a consistent pattern) and the nature of your relationship with the other person (regular interaction versus one-time collaboration). It's also helpful to remember that unconscious bias can sneakily alter our perceptions of who did what—and how much we contributed. Research by Harvard University professor Max H. Bazerman and others shows that when group members are asked what percentage of the group's work was done by each of them, the total "typically far exceeds 100 percent."

How do we respond? Publicly embarrassing the person or involving too many other people is neither helpful, nor a show of the principles listed above. If it's a minor first-time offense with no important consequences, consider yourself on alert and think about acting only if there is a second offense. You might speak to the person, and give them a chance to explain, apologize, and take responsibility (or even correct the misunderstanding). If it's a more serious issue, you can speak to your boss, Human

Resources, another senior person, or an Ombuds service. Or you might sidestep it: armed with confidence in your own contributions, ask for more responsibilities and prove yourself with another assignment.

Do create space for others to grant credit. I ask my Stanford students to report team members' exceptional work after team projects are completed. If you're tempted to accept undue credit by not correcting someone else's assumption, consider the impact on your reputation—the undermining of trust and relationships, not to mention how it might affect your performance evaluations and subsequent recommendations for promotions. And what do you do when your boss asks you to complete a similar task, but you don't really have the skills? That is the danger of contagion of unethical behavior; accepting credit for someone else's work sets a number of ethical violations in motion—the ramifications of which can be hard to foresee.

How would you respond if you witnessed a boss sexually harassing or bullying a more junior colleague?

At the company you work for, you notice some uncomfortable behavior on the part of a manager. At staff meetings, he ignores a female coworker who tries to ask a question. When someone else invites the woman to speak, the manager interrupts, drowning her out. A week later, you overhear him berating the employee at her desk, using inappropriate language. You ask her about it later, but she refuses to talk.

You are a bystander—someone who witnessed bullying and harassment but is not personally involved.

Exploration

As an ethics advisor, I encounter stories of bullying and harassment in organizations of all sizes and with all combinations of seniority.

Bullying often falls on a spectrum, with irritating banter at one end, and sexually or racially charged behavior at the other. Two hallmarks of bullying are the repetition and the targeting of an individual or group. The behavior may range from subtle verbal digs, "accidentally" omitting someone from an email chain, or sabotaging one's ability to do their job—to blatant disrespect or aggression. The tricky cases to resolve are those that are not explicit enough to trigger the company's antibullying policy and don't involve racist or sexual content. Regardless, all types of bullying and harassment are unacceptable.

First, check your company's policy to determine if you have a responsibility to intervene, regardless of whether you are a manager. It may also indicate if you are protected from potential retaliation and offer guidance on whether the behavior you witnessed is bullying, harassment, or sexual misconduct. To me, safety and respect are the most important considerations in this situation. If a colleague's safety or well-being is at stake, I would consider intervening early and quickly.

One potential consequence of not taking action is the continuation or even escalation of the behavior. If the manager's actions are not investigated, your colleague will continue to suffer, potentially undermining trust in the organization. Others may begin to see the manager's behavior as normal, or even copy it to curry favor.

If your colleague declines having you act on her behalf, perhaps she would agree to your sharing just one aspect of the behavior. Or if the manager's actions make you and others uncomfortable, you might consider reporting the impact of the behavior on you, or joining others in reporting it. Consider consulting with a confidential source—your

Human Resources manager, an Ombuds service, an external lawyer, or your own manager. And you can continue to show understanding and support to your colleague and be available to step in if she changes her mind.

Bystander scenarios can occur anywhere: on the street, at the gym, at the movies. Certain situations require immediate action, such as calling the police if someone is in physical danger. (That said, you have no obligation to put yourself in harm's way by intervening directly.) In the workplace, you are operating within a structure in which you are *automatically involved—a stakeholder*. You have company regulations and guidelines to help you; you are more likely to be personally affected by the behavior and require protection from retaliation.

Reporting the abuse could result in conflict with your colleague if she doesn't want your involvement and feels you are disrespecting her privacy. And I would be remiss in not acknowledging that taking action could result in retaliation against you or your coworkers by the person accused and those who support them. None of us want to cause more harm by trying to help. Unfortunately, there are no guarantees in this situation.

Should CEOs speak out about important social and political issues of the day?

I n March 2021, CEOs from over one hundred companies, including major airlines, retailers, and manufacturers, gathered to discuss taking action against restrictive voting laws that had been enacted in Georgia and were being considered in several states. Kenneth Chenault, former CEO of American Express, and Kenneth Frazier, then CEO of Merck & Co., led an effort to organize seventy-two Black business leaders to sign a letter to band together to fight restrictive voting rights in Georgia and forty-two other states. Delta CEO Ed Bastian called the Georgia voting bill "unacceptable." Alfredo Rivera, the president of North America for Coca-Cola, which is headquartered in Georgia, also spoke out over the new laws, as did Apple CEO Tim Cook. Major League Baseball moved the Draft and the All-Star Game from Atlanta on April 2, 2021, in response to the new voting laws. In contrast, after considerable thought, McDonald's CEO Chris Kempczinski did not speak out against restrictive voting laws. He said, "In the case of voting rights, it wasn't our business. It wasn't aligned with one of our leadership platforms. And we didn't feel like our voice was going to be particularly helpful to addressing the issues."

Senate minority leader Mitch McConnell denounced such efforts, urging corporate leaders to "stay out of politics."

Exploration

While this question might seem just for corporate CEOs and boards, it's one for all of us to consider as employees, consumers, citizens, shareholders, and other stakeholders, about some of the most critical issues affecting society today—and the role and influence business has in these issues and our lives.

CEOs are free to choose what societal issues they speak up about. Importantly, in contrast, CEOs have an *obligation* to speak up about issues clearly within the company's responsibility, like product safety, customer data privacy, or antitrust regulation. In addition, every CEO I know of feels an ethical and legal responsibility to combat racism and other forms of bias and discrimination within their organization (including requiring suppliers, service providers, and other stakeholders to comply with their antidiscrimination policies), and they would owe transparency about any serious misconduct.

When speaking out about societal issues, I recommend CEOs advocate for an organization's lasting principles rather than supporting social movements (in favor of sustainability rather than to promote a particular group or hashtag). Movements can take unpredictable directions, create reputational risk on social media (or worse), and have rogue actors or splinter groups. CEOs should communicate the company's actions to further its principles, while acknowledging mistakes and the work still to be done.

Some CEOs may decide to establish a "no go" zone. For example, multinational companies might take the view that they never speak out to promote or critique a government's political stance—whether authoritarian regimes or democracies. Such blanket bans help leadership to sidestep government requests, and potentially threats, especially to the safety of employees.

Many CEOs stick exclusively to issues that directly affect their business. Kempczinski said in an interview in the *New York Times*, "Where do we speak up on an issue? . . . Is it either directly in our industry . . . or does it go specifically to the pillars that we've said are going to matter to us? So we've talked about jobs and opportunity. We've talked about helping communities in crisis."

Once a CEO has spoken, he or she has started a conversation. Often pressure mounts to continue to speak out or monitor and act on the issue as it evolves. Critics may query why a CEO spoke out on one issue but isn't speaking out on the issue they care most about—like the 145 CEOs who sent Congress a letter demanding action on gun control in 2019, but may not have said anything publicly about the U.S. southern border crisis. No CEO owes us to speak out on our issues or to agree with our views. They do owe us and society to *behave and run their business ethically.*

Would you hire someone who has made a mistake and is looking for a second chance?

I find in my ethics advisory work that organizations are beginning to integrate ethics into the recruiting process: verifying records and behavior, checking social media history, probing references, hiring me to do special ethics-focused interviews. Some job descriptions now highlight a track record of ethical behavior as a necessary qualification. Global organizations take extra care with references to ensure cultural sensitivity. Whether explicitly or not, the attitude is often zero tolerance: past offenders need not apply.

In our personal lives, too, our ethics antennae are up with respect to babysitters, music teachers, and school sports coaches who will interact with our children, and even painters, plumbers, electricians, and other service providers who will be working in our homes.

Exploration

To begin, a few key assumptions: We're not talking about minor offenses, like swiping a pack of gum when we were ten years old. Nor are we talking about the other extreme, like sex offenders or violent criminals whose postprison rights may be a matter of law. We're in the space in between, in which ethics really matter, but the law doesn't offer guidance.

The point here is not forgiveness. We were not the ones harmed by their earlier conduct. And we don't owe anyone a job or a second chance. But here are a few questions that bring considerations such as nonjudgment, compassion, and generosity into practice to help us determine if we are willing to try.

The first question to ask is, Who is this person *today*? You need in-depth information about the precise nature of both the misbehavior and the person's efforts to remedy that behavior and demonstrate permanent change. Ask yourself if the incident was a one-off (a one-time misstatement to save face), or if there is evidence of a pattern of misbehavior (repeatedly posting hate speech on social media). Check whether they have guardrails in place to ensure they don't slip again. The more time that has passed without further incidents, the more credibility they have.

Next, look outward. Has the world changed? Many women in my mother's generation smoked while pregnant because in 1960 no one knew any better. People's attitudes and beliefs about racism, sexism, and LGBTQ+ rights, for example, can evolve over time as they learn more. (To be clear, sexual harassment, discrimination, and racism were never ethically acceptable.)

Consider the relationship between the job and the misbehavior. Most important, consider the other people for whom you are responsible (employees, children, an elderly parent). For example, I wouldn't put someone who has stolen money in charge of finances or hire someone with a DUI (driving under the influence citation) to be a driver.

There are some red lines. Candidates with a history of hate speech should not be put in situations of responsibility for vulnerable people, like caring for children, working in hospitals or assisted living facilities, or working with people with disabilities, addictions, or mental health issues.

If we reject someone who has made a past mistake, where does that leave us when we err ourselves? We could be missing an opportunity to make a difference in someone else's life—and our own. We each have the power to model and spread ethical behavior; giving others a second chance can be an opportunity to spread hope, compassion, and transparency. Not giving others (and ourselves) space to learn and change can also catalyze insidious drivers of unethical behavior—particularly perfectionism, shame, and the sense that there's no point in trying. That said, while a second chance might be the ethical path, a twenty-second chance is willful blindness.

Are we responsible for acting on information obtained without permission?

Imagine that you glanced at your colleague's computer screen while she steps away to refill her coffee or attend a meeting. The details aren't important except one: you didn't have permission to look. Now you have information that you wouldn't otherwise have. It appears as if your colleague is claiming some remote workdays that she took as vacation days recently. No one else would know, as she does a lot of independent work on projects remotely.

Or consider a variation of that scenario: you see a text on your spouse's or partner's phone without permission, a reminder for a Gamblers Anonymous (GA) meeting. An addiction can be very difficult for even those close to the person to detect. You had no idea, and you are very concerned, not least because your partner kept it from you. And you can't help but wonder—if your partner has been gambling, where has the money come from? How long has this been going on?

Exploration

This question hinges on whether how we *obtain* information affects the ethics of our decision.

Whether a discovery is accidental or intentional, remember, you may not know what you think you know. Perhaps your colleague's boss gave special permission for additional vacation days. Or maybe she misunderstood the policy and made an honest mistake. You don't know whether this is a first offense or an escalating pattern—or even if she followed through with the request. And your partner's Gamblers Anonymous meeting may have been an appointment to support a friend. (Whatever the situation is, seeking help, and helping others to seek help, is admirable and courageous.) Ethics start with questioning rather than accusing.

Next, consider the potential consequences of your decision, particularly those that are important and irreparable. What if you accidentally see an email in which a colleague asks an employee to delete an inspection report, or an email that contains harassment—behaviors that could result in real harm? Or some financial dishonesty that affects clients and the reputation of the company? Failure to report more serious situations could result in the person continuing the wrongdoing, harm to the company and others, and consequences for you if you have an obligation under company policies to report misconduct. Consider also the extent to which the issue is within your own realm of responsibility. And yes, reporting also risks rupturing your relationship with your colleague.

When ethical decisions go awry, we should ask what the perpetrator *knew*, *could have known*, or *should have known*. Unfortunately, the first perpetrator here is *you—you* obtained information without permission. The twist here is that you know, but should not have known.

The next challenge is whether and how to divulge the information you have. Ask the person directly involved; don't consult Human Resources, the person's manager, or another third party. Once you share information, you can't un-share it. If you're wrong, you don't want false accusations floating around—or accurate reports that you're not minding your own business. You owe the other person privacy and the benefit of the doubt. Give the person a chance to fix the problem or come clean proactively. If they don't take action, then you can escalate your concern if the matter is serious enough.

What about your spouse or partner and Gamblers Anonymous? If you discover clues indicating that you are in a relationship with a compulsive gambler, speak directly to your partner. Addiction is a serious illness that scatters shrapnel far and wide, from co-addiction, to financial irresponsibility, to violating the law. It is a heartbreaking disease.

The bottom line is, if you come into the possession of important information, you have responsibility to prevent possible serious harm, however you obtained it. Make sure one ethical misstep doesn't beget another, such as by lying to cover up what you know. There's a fine line between "it's not your story to tell" and "it's a story you must tell even if doing so reveals the questionable way you learned of the story in the first place."

Would you apply for a job that your friend is also applying for?

Imagine that you have been working hard in the marketing department of a company for several years, when you learn of an opening for an art director. These roles are rare, and it seems like a fantastic opportunity. But your best friend heard of it online, too, and confides in you excitedly that she is sending in her résumé. Do you still pursue it?

Exploration

Lebanese poet and author Kahlil Gibran wrote that "friendship is always a sweet responsibility, never an opportunity." Of the many conversations I had in researching this book, this one turned out to be one of the most difficult for many people because it challenges us to consider more broadly how we would behave as a friend.

Start with the principles at stake, because they establish who you are and how you want to behave toward others: respect, accountability, kindness, nonjudgment, and honesty.

These principles would most likely encourage you to tell your friend that you are applying for the job as soon as you make the decision—not after you have the third round of interviews. Whatever your friend's response, you will have given her a chance to discuss this with you before you proceed. You will have acted in a way that builds trust over time, even if it introduces strain.

Consider what and who else matters. Is this truly your dream job? Are you desperately in need of it to meet family obligations? Or are you in a rewarding role already and just interested in testing the waters? Answer the same questions for your friend. Then let her answer these questions. Friendships based on honesty and respect should be able to withstand this effort to grapple with the situation, over time. Does your friendship genuinely support you in seizing new opportunities and being your best self? Is there anything in your situation that would suggest that the risk to your friendship is not worth it? Would your evaluation of the situation change if your friend is recovering from a serious illness, or is a single parent with young children to care for?

Remember, you are not making the decision about who gets the job. The employer is. Most employers take a number of factors into account—skills and experience, diversity in hiring, passion, a candidate's commitment to the job, longer-term ambitions, and culture fit. Deciding not to apply may have no bearing over whether your friend gets the job.

We don't have an ethical responsibility to give up job

opportunities—or our dreams. Nor do we get a pass for not telling our friend, applying, and not getting the job. There's no risk-free option here.

Friends frequently try out for the same sports teams, audition for the same plays, pursue the same senior roles in a company. Trust is built on truth—not on winning or losing a job or a sporting event.

There are some hard lines—you don't try to nudge a friend out of applying for the job, or speak ill of your friend during the recruiting process, should that occasion arise. Now, consider this variation: you only learn about this dream job through your friend. Does that change your answer?

Sometimes the seemingly commonplace dilemmas are the most difficult of all.

What are the ethical considerations of blind hiring?

In 1969, the New York Philharmonic was accused of racial discrimination by two Black musicians. The New York City Commission on Human Rights ruled against the musicians but concluded that aspects of the way the orchestra hired were discriminatory. At the time, American orchestras were made up primarily of white male musicians. In an attempt to avoid bias, a number of orchestras in the 1970s and 1980s began using blind auditions, whereby candidates perform behind a screen so that judges base their decisions of whom to hire on their ears rather than potentially prejudging a candidate based on their own biases regarding race or gender. While this hiring system has appeared to significantly increase the number of female musicians among American orchestras, a 2016 report by the League of American Orchestras stated that between 2002 and 2014, "the proportion of Hispanic/Latino musicians started at 1.8 percent . . . and grew to just 2.5 percent," and "the proportion of African American musicians hovered at around 1.8 percent."

Exploration

Most of us aren't auditioning musicians in our daily lives. But there is increasing pressure on employers across industries from start-ups to major financial services firms to hire diverse staff. Blind hiring practices remove key candidate information from the recruiting process, such as one's photo, name, and identity, in an effort to prevent bias on the basis of gender, race, age, religion, and background. New technology has facilitated early-stage filtering of candidate information.

Arguments against blind hiring include the fact that candidates' personal information can only be hidden during the initial stage; in the interview stage, various aspects of identity are revealed. Additionally, candidates lose the opportunity to explain any negatives on their résumé that might eliminate them early on, such as a candidate who temporarily left the workforce to care for children or an elderly parent. Blind hiring may dismantle affirmative action efforts where they exist. And the technology used to screen candidates can skew results. In 2015, Amazon discovered that the AI in the experimental hiring tool they used to evaluate candidates was biased against women, because the data it relied on came from a time when most résumés were from men.

Blind recruiting processes work best where technical skills are a priority. Where people skills are critical, employers or recruiters should be more flexible to fit the job with the skills needed.

When I chair search committees, I ask search firms to explain their own efforts to seek out diversity and inclusion, and to show me their data. I also always ask to see stretch candidates who may not seem like an obvious fit or quite ready for the role but who might be able to grow into the role.

In all cases, what comes next is just as important: the commitment on the part of the organization to assure integration into the position, mentoring opportunities, providing resources to facilitate a new hire's success, and oversight of compensation and career advancement. Being hired is just the first step in becoming a valued and successful employee, just as hiring is just the first step in employers' responsibility to assure a diverse and thriving work environment.

Should employers be permitted to consult candidates' social media accounts as part of the recruiting process?

You are applying for a job you really want, whether it's a dream career move or a temporary stint to help you supplement income. And you're wondering whether the employer will check your social media. After all, you found the job through a listing on a social media site. The job description and recruiting instructions didn't mention anything about it. You're wondering what you can reasonably expect, and how you might respond to inquiries about any questionable postings you might have if they do check your social media.

According to Pew Research Center, seven in ten adults are on Facebook, and seven out of ten of those users visit the site at least once a day. LinkedIn, the professional networking site, now has 800 million members, with 99 percent of the Fortune 500 having a presence on LinkedIn. Many employers today use social media, including Facebook, LinkedIn, Twitter, and Instagram, to post jobs and look up information on potential candidates. Even families use social media to vet babysitters and other household service providers.

Exploration

So far there is seemingly little that candidates can do about employers using social media research in recruiting. On the other hand, social media has facilitated employment opportunities globally through job postings, helping connect companies and candidates.

Given how many people use social media professionally and personally, it has become one of the ways that many people present themselves to the world, and in the process the lines between our personal and professional lives have blurred.

Companies currently look on social media since it can indicate whether candidates might be respectful, creative, curious, and helpful—as well as reveal potentially worrisome content.

So how should employers think about their use of social media in the recruiting process? What should candidates know?

Employers should have a clear job description on social media and in all postings for any positions they are looking to fill, listing the skills required, responsibilities, pay structure, hours, and any other unique considerations. Employers should be *transparent about whether they are consulting social media in making a hiring decision*. Hiring should involve a multipronged process, which, depending on the role, may include: résumé, statement of reasons for interest in the role, qualifications, interviews, references, and skills and personality tests. (In a family or other personal situation some of this may be less formal, but interviews and references are essential.) All of these steps underpin accountability for hiring for the right reasons, and putting any investigation into a candidate's social media in perspective.

Employers should give candidates an opportunity to explain anything troubling that appears on their social media—perhaps providing context or acknowledging a mistake. Employers will likely learn information on social media that could not be legally or ethically asked in an interview, so they should take extra care to handle properly any information that could trigger bias with regard to age, race, gender, sexual orientation, religious affiliation, marital status, children, and other protected characteristics. On the other hand, I wonder how employers can completely disregard ("un-know") information obtained without asking the candidate.

There are boundaries of privacy that companies should not cross, such as asking for candidates' passwords or raising questions about other individuals who appear in posts. Probing a candidate's understanding of what is and isn't appropriate to post on social media when in the role, however, is fair game.

As a candidate, when an employer does an internet search, your social media will appear. It is unrealistic to think that your public postings will not be seen (both past and future posts, once you are hired). Assume everything you post could end up in employers' hands. (I had one case where a former college roommate of a candidate sent a screenshot of a now twenty-eight-year-old's racist tweets from college to a new employer. He was immediately fired.) And be honest in the interview. Whatever you may have posted, or done, dishonesty will only further undermine the ethics and destroy trust.

Are you obligated to
report colleagues having
a relationship?

You become aware that a manager of another group in your company has started to date someone more junior in her department—perhaps one of them has told you they went out to dinner or went dancing together. You're not sure if you have an obligation to say anything to Human Resources, or to the manager's boss.

I have seen many examples like this in my work as an ethics advisor: The head of the London office of a company dating the head of a division. A junior manager who didn't know how to handle her (unverified) sense that two of her direct reports were in a budding relationship. A story that hit the media of a CEO dating an outside consultant hired by the company. But uncomfortable situations can arise in nonromantic situations, as well. In one such case two senior managers had been college dorm buddies. Each hired extensively from their college and continued to socialize as a pack; those who weren't graduates of the university felt increasingly excluded.

Exploration

This question hinges on conflicts of interest—situations in which people might act out of personal interest (protecting their relationships) rather than in line with their professional responsibilities and in the best interest of the organization. Conflicts of interest can spur the spreading of unethical behavior, including unfairness or impunity, to fear, secrets, gossip, and even sexual harassment or bullying.

The practical fallout is that office environments become uncomfortable, trust falters because everyone knows about the secret, stress levels skyrocket, and the potential for unfairness increases.

Companies should require employees involved in a relationship with other employees or external providers to disclose the relationship confidentially to Human Resources or a manager relatively early on. The trouble comes with determining what "early on" means. It's tricky. Not after a first date, certainly, but well before your relationship has become office gossip.

Work relationships should be off limits for anyone in a senior leadership role. There is such a power imbalance with senior leaders, and their reach is so broad, that there is no conflict-free space. The same is true for compliance, Human Resources, and legal teams, even at more junior levels, because they have access to, and responsibility over, confidential files and decisions. On the other hand, junior employees, particularly in different offices, divisions, or specialties and reporting lines (no common boss or dependency on each other's work such as colleagues on a team), should be able to have properly reported relationships. People meet romantic partners at work. I believe companies should set clear and reasonable boundaries and reporting requirements, and then stay out of employees' private lives.

By reporting confidentially to an Ombuds service or to Human Resources, you're (rightly) making the ethics question the company's responsibility to determine whether the relationship is appropriate, and how to manage it. I don't recommend speaking to the individuals involved directly, unless one of them has confided in you (in which case you can urge them to report the relationship themselves). It could damage your office relationships or position you as a meddler, and you may not have accurate information about the relationship, or whether or not it was already reported. The best option may be to stay silent if the situation has no impact on your own work.

If and when you do report a relationship, keep in mind that the company doesn't owe you an explanation for how and why they resolved the issue. Potential solutions may include moving one or both employees into different roles, or locations, or one participant leaving the organization. Companies should take extra care to ensure that women and the more junior employees are not unfairly penalized.

Personal behavior belongs outside the office, whether or not relationships are reported.

Do I need to take unconscious bias training every year?

In the late 1980s when I started out as a young lawyer, a friend who worked at an investment bank described something called diversity training as part of her introduction for new hires. She saw it as a good-faith initiative from well-intentioned leaders, but felt the questions were absurd (even by late 1980s standards). One hypothetical scenario probed what they should do if an important client inappropriately suggested a wet T-shirt contest at a deal-closing event. Another was blatantly homophobic. This training primarily targeted new recruits; she never received an invitation to a second round of training. It also seemed more focused on getting the "right answer" to various scenarios than actually training young bankers to recognize, and commit to eradicating, bias, discrimination, and inequality in real life.

The term "implicit bias" or "unconscious bias" refers to our "attitudes and beliefs that occur outside of our conscious awareness and control."

Exploration

I have learned from research, experts, and professional situations that all humans experience unconscious bias regardless of their level of education, socioeconomic situation, seniority within an organization, and other factors—and that it wreaks havoc on our ethics. Eradicating unconscious bias requires a sustained lifelong commitment to learning to make us aware—conscious—of our biases. As professors Max H. Bazerman of Harvard and his co-author Ann E. Tenbrunsel point out in their book *Blind Spots: Why We Fail to Do What's Right and What to Do About It*, we're not as ethical in our decision making as we like to think we are. Unconscious bias is one reason for that. Racism and other forms of bias are enmeshed in our systems and institutions. But we as individuals have a responsibility to do our part as well.

Why is *regular* training so important? Bias cannot be eradicated through a single event or training session. Regular training can bring us up to date on how unconscious bias evolves, as our society evolves—such as how social media and photo-enhancing apps turbocharge bias, discrimination, and narrow-mindedness. In other words, bias training is never done.

Regular training can also help stop the spread—the normalization—of bias and the slipping back into blind spots. But it's like a medical checkup: you need to have it done periodically. Regular training can also hold a mirror up to arrogance, the belief that we know enough, or that we're somehow special and exempt from this all-too-human foible.

Unconscious bias training can be particularly helpful in hiring decisions, including by reinforcing good listening skills and questioning our own perspectives. It is a way of pressing pause—reminding us that bias can cause us to leap to uninformed decisions and helping us to *see people for who they are* instead of the broad brushstrokes that fit them neatly into easily identifiable buckets such as race, creed, sexual orientation, or political party affiliation.

Some people claim that training isn't helpful or enough. I don't comment here on the specifics of any particular approach to training. Quality varies. And no one strategy suffices; training is one of many tools we should incorporate to increase our awareness of unconscious bias and change our behavior. In fact, one of the biggest mistakes organizations make is assuming unconscious bias training is the solution instead of part of the fight against bias.

But I have seen firsthand that by making the unconscious conscious, on an ongoing basis, we are better able to gain perspective on our ethics—better able to see our decisions while walking in someone else's shoes.

We're only as ethical as our last decisions. Regularly updated unconscious bias training can help us see some of our most important ethical weaknesses, decision by decision.

Chapter 4

Technology

Should social media
companies shut down
accounts of the president
of the United States and
other political leaders if
they incite violence?

In a post dated January 7, 2021—the day after the insur-
rection of the U.S. Capitol—Facebook CEO Mark Zuckerberg put an indefinite suspension on President Donald
Trump's Facebook and Instagram accounts, claiming he
was using "our platform to incite violent insurrection . . .
We believe the risks of allowing the President to continue
to use our service during this period are simply too great."
A day later, Twitter CEO Jack Dorsey suspended Donald
Trump's Twitter account, @realDonaldTrump, permanently.
In June 2021, Facebook announced Trump would be
banned until at least January 2023, when the company
would reevaluate his eligibility.

The Supreme Court has only recently begun to confront the impact of the internet and social media on First
Amendment issues. One example: in its unanimous 2017

opinion in *Packingham v. North Carolina*, the Court invalidated a North Carolina statute that made it a felony for a registered sex offender to log on to a commercial social networking site known to be accessible to minors. Even then, the Court recognized how quickly obsolete its rulings involving technology and the internet may be, with its "vast potential to alter how we think, express ourselves, and define who we want to be."

Exploration

Free speech is critical to ethics and democracy. Without it, truth, a nonnegotiable foundation for ethical decisions, collapses. Free speech can come under threat through government censorship, algorithms that spread disinformation, face-to-face, or online.

While the First Amendment to the Constitution prohibits the federal government from "abridging the freedom of speech, or of the press; or the right of the people peaceably to assemble," it doesn't prohibit corporations or private businesses like Twitter and Facebook from regulating speech, or establishing rules or terms of service. And they remain responsible for protecting and promoting free speech—and for setting boundaries to prevent real harm—as a matter of ethics. (Twitter and Facebook may not technically be media companies, but they function as such when they become both the access point for media and an influence on the media we see through their algorithms.)

Whenever considering a politically sensitive ethics

question, I suggest hypothetically replacing the political party in question with the party you support. Can you in good faith still dismantle the other side's arguments?

Second, safety and rule of law should prevail. We may need to shift our views of what words we consider "inciting violence" in a world in which social media instantaneously shares our messages to millions.

Who gets to decide? We don't want the CEOs of Amazon, Apple, Google, Facebook, TikTok, and Twitter arbitrating our societal conversations (and for the most part they don't want to), or becoming the determiners of truth. (Although they may do so indirectly as they did when Apple and Google removed Parler, the alternative social media app favored by conservatives, from their app stores for failing to remove dangerous content, and Amazon suspended Parler from its web hosting service.) And we rightly adhere to the First Amendment to prevent government censorship. But each of us individually also has a responsibility as we use these platforms, for the information we choose to post, read, and reshare. Without us, those inciting violence don't have an audience.

Ethical decisions require considering the actual and potential consequences: not what we know will happen, but what *could* happen. We had countless examples of unacceptable rhetoric and behavior on January 6—from politicians and ordinary citizens (including calls for combat and threats of revenge for failure to join the insurrection). It shouldn't take five people dying at the riot and more dying afterward to take action.

We must distinguish among various types of speech and determine which are to be protected (even if offensive) and which are to be prohibited, such as hate speech inciting violence, bullying, and harassment.

I believe in diverse voices, vigorous debate, and tolerating even offensive speech. But freedom of speech cannot mean freedom to harm.

Would you use the free Spotify service if you knew that artists are penalized financially?

In 2014, Taylor Swift pulled her discography from Spotify to protest what she saw as Spotify's unfair treatment of artists. Her battle highlighted the fact that Spotify offers consumers a choice between free music with advertising or paid subscriptions with no ads. "It's my opinion," Swift argued in a *Wall Street Journal* op-ed, "that music should not be free." She then released her album *1989* that same year, avoiding streaming platforms. Swift later returned to the platform in 2017 after a new licensing deal between her distributor Universal Music Group and Spotify allowed artists to withhold new releases from free subscribers for a period of time so the artists could potentially make more money.

With music streaming, you can listen to music without downloading song files to your computer hard drive. Spotify compensates the rights holders of music (e.g., record labels, distributors, aggregators, collection societies) through a concept called "streamshare": payment is based on the proportion of the streams of an artist's music (relative to the total number of streams) in a given month in a given market. Artists are then compensated by the rights holders, as spelled out in the terms of the artists' and labels' agreements. For example, Spotify says on its Loud & Clear microsite, if an artist (assuming they are the rights holder) received one in every 1,000 streams in Mexico in a given month, they would receive $1 of every $1,000 paid to rights holders from the royalty pool for the country. That includes subscription and music advertising revenue.

Spotify is the largest music-streaming service in the world in terms of the number of subscribers. In its 2021 third-quarter financial statement, Spotify reported that it had 172 million premium subscribers and 220 million ad-supported "monthly active users."

And independent and new, emerging artists may make very little in royalties. To give a sense of perspective, in 2020, the top 1 percent of artists accounted for 90 percent of all streams.

Exploration

On the positive side, Spotify provides access to a wide variety of music, encouraging a willingness to try new genres and artists given that we don't pay for each song we listen to. They offer lesser known artists access to a growing global audience. They spread culture, diversity, and even spirituality and joy. And they are sustainable: there is no packaging and no consumption of fossil fuels for transport. In addition, the advertising model makes music available for free to those who cannot afford the monthly premium subscription service or do not wish to pay.

By mid-2021, streaming accounted for 84 percent of recorded music revenue according to the Recording Industry Association of America. And it has increased recorded music revenue for musicians. As Princeton economics professor Alan B. Krueger noted in his book *Rockonomics*, from 2015 to 2017 revenue from recorded music—primarily as a result of streaming—increased by $2 billion, "erasing the last ten years of declines and providing a much-needed boost to the music industry." Paid subscription streaming services have continued to experience double-digit retail growth in the U.S., reaching 75.5 million in 2020 according to the RIAA.

On the other hand, Spotify, along with Apple Music, Google Play Music, Amazon Music, YouTube Music, and others, is also part of a trend in platform monopolization laden with ethics risks. Its technology disintermediates, or removes the middle players, such as retail stores. For many of us, our relationships with musicians now exist through a tech platform on which the royalty system can distort results. Users who spend more time on the platform and stream more often have a greater influence on which artists are paid more (even though users all pay the same subscription fee). These platforms feed arbitrariness (a driver of unethical behavior) by unlinking our purchasing choices from the financial reward—in this case, for artists and their art.

My view is that ethics should not, and need not, impede

this important innovation giving millions of people access to music and artists access to a vast listening public. It's a technological version of museums opening their doors for free to some patrons or putting virtual exhibits online free of charge. But the ethical responsibility is shared. Spotify must protect artists' intellectual property and monitor the fairness of the streaming business model, particularly for artists with smaller audience bases. As consumers we must recognize that opting for free by putting up with the occasional ad affects artists as well (unlike with our free use of social media in exchange for targeted ads). And artists should consider the economic and artistic benefits of a larger fan base and their responsibility to the public.

Should social media companies be required to offer users the option to pay a fee to avoid receiving targeted advertising?

I ordered a pair of flip-flops through a website, and now the company's advertisements pop up on my screen constantly. It's annoying. I don't need more footwear or other unsolicited recommendations. On the other hand, a friend's son was looking for an app to implement a tutoring service he and friends were setting up. Two weeks after an unsuccessful search, he was thrilled to receive an unsolicited targeted ad with just the product they needed.

Online advertising targets individuals based on data collected about each individual user, such as from their Facebook profile. Marketers can pinpoint ads to us based on what we like and what we buy. Depending on your sensitivity, targeting can seem invasive or even creepy. It assesses such characteristics as age, gender, income, attitudes, activity, location, and internet searches over time to predict your preferences.

Exploration

This is not a life-and-death situation. But it is one with consequences that will ripple throughout society, particularly as technology behemoths collect more and more data from us, and exercise the ability to control and use that data.

Targeted ads affect every one of us who has an online presence. They also raise broader societal questions about who should benefit from, and control, our personal data. In 2019, Facebook had ad revenue of $69.7 billion; more than 98 percent of the company's global revenue came from advertising. Facebook's share of the U.S. digital advertising market in 2020 was 25.2 percent, while Google's was even higher, at 28.9 percent.

Consider the positives: some consumers like seeing opportunities and find ads efficient; ad revenue makes Google Search and Calendar or Facebook and Messenger available free to billions of people around the world; small businesses are able to reach distant, otherwise inaccessible audiences; and sometimes lifesaving information pops up at just the right time—such as about the rising Covid-19 infections in your area during the pandemic.

A significant objection to a payment option is that it results in inequality: users who can't afford to pay would have no choice but continue to give up their data, and receive targeted ads, in exchange for the free service. Unlike other premium services like Amazon Prime or Apple TV+, social media can touch on our livelihood, family, and news sources.

And the data set could be skewed toward people who can't pay, which in turn might embed in the data additional inequality linked to race, gender, and access to technology; such skewed and distorted data could be dangerous in systems linked to health, voting, and other civic matters.

With or without payment, many stakeholders share responsibility for targeted advertising. Governments should regulate social media companies more carefully, particularly for issues such as truth in advertising, risk of fraud, and age appropriateness. And why couldn't social media companies make free services available to those who couldn't pay while diminishing the number of ads they are subjected to?

As much as search and social media companies have democratized access to these platforms, a fundamental question remains. Should the data these companies collect be allowed to be monopolized and controlled as private property (for shareholder benefit), or should the data be required to be made public (for public benefit such as mental health and education research)?

I often hear in conversations among experts that "people are just willing to live with the consequences" in exchange for free access to services. I'm not convinced of our willingness, or even our freedom of choice, when no one I know (including myself) is able to fully understand the terms of service of social media companies or articulate accurately the long-term ethical consequences of free social media.

Would you agree to let your elderly loved one be cared for by a robot?

Meet Zora. Just under five feet tall, "she" is a human-oid robot with sensors that allow her to "see" and "hear." She can tell stories, teach programming to her human companions, and play games. She is program-mable through a touch panel and is easily transportable. She shrugs her shoulders, dances, demonstrates gym moves as an exercise class leader—thanks to joints in her legs, arms, and digits. She has a built-in camera that allows her to scan barcodes. And she can interact with people of all age groups, from offering homework assistance for kids, to acting as a personal trainer for fitness-focused adults, to serving as a companion for older adults in elder care facilities. She was specifically designed to meet human social needs and "accompany you throughout your day with a positive attitude."

Zora is not alone. PARO is a therapeutic companion robot in the form of a stuffed seal that is found to ease patient stress and improve socialization. In early 2020, as

I entered the European office of a client I was advising, a humanoid robot, known as Pepper, greeted me. I had a touch screen exchange with Pepper, to which Pepper responded by flashing the organization's ethical principles.

South Korea stepped up its use of robots during Covid-19 with robots that spray disinfecting agents, check temperatures, and detect mask wearing (while protecting privacy by blurring faces).

Exploration

When discussing robots, it is important to start with humancentric ethics concerns, such as health and safety, respect, privacy, and compassion.

Robots are tools—no more human than washing machines. They are intended to supplement human care—a friend or a relative visiting, or other human contact—not replace it. We should prioritize human beings in making decisions about whether to use or deploy a robot. The goal is to maximize benefits to patients (reducing loneliness, increasing engagement, and augmenting care, such as checking blood pressure and providing medications) and mitigate risks (privacy violations or insufficient human oversight). The population of adults over the age of sixty-five is expected to more than double to more than 1.5 billion by 2050, according to the United Nations, making supplemental care increasingly important.

It's easy to assume that patients prefer interactions with other human beings. But nonhuman assistance might offer the person being cared for greater privacy and independence—such as in assisting with personal hygiene. Some caregivers have reported that the elderly share emotions more freely with robots that they wouldn't share with staff. Robots may also reduce the workload for caregivers, allowing staff more time to devote to more critical medical and psychological concerns.

As with any medical intervention, informed consent is vital. Not all elderly people have the capacity to grant consent, as in the case of dementia. Families need to be informed by hospitals and care centers before robot care is incorporated, and grant specific consent.

For perspective, we can look at this question on a spectrum of other options, from full-time human care, an option that may not be possible for many of us, to no human care. In between, there might be a mix of human care and robot care, with the engagement of the medical professionals in charge. Such care could include video check-ins or full medical sessions with caregivers, data gathered for caregivers via internet-connected devices, and online cognitive training.

Finally, how do we allocate responsibility for any harm (including misuse of data) to a person caused by a robot? Is the medical facility responsible? The individual caregiver deploying the robot? The manufacturer? For me, the physician or other human overseer must be held accountable—just as they would for a recommendation of any other treatment or use of a medical device. But we should be able to rely on proper transparency and safeguards from companies, as well, and regulators should sign off on robots' use for medical interventions.

As David Hanson, founder of Hanson Robotics and creator of the humanoid robot Sophia, told me, robots may call on us to be better human beings—perhaps even better caregivers, friends, and family members.

Should police departments be allowed to use facial recognition technology?

On a Thursday afternoon in 2020, Robert Julian-Borchak Williams, who worked in an automotive supply company, was arrested in his driveway by two police officers as his family looked on. Matched by a facial recognition algorithm to blurred video surveillance tape, Williams, who is Black, was charged with shoplifting at an upscale boutique in October 2018. But the algorithm was wrong: Williams was innocent.

Facial recognition technology, or FRT, uses computer algorithms to analyze details about a person's face, and compare that information against photographs in a database of known individuals.

Driven to a detention center, Williams was booked, fingerprinted, and held for over thirty hours. This became the first known case of an American mistakenly arrested due to faulty facial recognition software.

FRT can be used in two ways: for *verification*, where an image of a person is scanned and compared to a known image in a database, such as a passport photo; and for *identification*, where police take an unknown face off surveillance images and look for a match.

Verification, according to the National Institute of Standards and Technology (NIST), is highly accurate. With good-quality photos, the most accurate algorithms have miss rates of less than 1 percent. But identification, as in the case of Robert Williams, is far less accurate; it is much harder for a fixed camera to take high-quality photos of people on the move, obscured by shadows and other people.

Exploration

If we're trying to find a terrorist or a lost child, we would be in favor of facial recognition technology. If we're trying to eliminate racial and other types of profiling, and protect the privacy of innocent citizens, we would be vehemently against it. The paramount concerns to consider here are safety, privacy, respect, antidiscrimination, transparency, and legal compliance.

Many police departments, as well as the Department of Homeland Security, are embracing these FRT tools, saying they can help them more efficiently identify and arrest criminals. But FRT can result in misidentification, false positives, racial bias, and the apprehension of innocent citizens. In 2018, the American Civil Liberties Union reported that Amazon's FRT incorrectly matched twenty-eight members of Congress with people who had been arrested. A 2018 study of gender and skin-color bias in three commercial AI systems found an error rate that was never greater than 0.8 percent in light-skinned men, but which "ballooned" to as much as 46.8 percent for dark-skinned women.

In 2020, Massachusetts became the first state to join cities like Portland, Maine, and Portland, Oregon, as well as San Francisco and Oakland, to ban police use of facial recognition technology. In 2020, Microsoft announced that the company won't sell facial recognition technology to police departments until there is a "national law in place grounded in human rights." Amazon initially followed suit with a one-year moratorium, which they extended in 2021 until further notice.

The caution exhibited by Microsoft and Amazon has been emulated by Clearview AI, a start-up company that has "shrouded itself in secrecy," creating and selling a game-changing facial recognition app that has a database of 3 billion images that the company has taken from Facebook, YouTube, and the like. The *New York Times* reports that more than six hundred law enforcement agencies and a handful of companies have already started using it to identify people and potentially review their social contacts and where they live and work. But there has been pushback. Facebook announced the imminent closure worldwide of its facial recognition system. And in 2021 Clearview was banned from scraping images from websites in Australia; its services are already banned in Canada.

Lawmakers, corporations, police forces, and regulators

at least owe the public transparency about what FRT does, and how human checks and balances can be incorporated.

The bottom line is that we need to monitor progress in the technology; engage the public, corporations, and government in the debate; and press pause until we can eliminate bias and establish ethical and legal guardrails—while looking for ways to carve out exceptions in extreme cases such as a lost child or an active terrorist threat.

How do we handle the ethics of a deceased loved one's social media accounts?

One of my students told the class about her pursuit of the truth behind the kind of person her mother was by reading her late mother's diary. She discovered that her experience of growing up with her mother was skewed by the fact that she only partially understood her mother's past. Her lifelong condemnation of her mother's selfishness and indifference gave way to admiration for the quiet sacrifice her mother made to raise a family in the U.S., far from her country of birth. She learned how her mother navigated a multiracial marriage and parenting challenges. The diary shed light on her own multiracial identity growing up, her childhood family experiences, and her ability to rise to the highest echelons of business.

Her discovery of the truth about her mother and her family hinged on a single document—the diary, a physical object that only she could read and which she kept in her possession. Neither she nor her mother had posted it or made entries on social media. The daughter controlled whether or not to share it with others, and the decision of how much of it she might share. And who would inherit the diary after her own death.

She wondered what she would do if, like her own journal, the diary had been in the form of a Facebook, Instagram, or other social media accounts.

Exploration

Sharing a deceased person's private social media account is an ethical minefield. We cannot know what was happening in their heart or mind when they posted content, or how their views might have changed over time. We lack context. We don't know if an image was photoshopped, or our relative was having a bad day. We don't know how much of our loved one's account they would wish to share with us, let alone allow us to share with others.

Losing this content, however, might destroy the person's personal history with, and connection to, other relatives, not to mention erase an opportunity to honor a loved one's life.

There is a quagmire of ethics challenges for society, as well. Are social media accounts property, to be disposed of in a will just as a bank account or favorite necklace? Or is it a contract between you and the social media company to be disposed of according to their terms of service? State laws regarding posthumous privacy are evolving.

The diary of my student's mother was just as much a part of her belongings and inheritance as any family heirloom she received. Her mother likely could not have imagined that her diary would be shared with others beyond her immediate family, let alone potentially with strangers who with the click of a button could reshare. On the other hand, while her daughter had to consider her mother's privacy, I think her daughter's choice (to read it in confidence and then decide how to handle it) was the only option that didn't have important and irreparable consequences (destroying a family heirloom without knowing what's in it).

I am staunchly committed to truth and to avoiding "all or nothing" situations. I would be inclined to preserve the diary and pass it on to a very limited group of people who agreed to keep it confidential and respect the conditions of the deceased's will. I might share specific sections with individuals for whom it might bring joy or reassurance. I would never post, or repost, any of the diary on social media or in electronic form because technology dramatically increases the dissemination of material in ways that I cannot control.

We should also ask whether it's our story to tell. If our relative had wanted to share more widely, I assume they would have. And we are not the only stakeholder in our decision. The information that other people shared with the deceased was also private and not intended to be shared more broadly without permission.

Society's ethical norms have not caught up with the increasingly frequent decision of whether and when to expose social media without permission. Social media companies' terms of use should tell us in plain language what happens to our data upon our death. (Deletion? Appointing a guardian? Preserved as a memorial?)

If you are concerned about your own accounts, declare your wishes for posthumous social media, including in your will if you have one. Go to the sites and make choices about such things as legacy accounts and memorializing—and communicate your wishes to loved ones.

Would you consider using a bot therapist or recommending one for a family member or friend?

The daughter of someone I know has been diagnosed with depression. But their financial resources available to pay for individual therapy, which can cost $200 or more a session, several times a week, are limited.

One option the family considered is AI-powered Woebot, the "friendly little bot who's ready to listen 24/7." Woebot's mission, according to Woebot Health, is expanding access to mental health care. Woebot "works by inviting people to have a conversation," available any time of day or night "at a moment's notice." Woebot guides users to identify patterns in their moods and claims a 98.9 percent "accuracy rate in detecting crisis language"—but acknowledges that there is "no replacement for human connection." There are adolescent, maternal mental health, and substance use specialty options. Replika is a bot companion app (that doesn't claim to do therapy), allowing users to talk about their "thoughts, feelings, beliefs, experiences, memories, dreams" to a computer-generated digital companion, without humans in the loop. The app has been downloaded more than 2 million times. Other apps specialize, such as Pear Therapeutics' FDA-approved cognitive therapy apps for substance use disorders.

Mental health challenges are a global epidemic. The World Health Organization (WHO) reports that more than 700,000 people die around the world due to suicide every year. It is the fourth leading cause of death in people aged fifteen to nineteen worldwide. Nearly two thirds of those with a mental disorder "never seek help from a health professional," according to WHO.

Exploration

There are robust medical and professional ethics codes and oversight processes for human mental health professionals. This question targets what is ethically different about bot therapists, compared to human therapists.

The first challenge here is the huge gap in the information we need—we simply do not yet have sufficient data on the efficacy and risks of bot therapists trained on mountains of data versus a therapist's graduate degree and experience. This means that we cannot assess the immediate and longer-term consequences for patients, their families, and others affected. And without adequate information, our informed consent is not really informed.

What bot therapists potentially offer patients includes:

broad access to help for people who would otherwise be unable to afford a therapist, especially over an extended period of time; help for patients who are uncomfortable talking with another person about their struggles; and a complement to professional therapists. Some people may open up more knowing that they are talking to a bot. Risks of bot therapy include: data privacy breaches; therapeutic risk (what happens if a bot can't recognize an individual's suicidal tendencies, can't prescribe medication, or can't otherwise help the patient?); exacerbating medical care inequality by replacing trained therapists with a bot in underserved areas; and, again, a dearth of research on therapeutic efficacy and harm.

One crucial factor here is determining who is responsible for any potential harm to the user—the company that builds, programs, and sells the bot? Its shareholders? Regulators who allow its use? The patient? On the other hand, human therapists, too, have varying degrees of ethical and legal responsibility to patients when harm occurs.

My own view is that AI for health care requires human supervision—but without compromising confidentiality. Like all technology that affects health and data privacy, regulators should set rigorous standards for the technology, transparency about the risks, and medical intervention.

Bot therapists are one of many innovations blurring the boundaries of humanity—assuming a role in one of the most fundamentally human areas of our lives, involving our emotions, well-being, brain chemistry, and relationships with medical professionals. Our ethics (and ultimately our laws) must restore those boundaries of human responsibility and assure transparency and truly informed consent to users and the public—without sacrificing much-needed access to care.

Do you have an obligation to inform guests that you have a digital assistant on in your home when they visit?

One night, I was visiting a friend and as she was making dinner she turned to her Amazon Echo, and asked, "Alexa, what's the weather going to be in London tomorrow?" The device came to life at the sound of "Alexa," and gave her a forecast of rain. I was uncomfortable with the idea of Alexa "listening" to me. The device stayed quiet through dinner, and I forgot about it for the most part. But on my way home I couldn't help wondering if it was off, or listening, or perhaps listening and recording. I knew the Alexa personal assistant is only supposed to activate with key wake words. But there have been plenty of news reports of conversations accidentally recorded. Who knows if parts of our conversation had been recorded by Alexa and sent to the cloud and, if so, whether Amazon employees or others could access it?

Today in the U.S., one in four of us keep, on average, 2.6 smart speaker devices in our homes. At CES 2020, the largest technology convention in the world (originally known as the Consumer Electronics Show), Amazon announced there were now "hundreds of millions of Alexa-enabled devices" in the hands of customers around the world—more than double from a year earlier.

Exploration

Every day, people around the world "wake up" their speakers and ask their digital voice assistants to play music, check their calendars, call up recipes or instructions, or check the weather. Alexa has become so convenient that for many it has become a part of their everyday lives, an adopted habit, the incredibly efficient and reliable personal assistant you never had. But not everyone is comfortable with them. At their core, Alexa, Siri and Google Assistant are data-gathering machines that record our conversations, unless we turn off the microphone.

The widespread use of Alexa and similar devices is a clue about a potential ethics pitfall: the more something becomes normal, the less we question its use and the more its use spreads. And this is even more true when the habit involves a technology device with rapidly changing capabilities.

The people affected by our use of Alexa include you and any guests to your home, their families, anyone they may have spoken about while at your house, as well as Amazon or the device's company and partners. They could include other companies Amazon may acquire in the future, Amazon employees, and contractors. And *how* they are affected could change in ways you would never know. As Amazon notes in their terms of service, "Amazon processes and retains your Alexa interactions, such as your voice inputs, music playlists, and your Alexa to-do and shopping lists, in the cloud." Moreover, they state that you "and all other persons who use Alexa under your account" agree to their terms of service by using Alexa. It is difficult for the average user to understand what information the company records, or how the company uses that data. Given that police have obtained court-ordered warrants for recordings, others affected can potentially even include law enforcement and the courts.

To me, truth, privacy, transparency, and respect are at stake—all essential to trusted friendship. Friends and guests to your home can reasonably expect that their conversations are private. Leaving a device on when friends are in your house, and unintentionally exposing their conversations to being recorded, can be seen as a serious breach of their trust. Moreover, if your guests are not aware that Alexa is on, they are not making choices for themselves. (Informed consent refers to choices we make based on a full understanding of the risks and benefits.)

That said, we shouldn't miss the opportunities Alexa offers, whether convenience or, more importantly, for people with a wide range of emotional and physical challenges, from mobility to communication.

The solution here is simple: turn off Alexa when friends come over, or inform your friends that it's on so that they can make the choice for themselves.

Would you use the Robinhood trading app?

On Monday, January 25, 2021, individual investors snatched up shares in struggling retail game company GameStop (GME) in droves through retail brokers and the commission-free trading app Robinhood. Some traders on WallStreetBets (a message board in the social media and community network platform Reddit) banded together to inflict losses on institutional investors engaged in short selling.

Robinhood's stated mission is to democratize trading—to befriend the small investor. One investment expert likened the GameStop buying frenzy to purchasing a lottery ticket. The stock price skyrocketed from $20 on Monday, January 11 to a high of almost $500 on Thursday, January 28. Much of the GameStop bubble was disconnected from the company's fundamentals—their revenues, operating expenses, profits, and potential for growth.

At the height of the unprecedented rally in the stock price of GameStop and other companies, more than 24 billion shares were traded on U.S. exchanges, a level that was more than six times the previous single-day record on Wall Street. The rally was the result of a so-called short squeeze. In a short squeeze, investor buying causes a rise in the stock price, forcing sellers who have shorted the stock—in expectation that the price would fall—to cover their position to avoid further losses. It revealed the power individual investors could wield on financial markets if enough of them bought a stock to cause an artificial spike in the share price.

But the mania backfired on the Robinhood site. As a result of the trading volatility, Robinhood's Wall Street clearinghouse increased their cash deposit requirements tenfold, to ensure that their trades were settled smoothly. (Clearinghouses are responsible for settling accounts and clearing trades, among other things.) As a result, on Thursday, January 28, Robinhood had to limit trading. Investors could no longer buy the stock—they could only sell what they had. Investors, the media, and Washington cried foul, and Robinhood customers expressed their anger on social media.

Exploration

Robinhood is an example of scattered power, one of the most influential forces driving how we make decisions. Sometimes scattered power involves many individual acts organized into a movement, such as a storm of small stock market trades.

Companies that provide the technology are the scatterers of the power. Robinhood benefits from scattering power because the more customers trade on Robinhood, the more money the company makes despite not charging commissions. Robinhood earns revenue from third parties that pay the company for the right to fulfill its trades (so-called payment for order flow). So Robinhood shares responsibility for misuse of the product and reasonably warning users of serious risk.

Robinhood should have known the major risks that could affect their customers: cash requirements for clearing, individual users potentially suffering significant financial loss or even becoming addicted to trading as a form of online gambling, and manipulative speculation. There is a robust history of securities law focused on protecting unsophisticated investors. The tech landscape is littered with companies that moved too quickly and harmed individuals.

With Robinhood, I do not believe investors understand what they are signing on for. There is no real informed consent. Robinhood's customer agreement at the time was thirty-three pages of legalese in eye-straining print. I understood very little of it (including the company's responsibility to me), despite my years as a securities lawyer at a top Wall Street firm and decades of ethics advisory work. Most users are inexperienced traders who don't fully understand the underlying financial risks. And Robinhood's business model is spreading; today many companies offer commission-free trading. In 2021, the company announced plans to undertake a coffeehouse tour of colleges to attract students and younger investors.

A lofty mission is only ethical when deployed ethically. Taking actions based on principles such as customer well-being and transparency is a start. Companies must ensure that customers fully understand the risks and are equipped to make their own ethical choices. Robinhood is also responsible for assuring sufficient liquidity to settle trades.

While as a general matter users of technology also have responsibility with respect to how they deploy their power and inform themselves of risks (or a company's failure to adequately explain risks), we cannot blame users for Robinhood's management of their brokerage. Hedge funds are experts in financial risk; they can quickly determine how to recoup the significant losses they incurred shorting GameStop shares. But Robinhood's weaknesses ultimately harm all investors and the public by undermining trust in financial markets. Finally, regulators, too, should have addressed the potential for this kind of trading risk with Robinhood's business model and adopted rules to limit the damage, especially to inexperienced investors. The fact that trading happens through an app, or free of commissions, doesn't change the fundamental ethics risk and responsibility. Ultimately, individual traders and their families were harmed.

Should Apple be required to unlock encrypted iPhones at the request of the FBI in an investigation of a terrorist act?

I n December 2015, Syed Rizwan Farook, a county environmental inspector, and his wife, Tashfeen Malik, dressed in combat gear and wearing masks, entered the Inland Regional Center in San Bernardino, a nonprofit corporation that provides services and programs for people with disabilities, and opened fire with .223 caliber assault rifles. Firing over one hundred rounds within several minutes, they killed fourteen people and wounded twenty-two others before fleeing the scene. The two terrorists were killed in a shootout with police a few miles away.

The FBI, investigating the potential that others were involved in the San Bernardino attack, appealed to Apple to unlock Farook's encrypted iPhone. Apple and the Justice Department had been sparring with each other since the debut of the encrypted iOS 8 operating system in 2014. Apple said that the Justice Department was pushing them to create a backdoor—software code that would allow law enforcement to circumvent the password and unlock the encrypted devices. Apple resisted, offering alternative ways to obtain data from the phone. They explained that they didn't have a way to unlock the phone, without putting a team of software engineers on it to rewrite the operating system, which they refused to do.

In February, a federal district court judge issued a request to Apple to help unlock the phone. Apple appealed the request. CEO Tim Cook issued a letter to Apple customers, explaining the company's position: "We fear that this demand would undermine the very freedoms and liberty our government is meant to protect."

Ultimately, a third party—a little-known Australian cybersecurity firm called Azimuth Security—was able to unlock the phone, and the FBI withdrew its request to the court. But because the issue never went to trial, the long-running dispute between law enforcement and tech companies over privacy safeguards remains unresolved. (Apple is now suing Azimuth for their actions.) In fact, the situation recurred in December 2019 when the FBI asked Apple to help unlock two iPhones that belonged to the gunman who killed three sailors at Naval Air Station Pensacola. On its website, Apple claims that law enforcement departments have logged hundreds of requests with the company to unlock Apple phones.

Exploration

This case pits two critical principles against each other: safety and privacy. The FBI, investigating potential remaining threats from others who might have been involved in the San Bernardino shootings, was focused on ensuring the safety of American citizens.

Apple came down on the side of consumer privacy. But the company was also considering longer-term safety risks. As Tim Cook wrote, "Compromising the security of our personal information can ultimately put our personal safety at risk . . . Once created, the technique could be used over and over again." Apple also feared that foreign agents or authoritarian regimes could gain access to devices and put people at risk.

Privacy and consumer advocates supported Apple's position and Cook's response. Alex Abdo, then a staff lawyer for the American Civil Liberties Union, said, "Apple deserves praise for standing up for its right to offer secure devices." But law enforcement agencies criticized Apple just as strongly. Remember that the owner of the phone was a known terrorist (not a potential suspect), and he was dead (with potentially lesser privacy interests).

A few questions can help us test our views. How would the decision feel looking back on it from a future time? I asked a group of CEOs just after this incident how they would assess Cook's decision, or the opposite, weeks, months, even years out if a second related terrorist attack took place. And what would their decision look like from the perspective of different stakeholders—from other phone owners to law enforcement to potential victims of terrorist attacks?

Ethics, done well, should involve looking for alternatives. Apple did provide the data that they had on their servers, and suggested ways that the FBI could access some of the information on the phone. But they refused to help unlock the phone. The ultimate solution was an alternative actor (the Australian firm Azimuth).

Apple's promise to consumers, as they wrote on their website, was that "Apple cannot bypass your passcode and therefore cannot access this data." And so far, they have refused to create software that would give law enforcement a backdoor to unlock their phones. The commitment to keep their word to consumers is admirable. However, consumers deserve to know that while Apple might keep its promise not to bypass codes, other actors can.

Should robots have rights?

Sophia, the world's first humanoid robot, was invented by Hanson Robotics, and made "her" appearance before the public at the annual South by Southwest festival in Austin in 2016. The Hanson Robotics website describes Sophia as a humanlike robot that features "cutting edge robotics and AI research." Her face, made from patented elastic-rubber material, is strikingly human, modeled after ancient Egyptian queen Nefertiti and Hanson's wife in order to represent diverse physiques. She "can estimate your feelings during a conversation" and "has her own emotions too." She has appeared on *60 Minutes*, *The Tonight Show with Jimmy Fallon*, and *Good Morning Britain*.

Sophia's artificial intelligence enables her to "recognize human faces, see emotional expressions, and recognize various hand gestures." Sophia continually learns from the world around her through machine learning—the field within artificial intelligence "that gives computers the ability to learn without explicitly being programmed."

In 2017, Sophia became the first robot to be granted citizenship, by Saudi Arabia. The same year, the European Parliament adopted the resolution on Civil Law Rules on Robotics, which included a proposal to explore the creation of a special "legal status" for robots, allowing them to be "insured individually and held liable for damages if they go rogue." A backlash ensued, as over 156 experts from fourteen countries, in an open letter to the EU, expressed alarm, stating, "From an ethical and legal perspective, creating a legal personality for a robot is inappropriate."

Exploration

As robots and other versions of artificial intelligence increasingly infiltrate our lives, from flipping burgers to offering us viewing options based on our preferences on Netflix, the issue of whether robots should have rights is already squarely before society.

Robots may blur boundaries between human and machine, but in my view *human* rights must always take precedence. The question of robot rights is really a question of *human responsibility*.

We don't change our ethics foundations, such as safety, honesty, dignity, transparency, and compassion, just because robots are involved. People design, build, manufacture, program, and deploy robots; they must assure us that the robots they create act in furtherance of protecting and aiding us and preventing harm to humans. We shouldn't build driverless cars that preserve the car over saving the lives of passengers or pedestrians. We need to be assured that robots are ready to be trusted not to undercook a burger, mislabel a package, or spread hate speech on social media.

Whatever your view on robot rights, our behavior toward robots is important. We need more research on the impact of human interaction with robots, such as swearing at a robot nanny in front of our children or kicking a robot dog. But we can still ask ourselves what we think such behavior would say about us and what impact it could have on the humans observing it. Similarly, would we treat a robot that sorts packages and doesn't have a humanlike appearance any differently from a humanoid robot like Sophia?

If robots were accorded rights, how would they be enforced? Imagine taking a robot to court or an arbitration proceeding. Would the robot have its own human lawyer? Testify?

How we allocate responsibility for robots among the various stakeholders is a critical question: the companies manufacturing the robots, the companies and individuals who buy and use the robots, the regulators. The companies manufacturing and deploying robots with the public owe us transparency, an opportunity to grant our consent, and above all, safety.

I strongly oppose spending resources such as court time on metal machines when real people are deprived of desperately needed food, health care, and education. We have too far to go to guarantee human rights around the world before we get to robot rights.

This question reminds us that we may have to redraw lines in a world of increasingly blurred boundaries between humans and machines. Robot developers and experts should prevent machines and algorithms from achieving independent capacity to control or harm humans. I would flip this question instead to ask how we can assure that robots and other forms of AI cannot trample on our human rights. Technology should not redefine what it means to be human.

Chapter 5

Consumer Choices

Should we buy fast fashion?

The daughter of a close friend was giving away an extra-large Hefty trash bag with perfectly good clothes that still fit. My friend was shocked at the waste of money and materials. Yet the whole bag of inexpensive fast fashion clothes might have cost less than $100 at retail. What upset her was our throwaway mentality. An example: online British retailer Boohoo sold a bodycon minidress for £4 (around $5), about the cost of a vanilla spice latte at Starbucks in London (£3.75). According to the environmental organization Greenpeace, "In 1991, the average American bought 34 items of clothing each year. By 2007, they were buying 67 items every year." And only one quarter of those garments are later recycled.

What is fast fashion? One definition I came across calls it "landfill fashion." Fast fashion companies recreate high-fashion catwalk or runway trends and designs, and mass-produce them inexpensively. They are high volume, cheaply made, and designed to be quickly discarded. Sometimes fast fashion hits the stores almost before the models step off the catwalk. A fashionable knockoff that used to take six months can now be available to consumers in less than a week. The countermovement to it is sometimes called slow fashion—"mindful manufacturing . . . fair labor rights, natural materials, and lasting garments." Budget clothing, on the other hand, does not necessarily chase fashion trends, wear out, or even use synthetic materials so extensively.

Exploration

The guideposts of fast fashion appear to be short-termism, perpetuating our continuing addiction to new clothes and trends, a focus on revenues over principles, and a casual disregard for the environment.

Fast fashion companies may aim to make high-end designs more accessible for everyday consumers, but their approach to democratizing fashion comes at the cost of damage to the environment and exacerbating inequality. The UN Environment Program says that "it takes 3,781 liters of water to make one pair of jeans." According to a World Bank report, "The fashion industry is responsible for 10 percent of annual global carbon emissions—more than all international flights and maritime shipping combined." And that doesn't speak to the environmental impact of toxic chemicals and dyes, textile waste, water pollution, and pesticides.

Fast fashion also helps to foster what is known as planned obsolescence—designing clothes with an artificially limited useful life that need to be constantly replaced due to their poor quality and quickly outdated trendy fashion styles. It is the same concept smartphone manufacturers use to force expensive upgrades like changing the shape of the charger and using batteries that lose power quickly as they age.

We each have the power to buy or not buy disposable underpriced fashion clothing, as well as to seek quality (as well as other low-cost) brands. Or we can just purchase less, borrow and rent clothes from the companies now offering short-term rentals of designer clothing (renting an evening gown for a formal event), give away or sell our own used clothing, and seek out sustainable fabrics rather than environmentally dangerous synthetics. We can use social media to shift consumer discussions to a "less is more" culture (repurposing, sharing, handing down, re-cycling), moving from a throwaway culture that seeks out the latest fashion trends to searching for what lasts. Fast fashion retailers can't make money on what we don't buy.

But many stakeholders must contribute to reducing the impact of fast fashion and ensure a decent livelihood for fashion industry workers. Regulators should reinforce environmental impact standards; companies should offer more responsible budget clothing options.

Like fast food, I confess that I buy inexpensive fast fashion occasionally. The point is not to draw a line in the sand, or create feelings of guilt, but rather to consider how our purchasing power can help to influence and improve the choices companies make available to consumers, and improve company behavior.

Would you continue to support a nonprofit humanitarian organization that pays an illegal bribe to assure delivery of lifesaving medical treatments?

You volunteer with, or donate to, a highly reputable nonprofit organization that provides medical services to people in developing countries in high-risk, dire situations. In fact, they are often the only organization providing health care in the aftermath of a natural disaster, pandemic, or other emergency. In order to deliver these lifesaving medications and vaccinations to one country following a major disease outbreak, the organization has to bribe government officials. The bureaucracy is rife with corruption, and these payments are so regularly required that they are almost considered a tax. The bribes do not represent a significant sum (relative to the organization's budget for the region); however, they are illegal under United States and local law. (Most exceptions from the law for de minimis payments such as gifts wouldn't apply when paying off government officials.) There is no indication of danger of any other misconduct that could harm the local population the organization serves. The local population has no other source of the supplies your organization can provide.

Exploration

Barring highly unusual circumstances, respecting the law is the minimum standard of ethics—usually a nonnegotiable baseline.

This question encourages us to look at the short-, medium-, and long-term consequences of our decisions *at the time of the decision.* When we see words like "life-threatening," our temptation is to leap to fix the short-term problem and put off considering longer-term risks and opportunities. One short-term consequence is both important and irreparable: the potential (avoidable) loss of life. Many people would pay a modest bribe to save lives and worry about the fallout later. I might opt to pay the bribe myself. But the medium- and long-term consequences here are also important and could ultimately cost lives as well. Whatever our decision on bribery, the conversation about longer-term consequences should be part and parcel of our thinking *now*.

So what are these potential consequences?

First, because the organization has broken the law, legal sanctions could follow. These sanctions might include preventing the organization from providing assistance to this country in the future to help others in need; accusations of bribery resulting in the dismissal of key staff; and jeopardizing the nonprofit's tax-exempt status, and their ability to offer tax deduction incentives as a way to encourage donations.

Second, donor trust can easily be lost. Donors don't expect bribery as a cost of doing business in treating patients. I don't know of any organizations that are transparent about bribery, whether as a general warning that it may be necessary or that it has been done. Annual reports show photos of employees caring for children, not slipping an envelope of cash to a uniformed customs officer. Today social media and cell phone cameras greatly increase the reputational risk of exposure.

Also, bribery that is systemic quickly becomes a habit, and sometimes the price escalates. One act of wrongdoing often begets another (what I call contagion and mutation of unethical behavior). The organization would face further ethical dilemmas—including whether to lie to the media, regulators, donors, beneficiaries, and even their own employees. Soon what seems like a single justifiable (if illegal) bribe becomes the organization's brand identity. And donors may flee over time, particularly given the competition for donor funding and the many needs in the world today.

Still, even with all these potential consequences over time, this is one situation that may call for the unpalatable and illegal option to bribe to save lives now. Critically, there don't seem to be alternatives. At the very least, the organization could be transparent about the *general* risks of bribery and corruption in the countries in which they work (as many corporations must disclose doing business in countries known for high levels of corruption in their documents to regulators and shareholders).

I always urge that we ask how the person the most adversely affected by our decision would feel. And then imagine that person is you: How would you feel if your own child's life were on the line?

Is purchasing organic food and products a more ethical choice?

When I was sheltering at home in northern California, grocery store runs were pretty much the only outing. Masked, sanitizer in hand, I confess to lingering longer than usual over the produce aisle and the ice cream freezer. I was struck by the increasing number of parallel options: organic peaches for $4 per pound, side by side with regular peaches for $2.35 per pound. From ice cream to chicken wings, organic products were everywhere . . . and they were considerably more expensive. I also learned that organic products need not be edible: I discovered organic body lotion and shampoo, makeup, textiles (wool, cotton), and pet foods.

Even where there were labels (cereal boxes, for example), I had no idea what my extra investment was bringing me—ethically or practically.

A quick primer on the definition of "organic":

The U.S. Department of Agriculture (USDA) says that for a food to be "USDA certified organic" it must be "grown and processed according to federal guidelines addressing, among many factors, soil quality, animal raising practices, pest and weed control, and use of additives." The USDA categorizes organic products as: *100 percent organic* (all ingredients must be organic); *organic* (must contain 95 percent or more organic ingredients); and *made with organic ingredients* (must contain at least 70 percent organic ingredients, and cannot display the USDA organic seal). That said, customers (like me!) often see the *made with organic ingredients* label, and don't understand the USDA distinctions.

Exploration

In 2020, organic food sales in the U.S. surged by 12.4 percent to $61.9 billion.

On the one hand, a 2012 in-depth study from Stanford University's Center for Health Policy determined on average, organic foods were no more nutritious than their cheaper, nonorganic counterparts. On the other hand, organic farming *is* widely considered more sustainable, as it uses natural rather than synthetic pesticides. "The . . . wider variety of plants enhances biodiversity and results in better soil quality and reduced pollution," according to the Columbia University Climate School.

While buying organic may contribute to a more ethical food system, I do not view deciding not to buy organic as necessarily a lapse in ethics. Given the choice between consuming more fruits, vegetables, and proteins that are not grown organically, and purchasing fewer of these healthy foods in order to eat more expensive organic foods, I would choose the former. Also, because organic foods do not contain preservatives they often do not keep as long.

For those who can afford it, I do see Princeton University philosopher Peter Singer's point that buying organic is the better ethical choice because our food purchases contribute to a vast global industry with impact on animals, farmers, the environment, and future generations.

Organic purchases are one of many alternatives proactively to do good and reinforce our commitment to an ethical food supply. But there are many other ways to contribute to the community, the environment, and tackling inequality. Some experts suggest reducing the amount of meat in one's diet, reducing food waste, avoiding chemically processed foods, and paying attention to local sourcing. Check the information on the package or offered by the store about specific products to see if your highest priorities are being met (for some it may mean no artificial colors or sweeteners or organically raised animals).

To me, organic food is sometimes synonymous with luxury ethics. And unlike luxury clothing, we need food to live—so many people are struggling to feed their families, including those who have lost their jobs because of the Covid-19 pandemic. Twenty-five thousand people die of starvation throughout the world every day. In terms of food priorities, it seems to me that we should first ensure that the millions of people who are hungry in and outside the U.S. receive nutritious food before we call out people for not buying organic.

What are the steps to recovery from an ethics mishap?

I n December 2015, a 2014 working paper from Harvard Business School that found widespread discrimination on Airbnb's platform was reported in the media. The researchers claimed that Airbnb's platform encouraged racial profiling because hosts were able to view a prospective guest's picture and personal details before deciding whether to accept or deny requests. The paper concluded that renters with "distinctively African American names" were 16 percent less likely to be accepted by hosts compared to renters with "distinctively white names." Racial discrimination had been a known concern on the internet and was prohibited in the hospitality industry (including through the Civil Rights Act of 1964, which specifically prohibits "discrimination or segregation on the ground of race, color, religion, or national origin").

Airbnb was a blend of the internet and hospitality, on a technology platform that matches hosts and guests and that could only supercharge the risk of racism. In addition, Airbnb hosts were offering a blend of hotel stay (where discrimination is illegal) and private home (where discrimination is abhorrent but often legal). No one had determined what the law was in this new blended business model, but the ethics were clear. To their credit, the leaders of Airbnb took full responsibility. Brian Chesky, cofounder and CEO of Airbnb, acknowledged, "There were lots of things we didn't think about when we, as three white guys, designed the platform." Airbnb also took a number of comprehensive antidiscrimination steps, calling discrimination "the greatest challenge we face as a company." As Chesky said, "Our real innovation . . . is designing a framework to allow millions of people to trust one another . . . We intend to do everything possible to learn from these incidents when they occur."

Exploration

Every one of us makes mistakes. And we are all called on to respond to the mistakes of others.

In either case, ethical resilience and recovery requires three steps: telling the truth (to ourselves and others), owning our part of the responsibility, and committing to a plan of repair and prevention of future mishaps. All require a hefty dose of humility. All, I believe, rest on the late poet, memoirist, and civil rights activist Maya Angelou's famous advice: "Do the best you can until you know better. Then when you know better, do better."

Let's start with *knowing*. Start by asking whether you have the information you need in order to understand how to react to your own or someone else's error. Information is another way of gauging reality: a truthful assessment of what happened, why it happened, and what drove any spread of the regrettable behavior.

Information requires considering what *could* happen, not just what will happen when we make choices. Looking back, the same applies: what *could have* happened, not just what did happen. Just because we got away with a poor choice doesn't mean we don't face ethical recovery. Try to imagine the effect on people you will never meet—for example, the potential victims if you realize you have Covid-19 symptoms, decide not to self-isolate, and seriously infect another person or persons.

Identify the missing information (*the gap*), and the reason for it. Consider these scenarios:

- We had the information we needed but disregarded it and forged ahead anyway.

- We should have, or could have, had the information we needed, but didn't seek it out or use it.

- We couldn't have had the information we needed and made the best possible decision under the circumstances—and clarified the gaps in information to monitor events and behavior going forward.

Check for some common traps. Did you miss something that was right in front of you (as was the case with Airbnb)—which happens to us all? Did you make assumptions: base your decision on gut reactions, instinct, "everyone says," "I saw it on social media," or "the last time X happened, so I expected the same thing to happen again"? Did you wait for information to come to you rather than proactively seeking it out? Did you neglect to monitor changing information?

Now for the *doing*. The goal is to put your principles into action based on what you now know. Airbnb implemented a range of fixes, from removing the requirement to post customer photos, to new antidiscrimination policies, to denying hosts exhibiting racist behavior access to the platform. They have continued to monitor progress and consider further adjustments and changing information.

We can all strive to *know* better, and then when we do, *do* better—and honor others' efforts to do the same—with empathy and humility.

Are there ethical reasons that would persuade you to consider becoming a vegan?

A friend of mine who is the president of a California university noted that their dining halls are trying to nudge students toward plant-based choices in their diet, rather than emphasize options that feature beef, pork, fish, or chicken. Their view seems to be that vegan dishes are healthier for students or that vegan dishes are more sustainable food choices for the environment—or both. My own students are questioning their food choices as well.

The *Cambridge English Dictionary* defines veganism as "the practice of not eating or using animal products, such as meat, fish, eggs, cheese, or leather." An "ethical vegan" is someone who not only follows a vegan diet, but who also lives by the philosophy that animals should not be exploited for food, clothing, or other uses. According to the Vegan Society, the oldest vegan organization in the world, the ethical vegan avoids products tested on animals, and use of animals for sports or entertainment (such as racing), clothing and accessories, and makeup and personal hygiene items.

Exploration

Some people choose to be vegan or vegetarian for reasons of health, parenting, the environment, concern for animal welfare, or for other considerations. I focus here on the view of many vegans that it is morally wrong to consume animal products.

The *Stanford Encyclopedia of Philosophy* identifies a range of reasons that producing and consuming meat can be seen as morally wrong: it causes harm to the environment (veganism reduces our carbon footprint); industrial farming consumes vast quantities of water and energy, and produces enormous amounts of waste that must be treated and disposed of; it causes animals unnecessary pain (because of the conditions they're kept in); and it results in the unnecessary killing of animals (because we have other food options).

Exploring moral veganism presents an opportunity to banish "all or nothing" thinking. Taking partial steps toward veganism—such as eating vegan dishes several days a week—is better than taking no steps at all. Every choice matters. For example, Princeton philosophy professor and author Peter Singer calls himself a "flexible vegan," who allows himself to eat vegetarian when traveling. I agree that making some helpful choices is better than making none.

Put differently, even occasional vegans can do tremendous good by advocating for good choices rather than absolutes. Perfection is one of the most insidious drivers of the spread of unethical behavior. It is neither a laudable goal nor an achievable one and can trigger other forms of unethical behavior, like overstating the environmental impact of consuming meat, reducing the food supply for those in need, or lying about our eating habits.

Ethical veganism can also spotlight a decision-by-decision approach to ethics and allow us to evaluate choices, not stances. We're not condemning those who are not vegans, but rather choosing to praise the choices that make a better world for all of us. Veganism can prompt us to consider alternative ways to achieve common goals by creating better living conditions for livestock, reducing the amount of meat we consume that has the highest environmental impact, finding ways to reduce waste, and improving our diets. (All science and health matters should be based on expert advice.) There are many ways to reach these goals, and they don't all involve becoming vegan.

Ethical vegans help us connect to our own ethical principles and the identity they reflect—whether or not we are vegans. You and I might or might not wish to become vegans, or follow their practices, but I will learn from their choices, and become more informed and ethically resilient as a result.

Would you fly on a Boeing 737 Max plane?

I was grappling with whether my family should fly on Boeing planes. Here's why: In November 2020, the Federal Aviation Administration (FAA) rescinded the order grounding Boeing's 737 Max 8 and 9 planes that was issued in 2019 following two fatal crashes within a five-month period in Indonesia and Ethiopia. Disturbingly, Boeing knew that the software on its 737 Max planes—the Maneuvering Characteristics Augmentation System, or MCAS—was faulty. But they decided to wait years to fix it. And after the second crash, then CEO Dennis Muilenburg personally called President Trump to urge him to keep the Boeing 737 Max planes in the air, after sixty-five other nations decided to ground them. President Trump refused.

The ethics failure behind the crashes involves a complex history of poor decisions by Boeing executives and engineers, and regulators. The crux: first, due to competition from Airbus, Boeing ditched plans to build a new fuel-efficient passenger jet and instead redesigned the old 737 (first launched in 1967) with fuel-saving engines. Putting heavy new engines on the old plane changed the 737 Max's aerodynamics. The fix: the anti-stall software called

MCAS. Boeing made a pivotal decision that a single alert from one of its two sensors in the nose of the plane was enough, rather than relying on a second sensor alert as a fail-safe—an essential in an industry where redundancy is the key to safety. Another serious error involved Boeing's missing that a critical safety alert system to counter the risk of a faulty sensor was tied to an indicator that was a premium option (like luxury seating) rather than a mandatory feature. And Boeing did not notify customers or pilots about the need for the fix. In addition, Boeing cut corners with pilot training and testing. Meanwhile, the FAA gave Boeing increasing authority over its own safety certification process, thereby undermining the governmental independence of the review.

In rescinding the grounding of the planes, the FAA cited improvements in design and ordered operators to "meet all other applicable requirements, such as completing new training for pilots and conducting maintenance activity" before returning the planes to service.

Exploration

The question is when and under what circumstances passengers will be comfortable that Boeing has remedied the company's ethics failures enough to earn their trust to fly again on a 737 Max plane.

This is not a situation in which there are a few rogue individuals who can be fired (a CEO committing fraud), or where the flawed ethics don't affect consumers directly. This is the worst of all worlds: unpredictable ethics risks throughout the organization becoming life-threatening events for customers and employees. Worse, the then CEO did not prioritize passenger safety and perspective with his decisions that followed the accidents.

Ethical resilience and recovery require taking full responsibility for the mistakes and the underlying causes, then being transparent and having a plan going forward. Muilenburg ducked responsibility, suggesting after the two crashes that "procedures were not completely followed" by the pilots—in other words, the pilots, not Boeing, were to blame.

Ethics and safety are inextricably intertwined. Boeing did not just have a software problem, triggering tragic consequences that spread throughout the organization, to passengers, their families, the FAA, and the global airline industry. The company was mired in an uncontrollable contagion of failed ethics throughout Boeing affecting all stakeholders. The new CEO, David Calhoun, admitted that fixing Boeing was "more than I imagined it would be, honestly. And it speaks to the weaknesses of our leadership." He would later say, "The objective is to get the Max up safely. Period." The key lesson: We cannot just address the technical wrongdoing, insufficient training, and internal and external oversight failures. Genuine recovery—ethically and in terms of safety—requires identifying and eradicating all the *drivers* of the behavior that caused these tragedies to happen and be repeated. *Until we do, those same drivers will trigger other dangerous behaviors.*

Some of the causes of spreading unethical behavior at

play here include: competition and greed, fear (of losing business, as well as employees' fear of speaking up), impunity and failed regulatory oversight (the FAA's reliance on Boeing to control too much in self-certification), and weak leadership. All are exacerbated after the severe drop in business due to Covid-19.

Every one of these causes could affect the safety, security practices, and the oversight of *all Boeing planes*, not just the 737 Max. The ethics lapses in decision making cannot be limited to one product.

What other financial shortcuts did Boeing take that might not have surfaced yet? Are there other pilots flying without adequate training (no fault of the pilots)? How exactly did the FAA fix the *decision and regulatory oversight process*? Has Boeing shored up its decision making and manufacturing processes throughout the organization to regain our trust?

As consumers, we often don't have a choice of what plane we fly on. This question shows us how much we rely on other stakeholders, particularly regulators and the airlines that purchase and deploy Boeing planes, to assure ethical oversight of all aspects of travel.

Should you stop donating to a nonprofit organization if you find out about a sexual misconduct scandal?

The headlines can be deeply disturbing. "Sexual misconduct and management cover-up at humanitarian charity." "Government bans nonprofit organizations after claims of sexual misconduct." "NGO workers hired local prostitutes." "Well-intentioned employees pushed out after reporting allegations of sexual exploitation."

The headlines above are composites of headlines from around the world revealing sexual misconduct at nonprofit organizations of all sizes, missions, and locations—anonymized to avoid spotlighting any one organization.

In this question, I have also anonymized examples of the kind of horrific behavior that has come to light, to avoid targeting any one organization. Top of mind are instances of nonprofit employees pressuring beneficiaries (or their family or community members) for sex in exchange for desperately needed food, medicines, or other assistance. The abuse of power is particularly egregious in times of crisis—a pandemic, in the aftermath of a natural disaster, in a conflict zone. Misconduct can be more difficult to detect when employees and volunteers serve far from home; local laws and customs may be (wrongly) used as excuses for unacceptable behavior.

Exploration

All the global NGOs and other nonprofit organizations I have advised, researched, volunteered for, or donated to—and their peer organizations—have had some episodes of sexual misconduct. No organization in any sector can boast a spotless past, or guarantee a stainless future. That said, the overwhelming majority of employees at nonprofits work with impeccable integrity in terribly hard conditions, often for reduced pay—providing lifesaving assistance that would not otherwise be available.

This question pits our hearts—compassion for people in need and admiration for the good work done by non-profit organizations—against our repugnance at sexual misconduct. While this is not a question that affects most of us directly, through our donations and volunteering we have considerable power to affect the organization and the people it serves.

Sexual misconduct is one of the most virulently conta-gious forms of unethical behavior there is.

People receiving aid in crisis situations often have no other source of aid (giving nonprofit workers enormously greater power). Add to that impunity (conduct undetected or unpunished), information silos, arrogance, greed (or just financial pressure), cultural pressure (blaming women for an assault), and failed compliance systems. Moreover, victims may be unable to report transgressions due to language barriers, fear and shaming, or overly complicated reporting systems.

No organization can prevent all misconduct. But here are some questions you can ask to make an ethically informed choice: Did the organization investigate the scandal to determine the full scope of the problem (ideally with independent investigators)? Was the organization transparent with the public and donors as information came to light?

Did they then fix both the specific challenges (firing guilty individuals for cause) and systemic aspects of the problem (buttressing organization-wide compliance, more thoroughly vetting candidates when hiring, simplifying reporting processes)?

All of this can be difficult in nonprofit organizations with limited budgets, particularly those operating in many different countries with local customs and laws. Is the organization current with best practices? What precautions does the organization take to protect the most vulnerable (children, the elderly, the infirm, or those who have no other sources of life-critical health services)?

If you can answer yes—or they're working toward yes—to these questions, I would consider continuing support.

A few red flags might convince us to give our money elsewhere, such as a pattern of resorting to bribery to gain access, repeated failure to use donor funds for the specified purposes, failing to fire the perpetrators, or violation of medical ethics.

If you feel you need to withdraw support because the organization is just not handling the misconduct properly, tell them why you made the decision. And consider finding an alternative way to support the people the organization partners with and serves.

Should we buy clothing from companies that don't treat the people who work for them properly?

On April 23, 2013, deep cracks and fissures were discovered in the foundation walls of the Rana Plaza building in Bangladesh's Dhaka District, where thousands in the garment industry labored making clothes. Workers were reassured the building was safe and were told to return to their jobs the next morning. That afternoon, on April 24, the building collapsed and over 1,100 people were buried in the rubble; thousands more were injured. It was the deadliest garment factory disaster in history. "Soldiers, paramilitary police officers, firefighters and other citizens clawed through the wreckage, searching for survivors and bodies," reported the *New York Times*.

The factories housed in the Rana Plaza produced clothing for many Western fashion leaders. An investigation found that the building violated building codes; in fact, the top four floors had been built illegally without any permits at all. Scott Nova, executive director of Worker Rights Consortium (an independent labor rights monitoring organization), said in the aftermath, "The price pressure these buyers put on factories undermines any prospect that factories will undertake the costly repairs and renovations that are necessary to make these buildings safe." A spokesperson for one major brand, after expressing sympathy for the victims, said they were "committed" to urging stronger safety guidelines.

Exploration

This tragic event and similar stories ask us to decide whether, as consumers, we will stop purchasing from companies that don't guarantee decent working conditions throughout their supply chain—even if it means paying a few dollars more for (or going without) the product. There is a hidden cost many of us are unaware of to the $2 T-shirts we buy from discount stores, and even the promotions high-end retailers offer.

This isn't an instance where the products themselves are dangerous to consumers (like toxic baby powder), or an isolated case of wrongdoing (like sexual harassment by a senior leader). Rather, the ethics of these companies' entire *business models* are in question.

When buying clothing or other goods, none of us is perfect in considering our principles, such as safety, integrity, equality, and dignity. And many people do not have the means to have much choice when purchasing clothes. But many of us don't think about how easy it would be to live without these goods, find them elsewhere, or forgo a latte or two to pay a bit more.

Applying those principles is not so easy. What if our (or the company's) principles are in conflict? Women working in these factories depend on their wages to support their families. Many hardworking consumers simply don't have the extra few dollars. Would taking our business elsewhere hurt these people?

The ethical solution is not simply a factory closure or retail price increase—or our decision as consumers.

Companies can trim costs elsewhere, such as with executive compensation and perks. And they can eliminate products that just don't make sense when linking cost to humane business practices.

My own view is that companies are responsible for the ethics of every link in their supply chain. They can outsource everything from textile purchasing to contract negotiation, but *they cannot outsource their ethical responsibility.* Some companies claim they can't know everything because the supply chain is so complex or so long. My response: yes they can. Part of the challenge in monitoring the safety and well-being of "workers has been the difficulty of holding each party in the supply chain accountable"—the companies, people, resources, and distributors who turn raw materials into a finished product. One factory at Rana Plaza was making clothes without the retailer's knowledge, because the work had been subcontracted out by a wholesaler. But for companies it's a question of priorities, financial investment, and effort. The companies linked to the Rana Plaza tragedy could have, and should have, known about the unsafe working conditions.

We also need greater industry-wide transparency of company practices—like nutrition labels in the food industry—that clearly specify where products are made and a simplified certification of minimum standards. We need enhanced regulation and global advocacy.

Our individual purchasing decisions matter—in the case of retail goods, they can influence people we may never meet. They reflect our ethics, and they contribute to society's ethics.

Refusing to buy from brands that mistreat their workers is one option among so many ways to contribute to a solution, including speaking out, signing an online petition, and donating to nonprofit organizations that help people in these countries in need.

Should tax preparation for individual tax returns be free?

I n 2002, the George W. Bush administration proposed that the Internal Revenue Service (IRS) create a free online filing option for taxpayers. But the tax preparation industry, concerned about their profits, negotiated a compromise: companies would offer complimentary versions of their software, through a multiyear agreement between the IRS and the Free File Alliance, providing "free and secure online tax return preparation and filing services" to low- to moderate-income filers (those who generally earn $72,000 or less, although some tax companies have lower income limits). Their goal was to provide 60 percent or more of taxpayers with free online filing.

While more than 60 million returns have been filed since the program began in 2003, according to the alliance's website, the annual number of taxpayers using the free software dropped from 5 million in 2003 to half of that in 2020. Although 100 million Americans are eligible to use the free software, the Free File Alliance executive director reports, less than 3 million do so. According to interviews conducted with former employees of Intuit and H&R Block, their companies actively steer people away from the free services, and try to turn them into paying customers. H&R Block dropped out of the alliance in 2020. And in July 2021, Intuit, the maker of TurboTax, announced they would no longer be a part of the alliance.

Exploration

Paying taxes is a civic duty. It's also the law. The system for doing so should be accessible to all: easy to use, free of charge for basic returns, available on mobile devices, verifiable, and with access to a human in the loop to help where necessary.

Some countries such as Britain and Japan don't require taxpayers to file tax returns—the government just "withholds taxes from wage income and handles the paperwork." (Those with more complicated finances still need to file.) In 2006, Austan Goolsbee, who later served as chairman of President Obama's Council of Economic Advisers, suggested the idea of the "simple return," in which taxpayers review and sign off on already completed tax forms.

This question spotlights what appears to be an ethically charged uneven battle between the federal government and commercial tax prep providers, ensnaring average citizens just trying to pay taxes in a timely fashion in the cross fire.

With the Free File Alliance founded in 2003, the government created a monopoly that hadn't existed before. As a result of the alliance, the IRS agreed not to compete in providing free online services to taxpayers. Imagine if we had to go through private companies to receive Social Security checks. A series of exposés by ProPublica revealed that "free" often involved a series of paid enticements to purchase upgrades and additional assistance, playing on customers' fears to drive the tax preparation companies' growth despite the free service. And "free" applies to federal tax returns. Each company in the alliance was only required to cover 10 percent of taxpayers, so companies could manage their customer selection to keep their most lucrative customers. In my view, the system seems to rest on a quagmire of lobbyists, corporate advertising, social media strategy, and sophisticated product design, with respect to a fundamental civic duty that every American must fulfill.

The Free File Alliance argues that the tax collector—the IRS—should not also be the tax preparer. Doing both creates a conflict of interest.

Ethics must be made easy: the default option should not be an obstacle course. This is particularly crucial for anything involving citizenship—it applies to everything from obtaining Covid-19 vaccinations and voting to recycling and being able to report drunk drivers. If the federal government cannot dedicate the resources to a government-run free filing system, regulators should consider other ethics protections: eliminate the filing process for millions of Americans in lower income groups; ban the manipulative tactics used to steer consumers to paid tax preparation software; and require the companies in the Free File Alliance to display the free option prominently on websites, in Google searches, and in advertising. Governments have a responsibility to support well-intentioned citizens in efficiently and effectively complying with tax law by mitigating the risks that unnecessary government bureaucracy and the proliferation of for-profit intermediaries may pose to performing civic duties.

Should I switch my giving in response to Covid-19 or other emergencies?

Consider a situation in which you have decided you want to give money to your favorite charity—an animal adoption program, because you love animals. And your roommate or partner or best friend jumps in and takes you to task. How can you give money to animals, they argue, when people are dying from the Covid-19 pandemic, and millions are out of work and are struggling to get by? A lecture continues about how it doesn't matter whether you feel most connected to organizations that some would say aren't society's highest priority—a ballet program for underprivileged children or a neighborhood playground— we all should give to issues like supporting the victims of Covid-19, climate change, undernourished children, or the toxic lead in the water supply of Flint, Michigan.

The word "philanthropy" comes from the ancient Greek phrase "love of humankind." In 1835, when French civil servant Alexis de Tocqueville published the first volume of his famous work *Democracy in America*, he admired the American penchant for forming "associations"—coming together as citizens through nonprofit organizations that strengthened our social bonds and supported one another. Today, many of us include in our giving to others our time, our experience and talent, material goods, financial support, even our support in social and mainstream media.

Exploration

Charitable giving is a deeply personal decision. You don't owe anyone an explanation of how much and where you give, any more than you owe them an explanation of what is in your grocery cart or your Netflix selection. Only you can decide where you feel you can do the most good, have the greatest connection, and maximize your giving capacity (whether you are giving your time, your expertise, or your money).

Here are a few questions that can help you anchor your giving with ethics in mind. Ask yourself, Does the organization demonstrate a commitment to ethics essentials regardless of the mission? For example, are they transparent (telling you when things go wrong)? Do they fight discrimination and inequality? Do they hold themselves accountable for what they do and how they do it? Do they focus on *outcomes* (children acquiring skills) rather than actions (providing school books)?

When do you give? Perhaps during the pandemic you decided to continue to give to food banks, but chose those hit particularly hard by Covid-19. Or, alternatively, you decided to remain loyal to your favorite arts organization, which you realized will need help to restart when the pandemic subsides. Maybe this year you cannot afford to give money at all, but you help deliver food or medication to a neighbor who can't go out.

Will your gift make a difference? Médecins Sans Frontières/Doctors Without Borders (for which I have served on the U.S. advisory board for years) used to have a campaign called "a franc a day" (before the franc was replaced by the euro). A river of collective generosity from people from all walks of life became the bedrock of the Nobel Peace Prize–winning organization, even as individuals came and went. Other organizations are set up for only large donations. Effective altruism—a field of study using evidence and reasoning to try to do as much good as possible with available resources—is another lens for considering giving.

Lifting us all up and creating a compassionate society requires a complex tapestry of sustained efforts to support individuals and organizations—to further generosity and grateful assistance. As one chief executive of a global NGO said to me in 2020, given the nature of the Covid-19 pandemic and its resulting shrapnel, everything will be about, or at least touched by, Covid-19 for the foreseeable future. Organizations faced increased pressure and costs to protect staff and find alternative ways to serve beneficiaries. Many will face reduced donations because donors devoted more funds to address the impact of Covid-19; many donors may not have the capacity to continue giving at their previous levels.

Giving—in whatever way you give—should be a moment of joy, celebration, and gratitude that we are in a position to give, whatever and wherever and however you give.

Does buying (or not buying) a disposable plastic bottle of water really make a difference?

You have been on a hike and at the end you are very thirsty. But the convenience store at the trailhead doesn't have a water fountain. The only water available is sold in individual plastic bottles. You care deeply about the environment, and you are dismayed at the thought of purchasing a plastic water bottle, even if you dispose of it in a recycling bin. But you need water. Or perhaps you slipped up and forgot to bring your reusable water container to a concert or an outing, and resort to purchasing a bottle of water only to be confronted by a friend, family member, or colleague as they fix you with a withering stare. I have found myself in many such situations and bought the bottle.

Exploration

Many of us wonder whether, particularly without data, our one small decision will have an impact. In the case of plastic bottles, the data is striking. *National Geographic* reports that globally, "more than a million plastic bottles are sold every single minute." Further, "in the U.S., only 30% of these bottles are recycled." A single plastic bottle takes "about 450 years" to decompose. And plastic bottles are the third-most collected plastic trash in the Ocean Conservancy's annual international beach cleanup.

The ethics of our individual decisions matter because the small stuff adds up, especially when repeated by ourselves and others. They become habits that persist and spread among friends, within offices, across towns, on social media. Ethics contagion can be either positive or negative. For example, in offices that provide water fountains or sinks, few would *think* of displaying a plastic bottle on their desk.

There will be occasions when there are no alternatives. Sometimes there just doesn't seem to be another option to bottled water at an airport or at a concert. And there are places in the world where tap water isn't safe, and cheap plastic water bottles are the only affordable option. (Hopefully corporations that supply potable water will offer better choices. Bottled water is roughly 2,000 times more expensive than the equivalent amount of tap water, according to the American Water Works Association.)

My suggestion is to look for *additional* strategies rather than a license for a pass. Avoiding buying water in plastic bottles where possible is important, but we should also pursue a range of other measures, such as voting for tax credits for people and companies that recycle; educating our community about recycling; and using stainless steel reusable water bottles. And the water will be healthier (avoiding bisphenol A—or BPA—used in the manufacture of plastic bottles and linked to various health hazards).

Ultimately, our actions, no matter how small, make a difference.

Similarly, seeing the ethics opportunity in a single plastic water bottle can change our and others' individual and collective impacts on the world about many other issues, bottle by bottle, with seemingly little effort. I know I need to do better.

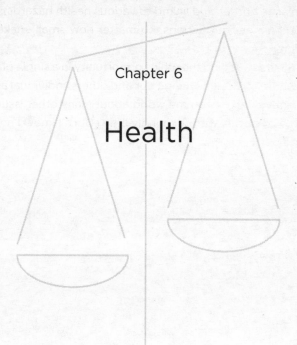

Chapter 6

Health

Should organ donation be opt-in or opt-out, from an ethical perspective?

As of this writing, 106,822 people in the U.S. were waiting for organs, and 17 people died waiting each day. Organ donation, as described by the Cleveland Clinic, is "the process of surgically removing an organ . . . from one person (the organ donor) and placing it into another person (the recipient)." Organs can be donated by living donors, as well as by deceased donors. There were 7,397 living donors in the U.S. in 2019, and 11,870 deceased donors according to the United Network for Organ Sharing (the nonprofit organization that manages the U.S. transplantation system). A single donor can supply organs for as many as eight different recipients.

Ninety percent of people in America favor organ donation, but only 60 percent actually sign up. Currently in the U.S., each of us has to actively register to donate our organs, in what is known as the opt-in or explicit consent system. The alternative is what is known as the opt-out system, where the government automatically enrolls individuals as organ donors, unless the individual has specifically selected not to donate their organs. The change in the default decision can make a significant difference. Germany, like the U.S., uses an opt-in system, and donation rates hover at 12 percent. Neighboring Austria, with a similar culture and economy, uses opt-out, and has a donation rate of 99.98 percent.

Exploration

Organ donation literally touches the core of our physical and spiritual selves. Among the stakeholders in organ donation are the organ donor, their family, the organ recipient and their family and loved ones, doctors, our spiritual advisors, and the general public.

As a society, our goal is to increase the number of organs available for transplant, by increasing organ donation. One way to do that is to shift the laws from an opt-in system where the individual must specifically request that their organs be donated, to an opt-out system. Twenty countries in the European Union, as well as Great Britain, have some form of opt-out system.

Switching to an opt-out system, however, while effective in increasing the supply of available organs for transplants, must rest on a foundation of robust transparency—making sure that the public understands what is at stake for them and offering a simple way to opt out if they wish. Our informed consent is not truly informed without both. Finally, ethics require monitoring—periodically notifying people who have, or have not, opted out—as our thinking on our decisions can change over time.

Complex ethical decisions benefit from looking for alternatives as well. The state of Illinois adopted in 2006 a policy of *mandated choice*, which required people applying for a driver's license to answer the "yes or no" question, "Do you wish to be an Organ Donor?" It is your choice, but you must make a choice.

Another potential solution is to offer tax incentives—a carrot, versus a stick—to those who donate an organ. But paying for organs is fraught with ethics risks. Educating the public about the importance of organ donation can also be effective and increase transparency.

Organ donation has a life-critical impact on another human being and their loved ones, in a way that most of the decisions we make may not. For some, the decision not to donate their organs is a matter of faith or religion. For others, it is an extraordinary opportunity to save or dramatically improve lives. Whatever our views, organ donation should be the result of a thoughtful decision, not something thrust upon us without choice.

As a society, our principles, policies, and practices say a great deal about how we balance individual autonomy versus saving lives.

Are you ethically obligated to tell your children if you have an inheritable disease?

The facts were unusual, but the case highlighted a life-critical decision that we are increasingly finding ourselves having to make. A woman in the U.K., known to the public only as ABC to preserve her confidentiality, sued NHS Trust, a group within the National Health Service in the U.K., for not informing her that her father had Huntington's disease. Huntington's is at present an incurable, inheritable degenerative brain disease. Symptoms, according to the Mayo Clinic, can include difficulty walking, difficulty speaking, tremors, depression, problems with impulse control, and bipolar disorder and other cognitive and psychiatric disorders.

With Huntington's disease, children have a 50/50 chance of inheriting the genetic mutation that causes the disease. Those with the mutation develop the disease. About 30,000 people in the U.S. have Huntington's disease, with another 200,000 at risk of developing it, including ABC, who ultimately tested positive for the genetic mutation.

Exploration

This story zeroes in on the gut-wrenching ethical quandaries behind a parent's decision on whether to tell their child and other family members that they have an inheritable disease—regardless of the parent's doctor's confidentiality obligations. Today, with increased genetic testing, including direct-to-consumer (DTC) genetic testing kits like 23andMe, we have the unprecedented ability to discover whether we have a predisposition for a genetically inheritable disease, without even consulting a doctor. The information discovered using DTC kits often affects others and varies significantly depending on one's situation, including the nature of the disease, family circumstances, the ages of the individuals most directly affected, and other factors.

This question puts many ethical considerations—health, honesty, courage, compassion, autonomy—in conflict with others that are also important, like privacy and confidentiality. At its core, this situation hinges on the most powerful force in ethics: truth. By truth, I mean the right to know, but also the right not to be burdened by knowledge that you can't un-know.

First, consider the rights of others who potentially need to be told. At the very top of the list are those who could inherit the disease (children and their children) and their parents if the children are minors. I would allow an adult child to make the decision about whether to tell their partner, spouse, family members, or others who might need to care for them. No one who is not directly affected needs to be told. Extenuating circumstances like mental health issues should also be considered.

If a parent doesn't tell their adult child, the child loses the power to make life-critical choices for themselves. That includes the ability to seek medical help and the decision to have children—and their choice to tell or not tell their own loved ones.

The father in the scenario robbed his daughter of the opportunity to decide whether to have a child. He valued his own privacy at the cost of his daughter's right to know.

Parents may wish to shield a child who is under the age of eighteen from this information so as not to burden them before they are emotionally ready, particularly if telling them wouldn't alter the choices available or the disease often presents in adulthood.

This question puts all involved in an impossible situation. The decision not to tell is so much more than a stand-alone decision: it effectively results in the parent controlling a series of follow-on decisions that are not theirs to make. The best you can do may be to consider the principles raised above, and what you would want done if you were in their shoes. Consider as well what you would think about what you did, looking back on your choice in the future. Ideally, we should consider how we might face these questions prior to using DTC kits. And as a society we will need to reflect on the implications of doctor-patient confidentiality obligations in this new world in which our own health care testing may reveal unprecedented information about the health of others.

What are the ethical considerations behind informed consent?

Henrietta Lacks, the subject of Rebecca Skloot's critically acclaimed book *The Immortal Life of Henrietta Lacks*, was a Black woman treated for cervical cancer when she was thirty-one years old at the Johns Hopkins Hospital in 1951. Lacks died, but her tissue and cells, harvested for research without her knowledge or consent, continue to live on. They became the first human cells successfully grown in a laboratory setting. Named HeLa cells (after the first two letters in Lacks's names), they were shared "freely and widely for scientific research," because her cells were found to be durable and prolific. Those HeLa cells have led to countless medical breakthroughs, from the polio and Covid-19 vaccines to AIDS research to cancer treatments.

Informed consent, one of the three pillars that support ethical decision making (along with transparency and effective listening), means agreeing to an action based on an understanding of the action and its consequences.

Exploration

Henrietta Lacks's story continues to raise disturbing questions about who controls the cells taken from a patient's body. This ethical dilemma emerges in procedures as varied as tonsil removal and the whisking away of a placenta after birth, to skin cells obtained through a biopsy. Too often consent really means "do it our way or we'll show you the highway." One hospital consent form I obtained stated, "I consent to the taking of pictures, videotapes or other electronic reproductions of the patient's medical or surgical condition or treatment . . . consistent with the Hospital's mission, such as education and research." Agree to the expansive terms or you can't get a medically necessary procedure. It's one thing to click "I agree" and skip the fine print on the Apple Music terms of service. It's quite another when it comes to our bodies. In either case, we don't actually have a choice.

Some believe such medical consent contributes to the good of society; others are concerned with the right to decide for yourself what happens to your tissues. Skloot, in a *New York Times* op-ed, highlights diverging views: "Some believe their souls live on in the disembodied cells," some feel "it's unethical not to use [these cells] to advance science," and others "worry that genetic information will be linked to them . . . in harmful or discriminatory ways—particularly minorities."

I want to banish "sign or you can't have a procedure" *binary thinking* about the ethics of our decisions. So how can we obtain genuine consent to maximize the good for society, and minimize the risk to privacy and more? One way to do that is for health care providers to make elements unrelated to the procedure (the "extras") *opt-in*. Here are examples you might not even notice if, like me, you felt too nervous about a procedure to read the fine print.

We should not be required to allow the hospital to sell or share our tissues (or videotapes and photos of our treatments) with *commercial third parties*.

The consent form could add a commitment to *data privacy* and add ironclad anonymity (although increasingly there is technology to reverse anonymity).

The form's reference to the "potential for overlapping surgery" (your doctor could leave the operating room and perform another operation somewhere else if needed . . . leaving you in the hands of another "qualified physician") should be limited to exceptional cases.

The form I obtained required the physician to "explain" the procedure and risks and benefits "to [your] satisfaction." This information should include not only everything that will be done, but why, the pros and cons, the *alternatives*, and the potential consequences. It's unlikely that institutions will change, but we can protect ourselves by forcing medical providers to take the time to explain until we feel we understand our choices.

The bottom line: if the consent form is overly broad, and we can't choose from a menu of options, we have no choice at all.

Would you tell someone who is suffering from dementia when a close relative has died?

Your mother, who suffers from late-stage dementia, lives in a nursing home. (The most common form of progressive dementia, according to the World Health Organization, is Alzheimer's, which may account for 60 to 80 percent of cases. The World Health Organization defines dementia as a "deterioration in cognitive function beyond what might be expected from the usual consequences of biological aging.") She is no longer able to care for herself. A close relative—a daughter or son, a brother or sister, her spouse or partner—dies. Do you tell her? While she has occasional moments of lucidity, her short-term memory is poor, and she struggles to recognize family when they visit.

If you do decide to tell her, you need to think about how much detail you share. On the other hand, if you have always had a very honest and trusting relationship, you may ask yourself how can you not tell her, even if it upsets her.

Many people suffering from advanced dementia lack

the capacity to understand, and/or suffer short-term memory loss. You may have to repeat—and have her hear, process, and experience—a painful truth and emotional distress over and over.

Exploration

Almost 6 million people are diagnosed with Alzheimer's and related dementias in the U.S. today. And more than 55 million people worldwide have dementia, according to the World Health Organization.

So many caring relatives experience this deeply painful and personal question as a moral dilemma, as well as an emotional and practical challenge. The ethics focus here is on what is in the *best interest of the person diagnosed with dementia*. The prerequisite to acting is getting medical advice about the person's capacity to understand the information.

This is a rare situation when we may turn two forces that drive the ethics of virtually every decision we make—transparency and truth—on their head. One way of thinking about transparency is ensuring that we have the information important to understanding the potential consequences of our decision. Truth undergirds the ethics of all decisions. Both force us to ask whether there is a legitimate *reason* to prioritize transparency and truth over other considerations tugging at us, such as compassion, respect, autonomy, and dignity.

On the other hand, the person may feel unsafe or confused if they don't know what happened to the deceased person. Those who are able can use the information to grieve, to understand why the person close to them who has died is not communicating with them or visiting. But there is no obligation to give information to help the person make a choice because there are no choices to make at this stage. Consider whether there are alternative ways to make them feel safe, such as increasing your own visits, or working with medical staff for ideas.

Guilt has no place in ethics. It neither solves problems nor improves the quality of our decision making. In this case, it makes the decision about *us*, rather than about the relative living with dementia. Ethics are about decisions—not about labeling ourselves or others as "bad" or "good."

Some people believe that withholding the truth is wrong no matter what the circumstances or consequences. Lying almost always has consequences—even if not seemingly significant or immediate—and ethical decision making requires considering the consequences of our choices over time. But this is a very rare situation in which the consequences of truth may cause more harm. (I'm not arguing for lying if the person asks about the deceased relative.) And we should tread very carefully to assure that exceptional situations do not become excuses for, or a slippery slope to, compromising transparency and truth.

If you are making this heartbreaking decision in your own life, I am so sorry that you are going through this. Be compassionate with yourself as well. There is no one right answer, other than doing our best to reflect on the ethics of our decisions.

Would you be in favor
of editing the genes of
human embryos?

"Imagine a world where genetic engineering is determined mainly by individual free choice, with few government regulations and no pesky bioethics panels telling us what's permissible," postulates Walter Isaacson in his book *The Code Breaker*, about gene editing pioneer and Nobel laureate Jennifer A. Doudna. "You go into a fertility clinic and are given, as if at a genetic supermarket, a list of traits you can buy for your children." He concludes that most of us would choose to eliminate serious genetic diseases such as Huntington's or sickle cell. Personally, he tells us, he would eliminate blindness.

But it is easy to go careening down a slippery slope . . . what about editing genes to achieve a higher IQ? An individual's preferred height and build? If we leave use of this humanity-defining technology primarily to individual choice, Isaacson suggests that indeed "Without any gates or flags, we might all go barreling down at uncontrollable speed, taking society's diversity and the human genome along with us."

Gene editing allows genetic material in the cell to be added, removed, or changed. But there are two different kinds of gene editing, with very different ethical stakes. Editing the code of somatic, or nonreproductive cells, is not inheritable. For example, gene editing to cure cancer only affects the patient, not any future offspring. In contrast, so-called germline therapy, according to the National Human Genome Research Institute, "change[s] genes in reproductive cells (like sperm and eggs) . . . [which] would then be passed down from generation to generation."

Exploration

This question asks us to confront one of humanity's most critical challenges—as Jennifer A. Doudna says, "the general unease of humans taking control of their own evolution." I offer some key questions and my own (evolving) views to help you get your bearings—even if, like me, you don't fully understand the science.

First, think about who gets to decide when and how our genes can be edited. Among the potential list: governments, geneticists, doctors and hospitals, patients, parents, those planning to have children. All of the above have a role and responsibility *for individuals and for society.* Individuals should not have unregulated freedom to choose their children's genes. And regulators should not impede what Doudna calls "genetic surgery" to fix genetic defects in nonreproductive cells since the consequences cannot be passed down hereditarily from parent to children.

Next, how do we assure informed consent—that the

participants understand the *potential consequences* of gene editing. Science is complex and rapidly changing, and there is limited visibility of the clinical outcomes and side effects of gene editing in many cases. (As of this writing, editing embryos is generally not seen as ethically acceptable by the scientific community.)

Then we should ask how we prevent gene editing from being used as a weapon for bioterrorism. Certain types of gene editing can be done on a relatively low budget and by rogue individuals, unlike building a complex nuclear device.

Perhaps most importantly, gene editing should be seen as a potential opportunity for medical progress to improve human lives, not as an effort to fundamentally change who we are. Some people who have genetic diseases understandably wonder whether they would in fact want to edit their genes or the genes of their children, because they believe their illness is a fundamental part of who they are as a person. Isaacson introduces us to a young sickle cell patient who has suffered tremendously during his life but still isn't convinced he would choose to edit embryos to eliminate the disease.

My view is that we owe it to each other to consider whether eliminating the suffering of a life-threatening disease could offer patients greater health, autonomy, and respect and more *opportunity to make choices for themselves*. Scientists will have to tell us if and when it is safe, with proper oversight in place, to extend gene editing to human embryos. We all need to consider how we would explain to a child—our child—that we could have prevented their suffering but chose not to. Then there is the matter of equity. We will need to assure access to gene editing to cure diseases for all.

Losing out on an opportunity itself can be one of our biggest risks. Imagine losing the chance to cure cancer with gene editing (a nonheritable intervention). Now imagine the patient is you, or a loved one.

What is our ethical responsibility to get vaccinated?

I was taken aback when a friend's guitar teacher in London—a thirty-four-year-old accomplished teacher and performer—told her that he does not intend to get the Covid-19 vaccine. He has two young children who cannot yet be vaccinated and teaches in person at a middle school and secondary school. Usually very thoughtful, he seemed oblivious to the fact that the vaccine both protects him and diminishes transmission to colleagues, students, his family, and others. For him, it wasn't about religion, denying science, or politics—or even a particular fear or risk. He believed that the U.K. had already reached herd immunity (not true), and that others had done the heavy lifting on civic duty, so there was no need for him to make the effort to get a vaccine.

Contrast this with one fifty-seven-year-old friend of mine who faithfully gets all vaccinations (including the annual flu shot) but at the onset of the pandemic said she would rather quarantine than be a "guinea pig" with the Covid-19 vaccine. She changed her mind after seeing the lasting health and mental health consequences of the disease and of quarantine, not to mention how quickly the new variants can spread even with the best precautions.

As of April 2021, one in four Americans "would refuse a coronavirus vaccine outright if offered," according to an NPR/Marist survey. The CDC says the vaccines are highly effective at preventing severe illness and death resulting from a Covid-19 infection. All fifty states require mandatory vaccinations for diseases such as polio and measles with outstanding results. The World Health Organization and the Pan American Health Organization jointly declared that measles are officially eradicated in North and South America in 2016.

Exploration

Vaccine hesitancy is front and center with Covid-19, reinforcing the question of whether vaccines should be mandatory. The ethics start with science.

The choice is not simply whether to get vaccinated. It's a choice about what combination of steps we will take, and sacrifices we will make, to keep ourselves and others safe. This is even more true with the surge of new variants of the virus. At a minimum, those refusing vaccination must take every possible safety precaution, including wearing masks, social distancing, apprising others near them of their unvaccinated status, and getting tested frequently, while those who have been vaccinated may live, work, and socialize much more freely. In my view, we have no more right to expose others to Covid-19 than we do to drive while drunk. We don't get to free ride on others' vaccinations.

(To be clear, I'm not addressing those with doctor-excused medical reasons and sincerely held religious beliefs here; they might be exempt, as they were from mandatory measles vaccines decades ago.)

Vaccine hesitancy forces us to navigate principles that affect us all: health and safety (our own and that of others), truth (evidence-based science), and responsibility. To me, protecting human life in these unprecedented circumstances trumps some of the most important individual rights. I am particularly concerned about those who are at grave risk because their immune systems are compromised, children who cannot yet be vaccinated, and those who through no fault of their own don't have access to vaccines. We must also think of others who have no choice but to go to work and be exposed to the public.

Companies, schools and universities, and organizations have a duty to protect employees, customers, and the public. Everyone who enters a workplace should be required to prove vaccination—or provide a recent negative test, or demonstrate immunity from recent recovery from Covid-19. And with the rise of new variants, both vaccinations and masks (and even testing) might be necessary. Employees who refuse vaccines and are able to work remotely might need to continue to do so. Some may lose their jobs. French president Emmanuel Macron has declared proof of vaccination, or a very recent negative Covid-19 test, a prerequisite to entering cafés, restaurants, concert venues, and other public places.

Requiring transparency about one's vaccination status

is the only way to allow others to make informed decisions about whether they want to be in contact with an individual or enter an enclosed space. It's a minor compromise on privacy considering that we are each called to make potentially life-threatening choices as we work, socialize, and travel—and given that the carrot approach (access for those who are vaccinated to workplace gyms or free food) isn't working well enough to achieve herd immunity.

We all can fight for truth, calling on social media companies and the media not to disseminate false information about vaccines.

Intention is clear: the consequences of failing to vaccinate are widely known, so those declining vaccines are making a deliberate choice (even if few people consciously intend to harm others or get sick themselves).

We can encourage those who are hesitant to vaccinate to consider how they would feel if they caused someone else's illness or death. Think of the drunk driving videos used to educate high school students. We don't get to opt out of being responsible to others—whether we vaccinate or not and whatever our intentions may be.

Would you want artificial intelligence to contribute to diagnosing your medical condition?

An American friend of mine living in Paris made an appointment for a mammogram at the American Hospital of Paris. She emerged very excited, not just with the usual relief of a negative test, but with additional confidence: her radiologist had deployed artificial intelligence in analyzing the images, to be more efficient and effective. I was curious. For years I have had the privilege of serving on the board of governors of the American Hospital of Paris, as well as the hospital's ethics committee and patient care committee. When I checked the update to the hospital's website, I learned that the imaging department offers medical imaging "assisted by artificial intelligence ... artificial intelligence (AI) does not replace the radiologist. It helps the radiologist to be more efficient and make a diagnosis more quickly. We have AI tools for segmenting brain structures, and detecting pulmonary nodules and breast microcalcifications."

Algorithms can detect patterns in images, work in

seconds, and are inexpensively reproduced. They don't get sick or tired. They do require accurate and representative data to train for accuracy, but they continually improve as more data is added. That said, they don't have much bedside manner (yet), and they cannot understand what it's like to be human (yet).

According to the American Medical Association, an AI program "can now diagnose skin cancer more accurately than a board-certified dermatologist . . . faster and more efficiently." In addition to diagnosis, *Harvard Business Review* reported a wide variety of promising medical applications, including robot-assisted surgery and dosage error reduction.

Exploration

It is imperative that ethics do not become a barrier to innovation; that is even more true when human health is at stake. Put yourself in the shoes of the person lucky enough to receive a cancer diagnosis from a machine much earlier than a human doctor could detect it, resulting in minor treatment with a positive outcome rather than a torturous treatment or worse. And consider the systemic benefits. An analysis by consultancy Accenture found that "key clinical health AI applications can potentially create $150 billion in annual savings for the US healthcare economy by 2026."

First, AI is a supplement to, not a replacement for, human oversight. It should be used in combination with human medical expertise and proper clinical care—a blended solution. Another critical concern is the potential impact of limited or skewed data used to train AI for diagnostic accuracy (for example, training data that is racially skewed or disproportionately represents a particular age group). But missing an opportunity to maximize diagnostic insights, save costs, greatly increase speed of results, and potentially save lives could be the greatest risk of all.

Then consider other concerns for patients and for society, particularly transparency, privacy, and inequality.

Medical ethics experts tell me that consent forms do not generally specify when AI is being used. This is another instance in which informed consent is not fully informed. I would argue that medical providers should be obligated to tell you whether they use AI in diagnostics, both to obtain consent to the use and to be sure you're not missing an important health care benefit.

And with so many global health matters, inequality is a major ethics challenge.

Google and its sister company Verily are testing an AI system in India that they developed to diagnose diabetic retinopathy, a condition that can lead to blindness if untreated. The Google project is part of a widespread effort to deploy systems that can automatically detect signs of illness where few eye doctors are available. (According to the International Council of Ophthalmology, there are only eleven eye doctors in India for every 1 million people.)

AI can be a force multiplier to spread good (or ill) faster than ever before. Your individual doctor and the medical institution are just as responsible for the use and confidentiality of AI as they are for using a scalpel or a prescription pad. Experts claim that artificial intelligence will be applicable to a vast array of medical fields, from diagnosing breast cancer, to predicting osteoarthritis years before there are symptoms, to recognizing rare diseases with facial recognition technology. We should ensure not only safety, but also access for all who wish to benefit from it.

Should vaping be banned?

Banana Ice. Unicorn Puke. Sweet Tart. "Every flavor Skittle compressed into one." Those are some of the flavors I found in 2015 when first researching e-cigarettes, battery-powered devices that look like USB drives, which deliver nicotine through a flavored liquid that is then heated and vaporized. E-cigarettes and other electronic nicotine delivery systems, or ENDS—vapes, vape pens, hookah pens, e-pipes—contain nicotine and other ingredients that are harmful to our health. The most popular e-cigarette in the U.S. is JUUL.

In 2016, it became illegal to sell e-cigarettes and electronic nicotine delivery systems to people under eighteen. In 2019, Congress raised the federal legal age to twenty-one.

Kevin Burns, the CEO of Juul Labs, urged viewers on *CBS This Morning* not to start vaping if they weren't already smokers. "Don't start using nicotine if you don't have a preexisting relationship with nicotine . . . You're not our target consumer."

On October 12, 2021, the FDA, for the first time, authorized the sale of a specific brand of e-cigarettes in the U.S.

The agency explained that based on available data, "the authorized products' aerosols are significantly less toxic" than cigarettes. The FDA stated that it would continue to monitor the marketing of e-cigarettes and take further action "if credible evidence emerges of significant use by individuals who did not previously use a tobacco product, including youth."

Exploration

This is an area where science, health, and medicine must rule the ethics. Remember that ethics may apply differently to youth and adults.

I strongly agree with the ban on purchasing e-cigarettes under twenty-one—not least because we don't have the information we need to trust the safety of the product. The jury is also still out on a range of safety and addiction issues, in the eyes of Dr. Norman E. Sharpless, the director of the National Cancer Institute. As Johns Hopkins Medicine reports, even the secondhand vapor from e-cigarettes has chemicals that can be harmful to children. There is also a concern that vaping will lead youths to escalate to real cigarettes.

The case for vaping may be more compelling for adults. Some adults see vaping as a healthier alternative for a long-standing cigarette addiction.

Companies and regulators owe the public transparency (clear statements of the risks *and the unknowns* in plain language like SMOKING KILLS on cigarette packages) and bans on manipulative advertising. (The five major U.S. smokeless tobacco companies spent $576.1 million on advertising and promotion in the U.S. in 2019, according to the Federal Trade Commission cigarette report.) Early studies suggest that vaping in order to quit smoking may lead to doing both interchangeably. Quitting smoking is incredibly difficult. But there are medically approved alternatives to vaping that can help smokers, from medications to nicotine patches to lozenges and gums.

These products engage a host of drivers in the spread of unwanted behavior: peer pressure, impunity, failed compliance (USB-size nicotine discs are extremely easy to hide), falsity (misleading advertising and social media), endorsements from celebrities, and greed as tobacco companies look for alternative revenue as smoking declines. All increase the popularity of vaping and illicit use by those underage and could renormalize and raise rates of smoking—which have been in decline for years—in the view of the American Heart Association.

We don't have enough information or studies on the long-term impact of vaping yet. Until we do, I believe it makes sense ethically to maintain laws prohibiting sale to minors and discourage the marketing and use of such products, but leave the choice to consenting adults and their medical advisors. It's easy to think that our ethical responsibility ends once a law is enacted. But as the FDA rightly emphasized, laws require monitoring, particularly as science reveals new information (as we learned from regulations on cigarette smoking, where we did far too little for far too long and adult behavior was copied by children and teens). Vaping is a reminder that we need other stakeholders such as companies and regulators to do their part to support our choices.

How do you decide if you should donate a kidney to a close friend or relative?

A close relative—your child or sister—is experiencing kidney failure. They need a transplant to save their life. After getting tested and examined, doctors determine you are a match and that the surgery would be safe for both of you.

There are 100,000 patients on the kidney transplant list. According to the Donor Care Network, there are 5,000 living donors in the U.S. every year who donate a kidney. In 2020, only 21,000 donor organs (from living and deceased donors) were available for transplant.

Exploration

This is a highly personal and emotional question that hinges on the individual facts and your personal perspective.

You have the power to save a life. But this is one time when you don't have a responsibility to use it. Nor are you responsible for the health consequences of the recipient. You do not owe anyone one of your organs. Similarly, the recipient can refuse a donation—for any number of reasons, not the least of which is concern over the donor's health or family relationships if a family member is involved.

The threshold question we have to answer before anything else is medical, not ethical: Get all the information you can get about *your specific situation*, from experts. Ask whether there is anything you don't know that you should. You might also confirm whether, in your situation, patients who receive an organ from a living donor have a higher success rate than those who receive an organ from someone who had died.

The ability to save another person's life is a gift beyond words. But it does require that one think about the short-, medium-, and long-term consequences. Don't expect that exercising such generosity and compassion will change how the other person feels about you, or how willing they would be to help at a future time should you or your loved one be in need. Also, catapult yourself into the future: imagine if one of your children or grandchildren needs a kidney, and you no longer have the ability to donate one. Should you consider the recipient's life expectancy—an eighty-eight-year-old grandparent versus your fifty-year-old brother? Think about how close you are to your relative. Ask whether other donors are available.

Consider putting this question on a spectrum of potential family obligations, such as whether we owe family members medical care if they cannot afford it. Do family members have to earn our financial and emotional support, or do you feel they have some sort of inherent right based on the family ties? Organ donation is at the extreme end of the spectrum—again, in my view we do not owe anyone the donation of a kidney.

This question forces us to broaden the lens: it reminds us that the personal ethical questions we face and the broader societal questions are interlinked. Family and friend donation decisions have a domino effect on a growing societal need for organs for transplant.

Donating an organ to a friend or relative can be compassionate, courageous, and generous. But there are many valid reasons not to donate, depending on your circumstances, and theirs. There is no one right answer. Whatever the ethics analysis, the decision will be fraught with emotion. What we can do is to show compassion to anyone in a position to consider donating, or needing, an organ.

Conclusion:
We Can All Do Ethics

When I set out to write this book, the list of potential questions seemed unlimited. Just as I settled on a selection, new questions popped up on the morning news, at the supermarket, in my class at Stanford, on family Zoom calls, and beyond—whether concerns arising out of the Covid-19 pandemic, new state voting restrictions, children's mental health, or the killing of George Floyd and the subsequent murder trial and verdict.

With the help of wise advisors, I chose questions across a broad spectrum. My goal: to offer an ethics arena in which you, the reader, could grapple with a mix of familiar and "never heard of" dilemmas. But the book's learning applies to every question I could have selected. I thank you for joining the conversation, debating the challenges that I pose and their effects on you individually, on family and friends, on work, on society, on our hearts and minds, on technology and tradition, on today's politics and priorities, and on tomorrow's problems and promise. I thank you for probing areas that may initially have seemed outside your personal knowledge or comfort zone, or don't seem that relevant to your life.

Now, your journey continues. The book is an invitation to see ethics in every choice we make. Not as a burden, but as a helpful habit, and a way of exercising our personal power. I hope you feel better equipped to tackle the ethical challenges you will inevitably face, as well as to express and debate your views, and to accept that we all live with uncertainty, and even error. Ethics do not require physical fitness, a hefty bank account, a certain level of education, or a title. It's a way of thinking we can all participate in. And I believe that our progress as a society is dependent on everyone embracing ethics. No political or corporate leader, institution, regulator, or citizen can do it alone. As much as we need stronger systems and institutional change, our systems start with, and must be held account-able to, individuals.

I hope you have come to see ethics as stories . . . stories that show that each of us has the power . . . and responsibility . . . to influence one another for the better. We are never the only characters in our stories. The up-side: decision by decision we can craft a better story for ourselves and all whose lives we are privileged to touch.

Occasionally there is a single right answer—eradicate racism, counter disinformation on the internet, expose and oppose sexual misconduct. More often, there are many possible outcomes or narratives. Our task is to cou-rageously wade through the gray areas in life—to seek opportunity and mitigate risk.

Ethics happen in real time . . . with no guarantees. We cannot control the actions or behaviors of others. We cannot custom design the world as we wish it were. Our power comes not from an unrealistic quest for control but rather from navigating the real world in which we often lack control. From building on truth, not wishful thinking. The world does not owe us to be the way we want it to be. And just because we believe it to be a particular way will not make it so.

Ethics are *proactive*. All manner of unfortunate outcomes, from unconscious bias to lack of compassion, can be traced back to our neutrality or passivity.

Ethics are *inclusive*. Questions that may seem far from our everyday concerns in fact touch us more directly than we might have imagined. Dilemmas that may seem separate and distinct often have a shared foundation. There is common ground among virtually every ethical conundrum in the book, as well as those you will face in your own life.

We're only as ethical as our last decision. Labels or categories—even "ethical" or "unethical"—are shortcuts, not thoughtful ethics. They create divisiveness and polarization rather than informed, compassionate connection.

When in doubt, we all should ask what our decision looks like from the point of view of the person most adversely affected. Then imagine that person is us or a loved one.

Before we judge, we all should query whether we really know as much as we think we know—where might assumptions (shortcuts, gut feelings, unverified social media posts, casual or even lazy thinking) be driving (or justifying) our choices?

We can be ethically resilient when we tell the truth, take

responsibility, and make a concrete plan to ensure that any unwanted behavior isn't repeated.

As you share stories, always ask if it's your story to tell. Look for every opportunity to shout out someone else's success—and pass up every chance to call out a weakness or error. Then ask if it's a story you must tell.

We must always keep human beings and humanity front and center. We should require our leaders to prioritize ethical decision making and to listen to those they have responsibility to lead—rather than attempting to dictate society's ethics or, worse, give themselves a pass.

Trust yourself. Enjoy your ethics. As mythologist and author Joseph Campbell said, "The privilege of a lifetime is being who you are." Ethics are a path for each of us becoming who we are. I believe that ethics are the greatest connector—binding us to one another and to our shared humanity.

The Six Forces Driving Ethics

Throughout this book, you will have seen references to six forces that I believe influence the ethics of every choice we make. You will quickly come to recognize these forces in the questions and explorations in the book (whether or not explicitly stated) and in your own life. Here is a quick primer.

Banish the binary: Ethics are not a "yes or no" or "do it or don't do it" choice. Some ethics failures are indeed straight-up unacceptable: racism, sexual misconduct, and disregarding science-based evidence about Covid-19. But most questions we face require navigating a gray zone. Rather than just labeling options as "right or wrong" or "ethical or unethical," banishing the binary prompts us to ask, *When and under what circumstances should we proceed?* You will have seen throughout the book an emphasis on *seizing opportunity* and *mitigating risk* rather than choosing sides.

Scattered power: Today, power is no longer concentrated only in the hands of a few; it's more scattered than ever.

Think of the power you have with your cell phone—to contribute to a political campaign or tutor a child across the country . . . or incite violence. The challenge today is to reconnect power to ethical responsibility . . . and to recognize that we each have a role: no president or corporate behemoth can deliver, or repair, moral decline alone. Every choice matters. Every choice is an opportunity to reconnect our power to our ethics—whether wearing a mask or speaking up against a racist remark.

Contagion: Ethics are contagious—for good or for ill. But we often focus so much on the unwanted behavior (fraud, social media data privacy, not wearing masks) that we ignore the factors that drove the *spreading* of the behavior—leaving them to fester and spur further trouble. While we know fake news can distort our choices, we have not adequately addressed the contagion drivers such as the misuse of the internet, lack of user-friendly transparency, ineffective regulation, corporate greed, and extremism, to name a few. The hopeful news: once we identify and dismantle these drivers, and deploy them for good, our choices can have a lasting impact. We will learn from mistakes and stop seeing the same headlines over and over again in the news.

Pillars of ethics: Transparency and (un)informed consent are two long-standing pillars of ethical decision making. They depend on understanding what's at stake in our decisions (short- and longer-term) but are crumbling in today's complex, technological world. Think of getting your tonsils removed: you understand the benefits and risks well enough, and you're clear about the procedure and recovery steps like an ice cream diet for a few days. Now think of artificial intelligence diagnosing skin cancer. Or how you feel when you click "I agree" on social media terms of service. But we can learn to recalibrate what we mean by transparency and informed consent—particularly the information and commitment to our understanding prior to soliciting consent that we expect of companies and governments.

Blurred boundaries: Blurred boundaries are everywhere today: human and machine, human and animal, and increasingly work and home. We are in uncharted, sometimes uncomfortable, territory as we think about the role of robots in society (receptionists, caring for the elderly, nannies, driverless cars), looking to animals for medical treatment (growing organs in pigs for human transplant), and beyond. We must keep humanity front and center and assure that humans take responsibility for the blur . . . and for reclarifying boundaries.

Compromised truth: Ethics hinge on truth. There is no such thing as post-truth or alternatively factual ethics. Today, truth is under threat in unprecedented ways from denial of science and other factual information to distrust of experts to algorithmic distortion of our news feeds and social media bubbles shielding us from diverse views. This compromised truth removes our choices from reality. But as I tell my students, we can do ethics in a world of wishful thinking or cherry-picked la-la land all we want, but reality—truth—will come back to bite. It is very real for us, and for others, in terms of the consequences of our choices. Compromised truth topples social relationships and institutions (including democracy) and threatens ethics. And its impact lasts: today's skewed truth becomes tomorrow's distorted memory and history.

Acknowledgments

The Little Book of Big Ethical Questions started with a meeting I was fortunate to have with Simon & Schuster CEO Jonathan Karp; executive editor Stephanie Frerich; and my agent, Kathy Robbins, about my first book, *The Power of Ethics*. Jon's idea for a series of conversation starters, and the question-and-answer format, fit so perfectly with my own mission of democratizing ethics. I couldn't be more grateful to write this book with Simon & Schuster, and to have a second opportunity to work with Stephanie.

The work continued over several years, with many varied conversations. I have cherished every exchange— whether with my black-cab driver in London, a podcast interviewer, fellow passengers disembarking from a canceled flight, at a dinner with friends, in line for a coffee or even a Covid-19 vaccination, in class with students, or on family FaceTime calls. I learned so much from conversations that extraordinary writers recorded in their own works of nonfiction and fiction, in the media, and on social media—too many to name.

As one of my wise advisors noted, writing a book takes a village. It was a privilege to work with the Simon & Schuster team: associate editor Emily Simonson was professional, efficient, and so thoughtful in her commentary; Fred Chase, an extraordinary copy editor, improved every page; cover designer Ryan Raphael and art director Alison Forner created the perfect jacket design (including one that continued the visuals seamlessly from their design for *The Power of Ethics*); Sara Kitchen (production editor); Beth Maglione (production manager); Paul Dippolito (interior designer); Jordan Koluch (proofreader); and Amanda Mulholland (managing editor) turned these thoughts into an accessible visual experience. And my thanks to publicist Cat Boyd and marketer Leila Siddiqui for crafting the message.

I am grateful to Roger Scholl for bringing his decades of literary expertise and immense editing talent to the project. He was very patient with my insistence that things are not as obvious or settled as they may first appear—and with my struggle to stay within our set word count.

As I said in *The Power of Ethics*, meeting my agent, Kathy Robbins, was one of life's great moments. This project never would have come to life without her wisdom, editorial insights, and support. It was such a pleasure as well to work with her Robbins Office colleagues Janet Oshiro and Alexandra Sugarman, who assured that all ran smoothly.

Lisa Sweetingham provided such valuable perspective and commentary just when I needed it most. I so value her thoughtfulness, writing talent, and research rigor.

For the past several years, I have had the pleasure of teaching and working with many meticulous students, research assistants, and teaching assistants. I am especially grateful for the open-minded, committed, and effective contributions of Daria Lenz, Ariadne Nichol, Megan Olomu, and Carolina Sculti. Clint Akarmann's wise observations and Joseph Zabel's insightful commentary improved many of the questions.

My gratitude to my trusted colleague of many years, Anna Barberà i Aresté, whose efficacy and contributions have been essential to my nonprofit platform, The Ethics Incubator, and both books.

Finally, to my children, Luca, Olivia, Parker, Alexa, and Cristo, for believing in me, and my husband, Bernard. I learn from you every day with every question we face.

And my gratitude to you, the reader, for taking the time to read, explore, discuss, reflect, and challenge yourself and others.

Notes

INTRODUCTION: ETHICS FOR EVERYONE

3 *Impossible Burger*: "What are the ingredients in Impossible™ Burger?" Impossible Foods, accessed October 8, 2021, faq.impos siblefoods.com/hc/en-us/articles/360018937494-What-are-the-in gredients-in-Impossible-Burger-.

CHAPTER 1: FAMILY AND FRIENDS

18 *"Love thy neighbor"*: Matthew 22:36–39, New Testament, *The Bible*, cs monitor.com/Commentary/A-Christian-Science-Perspective/2008 /0327/p18s02-hfcs.html.

18 *"The more we care"*: Tenzin Gyatso (the fourteenth Dalai Lama), "Compassion and the Individual," *His Holiness the 14th Dalai Lama of Tibet*, accessed September 5, 2021, dalailama.com/messages /compassion-and-human-values/compassion.

21 *According to the U.S. Census Bureau*: Katherine Keisler-Starkey and Lisa N. Bunch, *Health Insurance Coverage in the United States: 2019*, United States Census Bureau, September 15, 2020, census.gov /library/publications/2020/demo/p60-271.html.

21 *the Census Bureau reports*: Ibid.

21 *National Health Service*: "How does universal health coverage work?" The Commonwealth Fund, commonwealthfund.org/international -health-policy-center/system-features/how-does-universal-health -coverage-work.

24 *widely read*: Mary McNamara, "The Diary of Anne Frank," *Los Angeles Times*, April 10, 2010, latimes.com/archives/la-xpm-2010-apr-10 -la-et-frank-review10-2010apr10-story.html.

25 *doctor-patient confidentiality*: Kristin E. Schleiter, JD, "When Patient-Physician Confidentiality Conflicts with the Law," *AMA Journal of Ethics* 11, no. 2 (February 2009): 146–48, journalofethics.ama-assn

.org/article/when-patient-physician-confidentiality-conflicts-law
/2009-02.

30   *adult children prevailed in court*: Palko Karasz, "French Rock Star's
Instagram Defeats His Widow in Inheritance Battle," *New York Times*,
May 29, 2019, nytimes.com/2019/05/29/world/europe/johnny-hally
day-instagram-will.html.

31   *Napoleonic Code*: *Encyclopaedia Britannica Online*, s.v. "Napoleonic
Code," accessed December 12, 2021, britannica.com/topic/Napo
leonic-Code.

31   *ethical wills*: Deborah Quilter, "The Ethical Will: Life Is About More
than Your Possessions," Next Avenue, April 11, 2019, nextavenue.org
/ethical-will; Wikipedia, s.v. "Ethical will," accessed September 22,
2021, en.wikipedia.org/wiki/Ethical_will.

33   *23andMe*: "How it works," 23andMe, accessed September 22, 2021,
23andme.com/en-gb/howitworks.

33   *more than 26 million*: Antonio Regalado, "Is the consumer genetics
fad over?" *MIT Technology Review*, January 23, 2020, technologyre
view.com/2020/01/23/276092/is-the-consumer-genetics-fad-over.

34   *23andMe warns on its website*: "Terms of Service," 23andMe, last
modified September 30, 2019, 23andme.com/about/tos.

35   *The American Society of Human Genetics*: Deborah Levenson, "American society of human genetics updates guidance on genetic testing
in children," *American Journal of Medical Ethics* 167, no. 10 (October
2015): viii–ix, onlinelibrary.wiley.com/doi/full/10.1002/ajmg.a.37357.

46   *.08 g/dL or higher*: "Drunk Driving," National Highway Traffic Safety
Administration, United States Department of Transportation, accessed September 22, 2021, nhtsa.gov/risky-driving/drunk driving.

46   *three drinks*: "Blood Alcohol Level Chart: Are You Too Drunk to Legally Drive?" DrivingLaws, accessed September 22, 2021, dui.driving
laws.org/drink-table.php.

47   *died in a drunk-driving accident*: "Drunk Driving," National Highway
Traffic Safety Administration, accessed September 22, 2021, nhtsa
.gov/risky-driving/drunk-driving.

47   *28 percent of all fatal car accidents*: "Traffic Safety Facts 2019," U.S.
Department of Transportation National Highway Traffic Safety Administration, August 2021, https://crashstats.nhtsa.dot.gov/Api/Pub
lic/ViewPublication/813141.

51   *The* Oxford Advanced Learner's Dictionary *defines cheating*: *Oxford
Advanced Learner's Dictionary*, s.v. "cheat (*n.*)," oxfordlearnersdictio
naries.com/definition/english/cheat_2.

51 *something for sale*: Michael Sandel, "Are There Things Money Shouldn't Be Able to Buy?" Oxford Union, video, May 10, 2015, you tube.com/watch?v=zMg9Gjz8PKs.

52 *Sandel makes a critical point*: Ibid.

56 *graduation speech*: "Adm. McRaven Urges Graduates to Find Courage to Change the World," UT News, May 16, 2014, news.utexas.edu /2014/05/16/mcraven-urges-graduates-to-find-courage-to-change -the-world.

57 *"will encourage you to do another task"*: Admiral William H. McRaven, *Make Your Bed: Little Things That Can Change Your Life . . . and Maybe the World* (New York: Grand Central Publishing, 2017).

57 *If you want to change*: Ibid., University of Texas's commencement speech to be found at the back of the book.

CHAPTER 2: POLITICS, COMMUNITY, AND CULTURE

63 *Hurricane Katrina*: History.com Editors, "Hurricane Katrina," History .com, August 31, 2021, accessed December 12, 2021, history.com/top ics/natural-disasters-and-environment/hurricane-katrina.

63 *There was almost no food*: German Lopez, "Hurricane Katrina, in 7 essential facts," *Vox*, August 28, 2015, vox.com/2015/8/23/9191907 /hurricane-katrina.

64 *one of the costliest hurricanes*: Eric S. Blake and Ethan J. Gibney, *The Deadliest, Costliest, and Most Intense United States Tropical Cyclones from 1851 to 2010 (And Other Frequently Requested Hurricane Facts)*, NOAA Technical Memorandum NWS NHC-6, August 2011, nhc.noaa.gov/pdf/nws-nhc-6.pdf.

64 *"looters floated"*: "Chaotic Conditions in New Orleans," CBS News, August 30, 2005, cbsnews.com/news/chaotic-conditions-in-new-or leans.

64 *Police responses were inconsistent*: Sabrina Shankman et al., "After Katrina, New Orleans Cops Were Told They Could Shoot Looters," ProPublica, July 24, 2012, propublica.org/article/nopd-order-to-shoot -looters-hurricane-katrina. See also Jeff Brady, "New Orleans Housing Prisoners in Bus Station," NPR, September 9, 2005, npr.org/tem plates/story/story.php?storyId=4838671.

70 *Compulsory or mandatory voting*: "What Is Compulsory Voting?" FindLaw, last modified March 16, 2020, findlaw.com/voting/how-u -s--elections-work/what-is-compulsory-voting-.html.

70 *More than twenty countries have mandatory voting requirements*:

Laura Santhanam, "22 countries where voting is mandatory," PBS, November 3, 2014, pbs.org/newshour/politics/22-countries-voting -mandatory.

70 *Australia passed mandatory voting*: Nina Jaffe-Geffner, "The Pros and Cons of Requiring Citizens to Vote," FairVote, October 23, 2015, fairvote.org/the_pros_and_cons_of_requiring_citizens_to_vote. See also "Prime Facts: Elections and voting in Australia," Australian Prime Ministers Centre, Museum of Australian Democracy, accessed December 1, 2021, static.moadoph.gov.au/ophgovau/media/images /apmc/docs/62-Elections.pdf.

70 *Over 91 percent*: "Turnout," *Australia Electoral Commission Annual Report 2018–19*, Australian Government Transparency Portal, ac- cessed December 1, 2021, transparency.gov.au/annual-reports/Aus tralian-electoral-commission/reporting-year/2018-2019-11.

70 *In the 2016 presidential election*: Gregory Wallace, "Voter turnout at 20-year low in 2016," CNN, last modified November 30, 2016, cnn .com/2016/11/11/politics/popular-vote-turnout-2016/index.html.

70 *In 2020*: Domenico Montanaro, "President-Elect Joe Biden Hits 80 Million Votes in Year of Record Turnout," NPR, November 25, 2020, npr.org/2020/11/25/937248659/president-elect-biden-hits-80-mil lion-votes-in-year-of-record-turnout; United States Census Bureau, "2020 Presidential Election Voting and Registration Tables Now Available," news release no. CB21-TPS.49, April 29, 2021, census.gov /newsroom/press-releases/2021/2020-presidential-election-voting -and-registration-tables-now-available.html.

70 *Georgia passed a slew of laws*: Nick Corasaniti and Reid J. Epstein, "What Georgia's Voting Law Really Does," *New York Times*, April 2, 2021, nytimes.com/2021/04/02/us/politics/georgia-voting-law-anno tated.html; Election Integrity Act of 2021, Georgia State Senate Bill 202 (2021), legiscan.com/GA/text/SB202/id/2348602/Georgia-2021 -SB202-Enrolled.pdf.

71 *Florida and Texas*: Corasaniti and Epstein, "What Georgia's Voting Law Really Does."

71 *Advocates of mandatory voting*: Melissa De Witte, "Stanford politi- cal scientist makes the case for mandatory voting," Stanford News, November 30, 2018, news.stanford.edu/2018/11/30/case-mandatory -voting.

74 *580,000 people experienced homelessness*: U.S. Department of Housing and Urban Development, *The 2020 Annual Homeless As-*

sessment Report (AHAR) to Congress, January 2021, huduser.gov
/portal/sites/default/files/pdf/2020-AHAR-Part-1.pdf.

75 2021 study in high-income countries: Stefan Gutwinski et al., "The
prevalence of mental disorders among homeless people in high-
income countries: An updated systematic review and meta-
regression analysis," PLoS Medicine 18, no. 8 (August 2021), journals
.plos.org/plosmedicine/article?id=10.1371/journal.pmed.1003750.

77 Benin Bronzes: Barnaby Phillips, "No Revolvers, Gentlemen, No Revolvers," chap. 4 in Loot: Britain and the Benin Bronzes (London: One-
world Publications, 2021). See also Alex Marshall, "This Art Was Looted
123 Years Ago; Will It Ever Be Returned?" New York Times, January 23,
2020, nytimes.com/2020/01/23/arts/design/benin-bronzes.html.

77 twenty-six of the stolen artifacts: Aaron Ross and Marine Pennetier,
"France returns 26 artworks to Benin as report urges restitution,"
Reuters, November 23, 2018, reuters.com/article/us-africa-france-art
-idUSKCN1NS1GH.

78 Netherlands announced: "Government: Redressing an injustice
by returning cultural heritage objects to their country of origin,"
Government of the Netherlands, January 29, 2021, government.nl
/latest/news/2021/01/29/government-redressing-an-injustice-by
-returning-cultural-heritage-objects-to-their-country-of-origin.

78 Metropolitan Museum of Art has had to reassess: Colin Moynihan,
"Met Museum to Return Prize Artifact Because It Was Stolen," New
York Times, February 15, 2019, nytimes.com/2019/02/15/arts/design
/met-museum-stolen-coffin.html.

81 Leaving Neverland: Anastasia Tsioulcas, "Michael Jackson: A Quarter-
Century of Sexual Abuse Allegations," NPR, March 5, 2019, npr.org
/2019/03/05/699995484/michael-jackson-a-quarter-century-of
-sexual-abuse-allegations.

81 Thriller: Tom Huddleston Jr., "Michael Jackson's iconic 'Thriller' is 36
today—and it's still the world's best-selling album," CNBC, November 30, 2018, cnbc.com/2018/11/30/michael-jacksons-thriller-anniver
sary-still-all-time-best-seller.html. See also "Gold & Platinum," Recording Industry Association of America, RIAA.com/gold-platinum
/?tab_active=top_tallies&ttt=TIA#search_section.

81 Michael Jackson was never convicted: Zack O'Malley Greenburg,
"Michael Jackson's Earnings: $825 Million in 2016," Forbes, Octo-
ber 14, 2016, forbes.com/sites/zackomalleygreenburg/2016/10/14
/michael-jacksons-earnings-825-million-in-2016/?sh=2ab87f393d72.

See also Ben Sisario, "What We Know About Michael Jackson's History of Sexual Abuse Accusations," *New York Times*, January 31, 2019, ny times.com/2019/01/31/arts/music/michael-jackson-timeline-sexual -abuse-accusations.html.

81 *twenty-three years in prison*: Jan Ransom, "Harvey Weinstein's Stunning Downfall: 23 Years in Prison," *New York Times*, last modified June 15, 2021, nytimes.com/2020/03/11/nyregion/harvey-weinstein -sentencing.html.

81 *nine counts*: Troy Closson, "R. Kelly Is Convicted of All Counts After Decades of Accusations of Abuse," *New York Times*, September 27, 2021, nytimes.com/2021/09/27/nyregion/r-kelly-verdict-racketeering -sex-trafficking.html.

84 *the youngest U.S. president*: Associated Press, "France's Emmanuel Macron joins Trudeau in ranks of youngest world leaders," CBC News, May 8, 2017, cbc.ca/news/world/france-macron-trudeau-youngest -world-leaders-1.4105670.

84 *U.S. Presidential candidates must be*: "Requirements for the President of the United States," Library of Congress, loc.gov/classroom -materials/elections/presidential-election-process/requirements-for -the-president-of-the-united-states.

84 *Neither the Democratic frontrunners nor President Trump*: Dan Diamond, "Democratic candidates, Trump agree: Their medical records are none of your business," *Politico*, February 19, 2020, politico.com /news/2020/02/19/2020-democrats-medical-histories-116039.

84 *some medical documents and letters*: Susan Milligan, "Biden Releases Medical Records," *U.S. News & World Report*, December 17, 2019, usnews.com/news/elections/articles/2019-12-17/Biden-releases -medical-records.

85 *passed away at eighty-seven*: Linda Greenhouse, "Ruth Bader Ginsburg, Supreme Court's Feminist Icon, Is Dead at 87," *New York Times*, September 18, 2020, nytimes.com/2020/09/18/us/ruth-bader-gins burg-dead.html.

86 *companies are permitted*: Age Discrimination in Employment Act of 1967, 29 U.S.C. § 621 (2011), eeoc.gov/statutes/age-discrimination -employment-act-1967.

86 *commercial airline pilots*: Federal Aviation Administration, *Fair Treatment of Experienced Pilots Act (The Age 65 Law) Information, Questions and Answers*, May 9, 2019, faa.gov/other_visit/aviation_industry /airline_operators/airline_safety/info/all_infos/media/age65_qa.pdf.

86 *military personnel*: Retirement for Age, 10 U.S.C. § 63 (2010), govinfo

.gov/content/pkg/USCODE-2010-title10/html/USCODE-2010-title10
-subtitleA-partII-chap63.htm.

88 *Crucial runoff elections*: Matthew Impelli, "Georgia Senate Runoffs
Finish as Most Expensive in History, At Least 171 Million More Than
Any Other," *Newsweek*, January 6, 2021. See also Emma Green,
"Georgia's Billion-Dollar Bonfire," *The Atlantic*, January 5, 2021, the
atlantic.com/politics/archive/2021/01/money-spent-georgia-senate
-runoffs/617545.

88 *According to FiveThirtyEight*: Chris Zubak-Skees, Nathaniel Rakich,
and Julia Wolfe, "Where Are Georgia's Senate Candidates Getting All
That Cash From?" FiveThirtyEight, December 9, 2020, fivethirtyeight
.com/features/where-are-georgias-senate-candidates-getting-all
-that-cash-from.

89 *And 92 percent*: Ibid.

89 *Current law often permits*: "State Limits on Contributions to Candidates, 2021–2022 Election Cycle, National Conference of State Legislatures," National Conference of State Legislatures, last modified June
2021, ncsl.org/Portals/1/Documents/Elections/Contribution_Limits
_to_Candidates_2020_2021.pdf.

90 *"stand your ground"*: FindLaw Staff, "States That Have Stand Your
Ground Laws," FindLaw, last modified June 2, 2020, findlaw.com
/criminal/criminal-law-basics/states-that-have-stand-your-ground
-laws.html.

90 Citizens United: Matt Bai, "How Much Has Citizens United Changed
the Political Game?" *New York Times*, July 17, 2012, nytimes.com/2012
/07/22/magazine/how-much-has-citizens-united-changed-the-polit
ical-game.html; "Citizens United v. FEC," U.S. Federal Election Commission, fec.gov/legal-resources/court-cases/citizens-united-v-fec.

90 *"have no consciences, no beliefs"*: Citizens United v. FEC, 558 U.S.
(2010), law.cornell.edu/supct/pdf/08-205P.ZX. See also "Citizens
United v. FEC," FEC, fec.gov/legal-resources/court-cases/citizens
-united-v-fec/, pp. 57, 81, 76.

91 *Justice Stevens believed*: Daniel Rothberg, "Retired Justice John
Paul Stevens tells Congress 'money is not speech,'" *Los Angeles
Times*, April 30, 2014, latimes.com/nation/politics/politicsnow/la-pn
-supreme-court-stevens-congress-money-speech-20140430-story
.html; *U.S. Senate Rules and Administration Committee Hearing on
campaign finance law*, 113th Cong. 2 (2014) (statement of Justice
John Paul Stevens [Ret.]), supremecourt.gov/publicinfo/speeches
/JPSSpeech(DC)04-30-2014.pdf.

92 *In a recent case*: National Collegiate Athletic Association v. Alston, 594 U.S. (2021), supremecourt.gov/opinions/20pdf/20-512_gfbh.pdf.

92 *The Court disagreed*: Ibid.

92 *"massive business"*: Ibid.

93 *total revenues*: "Finances of Intercollegiate Athletics," NCAA, accessed November 30, 2021, ncaa.org/about/resources/research/finances-intercollegiate-athletics.

93 *$16 million*: Jo Craven McGinty, "March Madness Is a Moneymaker. Most Schools Still Operate in Red," *Wall Street Journal*, March 12, 2021, wsj.com/articles/march-madness-is-a-moneymaker-most-schools-still-operate-in-red-11615545002.

93 *fifty hours a week training*: Thomas Wright-Piersanti, "Change Comes to the N.C.A.A.," *New York Times*, June 22, 2021, nytimes.com/2021/06/22/briefing/ncaa-scotus-ruling.html.

93 *scholarships*: "A Guide to College Basketball Scholarships for High School Students," Next College Student Athlete, ncsasports.org/mens-basketball/scholarships.

94 *Athletes hoping to turn professional*: Zack Lowe, "Memo: NBA draft eligibility could shift by 2021," ESPN.com, June 15, 2018, espn.com/nba/story/_/id/23804458/memo-states-nba-draft-eligibility-shift-21.

94 *1.2 percent of men's basketball players*: NCAA, *Estimated Probability of Competing in College Athletics*, April 8, 2020, ncaaorg.s3.amazonaws.com/research/pro_beyond/2019RES_ProbabilityBeyondHSFiguresMethod.pdf.

94 *Recent legal changes*: Meghan Roos, "26 States Now Allow College Athletes to Be Compensated for Image, Likeness," *Newsweek*, July 14, 2021, newsweek.com/26-states-now-allow-college-athletes-compensated-image-likeness-1609744.

95 *The NCAA announced*: Michelle Brutlag Hosick, "NCAA adopts interim name, image, and likeness policy," NCAA, June 30, 2021, ncaa.org/about/resources/media-center/news/ncaa-adopts-interim-name-image-and-likeness-policy.

95 *Justice Brett Kavanaugh*: National Collegiate Athletic Association v. Alston, 594 U.S. (2021).

96 *stop publishing six*: Bill Chappell, "Dr. Seuss Enterprises Will Shelve 6 Books, Citing 'Hurtful' Portrayals," NPR, March 2, 2021, npr.org/2021/03/02/972777841/dr-seuss-enterprises-will-shelve-6-books-citing-hurtful-portrayals.

96 *Among the six were*: Ibid.

97   If I Ran the Zoo: Ibid.; Jenny Gross, "6 Dr. Seuss Books Will No Longer Be Published Over Offensive Images," *New York Times*, March 2, 2021, nytimes.com/2021/03/02/books/dr-seuss-mulberry-street.html.

98   *Roald Dahl reimagined*: Alexandra Alter and Elizabeth A. Harris, "Dr. Seuss Books Are Pulled and a 'Cancel Culture' Controversy Erupts," *New York Times*, last modified October 20, 2021, nytimes.com/2021/03/04/books/dr-seuss-books.html. See also Kate Cantrell and David Burton, "From pygmies to puppets: what to do with Roald Dahl's enslaved Oompa-Loompas in modern adaptations?" The Conversation, September 15, 2021, theconversation.com/from-pygmies-to-puppets-what-to-do-with-Roald-Dahls-enslaved-oompa-loompas-in-modern-adaptations-166967.

98   *New Jersey state lawmakers*: Allison Pries, "Lawmakers want to expel Huckleberry Finn from N.J. schools," NJ.com, last modified March 23, 2019, nj.com/education/2019/03/lawmakers-want-to-expel-huckleberry-finn-from-nj-schools.html; Benedicte Page, "New Huckleberry Finn edition censors 'n-word,'" *The Guardian*, January 5, 2011, theguardian.com/books/2011/jan/05/huckleberry-finn-edition-censors-n-word.

99   *"In a cultural landscape"*: Ross Douthat, "Do Liberals Care if Books Disappear?" *New York Times*, March 6, 2021, nytimes.com/2021/03/06/opinion/dr-seuss-books-liberalism.html.

100   *a sixty-nine-year-old Dutchman*: "Emile Ratelband, 69, told he cannot legally change his age," BBC News, December 3, 2018, bbc.com/news/world-europe-46425774.

100   *"all kinds of legal problems"*: Ibid.

103   *Sha'Carri Richardson*: Kevin Draper and Juliet Macur, "Sha'Carri Richardson, a Track Sensation, Tests Positive for Marijuana," *New York Times*, last modified July 6, 2021, nytimes.com/2021/07/01/sports/olympics/shacarri-richardson-suspended-marijuana.html.

103   *4x100-meter relay*: Ibid.

103   *"I am human"*: Drew Weisholz, "Sha'Carri Richardson speaks out about failing drug test ahead of Olympics," *Today*, July 2, 2021, today.com/news/today-show-exclusive-sha-carri-richardson-speaks-out-about-failing-t224363.

104   *"Pretty convinced"*: Nicholas Thompson (@nxthompson), "Pretty convinced that marijuana is not a 'performance enhancing' drug for a sprinter," Twitter, July 2, 2021, twitter.com/nxthompson/status/1410917919467491333?.

104 *"rather than lend legitimacy to poor policy"*: Editorial Board, "Opinion: Sha'Carri Richardson's relay exclusion wasn't necessary. USA Track and Field did it anyway," *Washington Post*, July 10, 2021, washingtonpost.com/opinions/2021/07/10/shacarri-richardsons-relay-exclusion-wasnt-necessary-usa-track-field-did-it-anyway.

104 *substances prohibited*: "Marijuana FAQ: Your Questions Answered," USADA, accessed October 8, 2021, usada.org/athletes/substances/marijuana-faq. See also "World Anti-Doping Code International Standard Prohibited List 2022," World Anti-Doping Agency, wada-ama.org/sites/default/files/resources/files/2022list_final_en.pdf.

104 *WADA believes*: Marilyn A. Huestis, Irene Mazzoni, and Oliver Rabin, "Cannabis in Sport: Anti-Doping Perspective," *Sports Medicine* 41, no. 11 (2011): 949–66, ncbi.nlm.nih.gov/pmc/articles/PMC3717337.

104 *The minimum penalty*: Draper and Macur, "Sha'Carri Richardson, a Track Sensation."

105 *not a performance enhancement*: Claire Maldarelli, "Is marijuana a performance-enhancing drug? The best evidence says no," *Popular Science*, July 2, 2021, popsci.com/science/marijuana-performance-enhancing-drug-evidence.

105 *"an overview of the research"*: Matt Richtel, "Science Doesn't Support Idea That Marijuana Aids Athletes' Performance," *New York Times*, last modified July 23, 2021, nytimes.com/2021/07/09/sports/olympics/marijuana-sports-performance-enhancing.html.

105 *Major League Baseball*: "MLB, MLBPA agree to changes to joint drug program," MLB, December 12, 2019, mlb.com/press-release/press-release-mlb-mlbpa-agree-to-changes-to-joint-drug-program.

105 *caffeine may enhance athletic endurance*: Matthew S. Ganio et al., "Effect of caffeine on sport-specific endurance performance: A systematic review," *Journal of Strength and Conditioning Research* 23, no. 1 (January 2009): 315–24, pubmed.ncbi.nlm.nih.gov/19077738.

107 *Is voting an ethics choice*: Susan Liautaud, *The Power of Ethics* (New York: Simon & Schuster, 2021).

109 *fewer than . . . 80,000 votes*: Philip Bump, "Donald Trump will be president thanks to 80,000 people in three states," *Washington Post*, December 1, 2016, washingtonpost.com/news/the-fix/wp/2016/12/01/donald-trump-will-be-president-thanks-to-80000-people-in-three-states.

109 *Al Gore lost*: "US election 2020: Does this compare to 2000 Florida recount?" BBC News, November 12, 2020, bbc.co.uk/news/election-us-2020-54903188.

109 *two elections in Georgia*: "Georgia Highlights: Democrats Win the Senate as Ossoff Defeats Perdue," *New York Times*, last modified May 11, 2021, nytimes.com/live/2021/01/06/us/georgia-election-results. See also "Georgia U.S. Senate runoff results," *Washington Post*, last modified January 19, 2021, washingtonpost.com/elections/election-results/georgia-senate-runoffs-2021/.

CHAPTER 3: WORK

113 Financial Times *headline*: Madison Marriage, "Men Only: Inside the charity fundraiser where hostesses are put on show," *Financial Times*, January 23, 2018, ft.com/content/075d679e-0033-11e8-9650-9c0ad2d7c5b5.

122 *Percentage of the group's work*: Max H. Bazerman and Dolly Chugh, "Decisions Without Blinders," *Harvard Business Review*, January 2006, hbr.org/2006/01/decisions-without-blinders.

124 *You are a bystander*: Susan Liautaud, *The Power of Ethics* (New York: Simon & Schuster, 2021).

127 *Restrictive voting*: Andrew Ross Sorkin and David Gelles, "Black Executives Call on Corporations to Fight Restrictive Voting Laws," *New York Times*, March 31, 2021, nytimes.com/2021/03/31/business/voting-rights-georgia-corporations.html.

127 *Black business leaders to sign a letter*: Associated Press, "CEOs gather to speak out against voting law changes," AP News, April 11, 2021, apnews.com/article/nfl-legislation-football-voting-rights-kenneth-frazier-0184a15a63fc2accfd5aeab973d341ae.

127 *spoke out over the new laws*: Matthew Impelli, "A Full List of Companies That Have Advocated Against Georgia's New Voting Law," *Newsweek*, April 1, 2021, newsweek.com/full-list-companies-that-have-advocated-against-georgias-new-voting-law-1580435.

127 *Major League Baseball moved the Draft and the All-Star Game*: Vanessa Romo, "MLB Moves All-Star Game From Atlanta Over Georgia's New Voting Law," NPR, April 2, 2021, npr.org/2021/04/02/983970361/mlb-moves-all-star-game-from-atlanta-over-georgias-new-voting-law?t=1630252451349.

127 *"it wasn't our business"*: David Gelles, "'Our Menu Is Very Darwinian.' Leading McDonald's in 2021," *New York Times*, July 2, 2021, nytimes.com/2021/07/02/business/chris-kempczinski-mcdonalds-corner-office.html.

128 *Mitch McConnell*: Richard Cowan, "'Stay out of politics,' Republican

leader McConnell tells U.S. CEOs, warns of 'consequences,'" Reuters, April 5, 2021, reuters.com/article/us-usa-georgia-mcconnell-idUKKB N2BS1R8.

129 *"Where do we speak up on an issue?"*: Ibid.

137 *"Friendship is always a sweet responsibility"*: Kahlil Gibran, "Quotes," Goodreads, accessed December 1, 2021, goodreads.com/quotes /198892-friendship-is-always-a-sweet-responsibility-never-an-op portunity?page=4. See also personal.umich.edu/~jrcole/gibran/sand foam/sandfoam.html.

140 *the way the orchestra hired*: Anthony Tommasini, "To Make Orches- tras More Diverse, End Blind Auditions," *New York Times*, last mod- ified Aug 6, 2021, nytimes.com/2020/07/16/arts/music/blind-audi tions-orchestras-race.html.

140 *began using blind auditions*: Ibid.

140 *While this hiring system*: James Doeser, PhD, *Racial/Ethnic and Gender Diversity in the Orchestra Field*, League of American Orchestras, Sep- tember 2016, ppv.issuelab.org/resources/25840/25840.pdf, p. 3–4.

141 *New technology has facilitated*: Daniel Bortz, "Can Blind Hiring Im- prove Workplace Diversity?" Society for Human Resource Manage- ment, March 20, 2018, shrm.org/hr-today/news/hr-magazine/0418 /pages/can-blind-hiring-improve-workplace-diversity.aspx.

141 *AI in the experimental hiring tool*: Jeffrey Dastin, "Amazon scraps secret AI recruiting tool that showed bias against women," Reuters, October 10, 2018, reuters.com/article/us-amazon-com-jobs-automa tion-insight/amazon-scraps-secret-ai-recruiting-tool-that-showed -bias-against-women-idUSKCN1MK08G.

143 *Pew Research Center*: John Gramlich, "10 facts about Americans and Facebook," Pew Research Center, June 1, 2021, pewresearch.org/fact -tank/2021/06/01/facts-about-americans-and-facebook.

143 *LinkedIn . . . now has 800 million members*: "About LinkedIn," LinkedIn, accessed December 14, 2021, about.linkedin.com.

143 *99 percent*: Nora Ganim Barnes, PhD; Ashley Mazzola; and Mae Killeen, "Oversaturation & Disengagement: The 2019 Fortune 500 Social Media Dance," Center for Marketing Research, UMass Dart- mouth, last modified February 11, 2020, umassd.edu/cmr/research /2019-fortune-500.html.

143 *Many employers today use social media*: "Use of Social Media in Hiring," Justia, last modified October 2021, justia.com/employment /hiring-employment-contracts/use-of-social-media-in-hiring.

150 *"implicit bias" or "unconscious bias"*: Charlotte Ruhl, "Implicit or Un-

conscious Bias," Simply Psychology, July 1, 2020, simplypsychology
.org/implicit-bias.html.

151 *we're not as ethical in our decision making*: Max H. Bazerman and
Ann E. Tenbrunsel, *Blind Spots: Why We Fail to Do What's Right and
What to Do About It* (Princeton, NJ: Princeton University Press, 2011).

CHAPTER 4: TECHNOLOGY

155 *In a post dated January 7, 2021*: Mark Zuckerberg, "The shocking
events of the last 24 hours," Facebook, January 7, 2021, facebook
.com/zuck/posts/10112681480907401.

155 *In June 2021, Facebook announced*: "Facebook suspends Trump
until 2023, shifts rules for world leaders," Reuters, June 5, 2021,
reuters.com/world/us/facebook-suspends-former-us-president
-trumps-account-two-years-2021-06-04/.

155 *Jack Dorsey suspended Donald Trump's Twitter account*: Nitasha Tiku,
Tony Romm, and Craig Timberg, "Twitter Bans Trump's Account, Citing Risk of Furthering Violence," *Washington Post*, January 8, 2021,
washingtonpost.com/technology/2021/01/08/twitter-trump-dorsey.
See also "Permanent suspension of @realDonaldTrump," Twitter Inc.,
January 8, 2021, blog.twitter.com/en_us/topics/company/2020/sus
pension.

156 Packingham v. North Carolina: Packingham v. North Carolina, 582
U.S. (2017), supremecourt.gov/opinions/16pdf/15-1194_08l1.pdf.

156 *the Court recognized*: Stuart Benjamin, "Opinion: What is the 'do no
harm' position on the First Amendment in cyberspace?" *Washington Post*, June 19, 2017, washingtonpost.com/news/volokh-conspir
acy/wp/2017/06/19/what-is-the-do-no-harm-position-on-the-first
-amendment-in-cyberspace.

156 *First Amendment*: U.S. Const. amend. I, constitution.congress.gov
/constitution/amendment-1.

157 *calls for combat*: Maggie Haberman, "Trump Told Crowd 'You Will
Never Take Back Our Country with Weakness,'" *New York Times*,
last modified January 15, 2021, nytimes.com/2021/01/06/us/politics
/trump-speech-capitol.html.

159 *"It's my opinion"*: Taylor Swift, "For Taylor Swift, the Future of Music Is a Love Story," *Wall Street Journal*, last modified July 7, 2014,
wsj.com/articles/for-taylor-swift-the-future-of-music-is-a-love-story
-1404763219.

159 *released her album* 1989: Victor Luckerson, "This Is Why Taylor

Swift's Album Isn't on Spotify," *Time*, October 28, 2014, time.com /3544039/taylor-swift-1989-spotify; Swift, "For Taylor Swift."

159 *new licensing deal*: Marc Schneider, "Spotify Signs Long-Term Deal with Universal to Give Artists 'Flexible' Releases, Opens Door on Windowing," *Billboard*, April 4, 2017, billboard.com/articles/business /7751373/spotify-universal-music-new-albums-access-windowing -licensing.

159 *Spotify compensates the rights holders*: "Streaming Numbers in Context" and "How is streamshare calculated?" Loud & Clear, ac- cessed October 5, 2021, loudandclear.byspotify.com.

160 *Artists are then compensated by the rights holders*: "How is stream- share calculated?" and "How is Spotify measuring payouts on this site? Why doesn't this focus on what artists actually take home?" Loud & Clear, accessed December 13, 2021, loudandclear.byspotify .com/?question=how-is-stream-share-calculated.

160 *largest music-streaming service*: Omri Wallach, "Which streaming ser- vice has the most subscriptions?" World Economic Forum, March 10, 2021, weforum.org/agenda/2021/03/streaming-service-subscriptions -lockdown-demand-netflix-amazon-prime-spotify-disney-plus-apple -music-movie-tv.

160 *2021 third-quarter*: Spotify Investors, Financials, 2020 Q4 press release, accessed December 31, 2021, s22.q4cdn.com/540910603 /files/doc_financials/2021/q3/Shareholder-Letter-Q3-2021_FINAL .pdf.

160 *emerging artists may make very little*: Emily Blake, "Data Shows 90 Percent of Streams Go to the Top 1 Percent of Artists," *Rolling Stone*, September 9, 2020, rollingstone.com/pro/news/top-1-percent -streaming-1055005.

161 *streaming accounts for 84 percent*: Joshua P. Friedlander and Mat- thew Bass, "Mid-Year 2021 RIAA Revenue Statistics," Recording In- dustry Association of America, accessed December 13, 2021, riaa .com/wp-content/uploads/2021/09/Mid-Year-2021-RIAA-Music -Revenue-Report.pdf. See also Alan B. Krueger, "Streaming Is Changing Everything," chap. 8 in *Rockonomics* (New York: Currency, 2019). See also Friedlander and Bass, "Year-End 2020 RIAA Revenue Statistics," Recording Industry Association of America, accessed De- cember 13, 2021, riaa.com/wp-content/uploads/2021/02/2020-Year -End-Music-Industry-Revenue-Report.pdf.

161 *"boost to the music industry"*: Ibid.

161 *$75.5 million*: Friedlander and Bass, "Year-End 2020 RIAA Revenue."

164 *Facebook had ad revenue*: Facebook, Inc., "Facebook Reports Fourth Quarter and Full Year 2019 Results," PR Newswire, January 29, 2020, investor.fb.com/investor-news/press-release-details/2020/Face book-Reports-Fourth-Quarter-and-Full-Year-2019-Results/default .aspx; Rishi Iyengar, "Here's how big Facebook's ad business really is," CNN Business, last modified July 1, 2020, cnn.com/2020/06/30 /tech/facebook-ad-business-boycott/index.html.

164 *Facebook's share*: Megan Graham, "Digital ad spend grew 12% in 2020 despite hit from pandemic," CNBC, last modified April 7, 2021, cnbc .com/2021/04/07/digital-ad-spend-grew-12percent-in-2020-despite -hit-from-pandemic.html.

166 *Just under five feet tall*: Zorabots, accessed October 9, 2021, zoraro botics.be.

166 *she can interact with people*: Adam Satariano, Elian Peltier, and Dmitry Kostyukov, "Meet Zora, the Robot Caregiver," *New York Times*, November 23, 2018, nytimes.com/interactive/2018/11/23/technology /robot-nurse-zora.html.

166 *"accompany you throughout your day"*: "Zbos by Zora," Zorabots, accessed October 9, 2021, zorarobotics.be/zbos-zora.

166 *therapeutic companion robot*: "PARO Therapeutic Robot," PARO, accessed December 24, 2021, parorobots.com. See also Facebook, Inc., "Facebook Reports Fourth Quarter."

167 *South Korea stepped up its use of robots*: Arirang News, "S. Korean developers create AI robot to help prevent spread of COVID-19," video, June 13, 2020, youtube.com/watch?v=rTTI44cY4n8.

167 *more than 1.5 billion*: United Nations Department of Economic and Social Affairs, *World Population Ageing 2019: Highlights*, 2019, accessed September 11, 2021, un.org/en/development/desa/population /publications/pdf/ageing/WorldPopulationAgeing2019-Highlights .pdf.

168 *elderly share emotions more freely with robots*: Satariano, Peltier, and Kostyukov, "Meet Zora."

169 *David Hanson*: David Hanson, "On Humanoid Robots: Relationships, Rights, Risks and Responsibilities," interviewed by Susan Liautaud, Ethics Incubator, April 2019, ethicsincubator.net/ethics-and-truth-in terviews/david-hanson-interview.

170 *Robert Julian-Borchak Williams*: Kashmir Hill, "Wrongfully Accused by an Algorithm," *New York Times*, last modified August 3, 2020, ny times.com/2020/06/24/technology/facial-recognition-arrest.html.

170 *first known case*: Ibid.

171 *With good-quality photos*: Patrick Grother, Mei Ngan, and Kayee Hanaoka, "FRVT Part 2: Identification," National Institute of Standards and Technology, March 27, 2020, nvlpubs.nist.gov/nistpubs/ir /2019/NIST.IR.8271.pdf.

171 *the American Civil Liberties Union reported*: Jacob Snow, "Amazon's Face Recognition Falsely Matched 28 Members of Congress with Mugshots," ACLU, July 26, 2018, aclu.org/blog/privacy-tech nology/surveillance-technologies/Amazons-face-recognition-falsely -matched-28.

171 *embracing these FRT tools*: Shirin Ghaffary and Rani Molla, "Here's where the US government is using facial recognition technology to surveil Americans," *Vox*, last modified December 10, 2019, vox.com /recode/2019/7/18/20698307/facial-recognition-technology-us -government-fight-for-the-future.

171 *Amazon's FRT*: Snow, "Amazon's Face Recognition."

171 *study of gender and skin-color bias*: Joy Buolamwini and Timnit Gebru, "Gender Shades: Intersectional Accuracy Disparities in Commercial Gender Classification," *Proceedings of Machine Learning Research* 81: 1–15, 2018, proceedings.mlr.press/v81/buolamwini18a/bud amwini18a.pdf.

172 *ban police use of facial recognition technology*: Kashmir Hill, "How One State Managed to Actually Write Rules on Facial Recognition," *New York Times*, last modified March 5, 2021, nytimes.com/2021/02 /27/technology/Massachusetts-facial-recognition-rules.html.

172 *Microsoft . . . won't sell facial recognition technology*: Jay Greene, "Microsoft won't sell police its facial-recognition technology, following similar moves by Amazon and IBM," *Washington Post*, June 11, 2020, washingtonpost.com/technology/2020/06/11/microsoft-facial -recognition.

172 *In 2020, Microsoft*: Washington Post Live (@PostLive), "Microsoft president @BradSmi says the company does not sell facial recognition software to police depts.," Twitter, June 11, 2020, twitter.com /postlive/status/1271116509625020417.

172 *Amazon . . . one-year moratorium*: Amazon Staff, "We are implementing a one-year moratorium on police use of Rekognition," Amazon, June 10, 2020, aboutamazon.com/news/policy-news-views/we-are -implementing-a-one-year-moratorium-on-police-use-of-rekogni tion. See also Drew Harwell, "Amazon extends ban on police use of its facial recognition technology indefinitely," *Washington Post*,

May 18, 2021, washingtonpost.com/technology/2021/05/18/amazon -facial-recognition-ban/.

172 *3 billion images*: Kate O'Flaherty, "Clearview AI's Database Has Amassed 3 Billion Photos. This Is How if You Want Yours Deleted, You Have to Opt Out," *Forbes*, January 26, 2020, forbes.com/sites /kateoflahertyuk/2020/01/26/clearview-ais-database-has-amassed -3-billion-photos-this-is-how-if-you-want-yours-deleted-you-have -to-opt-out/?sh=4ebd278360aa.

172 *More than six hundred law enforcement agencies*: Kashmir Hill, "The Secretive Company That Might End Privacy as We Know It," *New York Times*, last modified November 2, 2021, nytimes.com/2020/01 /18/technology/clearview-privacy-facial-recognition.html.

172 *Facebook announced*: David Meyer, "After Facebook abandons facial recognition, the technology takes another blow with new Clearview AI ban," *Fortune*, November 3, 2021, fortune.com/2021/11/03 /clearview-ai-Australia-facial-recognition-facebook/.

175 *State laws regarding posthumous privacy*: Natalie M. Banta, "Death and Privacy in the Digital Age," *North Carolina Law Review* 94, no. 3 (2016), scholarship.law.unc.edu/cgi/viewcontent.cgi?article =4765&context=nclr.

178 *"ready to listen"*: "Products & Pipeline," Woebot Health, accessed November 22, 2021, woebothealth.com/products-pipeline/. See also Arielle Pardes, "The Emotional Chatbots Are Here to Probe Our Feelings," *Wired*, January 31, 2018, wired.com/story/replika-open-source.

178 *works by inviting people*: "About us," Woebot Health, accessed November 22, 2021, woebothealth.com/about-us/.

178 *replacement for human connection*: "For users," Woebot Health, accessed November 22, 2021, woebothealth.com/for-users/.

178 *Replika*: "Our Story," Replika, replika.ai/about/story.

179 *downloaded more than 2 million times*: Pardes, "The Emotional Chatbots Are Here."

179 *FDA-approved cognitive therapy apps*: Christina Farr, "The FDA just approved the first app for treating substance abuse," CNBC, last modified September 14, 2017, cnbc.com/2017/09/14/the-fda-app proved-the-first-mobile-app-to-treat-substance-use-disorders.html.

179 *more than 700,000 people die*: "Suicide," World Health Organization, June 17, 2021, accessed September 11, 2021, who.int/news-room /fact-sheets/detail/suicide.

179 *mental disorder*: "The World Health Report 2001: Mental Disorders

affect one in four people," World Health Organization, September 28, 2001, who.int/news/item/28-09-2001-the-world-health-report-2001 -mental-disorders-affect-one-in-four-people.

180 *Risks of bot therapy*: Amelia Fiske, Peter Henningsen, and Alena Buyx, "Your Robot Therapist Will See You Now: Ethical Implications of Embodied Artificial Intelligence in Psychiatry, Psychology, and Psychotherapy," *Journal of Medical Internet Research* 21, no. 5 (May 2019): e13216, ncbi.nlm.nih.gov/pmc/articles/PMC6532335.

182 *Alexa*: Susan Liautaud, *The Power of Ethics* (New York: Simon & Schuster, 2021).

182 *2.6 smart speaker devices*: "NPR and Edison Research Report: 60M U.S. Adults 18+ Own a Smart Speaker," NPR, January 8, 2020, npr .org/about-npr/794588984/npr-and-edison-research-report-60m-u -s-adults-18-own-a-smart-speaker.

183 *"hundreds of millions of Alexa-enabled devices"*: Ben Fox Rubin, "Amazon sees Alexa devices more than double in just one year," CNET, January 6, 2020, cnet.com/home/smart-home/amazon-sees -alexa-devices-more-than-double-in-just-one-year.

184 *Amazon notes in their terms of service*: "Alexa Terms of Use," Amazon, last modified September 28, 2021, accessed November 30, 2021, amazon.com/gp/help/customer/display.html?nodeId=201809740.

185 *On Monday, January 25*: Yun Li, "GameStop jumps amid retail frenzy, shares double at one point in wild trading," CNBC, January 25, 2021, cnbc.com/2021/01/25/gamestop-shares-jump-another-40per cent-shake-off-analyst-downgrade-as-epic-short-squeeze-contin ues.html.

185 *purchasing a lottery ticket*: Yun Li, "GameStop, Reddit and Robin-hood: A full recap of the historic retail trading mania on Wall Street," CNBC, last modified January 30, 2021, cnbc.com/2021/01/30/game stop-reddit-and-robinhood-a-full-recap-of-the-historic-retail-trading -mania-on-wall-street.html.

185 *stock price skyrocketed*: Yahoo Finance, GameStop Corp. (GME), NYSE - Nasdaq Real Time Price, Jan 2011–Jan 30, 2021, finance.ya hoo.com/quote/GME/history?.

185 *disconnected*: Li, "GameStop, Reddit and Robinhood."

185 *more than six times the previous single-day record*: Annabel Smith, "The Reddit revolt: GameStop and the impact of social media on institutional investors," The TRADE, April 13, 2021, thetradenews.com /the-reddit-revolt-gamestop-and-the-impact-of-social-media-on -institutional-investors.

186 *tenfold*: "What happened this week," Robinhood blog, January 29, 2021, blog.robinhood.com/news/2021/1/29/what-happened-this-week.

186 *Robinhood had to limit trading*: Li, "GameStop, Reddit and Robinhood."

187 *coffeehouse tour*: Ron Lieber, "Robinhood Hits Campus, Where Credit Card Companies Fear to Tread," *New York Times*, September 25, 2021, nytimes.com/2021/09/25/your-money/robinhood-colleges.html.

189 *Firing over one hundred rounds*: Rich Braziel et al., "Bringing Calm to Chaos: A critical incident review of the San Bernardino public safety response to the December 2, 2015, terrorist shooting incident at the Inland Regional Center," Critical Response Initiative, Washington, D.C., Office of Community Oriented Policing Services, 2016, justice.gov/usao-cdca/file/891996/download.

189 *Apple and the Justice Department had been sparring*: Adam Satariano and Chris Strohm, "The Behind-the-Scenes Fight Between Apple and the FBI," Bloomberg, March 20, 2016, bloomberg.com/news/features/2016-03-20/the-behind-the-scenes-fight-between-apple-and-the-fbi.

190 *Tim Cook issued a letter*: Tim Cook, "A Message to Our Customers," Apple, February 16, 2016, apple.com/customer-letter.

190 *FBI withdrew its request*: Ellen Nakashima and Reed Albergotti, "The FBI wanted to unlock the San Bernardino shooter's iPhone. It turned to a little-known Australian firm," *Washington Post*, April 14, 2021, washingtonpost.com/technology/2021/04/14/azimuth-san-bernardino-apple-iphone-fbi.

190 *Apple is now suing Azimuth*: Ibid.

190 *Apple claims*: "Answers to your questions about Apple and security," Apple website, accessed December 13, 2021, apple.com/customer-letter/answers.

191 *San Bernardino shootings*: Adam Nagourney, Ian Lovett, and Richard Pérez-Peña, "San Bernardino Shooting Kills at Least 14; Two Suspects Are Dead," *New York Times*, December 2, 2015, nytimes.com/2015/12/03/us/san-bernardino-shooting.html. See also Mark Berman, Elahe Izadi, and Wesley Lowery, "At least 14 people killed, 17 injured in mass shooting in San Bernardino, Calif.; two suspects killed in shootout with police," *Washington Post*, December 2, 2015, washingtonpost.com/news/post-nation/wp/2015/12/02/police-in-san-bernadino-calif-responding-report-of-shooting/.

191 *Apple came down on the side*: Kifi Leswing, "Apple's fight with

Trump and the Justice Department is about more than two iPhones," CNBC, last modified January 16, 2020, cnbc.com/2020/01/16/apple -fbi-backdoor-battle-is-about-more-than-two-iphones.html.

191 *"compromising the security"*: Cook, "A Message to Our Customers."

191 *"Apple deserves"*: Eric Lichtblau and Katie Benner, "Apple Fights Order to Unlock San Bernardino Gunman's iPhone," *New York Times*, February 17, 2016, nytimes.com/2016/02/18/technology/apple-timothy -cook-fbi-san-bernardino.html.

192 *"Apple cannot bypass your passcode"*: Orin Kerr, "Apple's dangerous game," *Washington Post*, September 19, 2014, washingtonpost.com /news/volokh-conspiracy/wp/2014/09/19/apples-dangerous-game; "Privacy," Apple, accessed September 13, 2021, apple.com/privacy /government-information-requests.

193 *first humanoid robot*: "Sophia the Robot," Her Future Summit, accessed September 21, 2021, herfuturesummit.org/speaker/sophia -the-robot; "Sophia," Hanson Robotics, accessed September 21, 2021, hansonrobotics.com/sophia.

193 *The Hanson Robotics website describes Sophia*: "Sophia," Hanson Robotics.

193 *Her face*: Susan Liautaud, *The Power of Ethics* (New York: Simon & Schuster, 2021). See also Jack Kelly, "Sophia—The Humanoid Robot—Will Be Rolled Out This Year Potentially Replacing Workers," *Forbes*, January 26, 2021, forbes.com/sites/jackkelly/2021/01/26 /sophia-the-humanoid-robot-will-be-rolled-out-this-year-potential ly-replacing-workers/?sh=4d9900806df2.

193 *"can estimate your feelings"*: "Sophia," Hanson Robotics.

193 *Sophia's artificial intelligence*: Ibid.

193 *Sophia continually learns*: Sara Brown, "Machine learning, explained," MIT Sloan School of Management, April 21, 2021, mitsloan.mit.edu /ideas-made-to-matter/machine-learning-explained.

193 *granted citizenship*: Zara Stone, "Everything You Need to Know About Sophia, the World's First Robot Citizen," *Forbes*, November 7, 2017, forbes.com/sites/zarastone/2017/11/07/everything-you -need-to-know-about-sophia-the-worlds-first-robot-citizen/?sh =186ebd4046fa.

193 *European Parliament*: Janosch Delcker, "Europe divided over robot 'personhood,'" *Politico*, April 11, 2018, politico.eu/article/europe -divided-over-robot-ai-artificial-intelligence-personhood; Mady Delvaux, *Report with recommendations to the Commission on Civil*

Law Rules on Robotics (2015/2103(INL)), European Parliament, January 27, 2017, europarl.europa.eu/doceo/document/A-8-2017-0005
_EN.pdf.

194 *letter to the EU*: "Open Letter to the European Commission: Artificial Intelligence and Robotics," open letter, robotics-openletter.eu.

CHAPTER 5: CONSUMER CHOICES

199 *Boohoo sold a bodycon minidress*: Sandra Laville, "The story of a £4 Boohoo dress: cheap clothes at a high cost," *The Guardian*, June 22, 2019, theguardian.com/business/2019/jun/22/cost-cheap-fast-fash ion-workers-planet.

199 *vanilla spice latte at Starbucks*: "Starbucks UK Menu Prices," Fast Food Menu Prices, accessed September 11, 2021, fastfoodmenuprices .com/uk/starbucks-menu-prices-uk.

199 *"In 1991, the average American bought"*: United Nations Environment Programme, "Cleaning up couture: what's in your jeans?" December 14, 2018, unep.org/news-and-stories/story/cleaning-couture-whats -your-jeans.

199 *garments are later recycled*: Ibid.

199 *"landfill fashion"*: Jim Zarroli, "In Trendy World of Fast Fashion, Styles Aren't Made to Last," NPR, March 11, 2013, npr.org/2013/03/11 /174013774/in-trendy-world-of-fast-fashion-styles-aren't-made-to -last.

200 *"slow fashion"*: Audrey Stanton, "What Is Fast Fashion, Anyway?" Good Trade, accessed September 12, 2021, thegoodtrade.com/fea tures/what-is-fast-fashion.

200 *Fast fashion companies*: Shuk-Wah Chung, "Fast fashion is 'drowning' the world. We need a Fashion Revolution!" Greenpeace, April 21, 2016, greenpeace.org/international/story/7539/fast-fashion-is-drowning -the-world-we-need-a-fashion-revolution/. See also Terri Pous, "The Democratization of Fashion: A Brief History," *Time*, February 6, 2013, style.time.com/2013/02/06/the-democratization-of-fashion-a-brief -history.

200 *"3,781 liters of water"*: United Nations Environment Programme, "Cleaning up couture."

200 *"The fashion industry is responsible"*: United Nations Environment Programme, "UN Alliance for Sustainable Fashion addresses damage of 'fast fashion,'" March 14, 2019, unep.org/news-and-stories

/press-release/un-alliance-sustainable-fashion-addresses-damage -fast-fashion. See also "How Much Do Our Wardrobes Cost to the Environment?" World Bank, September 23, 2019, worldbank.org/en /news/feature/2019/09/23/costo-moda-medio-ambiente.

206 *U.S. Department of Agriculture (USDA) says*: Miles McEvoy, "Organic 101: What the USDA Organic Label Means," United States Department of Agriculture, March 13, 2019, usda.gov/media/blog/2012/03 /22/organic-101-what-usda-organic-label-means.

207 *USDA categorizes organic products*: "About Organic Labeling," United States Department of Agriculture, ams.usda.gov/rules-regula tions/organic/labeling.

207 *In 2020, organic food sales*: Dymond Green, "The rise of the organic food market," CNBC, September 22, 2021, cnbc.com/2021/09/22 /organic-food-sales-surged-in-2020-higher-demand-and-cheaper -costs.html; "U.S. Organic Industry Survey 2021," Organic Trade Association, accessed October 14, 2021, ota.com/market-analysis/or ganic-industry-survey/organic-industry-survey.

207 *a 2012 in-depth study*: Crystal Smith-Spangler et al., "Are organic foods safer or healthier than conventional alternatives?: a systematic review," *Annals of Internal Medicine* 157, no. 5 (September 2021): 348–66, pubmed.ncbi.nlm.nih.gov/22944875.

207 *Columbia University Climate School*: Anuradha Varanasi, "Is Organic Food Really Better for the Environment?" State of the Planet, October 22, 2019, news.climate.columbia.edu/2019/10/22/organic-food -better-environment.

208 *Peter Singer's point*: Jennie Richards, "Peter Singer: The Ethics of What We Eat," Humane Decisions, August 1, 2016, humanedecisions .com/peter-singer-the-ethics-of-what-we-eat.

208 *Twenty-five thousand people die of starvation*: John Holmes, "Losing 25,000 to Hunger Every Day," United Nations, un.org/en/chronicle /article/losing-25000-hunger-every-day.

210 *working paper from Harvard Business School*: The final version of their paper is at Benjamin Edelman and Michael Luca, "Racial Discrimination in the Sharing Economy: Evidence from a Field Experiment," *American Economic Journal: Applied Economics*, April 2017, 9 (2): 1–22, www.aeaweb.org/articles?id=10.1257/app.20160213.

210 *Civil Rights Act of 1964*: *Know Your Rights: Title II of the Civil Rights Act of 1964*, United States Department of Justice Civil Rights Division, justice.gov/crt/page/file/1251321/download. See also Rebecca Greenfield, "Study Finds Racist Discrimination by Airbnb Hosts,"

Bloomberg, December 10, 2015, bloomberg.com/news/articles/2015
-12-10/study-finds-racial-discrimination-by-airbnb-hosts.

211 *"There were lots"*: Brian Solomon, "Airbnb Confronts Racism As It
Hits 100 Million Guest Arrivals," *Forbes*, July 13, 2016, forbes.com
/sites/briansolomon/2016/07/13/airbnb-confronts-racism-as-it-hits
-100-million-guest-arrivals/?sh=64a036916b76.

214 *"Veganism": Cambridge Dictionary*, s.v. "veganism," Cambridge University Press, accessed November 16, 2021, dictionary.cambridge.org
/us/dictionary/english/veganism.

214 *An "ethical vegan"*: Jordi Casamitjana, "The foundations of ethical
veganism," Vegan Society, December 18, 2020, accessed August 28,
2021, vegansociety.com/news/blog/foundations-ethical-veganism.

214 *According to the Vegan Society*: "Definition of veganism," The Vegan
Society website, accessed November 23, 2021, vegansociety.com/go
-vegan/definition-veganism.

215 *I focus here on the view*: Kelsey Piper, "A no-beef diet is great, but
only if you don't replace it with chicken," *Vox*, May 22, 2021, vox.com
/future-perfect/22430749/beef-chichen-climate-diet-vegetarian.

215 Stanford Encyclopedia of Philosophy: Tyler Doggett, "Moral Veg-
etarianism," *Stanford Encyclopedia of Philosophy*, September 14,
2018, plato.stanford.edu/entries/vegetarianism.

215 *"flexible vegan"*: "I am largely vegan but I'm a flexible vegan. I don't
go to the supermarket and buy non-vegan stuff for myself. But when
I'm travelling or going to other people's places I will be quite happy
to eat vegetarian rather than vegan." From Dave Gilson, "Chew the
Right Thing," *Mother Jones*, May 3, 2006, motherjones.com/politics
/2006/05/chew-right-thing/.

217 *rescinded the order*: "Rescission of Emergency Order of Prohibition," United States Department of Transportation Federal Aviation
Administration, November 18, 2020, faa.gov/foia/electronic_read
ing_room/boeing_reading_room/media/737_MAX_Rescission_of
_Grounding_Order.pdf.

217 *Boeing's 737 Max 8 and 9 planes*: "737 Max Updates, Current Products and Services," accessed October 14, 2021, boeing.com/commer
cial/737max.

217 *Disturbingly, Boeing knew*: Theo Leggett, "Boeing admits knowing of
737 Max problem," BBC News, May 6, 2019, bbc.co.uk/news/business
-48174797.

217 *Dennis Muilenburg personally called President Trump*: Keith Brad-
sher, Kenneth P. Vogel, and Zach Wichter, "Two-Thirds of the 737

Max 8 Jets in the World Have Been Pulled from the Skies," *New York Times*, March 12, 2019, nytimes.com/2019/03/12/business/boeing-737-grounding-faa.html.

217 *poor decisions by Boeing*: David Gelles and James Glanz, "Boeing Built Deadly Assumptions Into 737 Max, Blind to a Late Design Change," *New York Times*, June 1, 2019, https://www.nytimes.com/2019/06/01/business/boeing-737-max-crash.html.

218 *In rescinding the grounding of the planes*: Curtis Tate, "Boeing's troubled 737 Max cleared to fly again. When will travelers start boarding?" *USA Today*, November 18, 2020, eu.usatoday.com/story/travel/airline-news/2020/11/18/boeing-737-max-when-american-united-southwest-alaska-fly/3766105001; "Rescission of Emergency Order of Prohibition."

219 *"procedures were not completely followed"*: Peter Economy, "Boeing CEO Puts Partial Blame on Pilots of Crashed 737 MAX Aircraft for Not 'Completely' Following Procedures," *Inc.*, April 30, 2019, inc.com/peter-economy/boeing-ceo-puts-partial-blame-on-pilots-of-crashed-737-max-aircraft-for-not-completely-following-procedures.html.

219 *fixing Boeing*: Natalie Kitroeff and David Gelles, "'It's More Than I Imagined': Boeing's New C.E.O. Confronts Its Challenges," *New York Times*, last modified March 6, 2020, nytimes.com/2020/03/05/business/boeing-david-calhoun.html.

219 *"The objective is to get the Max up safely."*: Ibid.

225 *On April 23, 2013, deep cracks and fissures*: Nadra Nittle, "What the Rana Plaza Disaster Changed About Worker Safety," *Racked*, April 13, 2018, racked.com/2018/4/13/17230770/rana-plaza-collapse-anniversary-garment-workers-safety; Dana Thomas, "Why Won't We Learn from the Survivors of the Rana Plaza Disaster?" *New York Times*, April 24, 2018, nytimes.com/2018/04/24/style/survivors-of-rana-plaza-disaster.html.

225 *"Soldiers, paramilitary police officers"*: Julfikar Ali Manik and Jim Yardley, "Building Collapse in Bangladesh Leaves Scores Dead," *New York Times*, April 24, 2013, nytimes.com/2013/04/25/world/asia/bangladesh-building-collapse.html.

225 *Western fashion leaders*: Ibid.; Nittle, "What the Rana Plaza Disaster Changed"; and "5 years after the world's largest garment factory collapse, is safety in Bangladesh any better?" PBS News Hour, April 6, 2018, pbs.org/newshour/world/5-years-after-the-worlds-largest-garment-factory-collapse-is-safety-in-bangladesh-any-better.

225 *An investigation found*: Ibid.

226 *"The price pressure"*: Manik and Yardley, "Building Collapse in Bangladesh."

226 *"committed"*: Matthew Mosk, "Wal-Mart Fires Supplier After Bangladesh Revelation," ABC News, May 15, 2013, abcnews.go.com/Blotter/Wal-Mart-fires-supplier-bangladesh-revelation/story?id=19188673.

227 *work had been subcontracted out*: Manik and Yardley, "Building Collapse in Bangladesh."

229 *In 2002, the George W. Bush*: "Most Americans Now Can Prepare & File Taxes Online for Free Treasury, OMB, IRS launch new Free File Website," U.S. Department of the Treasury, January 16, 2003, home.treasury.gov/news/press-releases/kd3771.

229 *multiyear agreement*: "Free File: About the Free File Alliance," Internal Revenue Service, last modified April 8, 2021, irs.gov/e-file-providers/about-the-free-file-alliance.

229 *moderate-income filers*: Ann Carrns, "Navigating the Many Offers of Free Tax Help," *New York Times*, February 3, 2017, nytimes.com/2017/02/03/your-money/taxes/navigating-the-many-offers-of-free-tax-help.html.

229 *$72,000 or less*: "Free File: Do your Federal Taxes for Free," IRS, accessed November 19, 2021, irs.gov/filing/free-file-do-your-federal-taxes-for-free.

229 *60 million returns*: "About: The Free File Alliance: Serving the American Taxpayer," Free File Alliance, freefilealliance.org/about.

229 *Although 100 million Americans are eligible*: Carrns, "Navigating the Many Offers."

230 *paying customers*: Justin Elliott and Paul Kiel, "TurboTax and H&R Block Saw Free Tax Filing as a Threat—and Gutted It," ProPublica, May 2, 2019, propublica.org/article/intuit-turbotax-h-r-block-gutted-free-tax-filing-internal-memo.

230 *H&R Block dropped out*: Allyson Versprille, "IRS's Free File Partners Moving Forward Without H&R Block," Bloomberg Tax, June 18, 2020, news.bloombergtax.com/daily-tax-report/irss-free-file-partners-moving-forward-without-h-r-block.

230 *and in July 2021*: Carmen Reinicke, "Intuit will no longer be a part of an IRS program that helps millions of Americans file taxes for free," CNBC, last modified July 16, 2021, cnbc.com/2021/07/16/intuit-will-no-longer-participate-in-an-irs-free-tax-filing-program-.html.

230 *Britain and Japan don't require*: T. R. Reid, "Filing Taxes in Japan Is a Breeze. Why Not Here?" *New York Times*, April 14, 2017, nytimes

.com/2017/04/14/opinion/filing-taxes-in-japan-is-a-breeze-why-not
-here.html. See also Binyamin Appelbaum, "Good Riddance, Turbo-
Tax. Americans Need a Real 'Free File' Program," *New York Times*,
July 19, 2021, nytimes.com/2021/07/19/opinion/intuit-turbotax-free
-filing.html.

230 *In 2006, Austan Goolsbee*: Austan Goolsbee, "The Simple Return:
Reducing America's Tax Burden Through Return-Free Filing," Brook-
ings, July 1, 2006, brookings.edu/research/the-simple-return-reduc
ing-Americas-tax-burden-through-return-free-filing/.

230 *chairman of President Obama's*: "Former Chairs of the Council of
Economic Advisers," The White House: President Barack Obama,
obamawhitehouse.archives.gov/administration/eop/cea/about/for
mer-chairs.

230 *agreed not to compete*: Elliott and Kiel, "TurboTax and H&R Block."

231 *ProPublica revealed*: Ibid.

231 *Each company in the alliance*: Ibid. See also "Independent Assessment of the Free File Program," IRS, September 13, 2019, irs.gov/pub
/newsroom/02-appendix-a-economics-of-irs-free-file.pdf.

233 *The word "philanthropy"*: Lexico, s.v. "philanthropia (*n.*)," accessed
August 28, 2021, lexico.com/definition/philanthropia.

237 National Geographic *reports*: Laura Parker, "How the plastic bottle
went from miracle container to hated garbage," *National Geographic*,
August 23, 2019, nationalgeographic.com/environment/article/pla
stic-bottles.

237 *2,000 times more expensive*: Matthew Boesler, "Bottled Water Costs
2000 Times as Much as Tap Water," *Business Insider*, July 13, 2013, busi
nessinsider.com.au/bottled-water-costs-2000x-more-than-tap-2013-7.

238 *And the water will be healthier*: Brent A. Bauer, MD, "What is BPA,
and what are the concerns about BPA?" Mayo Clinic, May 14, 2021,
mayoclinic.org/healthy-lifestyle/nutrition-and-healthy-eating/ex
pert-answers/bpa/faq-20058331.

CHAPTER 6: HEALTH

241 *waiting for organs*: "Organ Donation Statistics," Health Resources &
Services Administration, last modified October 2021, organdonor
.gov/statistics-stories/statistics.html.

241 *Organ donation, as described*: "Organ Donation and Transplantation," Cleveland Clinic, last modified May 4, 2021, my.clevelandclinic
.org/health/articles/11750-organ-donation-and-transplantation.

241 *There were 7,397 living donors*: "Organ donation again sets record in 2019," United Network for Organ Sharing, January 9, 2020, unos.org /news/organ-donation-sets-record-in-2019/.

241 *A single donor can supply organs*: "The Impact of One Organ Donor," University of Pittsburgh Medical Center HealthBeat, April 26, 2015, share.upmc.com/2015/04/the-impact-of-one-organ-donor.

241 *only 60 percent actually sign up*: "Organ Donation Statistics," Health Resources & Services Administration.

242 *Germany, like the U.S., uses an opt-in system*: Ghazi Ahmad and Sadia Iftikhar, "An Analysis of Organ Donation Policy in the United States," *Rhode Island Medical Journal* 99, no. 5 (May 2016): 25–27, rimed.org/rimedicaljournal/2016/05/2016-05-25-cont-ahmad.pdf.

242 *Austria . . . uses opt-out*: Richard H. Thaler, "Opting in vs. Opting Out," *New York Times*, September 26, 2009, nytimes.com/2009/09 /27/business/economy/27view.html.

242 *Twenty countries in the European Union*: Nicole Scholz, *Organ donation and transplantation: Facts, figures and European Union action*, European Parliamentary Research Service, April 2020, europarl .europa.eu/RegData/etudes/BRIE/2020/649363/EPRS_BRI(2020) 649363_EN.pdf.

243 *state of Illinois*: Thaler, "Opting in vs. Opting Out."

244 *sued NHS Trust*: The decision of Honourable Mrs. Justice Yip in ABC v (1) St. George's Healthcare NHS Trust, (2) South West London and St George's Mental Health NHS Trust, and (3) Sussex Partnership NHS Foundation Trust, 2020 EWHC 455 (QB), bailii.org/ew/cases /EWHC/QB/2020/455.html.

244 *Symptoms, according to the Mayo Clinic*: Mayo Clinic Staff, "Huntington's disease," Mayo Clinic, April 14, 2020, mayoclinic.org/diseases -conditions/huntingtons-disease/symptoms-causes/syc-2035 6117.

244 *With Huntington's disease*: "Huntington's Disease," National Organization for Rare Disorders, rarediseases.org/rare-diseases/hunting tons-disease.

244 *About 30,000 people in the U.S.*: Ibid.

244 *tested positive*: The decision of Honourable Mrs. Justice Yip.

247 *"freely and widely for scientific research"*: "The Importance of HeLa Cells," Johns Hopkins Medicine, accessed August 28, 2021, hopkins medicine.org/henriettalacks/importance-of-hela-cells.html.

247 *countless medical breakthroughs*: Ibid.

248 *who controls the cells taken*: "Henrietta Lacks: Science must right a

historical wrong," *Nature* 585, no. 7, nature.com/articles/d41586-020
-02494-z.

248 *One hospital consent form*: "Consent to Operation, Procedure and
Administration of Anaesthesia," Stanford Hospital and Clinics, stan
fordhealthcare.org/content/dam/SHC/for-patients-component
/womens-imaging/docs/15-01-consent-to-operation-admin-of-an
esthesia.pdf.

248 *diverging views*: Rebecca Skloot, "Your Cells. Their Research. Your
Permission?" *New York Times*, December 30, 2015, nytimes.com/2015
/12/30/opinion/your-cells-their-research-your-permission.html.

248 *genetic information will be linked*: Ibid.

250 *Alzheimer's*: "Dementia," World Health Organization, accessed August 29, 2021, who.int/news-room/fact-sheets/detail/dementia.
See also "What is Alzheimer's Disease?" Alzheimer's Association,
accessed December 30, 2021, alz.org/alzheimers-dementia/what-is
-alzheimers.

251 *Almost 6 million people*: "Minorities and Women Are at Greater Risk
for Alzheimer's Disease," Centers for Disease Control and Prevention, accessed December 8, 2021, cdc.gov/aging/publications/fea
tures/Alz-Greater-Risk.html.

251 *more than 55 million people worldwide*: "Dementia," World Health
Organization.

253 *"Imagine a world"*: Walter Isaacson, "Who Should Decide?" chap. 42
in *The Code Breaker: Jennifer Doudna, Gene Editing, and the Future
of the Human Race* (New York: Simon & Schuster, 2021).

253 *"we might all go barreling down"*: Ibid.

254 *In contrast, so-called germline therapy*: "How Is Genome Editing
Used?" National Human Genome Research Institute, last modified August 3, 2017, accessed October 3, 2021, genome.gov/about-genomics
/policy-issues/genome-editing/how-genome-editing-is-used.

254 *"control of their own evolution"*: Jennifer A. Doudna and Samuel H
Sternberg, "What Lies Ahead," chap. 8 in *A Crack in Creation: Gene
Editing and the Unthinkable Power to Control Evolution* (Boston:
Mariner Books, 2017).

255 *young sickle cell patient*: Walter Isaacson, "Thought Experiments,"
chap. 41 in *The Code Breaker: Jennifer Doudna, Gene Editing, and the
Future of the Human Race* (New York: Simon & Schuster, 2021).

258 *NPR/Marist survey*: Geoff Brumfiel, "Vaccine Refusal May Put Herd
Immunity at Risk, Researchers Warn," NPR, April 7, 2021, npr.org

/sections/health-shots/2021/04/07/984697573/vaccine-refusal
-may-put-herd-immunity-at-risk-researchers-warn.

258 *The CDC says*: Wesley H. Self, MD, et al.,"Comparative Effective-
ness of Moderna, Pfizer–BioNTech and Janssen (Johnson & Johnson) Vaccines in Preventing COVID-19 Hospitalizations Among
Adults Without Immunocompromising Conditions—United States,
March–August 2021," *Morbidity and Mortality Weekly Report* 70,
no. 38 (September 24, 2021): 1337–43, cdc.gov/mmwr/volumes/70
/wr/mm7038e1.htm?s_cid=mm7038e1_w.

258 *All fifty states*: Drew DeSilver, "States have mandated vaccinations
since long before Covid-19," Pew Research Center, October 8, 2021,
pewresearch.org/fact-tank/2021/10/08/states-have-mandated-vac
cinations-since-long-before-Covid-19.

258 *officially eradicated*: "Region of the Americas is declared free of
measles," Pan American Health Organization, September, 27, 2016,
paho.org/hq/index.php?option=com_content&view=article&id=12
528:region-americas-declared-free-measles&Itemid=1926&lang=en.

261 *I learned that the imaging department*: "Medical Imaging," American
Hospital of Paris, accessed August 29, 2021, american-hospital.org
/en/our-specialties/imaging-center.

262 *According to the American Medical Association*: Michael J. Rigby,
"Ethical Dimensions of Using Artificial Intelligence in Health Care,"
AMA Journal of Ethics 21, no. 2 (February 2019): 121–24, journalof
ethics.ama-assn.org/article/ethical-dimensions-using-artificial-intel
ligence-health-care/2019-02.

262 *in addition to diagnosis*: Brian Kalis, Matt Collier, and Richard Fu,
"10 Promising AI Applications in Health Care," Harvard Business Review, May 10, 2018, hbr.org/2018/05/10-promising-ai-applications-in
-health-care.

262 *Accenture found that*: "AI: Healthcare's new nervous system," Accenture, accessed December 13, 2021, accenture.com/au-en/insights
/health/artificial-intelligence-healthcare.

263 *Medical ethics experts*: David Magnus, PhD, and Thomas A. Raffin,
email message to author, October 19, 2020.

263 *diabetic retinopathy*: Cade Metz, "India Fights Diabetic Blindness
with Help from A.I.," *New York Times*, March 10, 2019, nytimes.com
/2019/03/10/technology/artificial-intelligence-eye-hospital-india
.html. See also Christina Farr, "Google launches India program
to screen diabetics for eye conditions that can cause blindness,"

CNBC, last modified February 25, 2019, cnbc.com/2019/02/25 /google-verily-launch-diabetic-eye-condition-screening-tech-in -india.html.

263 *eleven eye doctors in India for every 1 million people*: Ibid.

264 *facial recognition technology*: Robert Glatter, MD, "AI Can Read a Cardiac MRI in 4 Seconds: Do We Still Need Human Input?" *Forbes*, September 28, 2019, forbes.com/sites/robertglatter/2019/09/28/ai -can-read-a-cardiac-mri-in-4-seconds-do-we-still-need-human-in put/#220ca676a401.

265 *"Every flavor Skittle compressed into one"*: Sabrina Tavernise, "Use of E-Cigarettes Rises Sharply Among Teenagers, Report Says," *New York Times*, April 16, 2015, nytimes.com/2015/04/17/health/use-of-e -cigarettes-rises-sharply-among-teenagers-report-says.html.

265 *The most popular e-cigarette in the U.S.*: Jamie Ducharme, "Tobacco Giant Altria Just Made a $12.8 Billion Investment in Juul," *Time*, December 20, 2018, time.com/5485247/juul-altria-investment.

265 *In 2016, it became illegal*: Ned Sharpless, MD, "How FDA Is Regulating E-Cigarettes," U.S. Food and Drug Administration, last modified September 10, 2019, fda.gov/news-events/fda-voices/how-fda-regu lating-e-cigarettes.

265 *legal age to twenty-one*: "Newly Signed Legislation Raises Federal Minimum Age of Sale of Tobacco Production to 21," U.S. Food and Drug Administration, January 15, 2020, fda.gov/tobacco-products /ctp-newsroom/newly-signed-legislation-raises-federal-minimum -age-sale-tobacco-products-21.

265 *CEO of Juul Labs*: "Juul CEO Tells Non-Smokers Not to Vape or Use His Company's Product," CBS News, last modified August 29, 2019, cbsnews.com/news/juul-ceo-kevin-burns-tells-non-smokers-not-to -vape-or-use-his-companys-product.

265 *on October 12, 2021*: "FDA Permits Marketing of E-Cigarette Prod-ucts, Marking First Authorization of Its Kind by the Agency," U.S. Food & Drug Administration, October 12, 2021, fda.gov/news-events /press-announcements/fda-permits-marketing-e-cigarette-prod ucts-marking-first-authorization-its-kind-agency.

266 *"if credible evidence emerges"*: Ibid.

266 *Dr. Norman E. Sharpless*: Sharpless, "How FDA Is Regulating E-Cigarettes."

266 *harmful to children*: "Is It Safe to Vape Around Children?" Johns Hopkins All Children's Hospital, accessed August 29, 2021, hopkins

allchildrens.org/Patients-Families/Health-Library/HealthDocNew/Is
-It-Safe-to-Vape-Around-Children.

267 *advertising and promotion*: "Tobacco Industry Marketing," Centers
for Disease Control and Prevention, last modified May 14, 2021, accessed November 26, 2021, cdc.gov/system/files/documents/re
ports/federal-trade-commission-cigarette-report-2019-smokeless
-tobacco-report-2019/2019_smokeless_tobacco_report.pdf.

267 *doing both interchangeably*: Blaha, "5 Vaping Facts."

269 *21,000 donor organs*: "The Kidney Project," University of California
San Francisco, accessed August 29, 2021, pharm.ucsf.edu/kidney
/need/statistics.

270 *higher success rate*: "What is living kidney donation?" NHS Blood
and Transplant, accessed August 29, 2021, organdonation.nhs.uk
/become-a-living-donor/donating-your-kidney/what-is-living-kidney
-donation.

276 *"The privilege of a lifetime"*: *A Joseph Campbell Companion: Reflec-
tions on the Art of Living*, ed. Diane K. Osbon (New York: Harper
Perennial, 1995).

P9-BJD-416

Chicken Soup for the Soul

for the Soul®

Teens Talk

Our
101
BEST
STORIES

Relationships

Chicken Soup for the Soul® Our 101 Best Stories:
Teens Talk Relationships; Stories about Family, Friends and Love
by Jack Canfield, Mark Victor Hansen & Amy Newmark

Published by Chicken Soup for the Soul Publishing, LLC   www.chickensoup.com

Copyright © 2008 by Chicken Soup for the Soul Publishing, LLC. All Rights Reserved. No part
of this publication may be reproduced, stored in a retrieval system or transmitted in any form
or by any means, electronic, mechanical, photocopying, recording or otherwise, without the
written permission of the publisher.

CSS, Chicken Soup for the Soul, and its Logo and Marks are trademarks of
Chicken Soup for the Soul Publishing LLC.

The publisher gratefully acknowledges the many publishers and individuals who granted
Chicken Soup for the Soul permission to reprint the cited material.

Cover photos courtesy of Jupiterimages/Picturequest/Photos.com and Rubberball/Mike Kemp, and also
iStockPhoto/Yuri_Arcurs. Cover and interior illustration courtesy of iStockphoto/-m-i-s-a

Cover and Interior Design & Layout by Pneuma Books, LLC
For more info on Pneuma Books, visit www.pneumabooks.com

Distributed to the booktrade by Simon & Schuster. SAN: 200-2442

Publisher's Cataloging-in-Publication Data
(Prepared by The Donohue Group)

Chicken soup for the soul. Selections.
   Chicken soup for the soul : teens talk relationships : stories about
family, friends, and love / [compiled by] Jack Canfield [and] Mark Victor
Hansen ; [edited by] Amy Newmark.

   p. ; cm. -- (Our 101 best stories)

 ISBN-13: 978-1-935096-06-1
 ISBN-10: 1-935096-06-0

1. Teenagers--Literary collections. 2. Teenagers' writings. 3. Teenagers--Conduct of life--Anec-
dotes. 4. Teenagers--Family relationships--Anecdotes. 5. Dating (Social customs)--Anecdotes.
I. Canfield, Jack, 1944- II. Hansen, Mark Victor. III. Newmark, Amy. IV. Title.

PS508.Y68 C292 2008
810.8/09283   2008930430

PRINTED IN THE UNITED STATES OF AMERICA
on acid∞free paper
16 15 14 13 12 10 09 08   01 02 03 04 05 06 07 08

Chicken Soup for the Soul

for the Soul®

Teens Talk

Our **101** BEST STORIES

Relationships

Stories about
Family, Friends and Love

Jack Canfield
Mark Victor Hansen
Amy Newmark

Chicken Soup for the Soul Publishing, LLC
Cos Cob, CT

Chicken Soup
for the Soul

Contents

❸
~The First Kiss~

❹
~Friendships that Go the Distance~

❺
~Betrayal... or Not~

❿

~Putting Yourself Out There~

⓫

~Growing Apart~

Chicken Soup for the Soul

A Special Foreword

by Jack and Mark

For us, 101 has always been a magical number. It was the number of stories in the first *Chicken Soup for the Soul* book, and it is the number of stories and poems we have always aimed for in our books. We love the number 101 because it signifies a beginning, not an end. After 100, we start anew with 101.

We hope that when you finish reading one of our books, it is only a beginning for you too—a new outlook on life, a renewed sense of purpose, a strengthened resolve to deal with an issue that has been bothering you. Perhaps you will pick up the phone and share one of the stories with a friend or a loved one. Perhaps you will turn to your keyboard and express yourself by writing a Chicken Soup story of your own, to share with other readers who are just like you.

This volume contains our 101 best stories and poems about teenage relationships with family, with friends, and with boyfriends and girlfriends. We share this with you at a very special time for us, the fifteenth anniversary of our *Chicken Soup for the Soul* series. When we published our first book in 1993, we never dreamed that we had started what would become a publishing sensation, one of the best-selling lines of books in history.

We did not set out to sell more than one hundred million books, or to publish more than 150 titles. We set out to touch the heart of one person at a time, hoping that person would in turn touch another person, and so on down the line. Fifteen years later, we know that it has worked. Your letters and stories have poured in by the hundreds of thousands, affirming our life's work, and inspiring us to continue to make a difference in your lives.

On our fifteenth anniversary, we have new energy, new resolve, and new dreams. We have recommitted to our goal of 101 stories or poems per book, we have refreshed our cover designs and our interior layout, and we have grown the Chicken Soup for the Soul team, with new friends and partners across the country in New England.

We have chosen our 101 best stories and poems for teenagers from our rich fifteen year history to share with you in this new volume. We know that being a teenager is hard—we remember! Old friends drift away, new friends come with new issues, you fall in and out of love, your relationships with family members change.

You are not alone. We chose stories written by other teenagers just like you. They wrote about friends, family, love, loss, and many lessons learned. We hope that you will find these stories inspiring and supportive, and that you will share them with your families and friends. We have identified the 17 *Chicken Soup for the Soul* books in which the stories originally appeared, in case you would like to continue your journey among our other books. We hope you will also enjoy the additional titles for teenagers in "Our 101 Best Stories" series.

With our love, our thanks, and our respect,
~Jack Canfield and Mark Victor Hansen

Chapter 1

Teens Talk

Relationships

Head Over Heels

The mark of a true crush is that
you fall in love first and grope for reasons afterward.
~Shana Alexander

The Boy at Band Camp

If you're never scared or embarrassed or hurt,
it means you never take any chances.
~Julia Sorel (Rosalyn Drexler), See How She Runs, 1978

S trains of Mariah Carey floated in the background as we held each other close and swayed to the rhythm of the music. I hadn't expected us to be so intimate when I asked the guy who had been my best friend at summer camp to dance. But as my head rested on his shoulder and his arms wrapped around my torso, I realized that I had fallen head-over-heels for this guy. My timing had never been worse. It was the farewell dance at summer camp, the night before we left, and I was just realizing that I wanted to be with him. Furthermore, I had gone to middle school with him for the past two years, and I had never thought twice about the fact that I saw him literally six times a day. Then, he was just the annoying little boy who threw goldfish at my friends and me during lunch. But now he was the boy who would save me a seat at breakfast and write messages on my hand. The one with the cute smile and jokes that would make me giddy with laughter. And now I was dancing with him, the wonder boy. I had never been more content in my entire life. The song's last notes faded out and we just stood, locked in our embrace. Neither of us wanted to move; the moment was too perfect. However, we were soon interrupted by the loud drumbeat of a Blink-182 song.

We jumped apart, startled.

"Whoa," he said, shyly smiling. "That scared me." I smiled back at him and nodded in agreement. We were soon joined by a group of our friends and began jumping around to the muffled words of "All the Small Things."

It was now 9:30 P.M., time for us to crawl into our sleeping bags and whisper under the pillows. I was walking back to my cabin, grinning from ear to ear in the dark. Unexpectedly, someone jumped onto my back, causing me to stumble. I looked up to see who had attacked me and it turned out to be my friends Beth and Kari.

"So... Molly!" Beth said to me, with a smirk on her face.

"Y... yes?" I stammered, turning red.

"You and Brian, eh?" teased Kari.

All I could do was smile and laugh, but that was enough to send my friends into squealing fits of, "Oh my GOD!" and, "I knew it!" Satisfied that they had pulled the latest gossip out of me, they pranced off to tell the rest of my cabin. I didn't really care. They were all my best friends, and they would have found out sooner or later.

The next morning was concert day. We all had rehearsal in between packing our suitcases. I walked to the piano room for my ten o'clock run-through. I rushed through my piece and didn't bother to stick around for my feedback. Instead, I left the amphitheater where the orchestra was rehearsing and joined a group of my friends who were exchanging phone numbers and e-mail addresses.

"Molly! You're here!" said one of them.

"Yeah, I tried to get out of rehearsal as soon as possible," I replied as I grabbed a handful of pretzels from a bowl on the bench.

We started talking about nothing in particular, laughing and joking about anything and everything. Suddenly, Elise shouted "Hey Molly! Look who it is!" and pointed to my right. Snapping my head around, I saw Brian strolling up the hill to the amphitheater. I blushed and waved and quickly turned back to the conversation. He joined us and I could feel the rickety bench we were sitting on sink lower with his weight. Everyone's eyes were on me. I fidgeted with my bracelets while the silence grew.

"What's going on?" he asked, with a sincerely confused look on his face. Out of fear that one of my friends would embarrass me in front of him, I jumped up, mumbled something about forgetting to pack my sweatshirt and ran off in the direction of my cabin. Even though nothing extremely unordinary had happened, I couldn't help feeling embarrassed. I walked down to the beach instead of to my cabin and sat down on the sand. I felt like being alone for a while.

I wiped my tears on my sleeve while hugging all my friends. I couldn't believe it was time to go home already! Our time together had gone by so fast. I would have to wait a whole year before I would see these people again, I reminded myself as I heaved my overflowing duffel bag into the trunk of the car. All around me, cameras flashed, pens were scribbling digits, and people sobbed into each other's shoulders. Saying goodbye is always hard. But I was ready to go. I had seen everyone I needed to, until I heard my name being yelled from across the way.

"Molly!"

I turned around to see who had called my name. My heart skipped a beat. It was exactly who I hoped it would be.

"Are you about to leave?" Brian asked.

I nodded. I was afraid to speak; afraid of what would come out of my mouth.

"So, I'll see you at school then…" he said.

"Yeah, definitely!" I said, a little too enthusiastically.

"High school is a big place. I'll be sure to keep an eye out for you, though," I added.

"Okay, me too," he said, with a slight smile.

I stepped in to give him a hug, one (I thought) he eagerly accepted. For a few seconds I felt the peaceful bliss that had made me so content the night before. The head on the shoulder, the hands on my back... it was completely comfortable. But it ended in hardly enough time for me to even begin to enjoy it.

"So I'll see you later, then," he said, and turned to leave.

"Yeah, later," I whispered. "Umm, Brian?" He stopped and turned his attention back to me. "If you want to... you know... umm, like...

get together... or something... before school starts... just give me a call... I'll be around...." I stammered, my nerves trembling with anticipation.

He just looked at me standing in front of him, bright red and chewing my lips to death. Then he smiled, put his hand on my shoulder and said, "I'll keep that in mind."

After that, he turned and walked toward the parking lot. I watched his back get smaller and smaller until he disappeared behind a clump of trees. It was only then that I realized I was holding my breath.

~Molly Gaebler
Chicken Soup for the Teenage Soul on Love & Friendship

The 10:15 Vixen

To tell you the truth, I've had my share of girlfriends. I know how to pick them, too. Every girl I've ever been with is nothing short of a genius, and good looking to boot. And I'd imagine there are quite a few more girls out there who will eventually have the misfortune of thinking I'm the kind of guy they want to spend their time with. But as of right now, any kind of relationship that requires any schedule whatsoever—including calls every night, dates every weekend and/or the occasional use of the phrase "I love you"—is completely out of the question. Words cannot explain how sick and tired I am of regularity. It's predictable. It's boring. It's something that I really don't want to deal with right now.

But I'll let you in on a little secret. There's this girl at my school I see immediately after third period who simply drives me up the wall. Every day, at about 10:15—you can practically set your watch by it—this girl comes striding down the hallway wearing an outfit that would make an old man double over with excitement. And it's not just her outfit. Her hair is amazing. She has enough hair to give Rapunzel a run for her money. I've got a thing for girls with a ton of hair. And if I didn't before, she made me have one. I'm not even going to talk about the days when she wears pigtails and go-go boots.

I don't even know this girl's name. I don't know what grade she's in. I have no idea what her interests are, or if she plays any sports, or if she has a boyfriend who wouldn't even think twice before breaking my neck if he knew how much I studied his girl. I don't know if she's the worst person to ever grace this Earth, or if she's the much sexier form of Mother Teresa. The only thing I know about this girl is that her smile almost makes it worth rolling out of bed at five in the morning, and when I miss our daily 10:15 "date"—a quick glance and an attempted suave walk from me—my day is considerably worse. The funny thing is, I doubt she even acknowledges my existence.

Not that I do much to change that fact. I have to pretend I don't notice her either, because that's the cool thing to do. And I've discovered that it's much more difficult to be cool when you're actually trying to be cool. The other day I glanced over at her for two seconds and I ran straight into the back of an assistant principal who informed me, in not exactly the softest voice possible, that I need to watch where I'm going and get my head out of the clouds. I'm pretty sure she heard him. I'm also pretty sure the color of my face matched perfectly with the red tie worn by the man I collided with.

I know I could find out more about her. Word travels fast in high school, with rumors flying up and down the hallways like crazy. Surely a lot of people other than me find that girl intriguing. But honestly, I don't want to know. I don't want to know anything about that girl because I'm afraid it might ruin our "relationship" completely. I mean, what are the odds that she's the kind of person I'd imagine her to be? What if she only dates older boys, or treats everyone like crap or is one of those girls who leads you on only to have the nerve to want to stay friends after she beats your heart in with a bat? I don't think I could handle any information like that.

I think I've fallen in and out of love with this girl quite a few times. You're probably thinking that's stupid, that fifteen-year-olds can't fall in love with anyone. And you might be right to some extent. Teenagers don't fall in love with reality. They fall in love with false hopes and dreams that usually lead to heartache and digestive problems. That's where I am right now. And I don't think I mind all that much. Because as I write this on Monday night I know that tomorrow is Tuesday, and she often wears pigtails on Tuesday. Tuesday's a good day.

~Michael Wassmer
Chicken Soup for the Teenage Soul: The Real Deal School

Lucky

To win you have to risk loss.
~Jean-Claude Killy

My crush could have been the perfect boyfriend if I'd let him. He wasn't what most people would call cute, but I didn't care. I had a gigantic crush on him. My friends called me "obsessed." I preferred the word "infatuated."

I'm not sure why I never told him. The worst he could have done was say, "Yuck." But in my opinion, that's not so bad. You see, I'm pretty darn vocal; I say it how it is. Except when it comes to boys. If there is a hot guy anywhere close to me, I completely clam up. My voice goes quiet and a bit squeaky, my hands slap together in a twisted glob, and I practically bite my lip off, not to mention I can only look at the floor.

When it came to my crush, it was the same. I was petrified. I was so worried about rejection, embarrassment and looking like an idiot, I didn't even consider a positive outcome. I couldn't see the doughnut itself, only that there was a hole.

When I heard the news that he was moving away, I was devastated. His dad, who was a doctor, had taken a job in another city. He told me that he might be coming back in the summer. But by summer, he meant July, and it was now only October. It was much too long to wait. I had to tell him. Maybe he'd try and figure out a way to stay.

Over the next few weeks, I tried to build up my nerve. I prepared to tell him that I liked him. I made up a gazillion scenarios, a billion different conversations, and a trillion ways to tell him my big secret. I played them over and over in my mind, scripting every word, every moment and action. I finally decided to tell him at the surprise goodbye party we were throwing for him. I would expose everything, including my feelings for him. Scary.

The party would have been fun if I hadn't been so nervous. I put on my happy face, trying to hide the fact that I was depressed. There were so many times when I wanted to tell him how I felt, but my brain always came up with a good excuse not to. Finally, as he was about to leave, I took a deep breath, walked up to him and said, "Peter?" I was surprised he heard me. I was so quiet, I could hardly hear myself.

"Yeah, Ambrosia?"

"Uh, um, I, I, I'm, I'm going to miss you," I stammered, hugging him with all my might.

"I'm going to miss you, too," he whispered, hugging me back. Then he turned and walked out the door with what looked like a little tear streaming down his cheek.

For the next few days, I moped around with little to say. All of my friends seemed worried.

"What's wrong?" my best friend finally asked. After making her promise not to tell anyone, I told her about Peter. She looked surprised.

"Really?" she asked.

"Yep," I said, regretfully.

"Wow! He had a crush on you, too!" she screamed.

"No way. I don't believe you," I said quietly. I was floored.

"I'm serious! He was going to tell you the day he left, but I guess he chickened out," she said. "Kinda like you."

"Yeah. Kinda like me," I replied, smiling into the sun.

A few days later the phone rang, and my dad picked it up. He said it was my "boyfriend." I figured it was one of the guys from class wanting to get the homework assignment. But I figured wrong. It was Peter. My "secret" had leaked out to one of his buddies, and he wanted to know if it was true or not. I took a deep breath. "It's true," I said. I couldn't believe it. The words were so easy to say.

"I really like you, too," he said. I wanted to store his words in my ear forever.

That's when Peter and I became a couple. And I learned that although feelings can be scary, they can also be liberating, opening up new doors to happy endings.

~Ambrosia Gilchrist
Chicken Soup for the Teenage Soul on Love & Friendship

Eternity

I lie in bed at night and pray
that you will think of me.
I cry until my eyelids close
and dream—eternity.

I wake to sunlight on my face.
For a moment I forget.
Then a cloud passes by,
and I realize, this is it.

I carry on throughout the day,
feigning joy and feeling pain.
I long to gaze upon your face,
and share a smile, an embrace.

The day is drawing to an end,
and still I think of you.
I try to relax, yet in my mind,
I wonder what to do.

So now I lay me down to sleep,
I pray the Lord my soul will keep.
And should you chance to think of me,
know that I love you — eternally.

~Deiah Haddock
Chicken Soup for the Teenage Soul IV

Just One Look, That's All It Took

Pleasure is very seldom found where it is sought. Our brightest blazes are commonly kindled by unexpected sparks.

~Samuel Johnson

My cousin was getting married, and I was asked to be a participant in the wedding—a groomsman to be exact. Needless to say, I was pretty excited. My cousin lived in California and I lived in Washington, but since my cousin and I were very close, my family and I knew we had to be there for the wedding.

It was a gorgeous fall day in California, a perfect day for a wedding. The church was beautifully decorated and colors danced all over the room as the sun shone through the stained glass windows. I looked as fashionable as ever in my black tux and emerald green vest. The bride was stunning. I never saw two people more happy just to be in each other's presence than I did that day standing at the altar. You could see in their eyes that this was true love. They had each found their other half.

I couldn't help but think about my relationship at home. As much as I wanted to deny it, it was falling apart. She was my first serious girlfriend. I loved her a lot, but when you start to forget the reasons why you got together in the first place and when the negatives start outnumbering the positives, it's time to say goodbye. I wasn't excited to go back home, to say the least, but my family had other obligations so we had to leave the following day.

Our plane left Los Angeles at 4:00 P.M. the next day. We had a two hour layover in Seattle. My parents have a tradition of visiting the gift shops before flights. I decided I would stay at the boarding gate and do some homework. I started to pull out my math book when I looked up and saw HER. I couldn't believe my eyes.

She had on black sandals, black Capri pants and a yellow tank top. She was sitting in the seat across from me, reading a book on the Holocaust. Her shiny black hair hung down over her face and when she brushed it back, I got a true glimpse of her beauty. I was completely entranced before she even knew I existed. I had to say something; I couldn't let this go. How often does an opportunity like this come along? So I decided to introduce myself. I stood up and started to walk toward her. As I got closer, I realized that I wasn't ready to talk to her yet. I had no idea of what to say or how to say it, so I walked right by her and straight into the bathroom. Yes, I know, smooth. After I conquered my nervousness, I walked up to the mirror and practiced. Yes, I practiced—and all you guys out there know exactly what I'm talking about. I looked in the mirror and went through every single possible way of introducing myself to her. Hello... Hey... How's it goin'?... Haven't I seen you somewhere before? I left the bathroom and, as I walked by her again, I paused then sat back down.

Finally, a breakthrough. It just so happened that when I looked up at her again, she was looking back. Our eyes connected. A warm feeling covered my body. Not a sweaty warmth, but an inner warmth that was beyond comparison. It was more than just a look; we made a connection, and I didn't even know her name.

Something had to be done. I mustered up enough courage to casually look over at her luggage, which was under her chair, to see if I could read her name and where she was from.

Then, the worst possible thing that could happen in a situation like this happened. Her plane was leaving, and I had to do something. She started gathering up all her things and I started to panic. This could be something special, and I was in jeopardy of letting it slip through my fingers. Then, all of a sudden, she stopped. She pulled out a piece of paper from her planner and started to write something. She stood up, walked over to me, handed me the piece of paper and left without a word. Written on it was, "Just in case you ever get bored," followed by her address.

You know that feeling of complete and utter shock that you can't even speak? Triple it, and that was me. I had no idea of what to do next. She had walked to her gate, and I was left wide-mouthed and speechless. No way was I going to let it end there, so I stood up and ran to the gate from where she was leaving. When I got there, she had just handed in her boarding pass and was walking down the ramp. I prayed and prayed for her to turn around, just once, to see me, but all I saw was the back of her head going down the ramp to the plane. She was gone.

Back home, my relationship with my girlfriend eventually fizzled out. I got a handle on my life again and exactly one month after the encounter at the airport, I wrote her a letter hoping she would remember me. I got a letter back from her almost immediately saying not only did she remember me, but that she had hoped every day for a letter from me in her mailbox.

We are now celebrating our six month anniversary. The connection I made that afternoon at the airport was more than just a guy being attracted to a girl. It was a connection of souls, much as my cousin's was. We've had so many fun memories together, and we have plans for many more. Love found me that amazing day in September. It found my tired, doubtful self waiting at Gate C2D.

~Dan Mulhausen
Chicken Soup for the Teenage Soul on Love & Friendship

Girls Like Roses

Let us be grateful to people who make us happy,
they are the charming gardeners who make our souls blossom.
~Marcel Proust

irls like roses. Todd liked girls. Therefore, to get girls, Todd must have roses. This logic launched my thirteen-year-old son into the world of gardening.

"Dad, how much do roses cost?" Todd asked one day.

"That depends, son," his father said, lowering his newspaper. "Do you want a plant, or do you just want a rose to give to someone special—like your mom?"

"I dunno," Todd said, giving nothing away. "What do both of them cost?"

"Well, you can go to a florist and pay anywhere from two dollars on up, if that's what you want."

Todd did the math. Two dollars a rose! If you gave a girl a dozen roses, that'd be twenty-four bucks! That's a lot of money for a girl. Even for a girl named Michelle.

"But if you planted a rosebush," his dad continued, "you could get roses all season."

"How much does a rosebush cost?" Todd asked.

"They can be pretty expensive, but I'll tell you what: If you want to grow roses, I'll help with the cost and teach you how to care for them. But you'll have to do the work."

Todd thought about it. How much work was a girl worth, even

Michelle, who rode her bike by his house every day? He thought again of how she always waved and said, "Hi, Todd," and how her laughter made his throat tighten. "All right, I guess," he said, but he didn't look his dad directly in the eye.

So Todd and his dad went rose shopping. They picked out three rosebushes and his dad taught him how to plant and care for them. Todd fertilized, powdered and fussed over them. They grew and grew. One day he noticed rosebuds forming. "Hey, Dad! Come look what I've got! I've got roses starting! I'm going to have tons of roses!"

His dad laughed at his enthusiasm. "That's great, Todd. Now, you won't really have tons of roses, not the first year anyway. But if you keep taking such good care of your plants, you'll be sure to have some."

One day soon after, Michelle and her friend rode by. "Hi, Todd!" Michelle called out. "What are you doing?"

The perfect opportunity! "Oh, I'm just going to check on my roses," Todd said.

"What do you mean 'your roses'?" Michelle asked, smiling. Gee, she was pretty.

"Can we see them?" Michelle's friend asked.

"Sure, if you want to," Todd said, and they walked to the rosebushes in the backyard.

"Oh, come on!" Michelle teased. "You didn't grow these by yourself!"

"Yes, I did," Todd replied.

Michelle's friend looked at Todd with respect. She was quiet and didn't say much. She left that up to Michelle. Michelle kept teasing Todd, though.

"What are you going to do with them? I bet you're saving them for someone, aren't you? Who you going to give them to, Todd?"

Todd felt himself starting to blush. "Nobody, really. I just like to grow them. Do you want one?"

"Sure," she said, "why not? Don't you want one, too?" Michelle asked her friend.

Todd wasn't sure he liked Michelle offering her friend one of his flowers, but what could he say? He took out his pocketknife and selected a big, beautiful red rose for Michelle and a yellow rose for her friend. The friend smiled and carefully wrapped her rose in a napkin she had in her pocket. Michelle laughed. She took her rose, pointed it at Todd's nose and waved it about. "Who were you really saving them for, Todd?" she asked.

The large, special rose flopped up and down in front of Todd. Michelle was still talking, but he didn't see her. All he could see was his rose bobbing up and down one inch in front of his nose. Didn't she have any respect for his rose? Those roses were a lot of work!

Michelle's face seemed distorted to Todd. Horrid sounds were coming out of it — her laughter. His chest felt tight. A petal fell off the rose. It continued to wave up and down in front of him.

Michelle's friend spoke. "Thank you for the beautiful rose, Todd," she said. "I better hurry home now so I can put it in some water."

Michelle and her friend started to leave. Michelle was still talking and flapping her rose around. Todd looked at her friend as she gently held the wrapped rose in her hand, carefully got on her bike and turned to go.

"Hey," Todd called, "what's your name?"

~Janice Hasselius
Chicken Soup for the Gardener's Soul

A Crush

If you reveal your secrets to the wind,
you should not blame the wind for revealing them to the trees.
~Kahlil Gibran

"Aaarghhhmmmmm... Hello?"

It was about 10:00 on a beautiful July morning, and I had just been woken up from a deep slumber by the untimely ring of the telephone. Little did I know my destiny was on the other end of the line.

"Is Leigh there?" the rich tenor voice asked.

"Yeah. This is." I sat bolt upright, smacking my head on the headboard in the process. I rubbed my forehead and stared in disbelief at the receiver in my hand.

I met Josh while we worked together at the same pizza parlor. It was love at first sight for me, and the whole restaurant knew about it. Never mind that Josh was five years older than I was or that he didn't know my name (or so I thought, until this fateful phone call proved otherwise). I was 100 percent head over heels for the guy, the guy who was at this very moment on the other end of my telephone wire, calling my name....

"Leigh? Hello? Leigh?"

I regained my senses enough to answer. "Yes. I'm here. Um, hi."

"Leigh, I need to talk with you. Can I pick you up in a half hour?"

Could he? "Yeah. Sure." I responded, trying to sound casual. We hung up, and I stared at the telephone for another moment, until I realized that I had twenty-eight minutes left before the love of my life would arrive at my front door to confess his undying passion for me.

Thirty-two minutes later, I stood gazing up at Josh's figure in my doorway. This was simply too good to be true. He looked slightly uncomfortable as he stood, his tall, slim frame moving restlessly.

"Let's go," he said.

Josh led the way to his car, and we both got in. As we pulled out of my driveway, I again gazed at his beautiful face. His lips were full but firm, his nose straight and perfect, his hair sun-streaked blond (from a side job landscaping, as a little investigative research had revealed to me), and his eyes, his gorgeous, wide-set, polished mahogany eyes were... staring right back at me! I flushed in embarrassment, as I began to say something, but Josh interrupted me. He didn't bother with small talk, but got right down to business.

"I've been hearing some rumors at work," he began.

This was not the opening I had anticipated.

"What kind of rumors?" I ventured.

Josh presented me with an accusatory glance. "Oh, just that you and I are dating. That we're practically engaged. All sorts of great stuff." He gave me a pointed look. "Since I have never even talked to you until this morning, I don't know how anybody could have gotten that impression. Unless somebody," he paused dramatically, "told them."

I stared at him, shocked. I was speechless for a long minute, my mouth attempting to form denials that wouldn't make it past my throat. A vise took hold of my heart, squeezing painfully. Finally, I managed to collect myself enough to say, "I swear, I never said anything like that. I might have had a"—my throat began to close up, but I was able to continue in a humiliated whisper—"a little crush on you, and some people knew about it, but I promise, I swear to you, I never insinuated anything else. I'm sorry."

Josh looked at me. My shock at his accusation and every ounce of my humiliation were evident on my face. After a moment, he accepted my admission for the truth that it was, and he tried to change the topic to more lighthearted chit-chat, but I was too occupied trying to keep the tears from streaming down my face to be a good conversationalist.

After about five minutes, I requested that he take me to my friend Annette's house. As he pulled away, the tears overflowed down my cheeks. I turned to see Annette rushing outside. I ran toward her, sobs making my body shake, and she hugged me until I finally began to calm down. When my crying had diminished to random hiccuping sighs, my best friend took my face between her hands and said softly, with wisdom beyond her years, "If it were supposed to feel good, they wouldn't call it a crush."

~J. Leigh Turner
Chicken Soup for the Teenage Soul III

And There He Was

And there he was,
Staring into my eyes as a child stares at candy.
He was an image of perfection.
His sea blue eyes were as deep as the ocean,
And, oh, so full of mystery, like a treasure waiting to be opened.
He could win any girl's heart,
But he was awaiting my response to the question.
My stomach was churning like milk in a blender.
My heart was beating as if I had just run a marathon.
I was so excited that he had asked me,
Not just any girl, but me.
All I had to do was get the words out,
But it was hard.
His perfection stunned my thoughts,
Yet I managed to reply in a cool manner,
The words flowing off my lips as water flows through a stream.
"Sure, you can borrow my pencil."

~Joanna Long
Chicken Soup for the Teenage Soul on Love & Friendship

Teens Talk
Relationships

The Importance of Family

Other things may change us, but we start and end with family.
~Anthony Brandt

9

My Two Best Friends

Nine schools and nine cities in fifteen years.
Making friends is pretty pointless.
Foster kids easily learn how not to feel.
Then they came and expected me to be happy.
Promises given so often to my younger sister, Dani, and I.
Promises that quickly became lies.
Why should they be different?
So I didn't come willingly.
I almost had to be dragged out of the last home.
My hands touched none of my suitcases.
I would go to the new school,
But liking it was another question.
Her, I especially wanted to hate.
She wanted to cook for me, talk to me, even tuck me in...
All the things a "mother" would do.
Her warm words were quickly silenced by my cold ones.
He, the one who loved her so.
He was always quiet,
Surprisingly, never raising a hand.
Not even when Dani wet the bed purposefully
And threw the glass plate on the floor.
The breaking point—
The hand I raised and the words I said;
Even HBO would frown.

They both looked at me without speaking.
Finally, she said,
"We loved you before we ever saw you.
We had a choice, and you were it. Get it all out because we're
never letting you go.
When you get married, you still have to live here. Kids and all."
And I couldn't help but smile.
They were and continue to be a year later
Still ridiculously goofy.
But I've taught them about music and fashion,
And they, my mom and dad, my two best friends,
Have taught my sister and me about love.

~Jalesa Harper
Chicken Soup for the Teenage Soul: The Real Deal Friends

10

The Baseball Spirit

It was summer, and my parents sent me to spend time with my grandpa for my thirteenth birthday. He had been diagnosed with cancer the Christmas before. I was in this strange rebellious stage, and I decided to bring my skateboard and skates and not spend much time with him. I knew some kids down the street, and I was going to hang out with them. I was a major baseball fan (I strongly favored the Cardinals), so when I was packing, I slipped my baseball glove in my backpack too, thinking I could maybe play a little catch. I had planned everything.

Don't get me wrong, I wasn't trying to be mean or anything; I loved my grandparents, and it would be great to see my grandpa. I just wasn't planning on hanging out with him; but then, I never thought the spirit of baseball could bring two people together the way that it did that summer.

I was on the computer at my grandparent's house when Grandpa asked me if I wanted to play catch.

"Sure," I said, reluctantly.

We went outside to play catch, and at first I didn't think much of it, but with every throw, I realized that I was feeling more and more connected to him. I felt like I could have played catch with my grandpa forever. Later that night, he showed me his Mark McGwire first baseman's mitt and his Mickey Mantle bat. I thought those were the coolest things in the world.

On August 13, we went to a St. Louis Cardinals game at Busch

Stadium. While I was watching my heroes, like Fernando Vina, Albert Pujols, Jim Edmonds and Mark McGwire, my grandpa was telling me all about his childhood heroes. Through that whole game, I felt even more connected to him.

Toward the end of my time in Illinois, I found Grandpa's book about Mark McGwire's historic 1998 season. He caught me looking at it so much that he decided I could keep it, and he signed it to me:

> To: Caleb Mathewson
> From: Maynard Mathewson "MATTY"
> Remember the summer of 2001
> ~Grandpa

I didn't think much of the autograph then, but later, I treasured it more than anything.

That night I had to get ready to go home, and we decided to go outside and play catch for what turned out to be one last time. My grandpa and I laughed and talked while I did my best imitation of the top Major League pitchers, not knowing how much I would treasure this moment later in life.

I came back to Illinois the next summer with my family to see him. My grandpa was confined to his bed and barely able to walk. The cancer had spread to every bone in his body.

The very last time I saw him was the last night I was there. I was in his room watching a Cardinals game on television with him. He struggled to sit up and said, "If anything happens to me, I want you to have my Mark McGwire first baseman's mitt and my Mickey Mantle bat." It meant so much to me, I can't explain it. I could barely hold back my tears.

Two days later, his lungs filled up with fluid and on August 13, 2002, Maynard Mathewson died at 1:00 A.M., exactly one year to the day of attending that Cardinals game with me, which was still so fresh in my memory.

When I went to his funeral, on his casket there were two baseball caps. One was a Yankees cap and the other was the same

St. Louis Cardinals cap that he wore to the Cardinals game that we attended together.

Because of my grandpa and the love for the game that we shared, I know that I'll always have the baseball spirit in me. The bat, the glove and the book that he gave me are always with me to remind me that my grandpa, Maynard Mathewson, and I will forever be connected by the spirit of baseball and the summer we spent together.

~Caleb Mathewson
Chicken Soup for the Preteen Soul 2

11

Only Words

Words can make a deeper scar than silence can heal.
~Author Unknown

My father is a triathlete. That is, he has competed in several triathlons—a kind of marathon that includes running as well as swimming and bike riding. He's been doing it for years, and he really enjoys all the sports, but his favorite is bike riding. Ever since I was little, I've always loved going biking with my dad. We would leave the city behind and follow the bike trails way up into the woods of Wisconsin. We had a favorite spot where we would picnic. It was always our special time, and it kept me in great physical shape.

But as I grew older and became a teenager, I was distracted by other things to do with my time. Suddenly, it was very important to go shopping with friends or to a movie with a boy. I saw my dad every evening at home. Why did I have to devote my free Saturdays to all-day bike trips with him, too?

If my indifference hurt him, he never let on. He never asked me outright, but would always let me know when he was planning a bike trip in case I wanted to come.

I didn't, and as I approached my sixteenth birthday, I wanted to spend less and less time with my dad. Except for one thing—I didn't mind being with him when he was giving me a driving lesson.

More than anything else, I wanted that driver's license. It meant freedom. It meant no more waiting for parents to pick me up. No more carpools. It meant looking cool behind the wheel of a car as

I drove past my friends' houses. Of course, since I didn't have my own car, I would still be dependent on my parents, since they were allowing me to use theirs.

It was a Sunday morning, and I was in a terrible mood. Two of my friends had gone to the movies the night before and hadn't invited me. I was in my room thinking of ways to make them sorry when my father poked his head in. "Want to go for a ride, today, Beck? It's a beautiful day."

But I preferred to sit in my room and stew. I wasn't very polite when I said, "No! Please stop asking me!" It didn't matter that he hadn't asked me in months. Or that he was trying to cheer me up. It didn't even matter that he just wanted to be with me, as I knew he did.

"Leave me alone!" That was what I said. Leave me alone. Those were the last words I said to him before he left the house that morning.

My friends called and invited me to go to the mall with them a few hours later. I forgot to be mad at them and went. I came home to find the note propped up against the mirror on the mail table. My mother put it where I would be sure to see it.

"Dad has had an accident. Please meet us at Highland Park Hospital. Don't hurry, just drive carefully. The keys are in the drawer."

I grabbed the keys and tried hard not to speed or cry as I drove.

When I reached the hospital, I went in through the emergency room. I remembered the way because I had been there once before when I broke my arm. I thought about that incident now. I had fallen out of the apple tree in our backyard. I started to scream, but before the scream was out of my mouth, there was my dad, scooping me up, holding me and my injured arm. He held me while my mother drove us to the emergency room. And he held me as they set my arm and put a pink cast on it. I do remember the pain, but I also remember how safe I felt in my dad's strong arms. And I remember the chocolate ice cream afterward.

I saw my sister Debbie first. She told me our mom was in with our dad and that he was going up to surgery soon. She said I had to wait to see him until after the surgery. Just then, my mother came out.

She looked very old. I burst into tears without saying a word, and she put her arms around me.

My father's injuries were extensive. He had been riding on the sidewalk and, as he approached a stoplight, it had turned green. He had the right of way, but the white delivery truck making the right-hand turn didn't think so. At least, the sixteen-year-old driver didn't think so. Later, he admitted that he never saw my dad because he didn't look in his outside mirror.

The only reason my dad wasn't killed is that he ran into the van; the van did not run into him. He smashed head and face first into the side of the truck. His fiberglass helmet absorbed the blow, but he broke both shoulders and his left clavicle. The doctors put him in a horrible metal brace that attached to his body with screws. It braced his head and neck and looked horribly painful. My mom forewarned me about this apparatus before she let me see my dad because she was afraid that the sight of him would freak me out. She was right.

Still, as my mom said, it could have been much worse. My dad never lost consciousness. This proved to be a very good thing because the shaken boy who drove the truck wanted to move my dad, to help him up. Even I know you don't move someone who has been injured like that.

"Your father was able to tell the kid to leave him alone and just call 911, thank God! If he had moved Daddy, there's no telling what might have happened. A broken rib might have pierced a lung...."

My mother may have said more, but I didn't hear. I didn't hear anything except those terrible words: Leave me alone.

My dad said them to save himself from being hurt more. How much had I hurt him when I hurled those words at him earlier in the day?

I had to wait until the next afternoon to see him. When I did, he was in terrible pain. I tried to tell him how sorry I was, but I couldn't tell if he heard me.

It was several days later that he was finally able to have a conversation. I held his hand gently, afraid of hurting him.

"Daddy... I am so sorry...."

"It's okay, sweetheart. I'll be okay."

"No," I said, "I mean about what I said to you that day. You know, that morning?"

My father could no more tell a lie than he could fly. He looked at me blankly and said, "Sweetheart, I don't remember anything about that day, not before, during or after the accident. I remember kissing you goodnight the night before, though." He managed a weak smile.

I never wanted him to leave me alone. And to think it might have happened. If he had been killed, we all would have been left alone. It was too horrible to imagine. I felt incredible remorse for my thoughtless remark.

My English teacher, a very wise woman, once told me that words have immeasurable power. They can hurt or they can heal. And we all have the power to choose our words. I intend to do that very carefully from now on.

~Becky Steinberg
Chicken Soup for the Christian Teenage Soul

12

The Last Months

I was happy to be home that night, all bundled up in my fleece blanket, so soft, so warm. It was January first of the new millennium, and it was cool and breezy outside. My dad was looking at our Christmas tree, still decorated with a lifetime of memories. Dad had insisted on having the perfect tree, so we did. It was lushly green, and the smell of pine had permeated the entire house since the day it arrived. It was huge — ten feet tall and five feet wide. And now my dad was just staring at it.

Suddenly, I noticed that tears were rolling down his dark cheeks. I didn't understand this uncharacteristic show of emotion. It confused me, so I decided to leave him alone. I peered out from the kitchen to see what he was doing, but tried not to make it obvious that I was watching him. He touched each ornament and held it tightly. It looked as if he were trying to staunch the flow of dark and consuming thoughts.

That was the month I started to see my dad become weak and frail. Not knowing what was wrong, my mom took him to see the doctor. After undergoing X-rays and blood work, they returned home to anxiously await the results. Finally, the doctor called. My dad was in serious danger of having another heart attack, and he had to be checked into the hospital immediately.

I cannot remember a time when my dad was really well. He had already suffered a series of heart attacks, as well as complications from bypass surgery. This time, Dad was in the hospital for two long weeks. He was hooked up to so many IV tubes and monitors that it made it hard for him to communicate with us. Eventually, he progressed enough to be able to come home.

Every couple of days, a nurse would come to the house and help my dad with his rehabilitation. One day, as we waited for her to arrive, I noticed something unusual. My dad wasn't breathing. My mom ran over to him and shook him.

"What? What's wrong?" he asked.

"You weren't breathing," I told him.

He answered with a simple, "Oh," then fell back into an uneasy sleep. A few minutes later, I looked over at him.

"Mom…" I gasped and pointed at him. She woke him up again.

"Why don't we keep you up until the nurse gets here?" she asked him, her voice cracking. He slightly nodded his gray head in agreement. I didn't know what to say, so I didn't say a word.

The nurse finally arrived. She looked him over and said, "We have to get you to the emergency room."

My father frowned. He reminded me of a child not wanting to do what he is told. With a forlorn look on his face, he asked, "Do I have to?" The nurse nodded.

There were so many things to say, but no one was sure how to say them. When my dad was about to leave, I gave him a lingering hug and held him tight. I didn't want to let him go. As he got into the car, I told him I loved him.

He turned and smiled at me and nodded in acknowledgment. I watched as they pulled out of the driveway and down the street. I watched until the car vanished behind a big tree that stood on the side of the road. That was the last time I saw my dad.

Things have changed in my life over the past eight months. There is not as much laughter, and there are times I feel angry and depressed. Going places is not as enjoyable without my dad. When I see a family with their father, I feel envious. Sometimes when I come home, I forget that he is gone and go into his room to talk to him. I always feel empty when I realize he's not there.

My river of tears for him still floods every so often. I k

river will go on forever and never dry out, just as my love and memories of my dad will never dry up either. They will last forever, just like his spirit.

My time has come,
And so I'm gone.
To a better place,
Far beyond.
I love you all
As you can see.
But it's better now,
Because I'm free...

~Traci Kornhauser
Chicken Soup for the Teenage Soul on Tough Stuff

The Sisters I Never Had

Best friends are the siblings God forgot to give us.
~Anonymous

When I was in junior high school, the singer Sinead O'Connor released an album called *I Do Not Want What I Haven't Got.* If that's true, she's the only person who doesn't. Everyone longs for what they lack. The overweight imagine how perfect their lives would be if they could just lose whatever number of pounds. The bone-thin fantasize about how they would look if they could only grow breasts. The short want to be tall. The tall want to shrink out of sight. The single want a mate. The attached want independence. And, of course, all only children want a sibling.

Except me.

The only child of two wonderfully supportive, happily married parents, I drank in the attention. I got all the hugs and all the kisses. At holidays and birthdays, every dime went to my presents. When I needed my father's help with math, I didn't have to wait in line behind a crew of other perplexed kids.

I was first. I was only. And, being a fairly bright girl, I knew a good thing when I saw it. Why would I want some other kid to screw it up?

All my girlfriends with sisters were always complaining about some misdeed their sib had done — ignoring them, tagging along too much, borrowing clothes without asking, etc., etc.

Who needs it? I thought. I never want to have a sister.

Or so I thought. Ever the spoiled only child, I went to a private high school, an all-girls school. I know it makes a lot of people cringe, but to me, it was paradise. I had been an outcast in junior high, but here I found several girls to whom I related in ways I never thought possible. They didn't roll their eyes when I said something stupid. They forgave me when I lost my temper. They didn't think I was a loser because I liked school too much. They were more than friends. They were family. I truly felt they were the sisters I never had. And the school encouraged this view.

Every freshman was matched with a senior who would be her "big sister." Your big sister's friends, if they liked you, called themselves your "surrogate" big sister. Their little sisters then became your sisters by connection. Before I knew it, I went from being an only child to the member of a huge family, adopting sisters left and right.

Around that time, my friend Marjke (my friend since age five, and still my best), with whom I had been feuding for a few years, became my buddy again. She has a sister and two brothers and, as will happen, wasn't really thrilled with them all the time. She would tell me all her problems with school, her family and anything else that was bothering her. Then she would turn to me and say, "You're like the big sister I never had." Every time she said it, I was flattered. I loved the idea of being so close to someone that they considered you family. I still love it. Marjke is still like my sister. And her sister, Gretchen, also is like my sister. And my friends from high school that I keep in touch with are like my sisters.

After all those years of childhood, denying I wanted siblings, I went out and selected my own. And no, I don't always get along with them. We fight. We lose touch from time to time. We disappoint each other.

But always, at some core level, we share a connection with each other. We know how to make each other laugh, how to comfort each other in times of sadness. We know how to be there for each other. That is, after all, what sisterhood is all about.

~Amanda Cuda
Chicken Soup for the Teenage Soul on Love & Friendship

14

Dear Diary,

*D*rip. Drip. Drip. For three hours I've waited in this train station and for three hours I've heard the faint splash of waterfall from an old water fountain onto the cold, hardwood floor. The wood is old and worn but somehow doesn't allow any of the water drops to seep through. Funny, how something... Suddenly a horn whistles from a departing train, interrupting my thoughts and allowing them to come crashing back to reality.

I glance at my watch and realize I've missed my train, and the next one isn't going to leave this town for the next four hours. What am I going to do now? It's a quarter past midnight, and I'm cold and hungry. I have a meeting with the admissions officer in a college at 8:00 A.M., and by the look of things, I'm not going to make it on time. What a way to make a first impression, huh?

I begin to feel the tears burn the back of my eyes, and soon they are dancing upon my cheek. I am here alone. There isn't a familiar face around to comfort me. My mother was supposed to be here with me, to say one final goodbye before I enter adulthood. But with the many fights and broken promises we've shared, I didn't expect her to want to come here with me. Maybe I shouldn't have left the house this evening without saying I'm sorry. Sorry for the many disagreements and disappointments. Sorry for my hurtful words and actions. But we've passed the point where "sorry" heals things and makes them better again. Still, what I wouldn't give to have her here with me. Maybe she's right. Maybe I'm not the know-it-all mature adult I think I am. Maybe I am still just a scared kid who needs the protection of a mother's love.

It's almost 4:00 now, and the morning sun should be rising soon. I am able to grab a cup of coffee and change my clothes during the wait. I figure if I catch a 7:00 bus in Boston I can still make my appointment....

Until next time,

Me

Putting away my journal I reach into my bag to get out my ticket, but instead a plain white envelope emerges in my hand. I don't need to read the name on the front to know who it's from. She wants us to have a better relationship and put the past behind us. Have a fresh start. My mother even admitted she was sorry for all the arguments we've had over the course of the years. The note also said she would be waiting for me at the train station in Boston and we would walk into college together. Enclosed was an upgraded ticket and a "P.S." telling me to look in the bottom of my bag. There I would find money for a bite to eat and a sweater in case I got cold in the station. As I make my way to the train I pass the broken water fountain, which no longer drips, and I realize, for the first time in this life, I'm about to see a woman for who she truly is. My mother.

~Liz Correale
Chicken Soup for the Teenage Soul III

15

Sunshine

Having a sister is like having a best friend you can't get rid of.
You know whatever you do, they'll still be there.
~Amy Li

The silence was almost unbearably uncomfortable. I was too nervous to speak, and I think everyone else was, too. The car ride seemed endless. Once in a while, we would look at each other and force a smile, but our smiles were more nervous than warm.

I don't know what she was thinking about, but I know that memories flooded my mind. I was remembering my first day of school, when I felt like there was a spotlight shining on me and someone had written "new" on my forehead. She simply looked at me, took my hand and said, "Come on. I'll help you find your homeroom."

Then there was the time I missed the winning foul shot in a sixth grade basketball game. The other team was up by one point, and I got fouled just as the buzzer went off. I was allowed one-and-one foul shots, but I missed the first one and the other team won the game. I was angry at myself and apologetic to my team. I felt as though I had let the whole world down. I sat on the bleachers with my head in my hands. Suddenly, I felt her hand rest on my shoulder and a flood of warmth and understanding ran through me. When I looked up, she saw how crushed I was, and tears came to her eyes. She hugged me and told me the story of when she knocked herself out with her own hockey stick during a game. Laughter quickly overcame my tears.

She was also right there when my first boyfriend broke up with me. As I hung up the phone, I could feel tears making my throat close. I felt as though someone had taken my heart away from me in a matter of minutes. She hugged me, and I clung to her as though she were the only thing I had left in the world. Somehow I knew everything would be all right.

As I came back from my daydreams, I realized that our road trip was almost at its end. Only one hour left. She started twirling her hair like she does when she gets nervous. I saw a single tear roll down her cheek. It seemed to take the rest of the car ride for it to reach her chin.

When we drove onto the enormous campus, the rainstorm that had mysteriously appeared was subsiding. We found our way to her assigned dorm, unpacked her things and were standing at the car about to say our goodbyes; I couldn't do it. I couldn't say goodbye. We stared at each other, tears streaming down our faces. One long hug and a kiss on the cheek were our farewell. I climbed into the car and strapped on my seat belt.

She sat down in the grass and watched us pull out of the driveway. I stared through the rearview mirror at my best friend whom I was leaving behind at college. I stared until the car turned the corner and buildings blocked my view of my sister who was also my best friend. I looked up into the sky, and through the leftover clouds I saw one single bright ray of sunshine. It was going to be okay.

~Sarah Wood
Chicken Soup for the Girlfriend's Soul

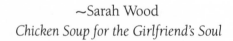

16

Don't Cry, Dad

Any man can be a father. It takes someone special to be a dad.
~Author Unknown

During my years in junior high, I developed an after school routine. Every day I walked in the back door of my home and proceeded up the three flights of stairs to my bedroom. I closed the door, turned my music up loud and lay on my bed for two hours until someone came to get me for dinner. I ate dinner in silence; I tried desperately to avoid talking to my family and even harder not to make eye contact with them. I hurriedly finished my dinner and rushed back to my room for more music. I locked myself in my room until it was time for school the next day.

Once in a while, my parents would ask me if there was anything wrong. I would snap at them, saying that I was just fine and to stop asking so many questions. The truth was, I couldn't answer them because I didn't know what was wrong. Looking back, I was very unhappy. I cried for no reason, and little things made me explode. I didn't eat well, either. It wasn't "cool" at that time to be seen actually eating lunch during school. I wasn't much of a breakfast eater, and if I weren't required to eat dinner with my family every night, I probably wouldn't have eaten at all.

The summer before my freshman year, my dad told me that he wanted to talk. I was not thrilled. In fact, I resented him. I did not want to talk to anyone, especially my dad.

We sat down, and he started the conversation by asking the usual questions: "Are you okay? Is everything all right?" I didn't answer; I refused to make eye contact.

"Every day I come home from work, and you're locked in your room, cut off from the rest of us." He paused a moment, his voice was a little shaky as he began again. "I feel like you're shutting me out of your life." Having said that, my father, a man who I thought was stronger than steel, began to cry. And I don't mean just a few tears rolling down his cheeks. Months of hidden pain flooded from his eyes. I felt like I had been slapped. Never in my fourteen years had I seen my dad cry. Through his tears he went on to tell me that he wanted to be a part of my life and how he ached to be my friend. I loved my dad more than anything in the world, and it killed me to think I had hurt him so deeply. His eyes shifted towards me. They looked tired and full of pain—pain that I had never seen, or maybe that I had ignored. I felt a lump forming in my throat as he continued to cry. Slowly, that lump turned to tears, and they started pouring from my eyes.

"Don't cry, Dad," I said, putting my hand on his shoulder.

"I hope I didn't embarrass you with my tears," he replied.

"Of course not."

We cried together a little more before he left. In the days that followed, I had a hard time breaking the pattern I had become so accustomed to over the last two years. I tried sitting in the living room with my parents while they drank their coffee. I felt lost in their world, while I was desperately trying to adjust to new habits. Still, I made an effort. It took almost another full year before I felt completely comfortable around my family again and included them in my personal life.

Now I'm a sophomore in high school, and almost every day when I come home from school, I sit down and tell my dad about my day while we have our coffee. We talk about my life, and he offers advice sometimes, but mostly, he just listens.

Looking back, I am so glad my father and I had that talk. Not only have I gained a better relationship with my father, I've gained a friend.

~Laura Loken
Chicken Soup for the Teenage Soul III

The Red Chevy

When you teach your son, you teach your son's son.
~The Talmud

My father loved cars. He tuned them up, rubbed them down, and knew every sound and smell and idiosyncrasy of every car he owned. He was also very picky about who drove his cars. So when I got my driver's license at sixteen, I was a little worried about the responsibility of leaving home in one of his beloved vehicles. He had a beautiful red Chevy pickup, a big white Suburban and a Mustang Convertible with a hot V8 engine. Every one of them was in prime condition. He also had a short temper and very little patience with carelessness, especially if his kids happened to be the careless ones.

One afternoon, he sent me to town in the Chevy truck with the assignment of bringing back a list of things he needed for some odd jobs around the house. It hadn't been long since I'd gotten my license, so it was still a novelty to be seen driving around, and Dad's red pickup was a good truck to be seen in. I carefully maneuvered my way toward downtown, watching carefully at each light, trying to drive as defensively as he'd always told me to do. The thought of a collision in one of Dad's cars was enough to make me the safest driver in town. I didn't even want to think about it.

I was heading through a green light and was in the middle of a main downtown intersection when an elderly man, who somehow hadn't seen the red light, plowed into the passenger side of the Chevy.

I slammed on the brakes, hit a slick spot in the road and spun into a curb; the pickup rolled over onto its side.

I was dazed at first, and my face was bleeding from a couple of glass cuts, but the seat belt had kept me from serious injury. I was vaguely concerned about the danger of fire, but the engine had died, and before long, I heard the sound of sirens. I had just begun to wonder how much longer I'd be trapped inside when a couple of firemen helped me get out, and soon I was sitting on the curb, my aching head in my hands, my face and shirt dripping with blood.

That's when I got a good look at Dad's red pickup. It was scraped and dented and crushed, and I was surprised that I had walked away from it in one piece. And by then I was sort of wishing I hadn't, because it suddenly dawned on me that I would soon have to face Dad with some very bad news about one of his pride and joy cars.

We lived in a small town, and several people who saw the accident knew me. Someone must have called Dad right away, because it wasn't long after I was rescued from the wreck that he came running up to me. I closed my eyes, not wanting to see his face.

"Dad, I'm so sorry—"

"Son, are you all right?" Dad's voice didn't sound at all like I thought it would. When I looked up, he was on his knees next to me on the curb, his hands gently lifting my cut face and studying my wounds. "Are you in a lot of pain?"

"I'm okay. I'm really sorry about your truck."

"Forget the truck, Son. The truck's a piece of machinery. I'm concerned about you, not the truck. Can you get up? Can you walk? I'll drive you to the hospital unless you think you need an ambulance."

I shook my head. "I don't need an ambulance. I'm fine."

Dad carefully put his hands under my arms and lifted me to my feet.

I looked up at him uncertainly and was amazed to see that his face was a study in compassion and concern. "Can you make it?" he asked, and his voice sounded scared.

"I'm fine, Dad. Really. Why don't we just go home? I don't need to go the hospital."

We compromised and went to the family doctor, who cleaned up my wounds, bandaged me and sent me on my way. I don't recall when the truck got towed, what I did for the rest of that night, or how long I was laid up. All I know is that for the first time in my life, I understood that my father loved me. I hadn't realized it before, but Dad loved me more than his truck, more than any of his cars, more than I could have possibly imagined.

Since that day we've had our ups and downs, and I've disappointed him enough to make him mad, but one thing remains unchanging. Dad loved me then, he loves me now and he'll love me for the rest of my life.

~Bob Carlisle
Chicken Soup for the Father's Soul

A Most Precious Gift

Things turn out best for the people
who make the best out of the way things turn out.
~Art Linkletter

Divorce. The word alone sends chills down some people's backs, but not mine. It may sound unusual, but my parents' divorce was, in a way, the best thing that ever happened to our family. You see, I can hardly recollect what it was like for my parents to be married. It all seems like a very distant memory, like a story from another lifetime.

It was the New Year's Eve right after my sixth birthday when my father moved out. All I remember was being in my family room and receiving a goodbye hug from him. My brother, who was four, consoled my mom and me. My dad left us all crying miserably. I thought I was never going to see my beloved daddy again. But the following Monday night, there he was. And our weekly dinner ritual was born.

He came to pick my brother and me up for dinner every Monday and Thursday night. And every other weekend he would take us to his new apartment where we would spend the night. For some reason, I learned to love my new life. I knew that every week I couldn't make other plans on our dinner nights; it was our precious time to spend with our dad. I learned how to pack a bag for the weekend trips to the apartment, trying hard not to miss a thing. Over the years our dinner ritual had to work around dance, basketball, tennis, art classes and golf leagues. But it always came first.

Three years after my parents got divorced, when I was nine, my mother got remarried to Marty. He's wonderful and has been making me giggle ever since with his brilliant sense of humor. Adding another man to his children's lives may have angered some fathers, but not mine. My dad took our new stepfather out and befriended him.

With our new stepfather came an older stepbrother and an enormous extended family. Three years later, my dad finally found the love of his life, and my brother and I were blessed with a not-at-all-wicked stepmother, Suzi. Suzi's son and daughter quickly became part of the family as well.

Now that my mom and Marty have been married for over nine years and my dad and Suzi for six, it has become impossible for me to even imagine my parents married to each other. Over the years, when people have been introduced to all of my parents and observe their relationships with each other, they tell me that my family is a prime example of how life should be after a divorce.

When I meet new people and they find out that my parents are divorced, they always apologize and sympathize. But to me, my parents' divorce is not something to be sorry about. A divorce in itself is sad, an ending, but the outcome in our case has been great for all of us. For our birthdays we all go out to dinner, the six of us. My parents have remained friends, and my mom and Suzi have even golfed together.

I wouldn't change anything about my life. I have eight grandparents, four parents, four siblings, too many aunts and uncles to count, and an endless amount of cousins. Love and support surround me no matter what or whose house I happen to be at. With the help of my family I have learned to cope during the hard times. But above all, I have learned that love is immeasurable and, when shared, the most precious gift of all.

~Jessica Colman
Chicken Soup for the Teenage Soul on Tough Stuff

Thanks, Mom!

When you are a mother, you are never really alone in your thoughts.
A mother always has to think twice, once for herself and once for her child.
~Sophia Loren, Women and Beauty

Dear Chicken Soup,

I want to thank you for your book *Chicken Soup for the Teenage Soul*. I have never read a book that made me cry so hard. I probably could relate to 97 percent of the stories.

I am a senior in high school. For four years I have been a member of the marching band at my school—four years of commitment to an organization of 150 kids, four teachers and 100 parents working from August to June of every school year. For four years, my mom has been there for me—never complaining, and never receiving a "Thanks, Mom." My mother is pretty much a supermom and, unfortunately, it took me some seventeen years to realize it.

"Chauffeur" is probably a more appropriate name for her. Every concert, every competition, every football game, my mom was there with a smile. She always stayed to watch—even through the football games. And when she couldn't be there, my mom would be waiting for me when the bus pulled into the school's parking lot.

The strange thing is, my mother actually enjoyed arriving at the school at 10:30 at night just for me to tell her that I was going out with my friends and that I needed twenty dollars instead of a ride home. She enjoyed selling cowbells and blankets, seat cushions and tickets—just as long as I was happy. Now that I'm a senior, I have my own car and drive myself to my football games and concerts. My mother still comes to watch me.

Recently, my band was invited to play for the fiftieth anniversary celebration of ETS (Educational Testing Service). When the bus pulled up to the flagpole in front of my high school I had the strangest feeling. Something was missing. I found myself desperately searching for my mom in the parking lot. I needed to tell her I didn't need a ride home; I was going out. I then realized my mother was at home and probably in bed. I never realized how much I took her for granted until she wasn't there.

When I got home that night, I woke her up and told her I loved her and I missed her. I told my mom that I really appreciated all the times she had driven my friends and me back and forth and around the world. I told her I was glad she embarrassed me all those times, because I knew that it just meant she loved me, too. My mom looked back at me with tears and a big smile.

Thank you for the wonderful books! They have inspired me to show my gratitude and my love to the people who matter. My mom thanks you, as well.

Sincerely,

~Rebecca Kross
Chicken Soup for the Teenage Soul Letters

Teens Talk

Relationships

The First Kiss

*To me, there is no greater act of courage than
being the one who kisses first.*
~Janeane Garofalo

First Kiss

*Kissing is a means of getting two people so close together that
they can't see anything wrong with each other.*
~René Yasenek

It's a beautiful day, the summer before I start seventh grade. For
Dee, it's the summer before eighth grade.

I'm watching TV. *Jenny Jones* is on. The guests argue about
their unfaithful husbands or wives, while their wives or husbands
deny all of the accusations of infidelity. Suddenly, Dee plops down
next to me on the couch, coming from the bathroom. She nuzzles
very close to me and rests her head on my shoulder, complaining
about how bony it is. I tell her to shut up. I feel very conscious of her
head on my shoulder, and then I feel conscious of her staring at me.
I look at her and smile.

"What's up?" I ask, confused.

"Nothing," she answers, shaking her head.

She nuzzles even closer to me, and I feel awkward. Her arm
slides in between my arm and my body, and she clings to me. A billion thoughts race through my head and then all of a sudden... nothing. I feel her staring at me, the heat of her face close to mine. I look
at her, and I see three eyes. She looks straight into my eyes, pinning
me with her gaze, locking my eyes with hers.

"Don't you wanna kiss me?" she asks sweetly.

My mouth drops open, and I quickly close it, realizing that it was
not the right look to give. I start to sweat a little. What's worse, I feel

her arms snake around my neck. I glance down for a second, sensing an awkwardness, like she doesn't know what she's doing. I look up again into her big green eyes. Her confidence suddenly blows me away, and I am intimidated. Time ceases to pass in minutes or even seconds... but in milliseconds. Actually, the only time that exists is measured by the small movements that she makes.

A smile slowly forms on her lips.

I start to blush, feeling my blood rush into my cheeks, and I feel stupid, like I don't know what I'm doing, which I don't. And in that moment I curse her for making me feel stupid; she knows what she's doing to me.

I have to do something. Her next move might be an embarrassing question, like, "Do you not know how to kiss or something?" or "Are you a prude?" or "What's wrong with you, boy?" She's too close to me. She's moving too fast for me. She's too close to my face! She's too intimidating. She's too... cute!

She stops smiling.

Oh no! What's she thinking now? I'm so stupid! I should've done something! She thinks I'm a prude! I am! So what?!?!? So I'm a prude. Give me a break! Give... me... a break!

She wets her lips.

Whoa.

Her face inches closer.

Oh, man. Only a breath away from my face now, I see her lips form a smile before she presses hers to mine.

Slow, soft and sweet. Only her arms around me keep me from flying.

After what seems like a few minutes, she stops kissing me and looks up. Her emerald eyes sparkle, and she smiles. She giggles and says that I'm cute. I stare at her. She nuzzles back against me and watches TV. I sit there, staring at her, dumbfounded... with a stupid smile pasted on my lips.

Wow.

~Ron Cheng
Chicken Soup for the Teenage Soul on Love & Friendship

Tom (my) Boy

You don't have to go looking for love when it's where you come from.
~Werner Erhard

When I was seven years old, I broke my wrist. I had gotten in a fight with Tommy Maducci over whether GI Joe was stronger than He-Man. Tommy had insisted that because I was a girl, I didn't know what I was talking about. To prove him wrong, I punched him in the nose. He came at me and pushed me off the jungle gym. My arm was in a cast and he had two black eyes and a broken nose, all in the name of GI Joe. I was one of the few girls in my neighborhood, and as a result, I was introduced to bands named after comic-book characters and anarchists. I grew up in a world of boxer shorts and baseball bats — where Tony Hawk was Hero, and Barbie was Bar-b-cued.

I wouldn't call myself a tomboy. Tomboys wore overalls and had their own treehouse club. I was somewhere in the middle. I never cared to sell lemonade on sidewalk corners or finger paint in smock and skirt. My weekends were spent catching crawdads in hair nets. On Sunday afternoons, I sneaked out of church to go play baseball with Danny and Tommy, who had forgiven me for the playground incident.

When Danny moved to the city, Tommy and I became best friends. We built skateboard mini ramps, mowed lawns together in the summers and shared slurpees and candy bars bought with our earnings.

Through elementary school, everything was cool. Tommy could care less if girls had cooties and I didn't see boys as anything but playmates. But one day we woke up and we were teenagers. Tommy stopped calling me after school and I traded my skateboarding shoes for flip-flops and bought myself a skirt. Nothing too feminine, denim cutoff. We said "hello" on the bus to and from Woodberry Middle School and partnered up in science class, but that was the extent of our relationship.

Tommy flirted with girls in class and I rolled my eyes and passed notes. It was annoying to me the way Tommy smiled at pretty girls. It made me mad because he didn't smile at me like that, not even as a friend. In the afternoons after school, while circling the cul-de-sac on my skateboard, I thought about Tommy a lot. One day I went down to the park, where we used to skateboard together, hoping that he would be there. The ramp was gone and Tommy was nowhere to be found.

The next day at school he was holding hands with Kelly Nicholson. I hated them both. The spectacle annoyed me. What made her hangout-worthy? What about me?

One day Tommy came up to my table during lunch with some of his new guy friends.

"Hey, Zoe, how's it going?"

"It's going," I said, unwrapping my turkey sandwich from the clear plastic Saran wrap.

"Jason is bringing the ramp over to Mike's house and we're all gonna skate on it after school if you want to come." Tommy nudged Mike and Mike winked at me.

"Gross," I thought. Mike was not my type at all, but skating sounded like fun and it was cool of Tommy to invite me along, so I agreed.

"Sure, I'll come along."

My friend Alice pinched me. "Mike's cute," she said.

"He's not my type," I chewed.

"No one's your type, Zoe. Good grief."

I changed the subject and finished my lunch.

When I arrived at Mike's house the boys were already there: Tommy, Mike, Jason and Tommy's brother, Scotty, who I used to push around when Tommy and I were friends. Alice came with me and Kelly Nicholson came with Tommy. They were an "item," but I knew it would never last. She wasn't Tommy's type, at least I didn't think so.

"Hey Zoe, I bet you can't do a crooked grind off that ledge."

"Yes I can," I huffed.

Mike shrugged. "Let's see it." And in the background I could see Jason shaking his head, flirting with Alice and muttering something stupid, making her laugh a little bit.

"All right boys. This is how it's done."

I wiped the sweat from my forehead and pushed off. I made my way up onto the ledge with a 180, but lost my balance and fell backwards, my skateboard launching into the air, feet twisted up and arms outstretched.

Instead of breaking my fall, I broke my wrist. I closed my eyes, trying to hold back my tears, more embarrassed than anything else.

When I opened my eyes, Tommy was next to me. His eyes were wide and he looked scared. He yelled for Mike to get his mom and the four of us drove to the hospital: Mike's mom, Mike, Tommy and me.

"It hurts, it hurts."

Tommy put his arm around me. "Be brave, Zoe. We're almost there."

I looked over at Tommy's sweaty face, hair matted to his forehead, acne around his nose and I nodded my head.

It turned out that I had broken my wrist in the same place as when I hit Tommy in second grade. The doctors put me in a cast, scolded me for skateboarding without wrist guards and sent me home. Tommy stayed with me the whole time and was the first to sign my cast.

I couldn't sleep that night and it wasn't because I was in pain. It was something else completely. Every time I tried to close my eyes, all I could see was Tommy's face and his crystal blue eyes pleading with me not to cry.

The next morning, Mom opened my bedroom door.

"You have a visitor," she said.

Tommy peered his head in the door, nodded at me and came over to give me a high five.

"Very funny," I coughed.

Tommy sat down next to me on my bed. "Because of me, now you've broken your wrist twice."

"It isn't your fault or anything. I can usually make that move without falling. Sometimes things just happen."

"Well, you know what I think?" Tommy pulled an old Barbie off my shelf, head shaved on the sides.

"That's Mohawk Barbie," I laughed.

"Oh yeah? Well I bet Mohawk Barbie is stronger than GI Joe and He-Man put together." Tommy dropped the doll on the floor and looked over at me.

"Oh you do, do you...?"

And with that, Tommy Maducci kissed me, right there with Mohawk Barbie as a witness and me in my big ugly arm cast, hair unwashed, stinky sneakers on the floor. The room started spinning, my knees got weak, and boy was I glad I broke my wrist.

"What about your girlfriend?" I asked, pulling away.

"She's not my girlfriend anymore," he said, shyly.

"Yeah, she wasn't your type anyway," I laughed.

"Nope." Tommy kissed my cheek.

That afternoon we took a walk down to the old 7-Eleven at the edge of the neighborhood. Tommy held my casted hand the whole way, and bought me a slurpee and a candy bar. Just like the old days, except everything was different now.

~Zoe Graye
Chicken Soup for the Teenage Soul IV

22

Seven Minutes in Heaven

People say you change many times in the course of your teenage years, and that your time in school will teach you lessons you will never forget. I think they were referring to classrooms and football fields, but one of my greatest learning experiences began in a parking lot. It was as I was waiting to be picked up one day that I met my first girlfriend.

Her name was Brittany. She was pretty, outgoing and two years older than I was—it seemed too good to be true that she was interested in me—but not long after we met, we became an official couple. At our age, "going out" meant that we talked on the phone every night, and saw each other at school in between classes. We never really had a lot of opportunity to see each other or get to know one another very well. But, never having been in a relationship before, I thought this was what they were like. It didn't seem like a big deal that we weren't that close, that I didn't get butterflies in my stomach when I saw her.

Not long after we got together, she called me and told me that she was going to a party with some friends, and that she wanted me to go with her. I said I would, and waited somewhat nervously that night for her to pick me up. When the small car packed with teenagers arrived, I squeezed in and wondered what I was getting myself into.

An hour into the party, I was feeling less self-conscious and a lot more comfortable. Though the people at the party were all older than me, they were people I knew or had seen around school. It all seemed innocent enough—we just sat around eating popcorn, watching a movie and having a good time—until the movie ended.

Someone suggested a game of "Spin the Bottle," and my heart began to beat a little faster. It can't be that bad, I thought to myself. It's just kissing even if it is in front of a bunch of other people. But after a while, some people wanted to take the game a little further. I heard somebody say "Seven Minutes in Heaven," and everyone answered "Yes!" with knowing smiles. I had no idea what it was, and looked at Brittany for help, but she just smiled and agreed that it was a good idea.

After the first few couples spent their seven minutes in heaven, I figured out what the object of the game was—going into a closet and kissing. My stomach flip-flopped and I felt dizzy as I waited for the inevitable, when it would be my turn with Brittany. I was scared. I had no experience with this kind of thing, and I was about to jump into it head first with a girl two years older than I was. I didn't know what she expected, or what she would tell the other older kids when we got out. I could see a sad reputation of being a lame boyfriend looming in the near future.

I really didn't have a lot of time to think about it, because our turn came, and Brittany pulled me after her into the closet. As it turned out, she was an experienced kisser—I didn't have time to think, or react, she just kind of took over. I was relieved and glad when it was over. When she took me home later, neither one of us said much. I don't know what she was thinking about, but I was still trying to let everything sink in. It wasn't as much fun as I had thought it would be—there was no romance or feeling in it.

It was never talked about, but in the weeks that followed the party, my relationship with Brittany slowly ended, and I returned to doing normal things with kids my own age. I thought it was strange that I didn't feel sad about it. It was almost a relief to not have to worry about another party or situation where I would feel out of my league.

I was at the beach with friends several months later when I started talking to a girl. As we talked, I realized I was strangely happy just listening to her and watching her smile while she told me about her life. There was something about her that made me enjoy just being with her. With no thoughts of what it meant, I knew I wanted to see her again so we planned to meet the following week, same time, same place.

I was completely comfortable as we sat on a blanket that night filling each other in on the events of the long week that preceded our reunion. We sat next to the bonfire and laughed, and suddenly, I wanted to kiss her... and I did. A pure, sweet, innocent kiss, one that made me feel warm and happy. And though it was nowhere near seven minutes, it was definitely a piece of heaven.

~Andrew Keegan as told to Kimberly Kirberger
Chicken Soup for the Teenage Soul II

23

Will He Kiss Me?

A kiss can be a comma, a question mark or an exclamation point.
That's basic spelling that every woman ought to know.
~Mistinguett (Jeanne Bourgeois), Theatre Arts, December 1955

I met Chris on a double date, only I was with his best friend. Chris of course was with his old girlfriend, Paula. As we sat at the restaurant, our eyes kept meeting. He had the most electrifying blue eyes I had ever seen. When he talked, I got lost in the sea of blue. He had the kind of eyes that could make all the girls swoon. I knew I should not stare at this boy across from me — he was not my date. His eyes were like magnets drawing me back. Every time I looked at him, I found him staring at me as well. I tried refocusing on my date but to no avail. I went home that night dreaming of those blue eyes and wondering if I ever would see them again.

A week later, Chris called. Oh, how my heart started racing. I got so excited I had to sit down. When he asked me out, the only thing I could think to ask was "What about Paula?" He responded, "What about her?" He then went on to tell me that the two of them were over. Nonchalantly, I agreed to go out. In reality, I was so ecstatic I could hardly contain myself.

Saturday: he arrived right on time. He came in, sat for a while and chatted with my mom. I couldn't take my eyes off him the entire time. I thought it was so sweet how he talked and listened to my mom, smiling and laughing with her. I was dancing on cloud nine.

Chris was a gentleman all evening. He opened my car door,

offered his arm for me as we walked and always ushered me through the door first. When he brought me home, he walked me to the house and greeted my mom. I fully expected a kiss at this time, but instead he said, "Thank you for going out with me tonight. I had a good time." Wondering what was wrong, I responded, "I had a very good time too." I thought maybe he wanted to make sure I had a good time before we kissed. But he said goodnight and left. I was bewildered. What had gone wrong? Half of me thought he didn't like me and that would be the end of it. The other half giggled at the thought of such a gentleman and was excited about the prospect of where this could go.

Monday: I was standing at my locker when Chris came up behind me and gently touched me on the arm. I was very surprised to see him since we had never seen each other at school before. The school is huge with three floors and four different wings. There are so many students that it is impossible to know or have seen even half of them. But here he was; he had sought me out. I was very excited and my heart raced as he asked me to go to a basketball game on Saturday. After he left, I was so flustered I couldn't remember what I was supposed to take from my locker. I closed it and floated down the hall. I'm sure I had a faraway look on my face, along with a silly grin.

I didn't have the right book for class, but I didn't care. All I could think about was Chris.

Saturday arrived and I was a bundle of nerves. I wanted our date to be perfect. I drove my mom crazy that day, with questions about my clothes, my hair, makeup and what I should say and how to act.

Chris was right on time to pick me up. He came in and again exchanged pleasantries with my mom. He was so polite and nice, and he genuinely had an interest in my mom and the conversation.

We arrived at the basketball game, and walking across the parking lot, Chris took my hand and held it until we reached the building. All the while my heart was racing. His hand, firm and strong, engulfed mine. I could sense his strength, but he held my hand with such caring and gentleness. He made me feel safe and protected.

When he took me home that night I was sure he would give me

a kiss. But again he just thanked me, and we departed. I couldn't believe it—again no kiss! What was wrong with me? Was I imagining something between us that wasn't there? I was very confused and frustrated. I talked to my mom, and she said, "I think he is a gentleman." I responded, "Okay, but does that mean he likes me?" She shrugged her shoulders and winked at me with a smile on her face. I was so bewildered. I had never met anyone like Chris before, and I really liked him. But I was not certain how he felt about me.

The next week I didn't see Chris until Wednesday afternoon. He found me on my way to lunch. He asked if I knew how to bowl. Sarcastically I thought, "Bowling—this guy doesn't like me in a romantic way at all."

I responded unenthusiastically, "Yes, I've been on bowling leagues before." Suddenly his face lit up. "Really!" he said with excitement. "We need another person for our team. Someone dropped out. Can you come tonight?" I shrugged one shoulder and said, "Sure," feeling disappointed that we were never going to be more than "just friends."

We went bowling that night. Our team won, and I really enjoyed being with Chris. Several times that night our eyes met and I searched for some kind of a sign that he might still like me.

When he brought me home, he walked me up to the front door. I thanked him for inviting me to join the bowling league. As I turned to go inside, he gently touched my arm. I stood there looking into his dreamy blue eyes. He cupped my face in his large gentle hands. We searched each other's eyes for what seemed like a lifetime. Then as if we could read each other's minds we embraced in a long, passionate kiss. I was intoxicated with the aroma of his leather coat. I breathed deeply to savor the moment. Oh, at last, the kiss I had dreamed about. It was better than I had imagined. I was swept away. It was worth the wait. I knew in that instance there was a bond between Chris and me that would last a lifetime.

To this day I still savor that first kiss with Chris. That was nearly twenty years ago, although it seems like yesterday. I can still smell the leather of his coat. Sometimes I even take his coat out of our closet and breathe deep into it, relishing the memory of that first kiss. As for Chris, he can't figure out why I want to keep that coat around. It hasn't fit him for years.

~Margaret E. Reed
Chicken Soup for the Romantic Soul

Never Been Kissed

Attitude is a little thing that makes a big difference.
~Winston Churchill

It was at a recent sleepover with my high school cross country team that I truly realized how bad things had gotten. I was feeling pretty mature and sophisticated as I looked around at the shy, innocent faces of the incoming freshmen. Had it really been only two years since I was one of them? It seemed like ages.

That is, until we played our annual "get to know each other" game. Here's how it works: Everyone takes a turn sharing an interesting fact about herself, and then those who have had the same experience raise their hands, so we can see what we all have in common and bond as a team. It's sort of like "Truth or Dare," except a lot less exciting because, well, there are no crazy or embarrassing dares.

Everything was fine as we went through the standard boring statements ("I have run cross country before," "I am an only child," "I have a pet goldfish named Stan"). Then some daredevil decided to spice things up by casually voicing the statement that has plagued my teenage years: "I have had my first kiss."

I watched with red-faced embarrassment as all around me arms began to go up. Only three of us kept our hands in our laps: me, a sixteen-year-old junior, and two other freshmen who looked so young that waitresses undoubtedly still offered them the twelve and under kids' menus and movie theaters still gave them the child's ticket price.

Yes, indeed, I'm part of a species that is slowly growing extinct. I'm sweet sixteen and I've never been kissed.

I never imagined it would be like this. When I was younger, I pictured high school as something straight out of television shows like *Saved by the Bell* or *Boy Meets World*. A bright, clean indoor campus where everyone wears letterman jackets, has his or her own shiny locker, and students wave pom-poms at football games. There was no doubt in my mind that by the time I was an oh-so-old, oh-so-cool teenager I would have experienced my unforgettably magical first kiss. I mean, duh, I would have a boyfriend. Every girl has a boyfriend in high school, right?

It came as a big shock when I entered my freshman year and discovered that the high school campus was littered with trash, math class was just as boring as it had been in middle school and our football team was horrible. As for having a boyfriend, well, a great majority of the guys in my classes were those I had known since elementary school. You know who I'm talking about. The ones who used to eat paste and make farting noises with their armpits. (And even though they're now in high school, most of them are still so immature it wouldn't surprise me to find they still do those things.)

As freshmen, my fellow "kissing virgin" friends and I made a pact that whoever was the first to touch lips with a boy would tell the others what it was like. You know, so we'd have a clue of what to expect. The thought of kissing was scary. What if we don't do it right? What if we were horrible? What if our braces got stuck together? Can that really even happen?

Weeks turned to months, months to years, and eventually most of my friends found that Nosepicker Nick wasn't nearly as gross as he used to be, and Dorky Dan the Stamp Collector really was a nice guy. One by one my friends jumped off the never-been-kissed diving board into the mysterious yet exciting waters of high school dating. But when I asked them about it, they suddenly became shy and didn't elaborate much besides, "It was really great."

Even my best friend backed out of our pact. When I asked her how she knew what to do when she kissed, she replied, "Oh, Dallas, it's something you just know. It's like in that movie *When Harry Met Sally*. Remember at the beginning, when they interview all those old couples, and that one lady says, 'I knew he was the one. I knew the same way you know a good melon?' It's like that. You just know."

So that, sadly, is the most helpful advice I've received on the subject: some things you just know, the same way you know a good melon.

But what if I'm not very good at choosing fruit? What if I take the time and energy to pick out a melon only to later discover it's bruised inside, or even rotten?

My mom tells me not to worry: Boys are just stupid. My dad tells me I'm too young to have a boyfriend anyway. (Funny, he wasn't too young to have a girlfriend when he was my age!)

I like to think it just hasn't been the right time yet. I mean, I'm not a total loser. I've been to a few school dances and even out on a date or two. But at the end of the night, when my date and I were standing on my front stoop under the fluorescent porch light my dad is always sure to turn on, it was actually me who initiated the hug first in order to preempt the goodnight kiss. For some reason it just didn't feel right—I really don't know why. And it turns out that the only guy I wouldn't have minded receiving my first kiss from ended up liking me just as a friend. Go figure. But that's another story altogether.

So, as for now, the closest thing I have to a boyfriend is my boxer puppy, Gar. He gives me lots of slobbery dog kisses and is actually a very good dance partner when I hold onto his two front paws. If only I could take him to the prom.

I'm trying to stop worrying so much about getting my first kiss and just let life take me where it will. In the meantime, I'm working on new facts about myself to share at next year's cross country sleepover. How many hands will raise when I ask who else has climbed Mt. Whitney? Or learned how to speak sign language? Or published a story in *Chicken Soup*? I bet not too many.

I've learned I don't need a boyfriend to make my life fun. As for my first kiss? I'll get it eventually. There are some things you just know—the same way you know a good melon.

~Dallas Nicole Woodburn
Chicken Soup for the Teenage Soul: The Real Deal School

25

Starlight, Star Bright

Why not go out on a limb? Isn't that where the fruit is?
~Frank Scully

When I was five years old, I took an extreme liking to my sister's toys. It made little difference that I had a trunk overflowing with dolls and toys of my own. Her "big girl" treasures were much easier to break, and much more appealing. Likewise, when I was ten and she was twelve, the earrings and makeup that she was slowly being permitted to experiment with held my attention, while my former obsession with catching bugs seemed to be a distant and fading memory.

It was a trend that continued year by year and except for a few bruises and threats of terrifying "haircuts" while I was sleeping, one that my sister handled with tolerance. My mother continually reminded her, as I entered junior high wearing her new hair clips, that it was actually a compliment to her sense of style. She told her, as I started my first day of high school wearing her clothes, that one day she would laugh and remind me of how she was always the cooler of the two of us.

I had always thought that my sister had good taste, but never more than when she started bringing home guys. I had a constant parade of sixteen-year-old boys going through my house, stuffing themselves with food in the kitchen, or playing basketball on the driveway.

I had recently become very aware that boys, in fact, weren't as "icky" as I had previously thought, and that maybe their cooties weren't such a terrible thing to catch after all. But the freshman guys who were my age, whom I had spent months giggling over at football games with my friends, suddenly seemed so young. They couldn't drive and they didn't wear varsity jackets. My sister's friends were tall, they were funny, and even though my sister was persistent in getting rid of me quickly, they were always nice to me as she pushed me out the door.

Every once in a while I would luck out, and they would stop by when she wasn't home. One in particular would have long conversations with me before leaving to do whatever sixteen-year-old boys did (it was still a mystery to me). He talked to me as he talked to everyone else, not like a kid, not like his friend's little sister... and he always hugged me goodbye before he left.

It wasn't surprising that before long I was positively giddy about him. My friends told me I had no chance with a junior. My sister looked concerned for my potentially broken heart. But you can't help who it is that you fall in love with, whether they are older or younger, taller or shorter, completely opposite or just like you. Emotion ran me over like a Mack Truck when I was with him, and I knew that it was too late to try to be sensible — I was in love.

It did not mean I didn't realize the possibility of being rejected. I knew that I was taking a big chance with my feelings and pride. If I didn't give him my heart there was no possibility that he would break it... but there was also no chance that he might not.

One night before he left, we sat on my front porch talking and looking for stars as they became visible. He looked at me quite seriously and asked me if I believed in wishing on stars. Surprised, but just as serious, I told him I had never tried.

"Well, then it's time you start," he said, and pointed to the sky. "Pick one out and wish for whatever you want the most." I looked and picked out the brightest star I could find. I squeezed my eyes shut and with what felt like an entire colony of butterflies in my stomach, I wished for courage. I opened my eyes and saw him smiling as he watched my tremendous wishing effort. He asked what I had wished for, and when I replied, he looked puzzled. "Courage? For what?" he questioned.

I took one last deep breath and replied, "To do this." And I kissed him—all driver's-license-holding, varsity jacket-wearing, sixteen years of him. It was bravery I didn't know I had, strength I owed completely to my heart, which gave up on my mind and took over.

When I pulled back, I saw the astonished look in his face, a look that turned into a smile and then laughter. After searching for something to say for what seemed to me like hours, he took my hand and said, "Well, I guess we're lucky tonight. Both our wishes came true."

~Kelly Garnett
Chicken Soup for the Teenage Soul II

26

Impossible Things Can Happen

Some guys in high school are "all that." They have everything going for them; they hang out with all the right people; they have all the good looks; they are so popular they have half the girl population in the school drooling over them; and they are totally unreachable. In so many words, that is how I would categorize Eddie. He had a great body, he was cool and I loved everything about him. I loved the way he made me feel every time he walked by. Most of all, I loved his bright brown eyes. He was perfect. I had a huge crush on him the moment I saw him but, of course, that was all he would be to me. A crush. I had always been this regular girl who just hung out with my friends during lunch, pretending not to care about anything but secretly glancing in his direction every now and then. He had always been the guy everybody knew and respected. Compared to him, I felt like I was insignificant.

My best friend, Angela, knew everything about my secret crush on him, and she would never fail to remind me that we were not meant to be. In fact, she would remind me, if people knew that I had a crush on him they would probably laugh their brains out. It was like I was this commoner with a huge crush on my king.

Although we were never formally introduced, somehow our paths crossed. He talked to me one day when we were both late for school. He said hi and asked me why I was late. Naturally, I pretended to be unaffected and answered him right back. After that, I headed to my class. I was happy. He had recognized me as a living, breathing object that went to the same school. If I were a gymnast, I would have done several back flips just to release this flying feeling in my chest. I mean, I already felt shivers up my spine every time I saw him. So when he spoke to me it felt like someone had just poured a glass of cold water on my head.

After that incident, we casually chatted when we would see each other during lunch. Nothing personal, just some small talk that would last for a minute or two. Although we were talking and all, I could never imagine myself being his girlfriend. Pigs would fly before anything like that would ever happen to me.

One day, Angela's cousin from abroad came to visit her. She would be staying with Angela for a week. Her name was Tasha. We were introduced, and I liked her immediately. She was nice, funny, totally cool and a model back home. She had beautiful blue eyes and, well, I just had eyes. There was nothing to hate about her. Angela and I both loved hanging out with her so much that I finally suggested that she join us in school one time. Unknowingly, I initiated my own suffering.

When we went to school with her the next day, everybody was looking. She had those foreign looks and, well, she was a model. Everything was fine until she saw Eddie. Guess what? She decided that she had a crush on him, too. Worse, she wanted to date him. She asked me to introduce them. I felt I had no other choice. I introduced them and told Eddie that she wanted to go out with him. To my disgust, he willingly agreed. I could have strangled myself.

So they went out, and I found out the next day that they had kissed. I can still feel the stabbing feeling in my chest when I found out. I couldn't believe that "my guy" was with this girl who liked him for just a second when I had been dreaming of him forever. It was unfair that she got to kiss him, and I didn't even get to tell him how I felt. I was too hurt to cry.

The day Tasha was leaving to go back home, Angela decided to stay at home and spend some time with her. I went to school. At the end of the day, Eddie approached me and asked if I could take him over to see Tasha before she left. After some persuasion, I finally gave in. But he would not be delivered to my rival without a cost. I got in his car and gave him directions to Angela's house, making sure he took the longest way possible to get there. When we were nearing the house I pretended to be lost, and I led him around in circles until he almost ran out of gas.

After talking and hugging and saying goodbye to Tasha (although I liked her a lot, I was secretly glad to see her go), it was time for us to leave. Eddie offered to take me home, and this time I gave him better directions. What a lame way to get even.

After Tasha left, Eddie and I were closer. We would go out sometimes and share more than just small talk. He would even join us for lunch sometimes. I now know why he was so popular. He was incredibly nice and absolutely fun to be with. I found myself falling for him more and more each day. Several times I wanted to let him know that I, too, wanted to date him. Maybe I would get a kiss, too.

One day he asked Angela and me to go to the mall. Angela never showed up so Eddie and I hung out by ourselves. I was overwhelmed. Deep inside I was thanking Angela for not making it. It was almost like a date, only he didn't know it. He asked me if I wanted to see a movie. I said yes. My heart was pounding. I swear he could hear it as we sat beside each other. I couldn't help but think of what it would be like if he knew that I liked him. I felt so strongly about him, and something inside me felt like he had to know. Since words are always so awkward for me, I decided that I wouldn't tell him; I would just kiss him. I gathered up all my strength and took a deep breath.

I leaned on him a little, and he didn't seem to mind. I slowly faced him to plant my trembling lips on his cheek. When I looked at him, I was surprised that he was looking at me, too. I was so nervous, I could have choked on my own tongue. Then suddenly, he kissed me. I must have looked really stupid because I had my eyes open the entire time. I was in heaven.

I found out later that Eddie had liked me even before he met Tasha. He admitted to me that he never had the courage to let me know because he never thought I would like him, especially after I had introduced him to Tasha. Eddie and I have been together for almost four years now, and everything is still like brand new. Not bad for two people who thought they would never be together. Surely, impossible things do happen.

~Pegah Vaghaye
Chicken Soup for the Teenage Soul on Love & Friendship

27

Guy Repellent

No one remains quite what he was when he recognizes himself.
~Thomas Mann

Dear *Chicken Soup for the Teenage Soul*,

I have always enjoyed the *Chicken Soup for the Teenage Soul* books, however I haven't really been able to relate to any of the stories in the "Relationships" chapter. You see, I have never been in a relationship before so I am not able to feel the emotions of the authors. The stories are either about people in relationships or having just come out of one. There don't seem to be any stories addressing the insecurities and sad feelings people have who have never been in a relationship and feel weird because of it.

I have always believed that I was born with a coating of guy repellent. Like bug repellent, it drives away guys instead of bugs. To me, relationships have always required time, patience and the big "L" word, love. The idea of being in a relationship has always made me sort of squeamish and reluctant. Kissing scenes on TV would bring me to close my eyes. Couples on the street, in the malls or any other public place showing affection towards each other annoyed me. Couldn't they do it elsewhere? Some people told me that I was going through a phase and things would soon change. They were sort of right. I developed my first crush, and secretly spent time thinking about that person. I had begun to accept the fact that people falling in love is part of our everyday lives.

When I began high school it suddenly hit me that everyone had grown up while I was still a child. Everyone seemed like they were experts on dating, since many had practically started at age four. They knew everything and could give advice as if they were trained professionals. I, on the other hand, had never gone out with a single person, nor had anyone shown the slightest bit of interest in me. Even though I wasn't interested in anyone either, it made me feel bad, and the more I thought about it, the worse I felt. Was I ugly? What was wrong with me?

I knew that I wasn't the most attractive person or the most popular, but I certainly wasn't ugly. I would observe girls who had dated an endless string of guys and wonder what it was about them that made the guys go crazy. Some of them were very ordinary, and not even pretty. Others acted like ditzes.

One day while talking to a girl in my music class, the topic of relationships came up. I mentioned to her how I always managed to end up empty-handed in the dating pool. I remember her saying, "There's nothing wrong with that. Besides, the only two boyfriends I have ever had, I had to ask out." Her response startled me. She was one of those girls who seemed to attract tons of guys. She was gorgeous, with thick hair, beautiful brown eyes with green flecks, and a great personality to match. I started feeling better about my relationship predicament. I realized there was really nothing wrong with me if even people like her had to work to make relationships happen.

Since that day, I've finally discovered that I have to accept myself for who I am, both my strengths and my weaknesses. I have a tendency to look serious most of the time, which makes me appear unfriendly and cold, even though that is not what I am. Yes, I focus on school and hang out in the library, but I've learned never to sacrifice the things that I believe in just to impress a guy. After all, you can only pretend for so long. Whoever I end up with will have to like me for who I am, the nice girl who, according to her classmates, is destined to become a future nun. I feel that's the way a relationship should be. Until I meet that special person, I will be busy enjoying who I am and all the things I love doing. Who knows, maybe I will become a nun.

My future is not really clear to me now. I'll just have to wait and see. Guy repellent or not, I'm going to be just fine.

Thanks,

~Erin Seto
Chicken Soup for the Teenage Soul Letters

Chapter
4

Teens Talk

Relationships

Friendships that Go the Distance

True friends are the ones who never leave your heart,
even if they leave your life for awhile.
~Author Unknown

28

The Gift of Friendship

The music blares, and Ashlee Simpson can be heard faintly over my four girlfriends and me singing along. The windows are all rolled down, sweeping that summer smell through the car and sending our slightly out of tune but proud voices onto the streets. We are five seniors-to-be, packed into my small Honda Civic, driving the winding river road for the last time this summer. We are going to our paradise—the lake. Each curve sends our bare, browned knees bumping together as we sit cramped but completely comfortable. I stop singing for a moment and look at the girls around me. Not noticing that I have stopped singing, each of them continues on without a thought, but my brain starts buzzing, and I have an epiphany. As I think about each of the girls, I realize how lucky I am to be blessed with the great gift of friendship. It is so often overlooked, but at moments like this, you catch a glimpse of the importance friendship truly holds.

I know these girls, and they know me. I remember all we have been through together, all the joy and, yes, at times, the pain. Each memory is tucked safely somewhere in my brain, but, more important, deep in my heart. Like the time the girls and I stayed up all night reading on the roof to finish a book that was due the next day. As the sun came up around the neighborhood, each of us put our books down and took a moment to watch the breathtaking sunrise. Or the day when a friend of thirteen years had to move away. We all cried together, but we knew that the move wouldn't change a thing between us. Now, five years later, she is singing along with us as if we never had missed a day.

It is at times like this that I can't help but wonder what I would be like without the influence of these girls. Would I be who and where I am today if I didn't have those girls to lean on, to learn from or to trust through my life? I can't imagine what it is like for those who walk throughout life without the love and companionship of close friendships.

Now, every time I pass that winding river road, I catch myself reminiscing about all the good times I have shared with my friends. I love that I have those friendships to think about, to warm my heart and to put a smile on my face. And I love that I will always have the gift of friendship to cherish.

~Jennifer Traylor
Chicken Soup for the Teenage Soul: The Real Deal Friends

29

Saying Goodbye

How lucky I am to have something that makes saying goodbye so hard.
~Carol Sobieski and Thomas Meehan, Annie

Today I said goodbye to my best friend—the one person I have been able to count on for so many years. She has been my companion through low self-esteem, hard tests and bad prom dates. She's someone who could finish my sentences, who never failed to understand me, yet whom I could talk to for hours on end. My friend when friends seemed scarce and life too hard. Who'd laugh with me at jokes no one else understood. Though it took me a while to realize that a best friend is more than a title or an old habit, she was always there.

High school flew by so quickly that I hardly knew what I always had in front of me until it was getting ready to end. Our last year together was spent with late night outings to 7-Eleven and the playground or to the river. Exploring our small town convinced me that we could discover something for ourselves. The realization that her home had become another home to me, her family an extension of my own. College applications, tears of frustration and anger, AP Exams and SATs, and, hardest of all, sitting there in my cap and gown with my classmates, listening to her speech. My best friend: intelligent, president of the student council, funny, beautiful, amazing. She's someone I'm honored to lean over and whisper about to a classmate: "She's my best friend."

A friend who didn't have to ask, "Are we going out Friday night?" but instead, "So, what are we doing Friday?" Attached at the hip through disloyal people, bad dates, long nights spent studying. And now, because we are "old enough," we must head our separate ways—her on one side of the country, me on the other. Tears and discussion, excitement and fear for weeks beforehand. Last movies, dinners—the last everything. All this pain, and always putting the goodbye off until the last moment. Funny how, at the last moment, as I drove to her home this morning and hugged her for the last time for four months, the tears fell only for a few minutes. Because I've realized that it's not goodbye forever, just until again. We'll always have e-mail and phone calls, and Christmas, spring and summer breaks. When you have a once-in-a-lifetime friend, you're always together, no matter how much distance is between you. Real love stretches and bends; it does not see state lines.

Or maybe the reason the tears dried up and the sobs stopped wracking my body as I drove away from her house, seeing her wave until I was out of sight, is because I've realized how amazingly lucky I am to have someone who is so hard to say goodbye to.

~Kathryn Litzenberger
Chicken Soup for the Teenage Soul on Love & Friendship

30

The History of Izzi and Me

I met Isabel on my first day of preschool. I had arrived well-groomed and eager, although a bit nervous about being away from my mother. The first day began with a tour graciously given by one of the teachers. I took note of the festive carpets and a sandbox that looked intriguing. However, what was shown to me last was by far the most inviting—a giant trunk of dress-up clothing. As soon as I was left to my own devices, I began digging through the trunk and didn't stop until I had found the prettiest princess costume. I put on the dress and then piled everything else I could find that appealed to me on top. After a half hour and many layers, I was convinced that I looked fabulous.

With the confidence I had gained from my new attire, I worked up the courage to walk over to the pink and blue playhouse in the middle of the room. I stood on the doorstep in my beautiful sparkly dress, poised and ready to make my first real friend. I took a deep breath and knocked on the door. There was no answer, so I waited and knocked again. A few seconds later, a small blond girl in a pink jumper poked her head through the window, looking around until her eyes settled on me. I looked down at the floor, and then worked up the courage to say, "Hi, my name is Ari. Can I play with you?" She looked at me for a second, thought about it, then abruptly proclaimed "no" and slammed the shutters.

I was devastated and ended up spending most of the day crying and waiting for my mom to come get me. But ever the resilient child, I returned the next day, put on a similar outfit, knocked on the same playhouse door and once again asked to play. The answer was still "no," but I wasn't discouraged. I kept up my efforts until at last I was admitted into the game of house and learned that the girl's name was Isabel. (I was forced to play the undesirable role of father, but at least I was playing.)

Weeks passed, and I began to play with Isabel every day. I no longer even had to ask. In fact, I had soon secured a monopoly on the role of sister to her role of mother in our epic games of house. Within two months, we had proclaimed each other best friends—we were inseparable.

As soon as preschool ended, we enrolled in a day camp together near her home. After that came ballet classes, swim lessons and gymnastics. Then there were the countless sleepovers. Our mothers even organized a New Year's Eve get-together that quickly became a tradition. I began and ended every year by Isabel's side.

Middle school rolled around, Isabel became "Izzi," and she moved twenty minutes farther away from me. Luckily, Izzi was still the same old Isabel, even with the location change, and we dedicated every weekend to each other. Middle school proved to be difficult, as both of us were put under tremendous pressure, but school was quickly forgotten when I pulled into her driveway for my weekly vacation.

In eighth grade, I spent New Year's Eve standing in Izzi's backyard watching nearby fireworks and blowing a noisemaker until my face was bright red. By that time, we had spent ten years together, going from loving the Power Rangers and the Spice Girls to going to Weezer concerts together.

That New Year's led me to the year when I reluctantly started high school. I had trouble making friends for a while, but I got through it by heading over to Izzi's at every possible occasion. It was a tough year, but eventually we both managed to make groups of friends at our respective schools.

Unfortunately for me, one of Izzi's new friends was an attractive boy with whom she soon became more than friends. Izzi began hanging out with him more and more, and hanging out with me less and less. Soon I was lucky if I got to see her once a month. It got to the point where we would go weeks without talking. Then, one day she called me for the first time in almost a month with shocking news—she and her boyfriend had broken up. She was upset, and while I felt bad for her, I couldn't help but be excited to have my friend back. I rushed over to her house to comfort her and ended up staying for the weekend.

The next weekend on the way to Izzi's house, everything seemed right with the world. But when I got there, things were different. Instead of running to the door and greeting me, Izzi sat in her room and let her mom answer the door. Izzi didn't get up for a while. I expected that she would be upset about the breakup, but I never realized that it would have impacted her so strongly.

After trying to cheer her up in every way I could think of, I gave up and just asked her what was so special about this guy. She told me that it wasn't the guy that she felt so bad about. What worried her was the way she had handled the whole relationship. Izzi told me that when they started dating, she became so involved that she ignored everything else. She convinced herself that her relationship with this boy was the most important thing in the world, so when it all fell apart she felt like she had lost everything. She felt even worse when she realized that she had sacrificed her relationships with everyone else, especially me. She burst into tears and told me how sorry she was, asking if we could go back to being friends like we had been before she started dating. I told her that, of course, we could.

The next weekend, I went up to her house again. We watched some TV and read magazines, and things felt like they were before. After that, we both made other friends and started dating, but we never went back to ignoring each other like we had before.

This past New Year's Eve, I found myself at Izzi's house again, ringing in the coming year. We blew noisemakers side-by-side, knowing that no matter what happened with college or boys or any-thing else, we would be able to face it together.

~Ariana Briski
Chicken Soup for the Teenage Soul: The Real Deal Friends

31

There Is No End in Friend

auren and I met during summer camp after fifth grade. We were stargazing. She was looking for Orion and I was lying on my back searching the night sky for the Little Dipper when she tripped over me and fell backwards.

"Oh sorry! I was trying to find the stars in Orion's belt and..."

I took her hand and pointed with it to the sky. "Just over there."

She smiled and introduced me to the Little Dipper. That was right where it all began, a chance encounter with a fellow camper as curious as I was about the stars.

Lauren and I were instant friends, spending the remainder of the summer together jumping rope, swimming in the lake, crushing over the cute camp counselor and gushing over our diaries by candlelight. We were attached at the hip—partners in crime, secret handshakes and lazy day promises over fresh-squeezed lemonade to remain friends forever. She beat me at checkers and I was the chess champion. We both had June birthdays, annoying younger brothers and last names that started with W. We both loved books, funny movies and laughing until we cried.

Lauren and I lived two hours apart, so during the school year we went months without seeing each other. We maintained our long distance friendship by telephone and e-mail. When boys broke my heart, she was there to console me at 2:00 A.M. on a school night and when Lauren's parents divorced when we were in ninth grade,

Lauren came to visit for a long weekend and cried on my shoulder into pockets full of Kleenex.

No matter what happened in our lives, we knew we would get through it because we had each other. We were convinced that a good friend was the best medicine, especially a friend who could make you laugh.

"There's no end in friend," Lauren said.

"You're right...."

"You are the sugar in my tea."

"Today I feel like coffee."

"Okay then. I'm the cream in your coffee."

"Half-and-half."

Through thick and thin, love lost and found, family tragedy and fair-weather friends, we always knew that the other was only a couple of hours drive up the coast, an instant message, an e-mail or a phone call away.

When Lauren met her high school sweetheart, she sent me photographs and made sure he called me on the phone so I could approve of him. His name was Isaac and he seemed really nice. She promised to dig up one of his friends so we could double date the next time I went to visit her.

"Awesome. I love you to death," I said, laughing.

"Oh yeah! Well, I love you to life!" Lauren exclaimed, voice creaking through the phone.

And she was right. She always knew how to rewrite the rules so that things made perfect sense. She modernized clichés and came up with secret passwords and sayings that suited us, like twin red dresses and matching pigtails.

The distance between our homes couldn't separate the bond we had. Lauren and I would be best friends forever. She was my soul mate, finishing my sentences and blowing me kisses from her backyard to mine.

Lauren and Isaac broke up about a year later, and I had just broken up with my boyfriend, Jake, a few weeks previously. Sweet sixteen was right around the corner for both of us and school was almost out for the summer. For some time, Lauren and I had been talking about going back to camp and now that we were old enough to attend as counselors with a summer salary to boot, we decided to return.

We spent our summer the same way we had six years earlier—stargazing, river rafting and crushing on the cute counselors over juice and pretzels. It was the first time since junior high we were able to spend the entire month together. We had grown up. Once upon a time we were little girls, whispering after "lights out" and misspelling words in our diaries. Now we had driver's licenses, SAT prep courses and unrequited love stories. We had mastered the art of kissing boys, acing English papers and coming up with good excuses for getting home after curfew. We swapped stories, gave advice, listened and talked through the night. Virtually exhausted every afternoon, we napped in a heap on the counselors' couch.

On the last night of camp, we hiked to the top of Silver Mountain with our flashlights, and sprawled out in the dirt and grass, young women giggling and reminiscing about the first night we met.

"It was right over there," I said, pointing.

"I tripped over you just like this!" Lauren laughed, pushing me into the dirt.

Lying on our backs, eyes to the sky Lauren raised her hand. "You see that up there? That's Gemini."

I looked over her shoulder. "Where?" I asked.

"See the two heads? And the legs coming down—like that."

I squinted and sure enough there they were. Twins joined at the hip, best friends forever hanging out in the sky.

~Rebecca Woolf
Chicken Soup for the Teenage Soul IV

32

Losing My Best Friend

ears streamed down my face as I hugged Kristen tightly. I whispered goodbye and got into the van to travel back home to Tennessee, which meant I would be leaving my best friend in the whole world hundreds of miles away at her new home in Texas. I didn't know how I would ever be able to deal with this terrible loss. As I left I clutched my favorite pillow close to me, wondering what my life would be like without Kristen in it. Trying to stop the pain, I shut my eyes and let all the memories of joy I had shared with her slowly flow into my thoughts. Pictures of smiling faces and the sound of laughter played out in my head.

For six years, we had shared every detail of our lives, big or small, with each other. We constantly helped each other deal with all the pain, suffering and joy that comes with the new experiences you face as a teenager. I depended on her for so many things, and she was unceasingly there for me. She always listened closely to my problems with a nonjudgmental ear and helped me solve them. When I desperately needed someone to laugh at my jokes and give me encouragement to follow my dreams, her words always reassured me. When I needed someone to help me understand why I cried because my heart was breaking, she simply cried with me. I shared every secret with her, causing me sometimes to wonder if she knew more about me than I did about myself. Being around Kristen helped me to learn who I was and who I wanted to be.

As I felt another teardrop roll slowly down my face, I was hit with the horrible memory of the night Kristen called me with the bad news.

"What? You have to move? Your dad is being transferred to Texas?" These questions tumbled out of my mouth. I felt myself panicking as my mind began to race, searching for some explanation that would help all of this make sense. Please, please let this be some cruel joke. I wanted to scream, but it was true. Kristen would be leaving in just a few months. I was devastated. This was one problem that we couldn't resolve. There was nothing either of us could do to change what was going to happen.

The memories of Kristen's farewell party flashed before me. Balloons, presents, food and friends filled the room. Kristen was opening her presents. As she opened mine, a photo album filled with pictures, I stood up to read her a poem I had written.

Remember Me Always
So many memories we've made together
As the years have slowly passed.
Tears may have been cried
But our laughter drowned them all out.
Sharing my deepest-most secrets
'Til one in the morning at your house.
Talking forever about things
Until our words just ran out.
But now you must leave,
And I stay behind.
Who will I call
When I just need to talk?
Who will you lean on
When your problems weigh you down?
Who will laugh at my jokes?
Who will make you smile?
I can't tell you the answers
To the questions I have.
But I want you to know

I will always love you as my friend.
And when your heart is troubled,
I want you to think of me.
Remember the times of joy
We have shared
And maybe it will make you smile.
And since you can't take me with you,
Take the memories we have made
And cherish them
As I always will.

I quickly pushed that memory aside, not wanting to relive the emotions written on everyone's faces as I read aloud. More images zipped through my head.

It was the week I traveled with her and her family to Texas. I remember sitting on Kristen's kitchen floor of her bare house waiting for the movers to finish packing some of the last belongings and feeling extremely lost. Once we arrived in Texas we stayed at a hotel for a few days while they moved into their new house. Kristen unpacked her keepsakes, placing everything down with care and asking me if it looked all right. No, of course it didn't. She wasn't supposed to be here and neither were any of her possessions. But I simply told her that it all looked fine. For the rest of the week, we went swimming and to the mall trying to make new memories that we could reminisce about later. We stayed up every night until the early morning hours just talking. Then the day came when I had to go back home. I wasn't going to relive that morning with all the tears and goodbyes. I popped open my eyes, snapping myself back into reality.

That dreadful week happened almost two years ago, but the memories of it are as vivid as if it happened yesterday. Kristen and I call each other all the time and write each other every detail about our lives. Sometimes when I talk to her on the phone, I forget she's hundreds of miles away. She's still as large a part of my life as she was before and vice versa. Our friendship is so strong that it can face anything. I am very lucky. I've found my soul sister, and I am able to share my life with her. The distance just doesn't matter.

~Amanda Russell
Chicken Soup for the Teenage Soul on Love & Friendship

Teens Talk

Relationships

Betrayal... or Not

Love is whatever you can still betray.
Betrayal can only happen if you love.
~John LeCarre

33

Breathing

(inhale.)
tears begin to flood my face like a cup left under a
running faucet well after the water has reached the rim,
my heart leaping to my throat,
getting caught,
squeezing,
twisting,
tearing.
my throat contracting around the emotions that threaten
to leap up & out of my lips,
my stomach
rumbling,
wrestling,
knotting.
my hands quiver as I reach up to blot the tiny teardrops,
leaving footprints down my cheeks.
the path that awaits me
suddenly seems like a pilgrimage,
one foot,
next foot,
step,
step,
I see you.
(I see her.)
you smile.

I smile.
(she leaves.)
you ask how I am.
(I lie.)
I reply that I'm fine
(even though my heart has just crept up into my mouth &
is jumping up & down on my tongue like an Olympic
diver waiting to hit the water).
I want to say that I miss you,
let you know that every moment I'm awake I think of you.
I want you to know that I miss your arms,
your smile,
your lips.
I want you to know that
(I'm incomplete)
my body hurts,
my soul bleeds.
I ask how you are
(hoping against all hope that you'll tell me what I want to hear).
you reply,
(your answer not including that you miss me,
that you miss my arms, my lips, my touch).
my eyes attempt to strip you down to your soul
(searching for what I once knew so well).
they get lost,
(but find their way back to reality when
they graze over the [ever-fading] hickey, just above
the collar of the shirt she bought you).
my heart leaps off the end of my tongue,
wanting you to see the way you've hurt me
wanting you to hurt the same way.
it falls to the ground.
(she calls you.)
you hastily say goodbye,
(as you trot over to her)

stomping,
squishing,
mutilating
my vulnerable, fallen heart.
(not even pausing long enough to scrape it off the
bottom of your shoe, like a discarded piece of gum.)
she wraps her arms around your neck,
brings her lips to yours…
(your ears still turn red.)
people pass, as if I don't even exist.
(I want to cry, scream, shout.)
I want someone to find my heart,
bring it back,
piece it together.
I turn away,
hoping that one day it won't hurt
(as much)
and hoping that I will again be able to call you
and have you come over to me,
be able to buy you shirts that match your eyes,
(and leave the telltale hickey just above the collar)
and will still be able to make your ears turn red from the
friction of our lips.
I walk away,
knowing my heart will not follow.
(exhale.)

~Michelle Siil
Chicken Soup for the Teenage Soul on Love & Friendship

Sometimes Things Are Never the Same

Forgive all who have offended you, not for them, but for yourself.
~Harriet Nelson

Michelle and I had been best friends since the fourth grade. She was a beautiful person inside and out, one of the kindest I'd ever met. We were like paper and glue—completely inseparable.

When we began junior high, the new social life was a tough adjustment. But our friendship endured, and we were there for each other. I took comfort in the fact that I could tell her anything and always trust her.

Sixth grade passed, as did seventh, and soon eighth grade was upon us. It was that year that things slowly started to change between Michelle and me. I became a social butterfly, fluttering around to different cliques of friends, discussing the hottest gossip and relishing my new categorization as "popular." Although I made many new friends that year, I still loved Michelle and wanted her to hang out with my new, fairly large social group. I attempted to drag her along to my social gatherings, but I soon noticed the disapproving looks and whispers about Michelle—a clear message that she was not "cool enough" to hang out with us.

My new, so-called friends made up lies and rumors about Michelle in order to ruin our friendship. And somewhere along the way, I fell into their trap. I started to believe that I shouldn't be friends with Michelle just because my other friends didn't like her.

One night, one of my new friends, Jamie, came over after school. I was thrilled that she wanted to come to my house and spend time with me. After a couple of hours of laughing and having a great time, Michelle's name came up in our conversation. Slowly, a mischievous grin formed on Jamie's face. Remembering that Michelle was madly in love with a boy named Zach, Jamie ordered me to tell Michelle that Jamie was going out with Zach and then rub it in her face. Afraid that my new friends would dislike me if I refused just like they did Michelle, I picked up the phone, dialed Michelle's number and blurted it out to her. She was more sad, heartbroken and furious than I'd expected, and as I listened to her hysterically cry over the phone, I remembered how close we used to be. At that moment, I realized how much I treasured her friendship, and the cruelty of my actions sunk in. Needing to think about what I had just done, I got off the phone.

I soon called Michelle back and told her the truth. Zach was not going out with Jamie, and I was deeply sorry that I decided to betray her. I was sorry for not being there for her in the last few months, and I was sorry for letting my friends pressure me into situations like these. I wanted to be her best friend again. But she was not as forgiving as I had hoped. "It's not that easy," she said solemnly.

For the next couple of weeks, I did everything I could to win back Michelle's friendship. I sent her a thousand apology notes, I gave her pictures of the two of us, and I called her every night. I even stopped hanging out with my new group of friends who had been so cruel to Michelle. They weren't true friends anyway.

One night, I was sitting on my bed doing homework when I heard the doorbell ring. Unsure of who was at the door, I opened it tentatively, and there stood Michelle. I was shocked. "I forgive you," she said. "I wanted to let you know."

"Really?" I responded excitedly. "So, do you want to come in? Maybe you could sleep over, and we can talk."

"No, I can't. I don't want to," she said.

"Well, maybe we can catch a movie this weekend," I said with a hint of desperation.

"No," she answered.

"I thought you forgave me, Michelle," I said, unable to hide the disappointment in my voice.

"I do forgive you, but what you did changed what we used to be and what we are now. There is still a hole in my heart from what you did; it will never be the same."

She turned away. "I'll see ya around," she said, without looking back.

Every once in a while, Michelle and I run into each other at school, and she waves without saying a word. I always held out hope that our friendship would rekindle. But it hasn't, and things between us will never be the same. I lost my best friend, and it changed my heart forever. I wish I could undo the damage and take back what I have done. Never again will I let the influences of others get in the way of genuine friendships. I owe that to Michelle.

~Celine Geday
Chicken Soup for the Teenage Soul III

35

Starting a New Path

"But I love you, Jessie," he says as we sit on the couch in my living room, his voice quivering and unstable. His pleading eyes look directly into mine, begging my forgiveness. I don't recognize these eyes that once provided me with a sense of comfort and security. The warm blue of his eyes that used to reassure me of a love that would last forever is replaced with a colder gray. I shiver and look away.

Tears cloud my eyes as I feel him breathing next to me on the edge of the couch. My mind wanders to a time a year earlier, a happier time, when I had also been acutely aware of his breathing as we sat in silence on that same couch. My heart had pounded that day as I glanced nervously into his eyes, unable to hold my stare, yet unable to look away. It was that particular day that my heart decided to surrender itself to the magic of first love. And as I sat beside him, overwhelmed by the certainty of my love for him, I struggled to say the words out loud for the first time. I wanted to scream to the world that my heart felt bigger than my whole body, that I was in love and nothing could ever take away that feeling, but no sounds came from my mouth. As I fidgeted with the edge of a pillow, he gently placed his hand on my arm and looked directly into my eyes. His soft stare soothed my nerves. "I love you, Jessie," he told me, his eyes holding my stare. A small smile formed on my face as my heart began to beat quickly and loudly. He had known that night, just as I had—and he had felt the power of the realization of love, just like I had.

But that power is gone now, I remind myself. That returns me from that distant memory to the present moment like a slap in the face.

"Doesn't it mean anything to you that I love you?" he asks. "Please, I'm so sorry." His hand reaches for my face to brush the hair out of my eyes. I duck my head to avoid his touch. It has become too painful since I found out. He had told me two days before that he had kissed another girl. I had sat in stunned silence, unable to move or speak.

I sit now in silence, not because I don't know what to say, but because I am afraid that my voice will deceive me and begin to quiver. As I start to speak, I look into his eyes and stop myself, wondering if I will be making a mistake. "Maybe it can work," I think, and I imagine his arms around me, hugging my head tightly to his chest, making everything okay like he had done so often in the past when I was in need of his comfort. Now, more than ever, I ache for the comfort of his arms and for the reassurance of his warm blue gaze. But it is not possible, for the trust is gone and our love has been scarred. His gaze is no longer a warm blue and his arms no longer provide comfort.

Now I struggle to find the words that I know must come from my mouth, not like before when I knew the words would lead us to a place of magic on the path of our relationship. I now struggle to find the words that will end that path. It's not that my love for him has been taken away, it's just that I know my heart can never again feel bigger than my whole body when I am with him. When he gets up from the couch to leave, the pain in my heart feels too strong to endure, and I have to stop myself from calling after him. I know that I have done the right thing. I know that I am strong, although at this moment I feel anything but strong.

I sit frozen on the couch for a long time after he has left; the only movement in the room is coming from the tears that run down my cheeks and soak the thighs of my jeans. I wonder how I can possibly go on when it feels like half of me is missing. And so I wait. I wait for time to heal the pain and raise me to my feet once again—so that I can start a new path, my own path, the one that will make me whole again.

~Jessie Braun
Chicken Soup for the Teenage Soul II

36

Never Been Dissed —— Until Now

Relationships are like glass. Sometimes it's better to leave them broken than try to hurt yourself putting it back together.
~Author Unknown

What can I say? Sometimes I'm a little dumb. I consider Cheetos a major food group. I play air guitar. I think burping is funny. And, worst of all, I screwed up my chance with Darcy by listening to a bunch of other jerks who were just as clueless as me.

Darcy was kinda like the Jewel CD I loved. I played that thing over and over on the way to school, but the second I pulled into the parking lot, it got stuffed under my seat for, uh, safekeeping and replaced with the Beastie Boys.

Imagine me confessing to my friends that I, captain of the basketball team, was dating Darcy, captain of the debate team. Believe me, I didn't plan on falling for the school brain. But I was blown away by the first words she ever spoke to me.

"Uh, are you lost? This is the li-brar-y. The gym is on the other side of the school, remember?" she said, enunciating the words like she was talking to a toddler. Ouch.

Even though we went to the same school, Darcy and I lived in completely different worlds. She spent her time with the Net nerds, and I roamed the halls like Moses parting the Red Sea of fans who worshipped the guys on my team. I was totally knocked for a loop when she broke the silence.

"Books. I need a book," I stammered, suddenly unable to remember my assignment. She pointed to a row of books on Thomas Edison—just the man I was looking for—and before I could turn to thank her, she was gone.

When I did catch up with her again, she was on her tippy toes reaching for an encyclopedia in the next aisle. "Need a ladder? Or how 'bout some platforms?" I asked giving her a taste of her own sarcasm.

"How about giving me a hand?" she replied. "Oh, that's right. Books are square, not round like a basketball. Think you can hold one?" Cha-ching! "This girl has guts," I thought. When I started laughing, Darcy totally cracked up and started snort-laughing. The number two pencils holding up her hair were shaking.

"I can't believe I said that to you. I can't believe you're laughing. This is so surreal," she laughed. "Oh, sorry, that's a big word. Do you need a dictionary?" More laughing, more snorting. We went on like that for a while, ripping on each other until I thought my sides would split.

For the rest of the day—okay, the rest of the week—every time I thought about her, I felt the same gut-socking dizzy feeling I get before a big game. Then I found myself taking different routes to get to class just to see if I'd bump into her, and when I did... doh! We didn't say a word to each other, but the joke was still going. I'd innocently make gorilla noises, and she'd die laughing. Or she'd take off her glasses and bump into walls, sending her books, pen and pro-tractor flying everywhere. She taped Brain Gum to my locker. I glued a pair of sweaty gym socks to hers. Two weeks into our secret game, Darcy asked me out. Correction: she blackmailed me into a date. I found a ransom note in my locker saying that if I ever wanted to see my lucky jockstrap again, I'd better meet her at a nearby coffee shop. What guy wouldn't love a girl with that sense of humor?

After that first date, we spent nearly every day together talking about everything—cheesy Kung Fu movies (our shared obsession), how I hated being judged as a jock despite my 3.5 GPA, why I hadn't lost my virginity—all of the things I could never talk about with the guys or would even think about mentioning to any of the other girls I had dated. Then again, Darcy wasn't like anyone I had ever been with before. She was a lot of firsts for me. She was the first girl who had the guts to ask me out. She was the first girl I didn't judge by her bra size or reputation. She was the first person who made me feel I had more to offer the world than a killer turnaround jumper. She was the first girl I dated who didn't obsess about her hair, her weight or what she was wearing. And she was the first girl I didn't blab about in the locker room when the guys started bragging about their weekend conquests.

It didn't take long for everyone to start wondering why I was flaking on basketball practice or missing the weekly Duke Nukem marathons at Kyle's. I had been making up the lamest excuses to cover for hanging out with Darcy and was feeling pretty skanky about it when the guys confronted me about it. So I told them about her.

"Who?" Steve asked.

"Not the girl in overalls and High Tops?" Eric asked.

"Why are you wasting time on that?" Kyle asked.

I sat there as they teased me about slumming with a "geeky chick," assuming that once they exhausted all of their lame jokes about Darcy, they'd move onto their next target. Wrong. After that day, whenever I told them I was doing stuff with Darcy, they unloaded on her again. At first, I didn't let it bother me. Then one morning, Dave asked, "Have you figured out how to get her to wear a bag over her head to the prom yet?" That really pissed me off and eventually the little things turned into big things, like "accidentally" forgetting to tell me about practice or suddenly not having enough room at the lunch table for me.

After a few weeks of getting the cold shoulder from my friends, I started to doubt my own judgment. Darcy wasn't one of the prettiest girls in the school. Was I actually planning to take her to my senior prom? She'd probably wear number two pencils in her hair and those hideous High Tops. Once I finished picking her apart, I was convinced she was totally wrong for me. Darcy didn't like basketball or my friends. She refused to go to any of the team parties. I'd been blowing off practices to be with her, and my game was totally suffering. In my mind, the relationship was doomed.

I tried to be subtle at first by taking different routes to my classes to avoid her. I'd promise to call her but never did. She finally cornered me in the hall one day and demanded an explanation, so I swore I'd meet her after school. Then I blew her off. I was hoping she'd get the hint and go away if I flaked, but she didn't let me off that easily. The next day, in front of the entire school, Darcy let me have it. She yelled at me, called me a coward, a jerk and an idiot, and, worst of all, tossed my friends a box of notes I'd written to her. I stood there speechless as they read each one aloud and laughed like hyenas. The funny thing was that for the first time (another first with Darcy) I didn't really care what the guys were saying or who saw me standing there like an idiot, because I knew she was right. When I looked at my friends howling and high-fiving each other, I finally realized that I was going to be the first guy in our pathetic circle to grow up.

I wish I could say there was a happy ending to the story, that I begged Darcy to take me back and she did, but it didn't happen. Well, at least not the part about her taking me back. I begged. I pleaded. I stuffed notes in her locker. I followed her around school. I was practically stalking her by the time I realized it was too late. She had already gotten over slumming with a dummy.

Last I heard, Darcy graduated early and got accepted to an out-of-state college. I still feel a little sad when I think about her and what could have been, but I'm also grateful that I learned what I did, when I did. I know a little bit more about who I am—the whole me, not just the big man on campus part—and who I can be, regardless of what my friends think or say. So, Darcy, if you're reading this... thanks.

~Shad Powers
Chicken Soup for the Teenage Soul III

37

On Shame and Shadowboxing

That summer I spent my days with a group of young men whose long, stringy hair was bleached from sun and saltwater. This was in Corpus Christi, Texas, on the Gulf Coast, and the boys went surfing in the mornings then returned in the afternoons to play football on my parents' lawn. My parents warned me about them. They knew about cars and smoked cigarettes, and when they took off their shirts for our games, their chests and arms were hard with muscle that came from paddling out into the ocean before dawn. Girls fawned over them, and that summer I idolized them, too. I've forgotten all but one of their names, Barry, though maybe another was called Todd. Always in this ever-present gang of boys there is one named Todd.

My father didn't like the boys smoking around me or their long hair, and he didn't like things he'd heard about them, things he wouldn't tell me. But he wanted me to spend more time outside and must have figured that since the games took place in our front yard, the shadow of our house would protect me from them, from their influence.

Earlier that year my father had taught me to throw a football, and by summer I could pass the length of two, sometimes three, lawns. These were high, arching throws that should not have come from the small arms of a boy who preferred books to ball games. Every time

I heaved the football, I expected it to veer off course into a window or under the tire of a passing car, but instead it almost always went where I wanted it to, into that pocket of my father's chest and arms. "Perfect," he would say. "Right in the numbers." When I played football with the boys, I was "All-Time Quarterback," which meant that I threw for both teams and got sacked a lot.

In addition to teaching me how to throw long bombs, my father also taught me how to fight. He stressed that I should never throw the first punch, but once it's thrown, I shouldn't hold back. My father had fought a lot: In his youth, in the army and once in a pool hall after a man made a vulgar innuendo toward my mother. He taught me how to shadowbox and how to hit someone, how to twist my fist just as it made impact so that it cut the skin. He encouraged me to bite, scratch and pull hair, to use sticks or attack from behind, to kick whoever had started the fight in the shins or between the legs, or to stomp the bridges of his feet. I nodded as my father told me these things, but I knew if the time came, I would worry that hitting someone would only make him hurt me worse. In the pool hall, my father had hit the man in the knee with a pool cue, and when I asked him if it had broken, he said, "The stick or his leg?"

Maybe I wanted so badly for Barry and Todd and the boys to accept me because each of them seemed more like the young man my father was than I did. And maybe, too, that's why my father worried about my time with them and taught me how to fight. He thought the boys would bully me, take advantage of my adoration, and he knew I would not snitch on them. I would suffer their insults and mockery because I feared bringing trouble to anyone, and he saw that these boys thrived on trouble, as probably he had.

But in the summer when I was fourteen, the boys tolerated me because of my quarterback abilities and my parents' long, even lawn. The target of their harassment that summer was a boy named Robert, but they called him Roberta. They called him Roberta because of a high voice and the feminine lightness in his stride, something like a prance. For three months, he stayed with his grandmother who lived across the street from my family. Robert usually left on his bicycle in the mornings and returned in the afternoons while we played football. When he rode past, the boys acted as if they were going to peg him with the football. Although they never actually threw it, every time one of them dropped back and took aim with the ball, Robert flinched. Sometimes he fell off the bicycle and turned red. If his grandmother tottered outside, the boys waved at her and asked Robert if he wanted to join the game. He never did.

I felt sorry for him and hated to see him turn the corner on his bicycle because I knew Barry and Todd would start insulting him. He made an easy target, and for all of their muscle and mouthing off, for all of their bragging and bravado, they were weak, insecure boys. But I never interfered with their cruel impressions of his prance or tried to silence the jokes they made about his voice; I just waited for the game to resume. As much as I wanted them to lay off of Robert, there was always the great sense of relief that the insults weren't being hurled at me.

After almost an entire summer of enduring their threats and slurs, something happened on a hot August afternoon. I'm not sure what changed that day; maybe they'd finally pushed him too far, or maybe he'd been planning it all summer. Maybe he'd been scouting our games like a coach from an opposing team, looking for weaknesses, trying to identify the player who would fumble or fall most easily. When Barry and Todd started in on Robert when he returned from his bike ride, he didn't retreat. Instead of sulking away, he stood flat-footed in his grandmother's driveway and started insulting me. I can still hear his high, girly voice coming across the street, across all of these years.

I hoped the boys would rush to my defense, but as Robert marched into my yard, they only laughed, their eyes boring into me as if it were the showdown they'd been waiting for all along. My knees trembled as they did when I had to speak with girls. With everything Robert said, the boys cackled louder. He fed off their laughter, his words growing louder and more harsh, and soon the boys rallied behind him and egged him on. They listened to him as a football team listens to its quarterback.

That afternoon when he gathered the courage and confidence to insult me, I did the one thing that would have disappointed my father: I threw the first punch. I whipped a hard, perfect spiral into Robert's face. Then as he brought up his hands, I exploded across the yard like a fullback charging for a touchdown, barreled into his chest and knocked him to the ground. The boys closed in around us, yelling and laughing. Robert and I grappled with each other—he was much stronger than I would have anticipated—then I managed to mount and straddle his chest. Aside from an awkward, frantic slap that bloodied my nose, I owned the fight. My fists flurried on his face, and his pale, freckled flesh tore between my knuckles and his cheekbones.

Soon my father broke through the boys around us and pulled me off him. Because he never learned the truth behind the fight—Robert, like me, would never tell—I knew he was proud of me. I felt ashamed, and even then wished I had the strength to walk into my house and leave the boys in the sun. The truth is, while I've grown to resemble my father in many ways—his stubborn optimism, his broad, round shoulders and his inclination to protect those he loves—on that day in the yard, I was the weak one. I think Robert understood this. He saw me as an outsider in the group, someone like himself who would never quite fit in, and he knew the boys would turn on me. If his eyes had been open, he would have seen that I winced with each strike, and was as scared and ashamed and in as much pain as he was. It was as if I were shadowboxing, throwing blows at my own image, and with each swing, I came that much closer to connecting.

~Bret Anthony Johnston
Chicken Soup for the Teenage Soul on Love & Friendship

38

Jonathon

f we hadn't thought our girlfriends were cheating on us with Jonathon, I don't think Ben and I would ever have become friends. Since our coach was making us run about three miles a day, and we ran at the same pace, we had plenty of time to talk about this weird thing we had in common.

Grace and I had been together for over a year, but we'd spent a lot of that time fighting. Jonathon had been my best friend since fifth grade; since he and Grace had become close friends, he frequently had to play referee.

Being our referee wasn't an easy job, because Grace and I fought about everything. We were a dramatic couple, as our whole school knew, and we probably spent as much time broken up as we spent together, maybe even more.

But Jonathon was having problems of his own. He and his mom hadn't been getting along, so he had been living with my family for several months. He slept upstairs, in the old bedroom I'd abandoned for the room my brother had vacated for college.

My new room downstairs was like a little bachelor pad, with a TV, its own bathroom and doors to the kitchen and outside. I could go anywhere and no one would know. Except for one thing: without my own car, "anywhere" meant "within walking distance."

Jonathon, on the other hand, had inherited a tiny white jalopy from a distant cousin that was years past its prime, but it was still a car. He could come and go as he pleased. My parents left him alone.

It was torture: with all the independence my new room conferred, I still needed my parents' permission to go anywhere.

Having Jonathon's car around changed things dramatically: instead of my mom and I sharing her car, with one of us dropping the other off at school or work, Jonathon was now my ride. I was completely dependent on him to get from home to school, from school to practice and everywhere else. But even though we were on the same team and spent a lot of time together, Jonathon had his own life. He skipped practices or went out late, and when he wasn't available, I had to beg other people for rides or call my mom. I felt like the only child in a family with three parents.

To make things worse, Grace and Jonathon were spending a lot of time together. Frequently, they would hang out at my house while I was at practice, though Jonathon and I played for the same team, our coach let him skip practices without consequence.

Jonathon and Grace had their inside jokes, like one where they would rub their feet together: they called it "foot sex." I was the monkey in the middle, supposed to play along. It seemed like I was always the butt of their jokes that I didn't understand. Jonathon was taking everything that was mine — my girlfriend, my house, my independence — leaving me running around in circles.

My running partner, Ben, was in the same boat. His girlfriend, Melisa, was also spending time with Jonathon while we were at practices that Jonathon was able to avoid. There were the same inside jokes, traded smirks and rolled eyes; he was growing uncomfortable, too.

Ben and I talked about it constantly for weeks, trying to figure out what the three of them were doing. I was much angrier, thanks to Jonathon's omnipresence in my life, but we were both confused and growing more irritated. Then, one day as we finished up a run, Ben turned to me and said, "Listen, I can't tell you why, but you don't have to worry about Jonathon and Grace."

I asked what he knew, and how.

"Just trust me. I guarantee she's not cheating on you. Not with him, at least."

"What about Melisa?" I asked.

"It's fine," he said. "I promise."

Unfortunately, I didn't believe him. His advice only made things worse. Now I was left out of another group—first my family, then my relationship with Grace and now the people who "knew" that nothing was going on.

Meanwhile, my relationship with Jonathon grew worse. I would barely speak to him when he came home, which made him come home later and later to avoid the discomfort. Finally, it all came to a head.

"Can we talk?" he asked. It'd been a while since we'd really spoken: he had as much reason to expect a "no" as a "yes."

My fists balled up as I said, "Yes."

He suggested we go for a walk, so I followed him out the door toward the wetlands behind my house. There were acres of dried-out swamp with train tracks cutting through the middle. We had played on the tracks as kids, placing coins on the rails to see them deform into blank strips of copper.

Barely concealing my rage, I stood in front of him with my fists still balled up behind me, ready to do anything at all to take back my girlfriend, my house and my sanity.

He looked at me and said quietly, "So you know how Grace and I have been spending a lot of time together lately?"

Prepared as I was, I couldn't believe he was about to say it. As my heart skipped, I glared back, too angry to respond.

"Well, she's been helping me figure something out. And we didn't tell you, but I know that Ben knows, and since you're my best friend, it's only fair that I tell you...."

As he trailed off, I pictured us wrestling on the tracks, a train approaching.

"...Dan, I'm gay."

"You're what?" I asked.

"I'm gay," he said. It was clearly not an easy thing for him to say. This wasn't what I had expected. He was still stealing my girlfriend, though, right? Slowly I began to piece together that if he were gay, he might not want a girlfriend.

I was still suspicious: "So, you're not sleeping with Grace?"

He laughed. "Um, I'm gay, Dan."

"Are you sure that that's it?" I asked. I still wasn't convinced.

"Uh, yeah, that's about it," he replied.

"Oh. Okay. I thought you were going to tell me something bad that could have ended our relationship."

That was the end of an ugly chapter in our lives. Jonathon returned home, and to refereeing other things Grace and I found to fight about. But I always found it funny that the one thing he seemed ashamed of was the only thing I wanted to hear.

~Dan Levine
Chicken Soup for the Teenage Soul IV

Chapter 6

Teens Talk

Relationships

Oh Brother, Oh Sister

I don't believe an accident of birth makes people sisters or brothers.
It makes them siblings, gives them mutuality of parentage.
Sisterhood and brotherhood is a condition people have to work at.
~Maya Angelou

39

Sugar River

Nothing can make everything okay after a hard experience,
but the simple act of giving a hug can come pretty close.
~Hannah Boyd

I t was the last day of our family camping trip in Wisconsin. We had been driving for nearly three hours. It was a really hot day, and I thought I couldn't stand another minute in the car. My younger brother and sister were squirming and fighting, and I had to sit between them, so, of course, I was getting the worst of it from both sides. I'm three years older than Aaron, and five years older than Emily, so my parents expected me to be more mature and try to keep the younger kids apart.

I was trying really hard to ignore them and just read my book, but then Aaron reached over and pinched my arm. I couldn't take it anymore. "Cut it out!" I screamed at him, grabbing both of his hands in anger.

"Ow, you're hurting me! Let go!" he cried.

My mother turned around and gave me a stern look. "Leave him alone! You know you have to be patient with him!" I let go of his hands with a sigh. My parents were always telling me to be more patient with him, but it really wasn't fair. Just because he had learning disabilities, just because he was a "special" kid, he shouldn't be allowed to get away with stuff like that. But he knew he could, and that I couldn't pinch him back. He grinned at me. I glared back at him. He was such a pain.

Finally we rounded the last turn on the dusty country road, and the sign came into view: "Sugar River Tubing." My brother and sister were out of the car almost before it stopped moving and raced toward the ticket booth.

I followed them more slowly, but I was pretty excited to be there, too. We would be provided with large inner tubes, driven several miles upstream in a van, and then would spend the afternoon lazily floating back down the river.

From the clearing where the shack stood, we couldn't see the river, since the trees were thick with leaves. We followed the attendant over to a beat-up old van and climbed inside. After about ten minutes, we reached the drop-off point a few miles upstream.

As we got out of the van, the driver went around to the back and pulled out our inner tubes.

"Just walk down that path to the river," he instructed us.

My mother gestured toward the inside of the van, where several life jackets lay tangled in a heap. "What about the life jackets?" she asked.

"Well, we're required by law to have those," he said, "but you won't need them. The water's really shallow. In some places you might even need to stand up and carry the tubes because they'll scrape the bottom."

We were already heading down the path, so despite her misgivings, my mother agreed to forgo the life jackets. She probably decided it wasn't worth the arguments she would get from us if she tried to make us wear them. After all, I wasn't a baby! I was fourteen, and I'd known how to swim since I was five. Emily knew how to keep her head above water for a long time, and even though Aaron was "disabled," he was a natural athlete and was a better swimmer than I was. As I followed my brother and sister down to the river, I heard the tires skidding on the loose gravel as the van turned around and disappeared down the road.

When I caught up with the kids, they were standing silently on the riverbank, surveying the water. Instead of a shallow stream, we saw a wide, quickly flowing river. My father stepped closer to the edge and studied the water for a moment.

"I think it looks okay," he said. "I can see the bottom; it doesn't look too deep. Just let me get in first, then I can help the kids get on their tubes."

He stepped off the riverbank with a splash; the water was up to his chest—and apparently colder than he had expected.

"Jeez Louise, that's cold!" he exclaimed, and then grinned at us. "Okay, who's first?"

Within a few minutes, the rest of us had managed to climb onto our inner tubes, and we started floating downstream. I quickly realized that this was not going to be quite as much fun as I had thought. The water was flowing so fast that it was difficult to steer the tubes. The current kept pushing us to the sides of the river, where we found ourselves constantly having to paddle and push off the riverbanks in order to avoid being scratched by the branches overhanging the water.

As we made our way down the river, our tubes began to drift away from each other. Whenever there was a bend in the river, we would lose sight of at least one of the others, and my mother began to get nervous.

"Can you see Aaron?" she asked me at one point, as we rounded a bend. She was always checking up on Aaron.

As we came around the bend, I spotted him. He was pretty far ahead of us, which wasn't surprising. He always insisted on being first, no matter what it was. Whenever we went somewhere in the car, he would push Emily and me out of the way to get in first, even though we all sat in the backseat anyway. And when my mother put a platter of food on the table, he would grab to take his piece first, as if there wasn't a whole refrigerator full of food. It was really annoying, but everyone was always making excuses for him because of his learning disability. I knew that I was getting too old to care about things like that, but I couldn't help it.

Aaron was still pretty far ahead of us on his tube, and I could tell that it was even making my father nervous. Since I was much closer to him than either of my parents, my father told me to try and catch up with him. I started kicking and paddling, and gradually began closing the distance between us.

As the river straightened out, I saw that there was a fallen tree extending nearly all the way across. Aaron was heading straight for it.

"Aaron, watch out!" my father yelled to him. "Try to paddle over to the right!"

Either Aaron was too far away to hear him, or he was just ignoring him, but he didn't even look up.

Suddenly I got scared. The current was pulling Aaron's tube really fast, and I could see that it would only be a matter of seconds before the tube would slam into the log. He was moving fast enough that he could be badly hurt. I kicked and paddled as hard as I could, and I had almost caught up to him. I screamed, "Grab my hand!" But just as I reached out for him, his tube smacked into the tree. The force of the impact caught him by surprise, and he was catapulted off the tube into the river. Instantly he disappeared under the water. I immediately jumped off my tube—and was shocked to realize that I couldn't touch the bottom. I grabbed onto the tree for support. The current was so strong that I was nearly sucked underneath. Frantically I looked for him—the tree's branches formed a dense thicket under the water, and I knew that if he were caught in there he would be trapped.

Suddenly I saw them—his two little hands sticking up out of the water, desperately grasping at the slippery trunk. With one hand hanging on to the tree, I grabbed his wrist with the other hand. With every ounce of my strength, I fought to pull him above the water.

He came up gasping and choking; he threw his arms around my neck and we hung there, sobbing with fear and relief. He had lost his glasses; his face and arms were scratched from the branches; but he was safe. A moment later my father was there. He helped us up onto our tubes.

I still couldn't stop crying, and I couldn't let go of Aaron's hand. After making sure that neither of us was hurt, my father said, "Let's get out of here. Maybe we can climb up out of the water and walk back the rest of the way."

I reluctantly released my grip on the trunk, and the three of us worked our way around the end of the tree and back into the current.

My mother and Emily were huddling under the branches of a small bush overhanging the water, where the current had dragged them. I could see the fear in my mother's face, and I was at that moment very thankful that she had not seen how close we had come to losing Aaron.

We surveyed the riverbank, but it was too steep to climb. We had no choice but to continue downstream on the tubes. We linked hands to form a chain and pushed off from the riverbank. The fifteen minutes it took to reach the dock seemed like an eternity. The young man who had dropped us off leaned over to help us off our tubes and out of the water.

"How was it?" he asked brightly.

My father just glared at him. The rest of us headed off to the car, leaving my father to fill him in on exactly "how it was." When he came to the car, he said simply, "He said they had a lot of rain last night and they didn't know the water was so deep. They're closing down for the rest of the day."

We set out toward the nearest city, in search of a mall that might have an optometrist, where my parents hoped to replace Aaron's glasses. Emily sat up front between my parents, and Aaron fell asleep with his head in my lap. For once, it wasn't annoying to have him leaning on me. It felt good. His hair was still damp and his face was streaked with mud, but he actually looked kind of cute.

As we drove into the mall parking lot, Aaron stirred. Gradually he sat up, his face flushed from the heat. He squinted in the late afternoon sun. I had never seen anything so beautiful.

"Are we there yet?" he asked.

I just smiled. "Yes," I said, "we're there."

"Can we get ice cream?"

"You bet," said my father, glancing at him with a grin.

One evening a few weeks later, my parents went to a movie, and I had to stay home and babysit. I was in Aaron's room, looking for his new glasses, which had flown off his face while he was doing back flips on his bed. After we found the glasses under the dresser, he put them on and adjusted the slightly bent frames. Then he looked up at me. "You saved my life," he said seriously. I was so surprised, I couldn't speak. Aaron rarely said anything nice to me, and he hadn't said anything at all about the incident. I didn't think it had made any impression on him at all. But before I could think of what to say, the moment was over, and Aaron resumed doing flips. I don't think he noticed the tears in my eyes.

Maybe it's just that I was getting older and I could see things in a more mature way. Now that I thought about it, Aaron hadn't been nearly so annoying lately. Not that his behavior was any different. He's still the same kid he always was. He still pushes me out of the way to get through the door first, and he still makes a big scene if he doesn't get to pick which TV show we watch. And my parents still give in to him. But lately I really don't mind.

Even though there are still some times when I can't stand him, it's a little easier for me to be patient with him. I can even see why my friends think he's cute and funny. In a way, I'm actually glad that he's my little brother.

Aaron knows what I did for him that day on the river. He knows that I saved his life. But I'm sure that he doesn't know what he did for me that day. Aaron showed me that I did have it in me, after all, to be the kind of big sister my parents wanted me to be, the kind of big sister I always knew I should be. Aaron helped me bring out my best that day, when I grabbed onto his slippery little hands in the water and held on as tightly as I possibly could. He needed me — and I needed him, too. I held on to him then as if both of our lives depended on it. And I'll never let go. That's what being a big sister means. Our lives depend on each other, and that's always and forever.

~Phyllis Nutkis
Chicken Soup for the Sister's Soul

40

No Longer an Only Child

A sister can be seen as someone who is both ourselves
and very much not ourselves — a special kind of double.
~Toni Morrison

I thought my parents were crazy when they announced over dinner one night that I was going to have a brother or sister in about nine months. Being fifteen years old and in high school, I figured I was out of the woods and free of siblings. Well, that wasn't the case.

My mom and dad had divorced when I was three years old, and several years later, my mom met a wonderful man named Randy. They got married, we moved out to the country on a hog farm in rural Illinois (yes, I was officially a farmer's daughter), and things were going fairly smoothly. A week after their wedding, I went to Japan for a study abroad program, and when I came back a month later, I had a newly decorated room waiting for me. It didn't take long before I was calling Randy "Dad." I loved him dearly, and he treated me as if I were his own daughter.

I always considered myself a fairly well-adjusted teenager, and things were going just fine for me. I was an only child and never had to go without anything, so you could say I had it made. About two years later, the big announcement that a baby was on the way left me feeling, well, not really feeling anything. I wasn't mad, upset or happy; I was just feeling neutral about the situation. I always wanted a little brother or sister, and now I was finally going to get one. However, I was at a point in my life where I was used to not having siblings, had learned to entertain myself, and was perfectly content with being the center of attention at every family function.

The next several months were filled with chaos as we prepared for the new addition to the family. My idea of a new addition would have been a deck and a pool or even a new car for my sixteenth birthday, but I'm referring to the little bundle of nightmare that would soon be living in my house. I knew things were going to change, but I had no idea the emotional roller coaster my mom would be on during this time. One day, Dad drank the last Diet Coke and I thought she was going to kill him, then the next moment she would be the most pleasant person on the planet.

My mom's two older sisters, Aunt Dorothy and Aunt Lynda, threw her a wonderful baby shower with all the trimmings. To my surprise, I also received presents, including a gift basket with earplugs. My family was very concerned about how I would feel once the baby was born, so they were putting forth extra effort to make me feel loved, and they showered me with attention. All of my friends were excited for me. In a way, I think they were looking forward to me experiencing the aches and pains of being an older sister.

The next few months went by rather quickly, and before I knew it, one summer morning in June, my mom was taken to the hospital. I was visiting my Aunt Lynda in Missouri when we got the call that my mom was in labor, so we loaded up the car and drove to Illinois, hoping and praying that we wouldn't miss the big event. I remember it like it was yesterday. We stepped into the hospital at 12:03 P.M., which was the exact same time my sister, Bekah, was born. I saw my dad coming out of the delivery room and he was glowing. Everything seemed to be going just fine when all of a sudden they were wheeling my mom in a mad dash to the operating room. She had some complications after the delivery, and what was supposed to be a time of celebration now became a life-or-death waiting game. My first instinct was to hate the baby, since I felt it was all her fault that this happened. I had my mom to myself for fifteen years of my life, and now it looked as if she was going to be taken away from me forever.

As soon as I saw Bekah for the first time, those feelings of hate went away, and I saw her as a helpless being who had no idea what was going on. At first, I didn't see what all the fuss was about. She looked like a raisin with hair and couldn't do anything. But as I continued to look at her, I could see that we possessed some of the same features, and I started to think about what kind of person she would be five years from now. I imagined all the things we could do together and how much I loved her already.

Everything was touch-and-go for about a week, but my mom pulled through, and soon it was time to go home. Our family was very supportive, and everyone took turns in shifts coming to our house to make sure we had meals and to help take care of Bekah. My mom was somewhat bedridden because she was still recovering, so it was comforting to have family around.

I look back now, and I find it hard to believe all of this took place about thirteen years ago. My sister and I are very close, and I see her as an extension of myself. I think about the future and how we will be a continual source of support for one another. It's hard to believe that at one time I dreaded her existence. Now I can't imagine life without her.

~Jessica Wilson
Chicken Soup for the Teenage Soul IV

No Time to Say I Love You

Present your family and friends with their eulogies now—
they won't be able to hear how much you love them and
appreciate them from inside the coffin.
~Anonymous

Sweat beads gathered on my forehead at just the thought of the first day of high school. I thought for sure that I was going to be singled out and embarrassed in every class and then be laughed out of the school. In first hour, when I was called to the office, being singled out became the least of my problems.

My twenty-year-old brother, Brian, stood filling out papers for me to leave. He turned to face me and my heart sank. His face was pale and blotchy, like someone had carelessly thrown red paint on a white sheet of paper. His eyes were swollen and red. This was the first I had ever seen my brother cry, I knew that something bad had happened. He grabbed my hand and leaned down until his face was level with mine.

"Amanda has been in a car accident, and she is in the hospital," he said.

Every inch of my body went numb as I absorbed what my brother was telling me.

My sister? In a car accident? How could that happen? At age seventeen, Amanda was the safest driver I knew.

Without a thought in my head, I pulled away from my brother and sprinted down the hallway.

I had to get to my locker, my class and out of that school as fast I could. Yet nothing was fast enough. It felt like everything around me had slowed to a painful crawl just when I wanted it to speed up.

Yelling over my shoulder that I would be out to the car in a minute, I opened the door to my classroom. My teacher didn't ask what I was doing; she knew. She knew just by looking at me that I was leaving even without a note. Nothing she could do was going to stand in my way.

People watched from class windows as I ran down the hall in a panic to my locker and then out of the school doors. I would get in trouble for not waiting to get a note from the office, but I didn't care. Nothing mattered more than getting out of that school and to where my sister was.

Brian and I drove to the trauma center at MidMichigan Regional Medical Center. We ran into the room, and then I saw her.

She was lying on her back on a bed with her head and neck in braces. Her face was covered from the eyebrows up and you could see blood everywhere. She was hooked to several different machines to monitor her body reactions. Her entire body convulsed with the effects of the trauma.

My mom and dad stood at her side crying. Our pastor, youth pastor and what seemed at the time to be half of our church congregation were also in the room.

I walked like a zombie to her bedside.

Nothing could explain the feeling that coursed through me when she looked up at me with blood-filled eyes. In her eyes, where I expected to see fear, I saw strength. Then her eyes softened, and she spoke. She said one thing to me while she was lying on that bed.

She looked up at me and said in a strained voice, "I love you, Renee." I couldn't handle the emotion that filled me at the realization that I rarely told my sister I loved her. I tried to answer her, but she wasn't listening anymore.

The doctors were taking her away to the X-ray room, and she was watching them carefully.

As they wheeled her broken body down the hallway with her

blood seeping into the bandages and onto the white sheets that covered the portable bed, every inch of my being wanted to scream out to her that I loved her, but I couldn't. I couldn't move, speak or even cry until she was around the corner and I could see her no more. Then the tears came.

I knelt on the floor and cried in the corner. I cried tears of hopelessness and frustration.

Though everyone kept telling me she would be all right, something in their voices spoke loudly of the doubt that everyone was secretly harboring in the back of their minds. All I wanted was for the doctor to say, "She's going to be fine."

He didn't. Every moment that passed allowed the doubt to grow stronger and bigger, like a dense black cloud that refused to allow the sunlight to come through. Finally, he walked tentatively down the hall and stood quietly in front of us.

I tried to read his face what he was going to say, but I couldn't. He started to tell us about her head.

When the tie rod on her car broke, the car hit the side of the ditch and flipped end over end, clearing the ditch and landing on the other side in a small patch of trees.

Her head struck an object, which was assumed to have been the dashboard, with the front part of her face. The impact drove all of the skin on her forehead back into her hair. Pieces of skin still remained in that cursed car.

I knew that head wounds were very dangerous and that they could result in many different injuries. At that moment, I really wished that I had paid more attention to my teacher when we talked about head wounds in health class.

It was then that the long-awaited words came. The only words, from the only person that I could accept them from—the doctor. Amanda was going to be okay.

My soul leaped and my heart raced as I realized I still had a sister. She would never look the same and would require hours of plastic surgery, but she was alive, and that's all that mattered to me.

A year later, I still have a sister, and even though we fight and nag at each other, every time that I see her face and I spot the large scar that stretches from her hairline across her forehead, down her eyelid and back up to her hair, I remember to tell her that I love her. I remember when I almost didn't have the chance to tell her again how much I really do love her, and I thank God I still can.

~Renee Simons
Chicken Soup for the Sister's Soul

Rikki's Hug

A hug is two hearts wrapped in arms.
~Author Unknown

I'm walking up the sidewalk to our brown, three bedroom condo. I've lived here for so many years that I can't even remember the day we moved in. I know that sidewalk, steps and porch so well that I could easily walk them blind. As I pause at the door to search for my key in my purse, I get a whiff of the familiar dryer sheet smell that is flowing from the vent near the porch. It's a comforting smell, one that most people would overlook. But I've always noticed it. I gaze up at the same old gray Connecticut sky. The cool breeze that frequents early spring in the Northeast whips my windbreaker around my shoulders and leaks through the sleeves, causing me to shiver. My day at school was pretty typical, although I didn't do as well in all of my classes as I wanted to. I'm behind in my outlining for history, which is usually the most lacking area of my schoolwork because I dread it so much.

Tonight I am supposed to go out for a mid-week dinner and then to the gym, but play rehearsal ran over. It's getting late, and I have so much work ahead of me this evening. What began as an ordinary day is now anything but ordinary. The breeze feels like a fierce, wintry gust. My head hurts, my liveliness fades to a shade of tired. It's too much. I can't do it anymore. I struggle to turn the key in the door when it swings wide open.

There she stands, her little body clad in OshKoshes that have

Pooh on them, her long brown curls free and flowing down her back to her waist. She lets me put her hair up very rarely; she prefers it to be let alone to do what it wants. She's wise beyond her years. Her eyes remind me of milk chocolate with a fleck of summer sunshine in them. They retain the gentle radiance of summer long after the leaves have fallen off the trees and have been replaced with frigid snow. But it's her smile that I notice. Her smile never ceases to amaze me. It lights up her face with an innocent and happy luminescence. It's a contagious smile. "Gaga is home!" She's called me that name since she first started talking. She's put behind her all of the other baby names for friends and family, but mine sticks. That's because I'm her favorite sister, her favorite person. Well, that's what she tells me and I choose not to acknowledge that she's only four and doesn't understand yet what the depths of the word "favorite" are. I understand what it means, so I can legitimately say that she's my favorite. Though she may not understand the extremity in this word, she sure understands me.

Her little arms wrap around me as I hug the little girl whom I still call, "Baby." Only when she misbehaves do I use her real name. Though she's at that age when babies no longer are babies and want to be "big girls," she never corrects me. And only when she's upset with me does she ever use my actual name. With that one gesture, everything's okay again. She puts a butterfly kiss on my cheek. Then come the sweetest words you could ever hear, which could easily be mistaken for the sound of an angel: "I missed you." Isn't it funny how with one simple display of affection, everything turns around? The world suddenly seems okay and I can no longer find a reason to be tired. And even though when that moment is over, the toils and troubles of life return, it's always waiting for me at my front door. All I have to do is turn the key.

~Kathryn Litzenberger
Chicken Soup for the Teenage Soul III

It's Not What You Think

You don't choose your family.
They are God's gift to you, as you are to them.
~Desmond Tutu

There's something about teenagers—they love to be together. Robert and our son, Calvin, had been best friends all throughout high school and it seemed quite natural that he should become part of our family. In our small town of Delburne, Alberta, a well-to-do German couple had adopted him when he was an infant, but Robert didn't want to be "well-to-do." He wanted with all his heart to be a mechanic. He felt more comfortable in a pair of greasy coveralls than he ever would in a three piece suit.

His mother didn't consider this vocation suitable to his status, and this caused a lot of friction. Calvin approached us with the idea of taking Robert into our home. And after talking to his parents and getting their consent, this is exactly what happened. Robert was a sweet lad with a mischievous mind, full of tricks and life, just like our own son. That meant there was never a dull moment in our home.

The rest of the youth group began hanging out at our place, usually Sunday evening after the service while my husband John, the pastor, and I were still at the church. And, as is usual with teenagers, they started pairing off. Robert already had a sweetheart. Debbie was a lovely young lady away studying at Bible College in another province. When he started paying attention to Cindy, a newcomer to the group, we became a bit concerned. We reminded him of Debbie, who was trusting him to remain faithful to her. But, to everyone's dismay, Robert continued to spend more and more time with Cindy. In a small community like ours, it's pretty hard to hide something like that.

Calvin hated to see his best friend being a cheat so he went to Robert's room one night and said, "Either you stop seeing Cindy or I'm phoning Debbie! How can you hurt her like this? She is bound to find out!"

Robert said nothing and just shrugged his shoulders. Meanwhile I had taken Cindy aside into our bedroom and told her more or less the same thing. She hugged me and cried, "Oh, but you don't understand! It's not what you think. Robert is like a brother I never had. We have so much in common, we just have to talk to each other. I wish you could see it our way."

Then came the day we all dreaded. Robert had taken time off work and Cindy skipped college for the day. They headed for Calgary, a four hour drive away. We were all disappointed and felt we had failed them along the way.

It was evening before they finally arrived home. Robert jumped out of his truck, ran around to the other side and hugged Cindy as she got out. They were both radiant as they came up the walk, hand in hand. As we watched through the dining room window our hearts sank. Here it comes, we thought.

"At least you could have been a little more discreet about it," I thought to myself. But I said nothing. Robert spoke first. "Mom and Dad [that's what he started to call us right after he arrived], can we have all the family together? We have some very important news to share with you." Our hearts sank. After Calvin and our two daughters came into the room, Robert began to speak.

"You know Cindy and I have been seeing a great deal of each other lately, and we know you don't approve. But honestly, we had to do it."

We sat silent, waiting for whatever type of excuse would come next. He went on, "The more we saw each other the more we realized how much we had in common. Cindy really seemed to draw me. We discovered that we were both of Russian ancestry, liked the same foods and even disliked the same things. The more we talked the more apparent it became. So we went to the provincial courthouse in Calgary today."

We gasped, "Oh no, you didn't go and get married?"

Then Cindy said, "We searched old records for hours until we finally found Robert's birth certificate." Then, with a huge grin on her face she announced: "Robert is my brother!"

There was a stunned silence as the words hit our ears.

"All these years, I've known that I had an older brother who was given up for adoption at birth. But I never thought I'd ever find him. And here he had been living less than thirty miles away all that time. We got suspicious when we found out we were both Russian, and bit by bit things fell into place. But we didn't want to tell anybody until we had proof and knew for sure."

We all gasped as we heard the story—first in disbelief—and then with great joy! Lots of hugging and crying followed! We were all apologizing to one another for our critical and judgmental attitudes and then rejoicing again. It was all too incredible. It was the wee hours of the morning before we finally went to bed. None of us got much sleep that night.

In the years that followed, Robert became a journeyman mechanic—fulfilling his own vision for his life. And oh yes, he and Debbie did get married after all—with his sister Cindy there to catch the bouquet!

~Greta Zwaan
Chicken Soup for the Sister's Soul

44

Kicki

Is solace anywhere more comforting than that in the arms of a sister?
~Alice Walker

Throughout my childhood, I constantly dreamed of being an only child—having no one around to fight with, to share with, to grab the remote away from me in the middle of a "big game." I would have the biggest bedroom in the house and be able to talk on the phone as long as I wanted, without being asked a million times, "Are you off yet?" But I was not born an only child; I was born with an older sister. I have always called my sister "Kicki," instead of her real name, Christie, because, when I was younger, I had trouble pronouncing the r and s. To this day, she is still "Kicki."

I started playing basketball when I was eight years old. My dad was the coach of my team, and my mom kept score. So my sister, not old enough to stay home alone, was forced to come to all of my games. I remember looking into the stands for my mother's approval during games and seeing my sister's face, confused. It was obvious that she wasn't thrilled to be there, but she cheered along with the crowd anyway. Her hair was cut short, almost as short as mine, and her teeth stuck out. I teased her often, calling her "bucky beaver." She wasn't a very attractive little girl, and she looked more like my older brother than my sister.

After the games, on the car rides home, my parents and I relived every move I had made on the court. My sister sat in the backseat with me in silence, not knowing how or when to enter the conversation.

Most nights she came into my room and said, "Good night, Brad. Good game." I would smile and thank her. I never really took her compliment seriously. I mean, she hardly understood what was going on in the games; she couldn't possibly know whether I had played well or not.

It wasn't until I reached high school that I realized what a truly beautiful person my sister was. Everybody knew her and thought highly of her, and I was referred to as "Christie's little brother." Kicki was on the Homecoming Court her senior year, and she stood tall and beautiful. I was astonished at the person she had become: smart, sweet and beautiful. To me, she was still the ten-year-old little girl with the boyish looks and buck teeth.

I played basketball in high school, and although Christie wasn't forced to attend my games anymore, she still came every week, cheering me on from the stands. I remember one game in particular, the last game of the season. My sister sat in the bleachers with her boyfriend and a large group of friends. Printed on her shirt, in big bright red letters, were the words "BRAD'S SISTER." Suddenly I was embarrassed. But it wasn't her presence that embarrassed me, rather, it was the fact that I had never appreciated her support before. She was never embarrassed to be my sister, even though I had been embarrassed to call her that so many years ago. She didn't care what anyone thought, and she never had.

I am an only child now; my sister left for college a few months after that last game. I finally have the biggest room in the house and the remote control all to myself. But now that she's gone, I kind of miss having someone to fight with for the phone, and the big bedroom isn't all that great anyway.

I went to visit her at college for a weekend, and as I stood outside her dorm, waiting for her to come out, a friend of hers walked past me and questioned, "Hey, aren't you Christie's brother?"

I beamed and said proudly, "Yeah, I am. I'm Christie's brother."

~Brad Dixon
Chicken Soup for the Teenage Soul III

45

More than Just Sisters

My sister and I have always had a special kind of bond. Being the only kids in the family, we were stuck with each other. Not that it was bad or anything, but we had our share of arguments and fights.

Although I would never admit it, I always looked up to her. Somewhere along the way, she became known as Sissy, and my nickname became Julie-Bug. I would try to hang out with her and her friends, only to be kicked out of her room, eventually eavesdropping at her door on their juicy conversations. Whenever she had a date, you could always catch my friend Ruth and me peeking out the window or hiding in the bushes, giggling. My sister and I even went through a "prank phase." I don't remember who started it, but we went through weeks of Saran Wrapped toilet seats, Vaseline covered phones, short-sheeted beds and frozen underwear — yes, frozen underwear. Eventually our parents had to break it up, for some of the tricks were getting out of hand, and although they were intended for each other, sometimes the effects ricocheted off our parents. Of course, being sisters, we also experienced our share of fighting over clothes and stealing, I mean borrowing, each other's things. Even though we occasionally… okay, daily, got in fights, we could never remain angry at each other for long.

When I was in middle school and she was in high school, she started letting me hang out with her friends. Once in a while she asked if I would like to go out with them, and I would eagerly reply yes. Sometimes she even let me tag along with her and her boyfriend to the movies or out to eat. Whenever I needed help with my homework she always made herself available to tutor me. When she turned sixteen and got her first car, she usually found time to take me to the Dairy Queen for a treat and on occasion brought me lunch at school.

The day we took her to college for her freshman year was the hardest day for me. Though my dad tried to comfort me on the long four-and-a-half-hour ride home, I cried from the time my sister and I said goodbye to when my parents and I reached our hometown. I missed her more than anything. I became the "only child" at home and, although I thought it was going to be great to receive all the extra attention, I hated it. I had more fights with Mom, more supervision and, worst of all, more chores. Adjusting to her absence at home wasn't easy, and occasionally I would catch myself walking out the door in the morning yelling, "Bye Mom, bye Dad, bye Ann Marie!"

Late one Saturday night, she called me, frustrated with school, friends, boys and life. We had always been able to call each other and talk about stuff, but this conversation was different. She told me her troubles and although I can't remember our conversation as well as she can, I tried my best to comfort her and give her good advice. That night I went from being her little sister to being a trusted source of listening and support. I told her that night, before we hung up, that she was my best friend. Later that week, I received a letter from her and this poem:

> *Sister*
> *I met my best friend last night.*
> *She's been under my nose for a while.*
> *How could I have been so blind?*
> *She's been with me all my life.*
> *Younger,*
> *and more intelligent than me,*
> *because she was the first one to see it:*
> *The tremendous friendship we possess,*

that binds us together as sisters,
and as friends.

That night we both came to the realization that we are more than just sisters, we are the best of friends.

~Julie Hoover
Chicken Soup for the Teenage Soul IV

The Bridge Between Verses

A friend is a brother who was once a bother.
~Author Unknown

My brother is the boy with the big black eyes. He has an aura about him that feels strange and nervous. My brother is different. He doesn't understand when jokes are made. He takes a long time to learn basic things. He often laughs for no reason.

He was pretty average until first grade. That year, his teacher complained about him laughing in class. As a punishment, she made him sit in the hall. He spent all his time on the fake mosaic tile outside the room. The next year, he took a test that showed he needed to be placed in a special education class.

As I grew older, I began to resent my brother. When I walked with him, people stared. Not that anything was physically wrong with him; it's just something that radiated from him that attracted attention. I would clench my teeth in anger sometimes, wishing he were like other people, wishing he were normal.

I would glare at him to make him uncomfortable. Every time my eyes met his, stark and too bright, I would say loudly, "What?" He'd turn his head quickly and mutter, "Nothing." I rarely called him by his name.

My friends would tell me I was being mean to him. I brushed it off, thinking that they were also horrible to their siblings. I did not consider the fact that their brothers and sisters could retaliate. Sometimes I would be nice to my brother just because they were around, but return to being mean the minute they left.

My cruelty and embarrassment continued until one day last summer. It was a holiday, but both my parents were working. I had an orthodontist appointment and was supposed to take my brother with me. The weather was warm, being a July afternoon. As spring was over, there was no fresh scent or taste of moisture in the air, only the empty feeling of summer. As we walked down the sidewalk, on impulse I began to talk to him.

I asked him how his summer was going, what his favorite kind of car was, what he planned to do in the future. His answers were rather boring, but I wasn't bored. It turns out I have a brother who loves Cadillacs, wants to be an engineer or a business person, and loves listening to what he calls "rap" music (the example he gave was Aerosmith). I also have a brother with an innocent grin that can light up a room or an already sunny day. I have a brother who is ambitious, kind, friendly, open and talkative.

The conversation we had that day was special. It was a new beginning for me.

A week later, we were on a family trip to Boston, and I was in the back seat of our van. I was reading a Stephen King novel, while my dad and my brother sat up front talking. A few of their words caught my attention, and I found myself listening to their conversation while pretending to be engrossed in my book. My brother said, "Last week, we were walking to the bus stop. We had a good conversation and she was nice to me."

That's all he said. As simple as his words were, they were heart-felt. He held no dislike toward me. He just accepted that I'd finally become the sister I should have been from the beginning. I closed the book and stared at the back cover. The author's face blurred as I realized I was crying.

I will not pretend everything is fine and dandy now. Unlike changes in a *Wonder Years* episode, nothing's perfect and nothing's permanent. What I will say is that I do not glare at my brother any more. I walk with him in public. I help him use the computer. I call him by his name. Best of all, I continue to have conversations with him. Conversations that are boring in the nicest possible way.

~Shashi Bhat
Chicken Soup for the Teenage Soul II

She's My Sister

Little deeds of kindness, little words of love, help to make Earth happy.
~Julia Carney

He was twelve years old and going on sixteen. He gelled his hair into spikes and wore his pants with the crotch below the knees. He listened to rap music, watched MTV, and generously bestowed on me the nickname, "Sister C."

Yet when I looked at my brother Matthew, I kept expecting to find the little kid he once had been—the sweet, eager boy who used to drag me outside by the arm, begging me to play football with him or to help him build a clubhouse or to catch salamanders in the creek. That Matthew had always looked up to me. I had been his hero, his big sister and—despite our age difference of several years—his best friend. Now everything was changing.

These days, instead of our usual hikes through the woods, Matthew spent his time indoors, talking on the phone. He refused to dive after the football when we played catch for fear of getting grass stains on his designer jeans, and he hollered at me whenever I bopped him playfully on the head, because how dare I mess up his perfectly sculpted hair.

Of course I had always known he would grow up eventually—I just hadn't expected it to happen overnight. Matthew was becoming a teenager faster than I thought possible. It was tough facing the fact that I was no longer the center of my brother's universe, and I worried about where I fit in this new life of his.

I discovered the answer during the spring of Matthew's seventh grade year. That was when the kids from my brother's small private school attended a weeklong outdoor education camp. I had always been involved with Matthew's school, and because I loved both the outdoors and kids, I volunteered to chaperone.

On the very first day of camp, I was playing catch with Matthew and some of his friends. We were tossing my brother's football back and forth when some older boys—older than Matthew, at any rate, a few around my age—sauntered over and began snatching the football in midair.

These boys were obviously part of the "in" crowd here at camp. They dressed like teen pop stars and strutted around like they owned the place. It wasn't long before they had joined my brother and his friends, starting up a competition to see who could throw the football the hardest.

A year ago Matthew would have stood quietly to the side, not sure how to handle himself around "cool" guys like these. But not anymore. Now, my formerly shy kid brother jumped right into the action, showing off exaggerated football player poses, playing the part of the goofball and making everybody laugh. I could hardly believe the change.

For the rest of the week I barely saw my brother. During meals he sat at the most crowded table in the cafeteria, the one packed with young teenagers sporting the latest styles and laughing loudly. Not only that, but my brother was usually the center of attention, making pyramids out of water glasses and blowing straw wrappers at all of his buddies. He was the wacky kid everybody in camp knew and loved. As for me, I quickly became known as "Matthew's big sister."

I was happy for him; I really was. For the first time in his life my brother had more friends than he knew what to do with. But a part of me resented being cast aside like an old shoe. I was the one who had taught Matthew how to blow the wrappers off of straws. I had taught him to play football. I had been with him for every major moment in his life until now, and suddenly it was as if none of that mattered.

Or so I thought.

Then, on the last evening of camp, Matthew ran up to me as I was heading back to my cabin. "Chrissy!" he called out. "We're gonna play football! You have to come!"

I blinked in surprise. "Are you sure you want me to?" I asked. "I won't embarrass you?"

"Not unless you stink up the place," he replied, but he was smiling. "It doesn't matter. Just play."

I followed Matthew to the football field. All his cool new friends were there waiting, and when they saw me, they laughed. "I thought you were getting a real player!" one of the guys exclaimed. "Why'd you bring a girl?"

"She's my sister," was Matthew's reply. "And she's really good!"

"Hey, girl!" another boy laughed. "Do you know what this thing is?" He held the football two inches from my face.

"Yeah." I grinned and jokingly shoved my fist in front of the boy's nose. "Do you know what this is?"

A few of the guys snickered, and we were able to get on with the game.

As bad luck would have it, I wound up on the opposite team from Matthew. Still, I wanted to score a hundred touchdowns to prove to my brother that his faith in me wasn't misplaced.

Unfortunately, I never got that chance. The guys on my team simply refused to pass the ball to a girl. In fact, they wouldn't let me anywhere near it. That football game might have been the most frustrating I'd ever played... had it not been for Matthew.

As soon as he realized what was happening, he began to stick up for me. He shouted loudly over at his teammates.

"It's a good thing they're not throwing the ball to my sister or we'd be losing big time! She's wide open during every play!

"Hey, if you hadn't pushed in front of my sister she could've gotten that kick return and made a touchdown! Lucky for us you're not letting the fast person touch the ball!

"At least my sister isn't guarding our good players or we'd never even score!"

Over and over, throughout the entire game, my brother stood

up for me in front of all his new friends. As badly as he wanted to be one of them, and as important as it was for him to be cool, Matthew proved that I was even more important. "She's my sister," he had said proudly. And the awesome thing was that he was still saying it, even though I couldn't even try to score a single touchdown. He claimed me even when his friends laughed.

That night I realized that I no longer had to worry about losing my brother as he became a teenager. I didn't have to worry about ever losing him. Because even though our relationship might change over time, it would always be strong.

That night Matthew proved that no matter what, he would always care about me, and on that night I had never been prouder to be called his sister.

~Christina Dotson
Chicken Soup for the Teenage Soul IV

A Closer Family

Dear *Chicken Soup for the Teenage Soul*,

I am writing to thank you for the story "Healing with Love" by Cecile Wood in your new edition of *Chicken Soup for the Teenage Soul III*. As soon as I started reading the first line and the words "reform school" leaped off the page, I knew I was going to be able to relate to the story.

My brother was dealing with a drug problem last year and had to be checked in to a center for kids with drug problems. He was eighteen at the time. Being at the center made him a whole new person. Before he went, we couldn't even speak to him. We would ask him how his day went, and he would respond with only a nod. He never even said "Hi" or "Bye" to us. We felt completely shut out of his life.

He was allowed no family contact at all for the first three weeks of the program. After the three weeks were over, my whole family went to visit him. He was waiting for us outside and greeted us all with big hugs. I was shocked and didn't hide it. I asked him what they had done to him, and he told me that he had just "grown up."

That entire day he couldn't stop talking about how much he enjoyed being there and thanking my parents for having sent him there. I was so happy for him. It felt like I finally had my brother back.

In the story in the book, Cecile wrote about not being able to have a meal at the center where she was visiting her brother without crying. I had the same experience. When I had lunch with my brother and the other residents later that day, it was a struggle for me to hold back my tears. It was sad to look at the kids working so hard to get themselves together and pull themselves back up. I wondered what had brought each of them down so low to begin with.

Not all of the kids were alone that weekend; there were some other parents there, too. Everyone seemed genuinely happy and proud of their sons or daughters. There were a lot of tears shed.

My brother and I were closer after that weekend. We would talk on the phone all the time. He called me once a week, and we would talk for hours and hours. I guess we had a lot of catching up to do.

He's nineteen now, and he just finished his treatment program. He's been sober and off drugs for almost an entire year now. I'm so happy for him, and my family feels closer than we've ever been. Yesterday I made my brother read the story "Healing with Love." He read it out loud in front of my parents and my twenty-two-year-old brother. He couldn't finish it because he started crying halfway through. I guess it was difficult to remember all the pain he had to go through to get to where he is today. I finished the story for him. My whole family could relate, and it made us all feel so grateful that my brother was able to "heal with love." Thank you again for this wonderful story of hope and healing.

Sincerely,

~Lissa Desjardins
Chicken Soup for the Teenage Soul Letters

Teens Talk

Relationships

The Dreaded "Let's Just Be Friends"

We must embrace pain and burn it as fuel for our journey.
~Kenji Miyazawa

49

Just Friends

Here's the story of a guy,
Who learns that no matter how hard you try,
"Best friends forever" means just that.
It all began one normal day,

When everything was fine.
The new girl sat down next to me,
Her heart beat close to mine.

We often said "hello" and "hi,"
Talked about things so dumb.
I never would have guessed then that
Such good friends we'd become.

Together we talked and laughed,
We knew what the other liked and desired.
She was funny, pretty and smart,
And that was everything I admired.

"Best friends 'til the end" we promised,
And soon the months passed.
You grew on me, I grew on you;
Time flew by so fast.

I took the plunge, I held my breath,

I meant those fateful words.
You said, "Can't we just be friends?"
But "no" is what I heard.

My heart was crushed and torn in half,
It was the moment that I'd dreaded.
You left me with no other choice,
So just friends we'll stay instead.

~Matthew Chee
Chicken Soup for the Teenage Soul: The Real Deal Friends

50

Love is Never Lost

hey say it's better to have loved and lost than never to have loved at all.

That thought wouldn't be very comforting to Mike Sanders. He had just been dumped by his girlfriend. Of course, she didn't put it quite that way. She said, "I do care about you, Mike, and I hope we can still be friends."

"Great," Mike thought. "Still be friends. You, me and your new boyfriend will go to the movies together."

Mike and Angie had been going together since they were freshman. But over the summer, she had met someone else. Now as he entered his senior year, Mike was alone. For three years they shared the same friends and favorite hangouts. The thought of returning to those surroundings without Angie made him feel — well, empty.

Football practice usually helped him take his mind off his troubles. Coaches have a way of running you until you are so tired, you can't really think of anything else. But lately, Mike's heart just wasn't in it. One day it caught up with him. He dropped passes he wouldn't normally miss and let himself get tackled by guys who had never been able to touch him before.

Mike knew better than to have the coach yell at him more than once, so he tried a littler harder and made it through the rest of the practice. As he was running off the field, he was told to report to the coach's office. "Girl, family or school? Which one is bothering you, son?" asked his coach.

"Girl," Mike responded. "How did you guess?"

"Sanders, I've been coaching football since before you were born, and every time I've seen an all-star play like a J.V. rookie, it's been because of one of those three."

Mike nodded. "Sorry, sir. It won't happen again."

His coach patted him on the shoulder. "This is a big year for you, Mike. There's no reason why you shouldn't get a full ride to the school of your choice. Just remember to focus on what's really important. The other things will take care of themselves."

Mike knew his coach was right. He should just let Angie go and move on with his life. But he still felt hurt, even betrayed. "It just makes me so mad, Coach. I trusted in her. I opened myself up to her. I gave her all I had, and what did it get me?"

His coach pulled out some paper and a pen from his desk drawer. "That's a really good question. What did it get you?" He handed Mike the pen and paper and said, "I want you to think about the time you spent with this girl and list as many experiences, good and bad, that you can remember. Then I want you to write down the things that you learned from each other. I'll be back in an hour." With that, the coach left Mike by himself.

Mike slumped in his chair as memories of Angie flooded his head. He recalled when he had first worked up the nerve to ask her out, and how happy he had been when she said yes. Had it not been for Angie's encouragement, Mike wouldn't have tried out for the football team.

Then he thought of the fights that they had. Though he couldn't remember all the reasons for fighting, he remembered the sense of accomplishment he got from working through their problems. He had learned to communicate and compromise. He remembered making up after fights, too. That was always the best part.

Mike remembered all the times she made him feel strong and needed and special. He filled the paper with their history, holidays, trips with each other's family, school dances and quiet picnics together. Line by line, he wrote of the experience they shared, and he realized how she had helped shape his life. He would have become a different person without her.

When the coach returned, Mike was gone. He had left a note on the desk that simply read:

Coach,

Thanks for the lesson. I guess it's true what they say about having loved and lost, after all. See you at practice.

~David J. Murcott
Chicken Soup for the Teenage Soul II

51

A Changing Season

When we are no longer able to change a situation,
we are challenged to change ourselves.
~Victor Frankl

I went to his soccer games, and he went to my shows. I thought I could count on him, and he could count on me. That's how best friends work. And that's exactly what Chris was — my best friend. At least, I thought he was. With his short blond hair and daydreaming blue eyes, he was my stability. Was, not is.

Our friendship was easy to figure out — not much was left to the imagination. Everyone knew we were the best of friends. If you couldn't find Chris, he was likely with me, and vice versa. He always had a girlfriend, and I was always flirting with his friends. I never cared if my shirt was wrinkled or I wasn't wearing makeup around him. I mean, it was just Chris. In my eyes, he never cared about those types of things. Chris was just my bud. We played video games for hours, and he taught me how to skateboard. I taught him how to develop a picture in a darkroom. And then there were those nightly expeditions where we'd lie in the middle of a field and talk about what we thought the future held for us and what part of New York City we'd live in one day. My favorite thing about Chris was his need to look you right in the eye. He felt you couldn't truly connect with someone until you looked him in the eyes.

I cried in his arms over my first broken heart and jumped into them when I got the part of Dorothy in *The Wizard of Oz*. He knew all about my life, and I was always up to date on his. My friends told me that boys and girls could never be good friends because the attraction part always got in the way. I told them they were wrong, that Chris and I were different. He was like my brother and I was like his sister. At least, that's how I viewed our relationship.

Well, apparently this wasn't a two way street. I found out one day that Chris viewed our relationship as something more when he confessed his love to me. Chris's vibrant blue eyes locked onto mine as I told him that I loved him, yet I wasn't in love with him. At first, he was fine with that decision, and we stayed close friends.

But freshman year slowly crept up on us, and things took a drastic turn. His soccer buddies began to tease him about the "girl next door" who had turned him down. Behind my back, his friends would sit and crack jokes about me, and soon Chris broke, joining in and slowly picking me apart. The way I dressed, the way I acted, my personality, my weight and my skin all became hot targets for teasing. Before I knew it, the teasing escalated to where there were no boundaries. He did it to my face.

All of a sudden, I didn't know Chris anymore. He had morphed into someone else. No more nightly field expeditions, no more CD swapping or sharing secrets. The Chris I knew was gone. My heart was broken, and my shoulder to cry on was missing. I started to question if my friends had been right in the first place. Is it possible for guys and girls to be just friends? My answer had always been "yes," but I began to doubt myself. I began to doubt everything. Did I ever truly know Chris? Was the guy I knew and trusted the real Chris?

As the months passed, I became more fed up. One day, before class began, I let it all out. I yelled at Chris. I yelled at him for changing and for not being the person I thought he was, for not being my stability when I needed him the most. His response was none other than a blank stare at the floor. I no longer recognized him. His hair was shaggy, he had gained weight, and he wasn't smiling. He was no longer my best friend.

A whole year later, the Chris I once knew has never fully returned, yet the mean Chris did dissolve. I have come to see that friends fade and people change, as do seasons, but at least you know what season is coming. I thought I knew Chris, and it took me a while to finally realize I didn't. One thing has changed since I came to that realization—he hasn't looked me in the eyes.

~Grace French
Chicken Soup for the Teenage Soul: The Real Deal School

52

One of Those Days

You have learned something.
That always feels at first as if you had lost something.
~H.G. Wells

Today is one of those days when I miss him—the lonely I-wonder-what-he-is-doing days. I don't have them often, hardly at all, but once in a while I do when I hear a song he used to sing or drive past his neighborhood. I am not sure why it is that I sometimes still miss him. It's been nearly eight months since we broke up for the second time. Maybe losing him bothers me a lot more than I let myself believe. Sometimes, I hate myself because I know that I am to blame.

The first time I met Justin I was completely infatuated with him. I just knew that I had to be with him, and two months later, I was. For a while, I thought my life was perfect. He was older and more mature than previous boyfriends were; he knew how to have a real relationship that meant something. I was always happy, and I always felt beautiful around him.

Eventually, my immaturity began to surface. Three and a half months into the relationship I started to feel like my freedom was dwindling. I still cared about him a lot, but I was feeling exhausted. I needed a break. He wasn't ready to let me go, but I wasn't going to let that stop me. Tearfully, I chose to take the road of independence and broke his heart in the process.

I dated other guys, but he would creep into my thoughts at least once a day. None of the guys measured up to him; none of them gave me the special feelings that I longed for day after day. Then, one day, about eight months after our breakup, he called out of the blue. Until then we had barely spoken, and I realized just how much I really missed him. We decided to get together and catch up. We went out to dinner, and he talked about his new girlfriend... a lot. I thought I was going to have to dump my glass of water on him to get him to shut up about her. After a long conversation he revealed that he wanted me back. And I wanted him back. So, after his breakup and a few more emotionally charged talks, we got back together. It almost felt as if no time had passed since we were last a couple. We were happy, and I felt complete again. I had matured a lot and could now handle committing to him. Sometimes my adoration for him would overwhelm me. Never before, and never after, have I cared about a boy so strongly.

After a while, though, I became too busy with my after school activities to be able to put so much energy into the relationship. He felt like I was betraying everything that we had, everything we had worked for. And in a moment of anger, I felt like he betrayed my trust in the worst way. We broke up. I held a grudge for a long time. My pride was wounded and my feelings torn.

With time we were able to be friends again. We had given it two tries, and it seemed it wasn't meant to be. What I learned from him and the relationship was worth all the painful times we went through. There were many happy memories, too. I heard a quote once that rang loud and true: "You always believe your first love to be your last, and your last to be your first." For me, he's been both. We shared secrets and laughs, rainy nights and sunny days. Though we experienced many storms together, we taught each other valuable lessons about life and love. The way that I was able to look at myself through his eyes was one of the most amazing feelings I've ever had. But, there comes a time when the feelings start to fade and the memories become bittersweet. A time when all that you can do is hope that somehow he will realize what a difference he made in your life and how he contributed to the person that you've become.

I can't ignore the feelings that once were. I can, however, let go and remember.

~Cassie Kirby
Chicken Soup for the Teenage Soul on Love & Friendship

53

I Had to Let Him Go

Giving up doesn't always mean you are weak;
sometimes it means that you are strong enough to let go.
~Author Unknown

"I'm sorry, I just don't really remember...."

His words tore through me, piercing every inch of my body and cutting jaggedly through to my heart. Just one week earlier, we had watched the sun set and held each other. He comforted me while I asked him why my best friend and I just couldn't get along anymore. But tonight, his mind was somewhere else; he couldn't remember that special night.

Why was he so distant? Was he so lost in the pain that had been haunting him for so long?

There were nights he cried himself to sleep, remembering the harsh words of his mother. He told me how much he dreaded the weekends spent with her, because it meant another seventy-two hours of being blamed for everything that went wrong. The nagging didn't stop—she harassed him because his grades were lower than his brother's and he wasn't the perfect son she wanted him to be. She said he was dumb; that he wouldn't get into college, wouldn't succeed in life. She called him a loser, a disappointment to her. His gift at art was undeniable, yet her criticism caused him to believe he had no talent, when actually, he was winning prizes for his work.

What kept him alive, he told me, was our love. Friends for years, and now dating, he needed me. He counted on me. In one letter I received from him, he said, "You're like my family. Just you. We can be a family. Do you need anyone else? I don't. Just keep loving me," he wrote, "and I'll be okay."

For a while, I believed him. I promised I would never hurt him like she had, never leave him, never stop loving him. I would be his family; the one he needed in good times and in bad, the one who held him when he was sick and cheered for him at track meets. I thought that if I held him tightly enough, his pain would disappear.

It was like a roller coaster, though, our relationship. Sometimes, he was the happiest kid I knew—laughing, joking, smiling and kissing. I always knew if he was happy by his eyes. Crystal clear and blue, they told me no lies. If he was happy, they sparkled. But if he was sad, they seemed more gray than blue. On those sad days, he didn't joke. When I tried to cheer him with a kiss, he would refuse. He wouldn't let me touch him. I couldn't show him how much I loved him. When he was hurt, all he knew was to return the hurt to those undeserving. He said things he knew were cruel, apologizing the next day. The cycle never ended—the cruelties, the apologies. Yet I knew why.

Though I loved him, I couldn't take away his pain. It stemmed from events that occurred long before I knew him. Soon I realized my love couldn't compete with his inner pain. Though it hurt, I realized that I couldn't help him; rather, he had to seek professional help. I had to let him go.

The night I told him this couldn't continue, the tears stung my eyes more painfully than ever before. He now would have to face his worst fear—to be alone to confront the real demons within him. He thought I had deceived him, that I had lied to him when I whispered the word forever. But I hadn't lied to anyone but myself because I believed that all he needed was my love. Right now, my love was only causing pain.

He had built a separate world in which only he and I existed. For a while, it had been nice to dream of such a happy place, a mystical Eden for just the two of us. Before long, however, I knew the walls would crumble if he kept relying only on me. Deep down I knew it wasn't healthy for either of us. I simply couldn't hold on to us and this fantasy any longer.

Yesterday, I saw him for the first time in a year. His eyes sparkled, and the light came from within. The darkness is lifting because he allowed other people into his life, people who helped him in more ways than I ever could have done on my own. Now, he sees the special gifts that he has, and although the painful memories will always remain, he is now beginning to believe in himself. Yesterday, I realized that even perfect love can't protect someone from himself. And sometimes, the most loving thing you can do for someone is to let him go.

~Andrea Barkoukis
Chicken Soup for the Teenage Soul III

Chapter 8

Teens Talk

Relationships

Breakups and Healing

Love is like a puzzle.
When you're in love, all the pieces fit but when
your heart gets broken, it takes a while to get everything back together.
~Author Unknown

The World Won't Stop

Sometimes I wish I were a little kid again,
skinned knees are easier to fix than broken hearts.
~Author Unknown

People say that a teenager's biggest fear is a broken heart. I think they're right. In past relationships I always ran, reasoning that if I didn't give anyone my heart, then they couldn't break it. But when I met Jake last summer, it was different. I fell in love with Jake the moment my eyes met his alluring smile.

We played Wiffle Ball that day under the blistering afternoon sun. I tried to steal second, and I ended up pinned beneath him in the scorching sand. I'll never forget looking up to see his almond eyes shining down into mine. I instantly let down my guard. By the end of the day, we were revealing our darkest secrets while we played Chicken in the refreshing ocean.

Eventually, Jake's hand found mine that day, and our lips met soon after. The monstrous waves crashed like thunder behind us, and somehow his hand fit perfectly into the curve of my waist. I'm surprised he didn't hear my pounding heart as the anxiety raced throughout my body.

As soon as I kissed Jake, I was afraid to love him. But my fears were soon replaced with a sense of security. So I gave Jake my heart and slowly fell for him.

Our personalities simply clicked, and the next few months were unforgettable. The times we shared were filled with intense talks, innocent kisses and genuine laughter. The words he spoke, no matter how trivial, always found their way to a place inside my heart.

He attempted to teach me how to play pool, and he proudly introduced me to all of his college friends. I loved how he would call just to hear the sound of my voice, making me feel as if I was the only girl in the world. My face would light up each time his car pulled up in front of my house. His car was old, and there was no mistaking the familiar sound of the rumbling engine and his blaring music. "Hey, sweetie," he would say as I climbed into the front seat.

I never questioned falling for Jake until he was no longer there to catch me. He disappeared from my life as quickly as he came. With him he took a part of my heart that I had never given before. Jake did precisely what he had promised he would never do—he left me defenseless and alone. To this day I'll never know exactly why, but Jake simply stopped calling.

Heartbroken, I found myself thinking about him constantly. I missed the scent of his clothes and the way he grasped my hand, carefully curling his fingers around mine. I missed him telling me he didn't ever want to lose me. I missed how I felt complete when we were together.

At night I would clutch my fists and bite my lip, too frightened to close my eyes because I would always end up picturing his silly grin. Every song reminded me of him. My heart wouldn't let go of the love it felt. Every time the doorbell rang I would race down the steps hoping that his familiar, loving face would be there waiting for me. My mom would walk into my room to find me staring out my window, gazing at the empty street below. Each day I concentrated on breathing, walking, talking and trying desperately not to feel.

Eventually, I began to heal my broken heart. My eyes were no longer swollen and red, and I began to accept my life without Jake in it. I slowly understood I was braver than I believed, and I was stronger than I seemed. A guy was not more important than myself. The world would not stop for my grief, and although my heart was broken, it would keep beating just the same.

The other day I returned to the desolate beach where it all began.

The wind swept strands of hair across my face as the tide slowly crept up the shore line. The waves then quickly retreated, leaving behind tiny remnants of the past. Through my tears I smiled and realized that love finds people when they are least expecting it, and unfortunately it sometimes leaves in the same way. However, the memories and lessons, no matter how short-lived, remain intact forever. Love never leaves; it stays in the heart, and eventually we stop thinking about what we lost and are grateful for what we gained.

There is a reason why I met Jake, loved Jake and lost Jake. I can't say I'm glad I felt so much pain, but there was also that warm, tingling feeling inside my heart. It's necessary for me to love beyond my fears and trust beyond my doubts if I want to truly live my life. And yes, perhaps my tears may fall, but I will not.

I guess a teenager's biggest fear is a broken heart. Mine used to be, but not anymore. Jake was worth it. After all, it is the wounded heart that makes us all human in the end.

~Meredith Wertz
Chicken Soup for the Christian Teenage Soul

Always

Love does not begin and end the way we seem to think it does.
Love is a battle, love is a war;
love is a growing up.
~James Baldwin

"So can I ride my bike to your house tonight? Give me directions."

I laughed at Adam's childish request. "Ad, I live in Washington. It'll take you hours to get there!" I stared into his dark brown eyes, waiting for a response.

As I studied his face, a look of seriousness washed over him, and he answered, "You know, I'd do anything to see you. I love you, Amy Catalano." He started to sing our favorite Bon Jovi song, "Always." I blushed and lowered my eyes. This wasn't the first time Adam had confessed his love for me. He was always saying things like that. But tonight, as we sat across from each other in the crowded restaurant, was the first time I said it back and really meant it.

"I love you, too, Adam Baldwin." He smiled and grabbed my hand. My mind raced. What did I just say? Did I just tell him I loved him? His smile told me everything I needed to know.

The year that followed was filled with many ups and downs for us. I spent much of the time battling a serious bout of depression, and we began to drift apart due to my lack of interest in the world surrounding me. Despite my mental state, I thought of him often and still loved him more than anyone. But I knew that before I could be with him, I had to get better. I couldn't let the weight of my world rest on his shoulders, and mine too. That just wasn't fair. My junior year of high school soon ended, and the summer brought relaxation and long-awaited happiness. The storm cloud that had been resting over me lifted, and I was myself again. I called Adam one hot August morning, and we talked for hours. Just as I was getting ready to hang up, he told me that he wanted to see me and invited me to go boating with him and his family that day. I agreed.

The forty minute car ride to his house was spent daydreaming of our reunion. I couldn't wait to have him back in my life. My heart had felt so empty without him. I was still very lost in thought when my mom pulled into his driveway. My stomach was tied in knots. I felt like I was meeting him for the first time all over again. I rang the doorbell. I caught my breath as the door opened. And there he stood — my Adam.

Adam and I sat in the bow of the boat talking while his parents sat in the back. I looked out over the water and the wind whipped violently around my face, causing my long blond hair to come loose from its messy braid.

"You're so beautiful," he suddenly said to me. I hadn't heard those words from him in so long. My heart pounded as I gave a shy "thanks." Then he said it, the one phrase that would change everything: "I don't know how I feel about you anymore, Amy." I sat in shock, staring out across the graying sky. This can't be true, I thought to myself. This can't be happening. I looked at him, hoping that he would laugh and say that it was all just a joke. But the serious look on his face proved that he wasn't joking. I knew from that moment on, nothing would be the same.

I was right.

We soon began fighting, which was very out of the ordinary for Adam and me. We had always gotten along so well. He started pushing me away when I tried to reconcile, saying things like, "People change. Feelings change. You just have to learn to live with that." I had never felt so hurt in all my life. What had I done wrong? I had given him all of me, and I thought he loved me, too. I felt as though the past two years had been nothing but lies. I was left without any reasons, wondering why I had lost him. I pored over his e-mails and notes, and cried for the memories that remained buried in my broken heart. The tears stung my cheeks as I remembered those terrible words. While he moved on, I just couldn't bear to let him go. He was my first love, the first and only boy I ever said those three precious words to. I couldn't forget. I was hurt, angry and lost. I wanted nothing more than to cry myself to sleep and never wake up.

That was almost a year ago. Although I've let go of all the hurt and sadness, I haven't forgotten. We may have been young, but we shared something most people wait a lifetime for. He showed me what it meant to love wholeheartedly. He never judged me. He loved me for the girl I was and made me feel beautiful even when I thought I wasn't. He changed my life in an incredible way, and for that I will always love him.

~Amy Catalano
Chicken Soup for the Teenage Soul on Love & Friendship

To Have a Boyfriend — or Not?

All of a sudden it seemed like all my friends were starting to have boyfriends. Last year in eighth grade, when we talked on the phone, we had talked about all kinds of stuff; like horses, our 'rents, homework and boys, but it wasn't all about boys. Now every conversation was all, "My boyfriend this, my boyfriend that," and I had nothing to contribute. The last straw was when one of my best friends told me about her upcoming birthday party.

"Since my birthday is so close to Valentine's Day, my mom said I can have a couples only party, Patty. Isn't that cool?"

"Huh? Cool? Definitely NOT," I thought. I am the only one without a member of the opposite sex in my life, and I sure won't have one by next weekend.

"Yeah, that's cool, Heather," I managed to stammer out, and I hung up the phone. Great. Just great.

The very next day that all changed when I ran into Tyrone Raymond—literally. I was late to one of my classes (as usual), and as I was barreling around the corner of the building, I ran right into Ty, scattering my books and homework everywhere. He bent down to help me pick up my papers and as he stacked up what he could reach, he looked up at me and grinned. Not bad, I realized with a shock. Not too bad at all. In fact, kinda cute.

Ty Raymond was in our class, but he was a year younger than the rest of us because he had skipped a year of school somewhere along the way to ninth grade. We all figured he must be really smart to have done that. I had heard that his parents had gotten a divorce over the summer and that it had been really hard on Ty and his three little brothers. Other than that, I didn't know much about him; except that now, looking at him, I realized that he was much better looking than I had remembered. His deep brown eyes were dark and sparkling under long eyelashes as he gazed up at me, and his black hair wasn't just a careless buzz cut anymore—it had actually grown into kind of a neat style.

"Patty…"

I snapped back into reality as I realized he was trying to hand me my papers.

"Huh?"

"I've got to get to class. Here's your stuff…."

"Oh… thanks. Ummm… hey, Ty, would you like to go to a party with me on Friday?" Ohmigod. I can't believe I just said that.

"Ahhhh… sure," he answered.

What?????? I was astounded.

He continued, "Give me your number, and I'll call you after school. Sounds like fun." I scribbled my phone number on one of the pieces of paper and gave it to him. Then he turned and walked away, leaving me with my jaw hanging open. That was the beginning.

Ty did call me that night. And every night after that. And he called me in the morning before school every morning to tell me where we would meet so that we could walk to school together. As we walked together, Ty would do one of three things to show the rest of the world that I was HIS—he would have his arm around my back with his hand in the back pocket of my jeans, or wrap his arm around my waist, or grab the back of my neck with his hand as we tried to maneuver though the busy school halls like some weird conjoined set of Siamese twins.

That first couple of days, I was in heaven. Ty obviously liked me a lot. No boy had ever shown me this kind of attention before, and I felt proud of his possessive attitude and that he was always by my side.

On Friday night, my dad drove me over to Ty's house to pick him up for the party. His mom seemed like a nice person but kind of frazzled. It looked like she depended on Ty to help her take care of his three wild little brothers, and she asked us more than once what time the party would be over and when he would be coming back home. Before we left, she asked if I could come over for a family dinner on Sunday, and when I looked to my dad for the answer, he nodded yes, so I accepted. More than ever, I was convinced that this was my first real relationship.

When we got to Heather's house, I was excited. Her family room was dimly lit, and love songs were coming from the sound system. It was the first time I had gone to a party with a guy, and it felt so romantic... at first.

After about two hours of slow dancing with our faces stuck together from nervous sweat and Ty's hands roaming around my back as he held me tightly against him, I was ready to go home. I realized, too late, that I hated kissing Ty. He mashed his mouth so hard against mine that it HURT. I turned my face away so that he couldn't kiss me anymore and managed to mumble something about my braces hurting my lips, so he stopped for a while—but then he started right up again. When I went to the bathroom, he followed me and waited outside the door until I was done. If I wanted food or something to drink, we visited the table together. I started to feel dizzy and sick from the sweating, the groping, the music, the lack of air in the room and Ty trying to kiss me. I felt trapped and suffocated.

Finally, FINALLY... my dad came to get us. As we dropped Ty off at his house, Ty turned to me, smiled and said, "I'll see you on Sunday, Patty."

"Uhhh... okay... see ya." When he closed the door of the car and went into his house, I heaved a sigh of relief. I couldn't wait to get home and hide beneath the covers of my bed. My bed in my room. Away from him.

All day Saturday, I thought about Ty and how I was feeling. Every time the phone rang, I let my mom or dad answer it. When he did call, I was conveniently too busy to answer. "If this is how a relationship is supposed to be," I thought, "I don't want any part of it." I felt like I couldn't breathe. I didn't know how to tell him that I just couldn't do this anymore, so I did the logical thing—I chickened out. On Sunday, I pleaded with my mom to call Ty's mom to let her know I wasn't feeling well enough to go to dinner at their house. It actually was the truth—just the thought of seeing Ty right then made my stomach turn.

As I expected, Ty called me the first thing on Monday morning.

"What happened to you yesterday, Patty? My mom was looking forward to having you for dinner, and she missed seeing you. And what about all day Saturday? I called and called but I never got you."

My mind was spinning like an animal in a cage. What am I going to say to get out of this?

"Never mind," Ty said. "You can tell me all about it on the way to school. I'll meet you at the usual corner."

"Uh, Ty, I'm not going to walk to school with you," I blurted.

"WHAT!!?" He shouted.

"I don't want to date you anymore. I want to break up," I ventured timidly.

"What are you talking about? Is there someone else? That's it—you have been seeing someone else behind my back. Who is it? I'm going to beat the snot out of him! I'm going to...."

"Ty!" I interrupted. "I'm not seeing anyone at all. It isn't that! I think I'm just not ready for a boyfriend. I don't want to date anyone yet." I was barely able to breathe from the pressure of trying to understand my own feelings and to explain myself. "I don't want to belong to someone. I... I just don't want to...."

"All right, you baby. Whatever!" And he slammed the phone down.

I barely made it to school at all that day. My mom had to give me a tardy excuse because it took me so long to stop crying and to do something about my red swollen eyes. But the reality is I did make it to school. And I made it the next day and the next—and I walked down the halls alone or with my girlfriends. I didn't need Ty to be glued to my side to be okay. He moved shortly after that, and luckily I didn't have to worry about running into him in the halls anymore.

It took me a while to realize that Ty's possessive behavior wasn't normal and that wasn't how a healthy relationship should be. You should never feel pressured into doing something you are not ready to do, like you are trapped or owned, or be made to feel guilty if you want to hang out with your friends or like you can't do anything on your own without making your boyfriend mad at you. It's just way better to be a boyfriend have-not!

~Patty Hansen
Chicken Soup for the Girl's Soul

The First

Wisdom begins at the end.
~Daniel Webster

It ended as abruptly as it began. A brief phone call, then the final goodbye. I hung up the phone and sat silently in a daze for a moment. Then reality sank in, and I began to cry. A friendly breakup of a far-from-perfect relationship, and yet it still hurt. A lot.

It was in the school gym, among all our friends, that he began to weave his magic. It began with a sweet smile and a light brush of his fingers across my arm. A half hour before the dance ended, he uttered the words I had been dying to hear:

"Want to go to a movie sometime?"

I responded with a calm smile and a confident "yes" that belied the excitement coursing through my body. I felt as though I had won the lottery. My life was now complete. I had a boyfriend.

We walked out to the parking lot together, and with his mother waiting in the car just out of sight, he gazed into my eyes and kissed me on the cheek. Then with a whispered promise to call, he left. It felt so unreal. In one night, we had gone from being mere acquaintances to being the closest of friends. We were a couple.

Soon, we were strolling down the halls hand-in-hand, and I could think of nothing but him. I was nuts about him. I had been eagerly awaiting the experience for what felt like forever—the special bond between first loves that is like no other, the closeness between a couple, and perhaps most of all, my first kiss.

It took four dates before it happened. Up until then, we had held hands and cuddled, sitting close together in the plush seats of a darkened movie theater. The cuddling was just as much fun as kissing turned out to be, if not better. He had this way of rubbing his thumb across my knuckles that gave me butterflies.

Finally, we kissed. I had always wondered what my first kiss would be like. One night his mom dropped me off at my house after a movie, and he walked me to my front door. We stood under the porch light, gazing at each other shyly. Then he slowly came toward me, lowered his head and kissed me. It was over before I even realized it had happened. I wish I could say that fireworks exploded, but they didn't. After all, it was only a two second meeting of lips. Nonetheless, it was everything I had hoped for. It was sweet and tender and caring, and just the tiniest bit awkward, because it was his first kiss, too.

If only the rest of the relationship had progressed as wonderfully. Sure, we had many good times, but the true meaning of the word "relationship" was missing. He never seemed to notice, but I was miserable for much of the time. It's hard to put a finger on what exactly bothered me. Mostly, it was a whole lot of little things. We used to go to a movie every weekend without fail. That was fun, but I never got to choose what movie we saw. Also, we never did anything but go to movies. He didn't like going out to eat or even talking. Sure, we discussed movies and recent releases by our favorite bands, but that's about as deep as our conversations got.

Yet, it still didn't occur to me to break up with him. I don't know if it was him that I was so infatuated with or if I was in love with the fact that I had a "boyfriend." I can't deny the pride and confidence I felt when I walked down the street holding his hand and saw how the other girls eyed me enviously, attracted by his good looks and sweet smile. I don't know why I felt that having a boyfriend was so important or why I somehow used it to judge my self-worth.

Finally, I couldn't take it any longer and I became honest with myself. I wanted the relationship to improve or I wanted to move on. And I told him just that when I called him one Friday night. To my astonishment and disappointment, he responded by saying we'd be better off as friends. I agreed. I didn't say anything; I think I was shocked at how easy it was for him. After promising to stay friends, I hung up and it was over.

After the initial shock wore off, my first feeling was one of relief. I no longer had to wonder what he was thinking all the time or ponder where we stood. Then it hit me: It was over. I cried. And then I got mad at myself for letting him make me cry. I blamed myself for not making it work. I cried some more.

And then one day I woke up and realized that life goes on. I experienced a lot of firsts with him—my first kiss, my first love and even my first heartbreak—and I'm grateful for all of it.

~Hannah Brandys
Chicken Soup for the Teenage Soul on Love & Friendship

58

Hopscotch and Tears

I watched the blue Toyota speed down my street and listened to the sound of the diesel engine fade. Tears collected in my eyes and trailed down my cheeks until I could taste them. I couldn't believe what had just happened. Making my way into the house, I quickly ran up the stairs, hoping that my brother wouldn't see the frozen look of terror in my eyes. Luckily that rainy day, his eyes were glued to the TV.

Plopping down on my unmade bed, I buried my face in my pillow. Light sniffles turned into cries, and cries into hysterics. I couldn't bear it; the pain was too strong, and my heart was broken.

We had been seeing each other for three months and two days (not that I had been counting). I had never been so happy. We had brought out the best in each other. But that day he threw it all away, out the window of his rusty blue Toyota, in a speech that still rings in my ears.

"I don't think we should see each other anymore...." his voice had trailed off. I wanted to ask him why, I wanted to scream at him, I wanted to hold him, but instead I whispered, "Whatever," afraid to look him in the eyes because I knew I would break down.

I lay there crying all afternoon and into the night, feeling so alone, so upset, so confused. For weeks I cried myself to sleep, but in the morning I'd put a plastic smile on my face to avoid having to talk about it. Everybody saw right through it.

My friends were concerned. I think they thought I would recover sooner than I did.

Even months after the breakup, when I heard a car drive up my street I'd jump up to the window to see if it was him. When the phone rang, a chill of hope would run down my spine. One night as I was cutting out magazine pictures and taping photos on my wall, a car came up my street, but I was too preoccupied to notice that it was the car I'd been listening for over the last two months.

"Chloe, it's me, it's…." It was him, calling me to come downstairs! On my way down, my heart was pounding and my thoughts were of a reconciliation. He had seen the error of his ways. When I got outside, there he stood, gorgeous as always.

"Chloe, I came to return your sweater. You left it at my house…. Remember?" I had forgotten all about it.

"Of course. Thank you," I lied. I hadn't seen him since the breakup and it hurt—it hurt a lot. I wanted to be able to love him again.

"Well, I guess I'll just see ya around then," he said. Then he was gone. I found myself alone in the darkness, listening to his car speed away. I slowly walked back to my room and continued to tape photos on my wall.

For weeks, I walked around like a zombie. I would stare at myself for hours in the mirror, trying to figure out what was wrong with me, trying to understand what I did wrong, searching for answers within the mirror. I'd talk to Rachel for hours. "Rachel, did you ever realize that when you fall in love, you only end up falling…." I'd say before breaking down in tears. Her comforting words did little but give me a reason to feel sorry for myself.

Pretty soon my sadness turned into madness. I began to hate him and blame him for my troubles, and I believed he had ruined my life. For months I thought only of him.

Then something changed. I understood I had to go on, and every day I grew a little happier. I even began to see someone new!

One day, as I was flipping through my wallet, I came upon a picture of him. I looked at it for a few minutes, reading his face like a book, a book that I knew I had finished and had to put down. I took out the picture and stuck it in a cluttered drawer.

I smiled to myself as I realized I could do the same in my heart. Tuck him away in a special place and move on. I loved, I lost and I suffered. Now it was time to forgive and forget. I forgave myself also, because so much of my pain was feeling like I did something wrong. I know better now.

My mom used to tell me, "Chloe, there are two kinds of people in this world: those that play hopscotch and sing in the shower, and those that lie alone at night with tears in their eyes." What I came to understand is that people have a choice as to which they want to be, and that each of us is a little of both.

That same day, I went outside and played hopscotch with my sister, and that night I sang louder than ever in the shower.

~Rebecca Woolf
Chicken Soup for the Teenage Soul II

59

Please Sign My Yearbook

The hardest of all is learning to be a well of affection, and not a fountain;
to show them we love them not when we feel like it, but when they do.
~Nan Fairbother

Sitting in class, I concentrated on the back of Brian's neck. Evil thoughts filled my mind; I was secretly waiting for his head to explode. It didn't, and I was forced to watch my ex-boyfriend laugh and chat with every person in the room while he blatantly ignored me.

After Brian and I broke up, third period became pure torture. While I was still nursing what I considered to be the world's worst broken heart, I was bombarded with the sight of my ex's excessive flirting, as if he were proving to me that he was so obviously over his heartache. During class, Brian would gossip loudly about his weekend, his latest party and his new car.

Maybe Brian was trying to get back at me for breaking off our six month relationship. Maybe he thought that if he looked happy, it would hurt me more than I had hurt him.

At the end of the relationship, I let him cry on my shoulder but held a strong heart as he begged me not to go. Of course, he covered his pain very well at school, as if our tearful goodbye had never occurred.

Immediately after the breakup, Brian started dating another girl. She was graduating that spring, as if that were a big feat for a junior boy. She took him to the prom and announced it right beside me in math class. I, too, had a date for the prom, but it still hurt. My hurt curdled and turned to anger. It felt like he was trying to upset me, trying to rub his happiness in my face. Every time I saw them together, I wanted to scream. It felt like the pain was going to tear me in half, or at least force me to consider tearing her in half.

School was coming to an end, and I eagerly waited for summer vacation, my savior. No more Algebra Two and that gnawing feeling in my stomach each day.

One day in dreaded third period, Brian leaned over to me, and to my surprise, he asked me to sign his yearbook. I must have sat there for a full minute before I got over the shock and said yes.

I thought to myself, "This is my chance." I could really let him have it! I could tell him that I knew what he was doing, that he was trying to hurt me, and that it wasn't fair. I could tell him that I saw through his act, that he and I both knew it was exactly that, an act. But then it hit me, what good would come of that? Would belittling him make me feel better, or would it just perpetuate the pain that we both needed to recover from?

Instead of writing of the pain I had endured, I listed all of the fun times we had shared. I wrote about the first place we had ever kissed, the gifts he had given me, the lessons I had learned—the ones he had taught me—and the first "I love you" that was whispered between us. It took up one page, and that quickly became two, until my hand was tired of writing. There were still a million more great memories crowding the corners of my mind, and I remembered many more throughout the day. It made me realize the things I learned from him and what great experiences we had shared. I finished by telling him I held no hard feelings, and I hoped he felt the same.

Maybe what I wrote in his yearbook made me look weak, maybe he thought I was pathetic for still holding onto the memories of our relationship. But writing all those things helped me; it helped me heal the wounds that still hurt in my heart. It felt liberating to let go of the grudge; I finally felt free from my anger.

I realized that Brian had taught me one final lesson: forgiveness. Someday, when he is fifty and has his own children, he may stumble upon his high school yearbook, and they will ask who Stacy was. I hope he can look back and say I was someone who really cared about him, loved him, and most importantly, that I was someone who taught him about forgiveness.

~Stacy Brakebush
Chicken Soup for the Teenage Soul III

60

Sharing an Intimate Moment

Dear *Chicken Soup*,

I have lived in Southern California my whole life. I was never part of the popular crowd in high school. I never had the best grades or kept up on my who-is-dating-who gossip. The only things that interested me were hanging out with my friends and being on time for my horseback riding lessons. I didn't set foot in an airport until I was sixteen and had my first boyfriend when I was seventeen.

I have never had much luck with guys. I don't like the idea of breaking up over something dumb and crying for a week about how much he hurt me, so I usually end things early. Just before my eighteenth birthday, I met the most beautiful guy. He was really sweet to me so I thought maybe he would be different from other guys. I really let myself like him; I trusted him.

On my eighteenth birthday, I went to school because I had two tests to take, one of which I failed. My friends had brought me balloons, but the wind took the biggest and prettiest one. Then the rain began to pour down on me. My birthday was not going very well, and worst of all, when I went to my boyfriend's house he broke up with me!

For the next day, I stayed in my room until my mom offered to take me to lunch. She presented me with *Chicken Soup for the Teenage*

Soul. Reading the stories made me feel so much better. Even though I didn't know the people who wrote the stories, I felt connected to them. They made me feel good inside.

I have written about something that happened to me at summer camp that I would like to share with others in hopes that they too can get something positive from it. I hope it makes at least someone feel better, like others have done for me.

Sincerely,

~Emily Ferry
Chicken Soup for the Teenage Soul Letters

Teens Talk

Relationships

Differences
Bring Us Closer

*If we build on a sure foundation in friendship, we must love our friends
for their sakes rather than for our own.*
~Charlotte Brontë

61

We're Different, That's Enough

*I don't need a friend who changes when I change and who nods when I nod;
my shadow does that much better.*
~Plutarch

first met Michael in junior high school. I was in seventh grade, he was in eighth. I had joined the school's drama club at my mom's persuasion. She thought my quiet ways were unhealthy and said that extracurricular activities would be good for me. As it was my first day, I mostly kept to myself like I always do. Not that I was being rude—I just didn't like talking with other people. I eventually started daydreaming while others were doing improvs and monologues. Then, hearing a torrent of laughter, I looked up to see a scrawny, dark-colored boy, about a foot taller than me, performing a monologue as Richard Simmons.

Later on, I found out that he already knew who I was. He was friends with my brother Nicholas, who had quite a large group of friends of his own. I saw Michael several times after that, at Drama Club meetings and when he came to visit my brother. Mike was loud and full of life, completely opposite of my personality. On more than one occasion, he reminded me of a comic relief character from some show, walking up to people with a laugh and a grin. Still, though, his presence in my life did not make that much of an impact. At least not yet.

Our first real one-on-one encounter happened three years later. It was a week after my birthday, in my sophomore year of high school. I had answered the phone and, upon hearing Mike's voice, immediately gave the phone to my brother, assuming the call was for him. After a moment, the phone was given back to me, my brother saying that the call was for me. Confused, I took the phone and heard the sentence that would change my life.

"Hey, a bunch of us are going to hang out at Stephanie's house. Wanna come?"

This was the first invitation to a group party I had ever received. I had been invited to visit other friends before, but always just with one person. I never had the courage to go to a gathering with a group of people before. I didn't want to sound rude, so I agreed. Once there, I was shocked at how easily they accepted me into their little group. Afterward, Mike gave me his number, saying, "We should definitely hang out more."

Soon after that, Mike and I began to see each other more often. I was wary at first. I figured that his attitude toward me was based on the laws of association and that the reason he wanted to be my friend was because he was friends with my brother. With time, however, he demonstrated that he wanted to be friends with me, Chris, and not just "Nicholas' brother." This meant a lot to me. While I never felt any contempt toward my brother, I did feel like I was seen as just a relation to him at times. Mike made me feel like an individual, like he liked me for the things that made me who I was. This was the major impact he had on my life.

Soon, Mike became one of my closest friends. We would visit one another constantly and spend the day playing video games, watching anime or just talking about school. One thing did bother me, though. The more we talked, the more I found it strange that we were friends. While he was outgoing and energetic, I was reserved and mostly kept to myself. A typical day between us would consist of Mike talking while I listened for most of the time. The idea that he would want to be friends with someone like me baffled me.

This became more of a concern when I saw how other people

reacted around him. People loved hanging out with Michael—he was the school's social icon, the one everyone wanted to know. He could sit down with anyone and become friends with them in a heartbeat. But instead, he chose me. And for a long time, I just kept wondering, why?

"I enjoy spending time with you. When I'm with most people, I have to be careful of what I say or do, because they get offended or hostile. You don't really judge me or anything. You just listen to what I have to say. Around you, I feel like I can really be myself," he explained.

He just said it out of the blue one day, while we were talking in my basement. That last phrase—"I feel like I can really be myself"—was the one thing I wanted most of all. Even though all I could do was listen to his problems without being able to offer advice, that was enough for him. I was someone he could turn to when he needed to get something off his chest. My friendship was important to him, and that made a world of difference for me.

Michael and I are very different; that much is obvious. It wasn't until that talk in my basement that I realized it was our differences that made our friendship tighter. I relied on his extrovert personality to draw me out of my social shell. This helped me gather the courage to make other friends and even get a girlfriend (going on six months now). In turn, I offered my ears and opinions whenever Mike needed someone to talk to about his problems. Our flaws cancelled each other out.

If someone told me that I would be friends with Michael on the day I met him, I probably would have given them the "You crazy?" look. Now, Mike's one of my best friends, and I wouldn't have it any other way.

~Christopher Boire
Chicken Soup for the Teenage Soul: The Real Deal School

62

When It Counts

Call it a clan, call it a network, call it a tribe, call it a family.
Whatever you call it, whoever you are, you need one.
~Jane Howard

My brother and I are only a year apart in age. When we were little, people would ask if we were twins. We lived in the mountains and only had each other for a long time, so we weren't just brother and sister. We were best friends. I was the artist. I came up with ideas. He was the scientist. Whatever ideas I came up with, he found a way to make them work.

Then our parents divorced. He went to live with my father, I with my mother. Sometimes he visited us, sometimes I visited them. But it got weirder each time. He had friends I didn't know because he was going to a different school, and it wasn't really cool to hang out with his sister who was a snob and a brain. Then there were my friends, who thought he wasn't cool because he wasn't in sports or in the Honor Society. By the time I was thirteen, we'd stopped hanging out altogether. I think the only time we ever spoke was at Christmas, and it was all very formal and awkward, like he was a complete stranger instead of my little brother.

Finally, my high school graduation day came. I had been accepted to a major university three thousand miles away. I had big plans for attaching a U-Haul to the back of my beat up Mustang and driving cross country. The problem was there was no one to go with me. I was more than happy to go alone. I didn't need anybody. But my parents conferred and decided that my brother would have to be my travel companion.

Needless to say, we were both furious about the idea. The last thing he wanted was to spend a week in a car with someone he barely knew and drive three thousand miles to a college he could care less about. The last thing I wanted was to spend a week in a car with someone I barely knew and drive three thousand miles with a babysitter when I was more than capable of taking care of myself. But it was settled. So two weeks later, I packed the car and the U-Haul and drove across town to pick up my brother. He flopped into the passenger seat and stared out the window. Neither of us really spoke for the next six hundred miles unless absolutely necessary.

Then fate stepped in. We'd already had several minor arguments about music, speeding and stopping. The last one, though, had been a bit more heated. It was getting dark and I wanted to stop for the night. He thought it was stupid to lose that much time. Eventually I agreed to drive for another two hours just to end the argument. But I was mad. There he was, not speaking, making me listen to his idiotic music, making me drive when I didn't want to, and rolling his eyes every time I wanted to stop for a bathroom break. This was supposed to be my trip! I didn't want him there in the first place!

I was so busy debating him in my head that I stopped concentrating on the road. Suddenly, a strip of shredded rubber from an eighteen-wheeler in the road flashed into my headlights.

"Look out!" my brother shouted.

I shrieked and swerved. The U-Haul and my car jackknifed, and we went flying into the shoulder. Thankfully, we were on a stretch of highway with only two lanes, pastureland on both sides of the road and not another car for miles.

When everything stopped moving, we sat there in stunned silence, only the sound of the car engine and my heartbeat in my ears. Then I started shaking and crying.

"Oh God! Are you okay? Are you hurt? Are you okay?" I demanded slightly hysterically. I didn't even know if I was hurt. All I cared about was that I might have hurt my brother.

"No—I'm cool. I promise. No damage, see," he held up his hands and smiled through his color drained face.

"Oh God, I'm so sorry! I'm so sorry," I repeated again and again.

He just held my hand and kept telling me everything was fine. I think he was a little unsure about whether I was going to have a nervous breakdown right there in the car. Then he did something he used to do when I would get upset. He made a joke.

"Come on! That was awesome! Are you kidding?? Let's do it again!" he grinned.

Reluctantly, I smiled a little. But he was relentless.

"No seriously! If I'd known there would be near death experiences on this trip, I would've been way more psyched to go!"

This provoked a slight giggle from me.

In the end, after several more comments and a few silly faces for my benefit, we were both outright laughing.

"All right," he clapped his hands together decisively, "Let's see if we're spending the night here tonight."

We got out, inspected the damage and spent the next two hours unhitching and re-hitching the trailer (which, unfortunately, also required some unpacking and repacking) and rocking the back tires of the Mustang out of a small ditch.

By the time we were back on the road, we couldn't stop laughing and talking about the whole scenario. I even admitted to him why I hadn't been concentrating, and he admitted he should have taken the shift since he was the one who wanted to drive at night. We crashed (the sleeping kind, not the dangerous vehicular kind) at the first motel we came to and promptly overslept.

Over the next six days we stopped at the Carlsbad Caverns and the Grand Canyon (which neither of us had seen). In the end, he did most of the driving, and I did most of the navigating. Already I was back to coming up with the ideas, and he was finding ways to make them work. When we arrived, he even helped me get settled.

The night before I had to drive him to the airport to fly home, we were sitting at Denny's, making jokes and reminiscing. We'd talked a lot in those last few days. I'd found out so much about him I never knew: things about school, friends, girlfriends, even my father. Suddenly, I was crushed. I couldn't tell him because it was just too "girly." But I had my little brother back, my long lost best friend... and he was leaving in a few hours.

Life is never as perfect as the movies. I never told him how much I loved him and missed him. But I hugged him for the first time in more than five years before he got on the plane.

I couldn't wait for Christmas, even though it was months away. But I found a perfect present. It was a wall map of the world, complete with pins. We decided at the Grand Canyon that, when I graduate, we're going to backpack together and mark all the places we go. Hey, I may have great ideas—but I need someone to help me get there.

And... maybe to drive at night, too.

~Heather Woodruff
Chicken Soup for the Teenage Soul IV

63

An Unexpected Reaction

If you judge people you have no time to love them.
~Mother Teresa

I hated my parents' divorce. Because of it, my mom could no longer afford to send me to private school and now everything was ruined. Instead of graduating from the eighth grade with all the friends that I'd had since I was six years old, this year I had to go to public school with strangers. I felt like life was against me, nothing was fair, and I was determined to hate the new school and everybody there.

My vow dissolved on the first day of my new school when I met Ally. She was pretty and popular. Ally wore cool clothes while I, on the other hand, had to make do with much less. But the difference in our backgrounds never made a difference to our friendship. Ally and I had many common interests; we giggled and talked and even sang in the school choir together. We became so close that, in a way, I felt like I had known her even longer than my old friends. Ally's popularity helped open doors that might have remained firmly shut to me in the preteen world of cliques. Because of her, I felt as if I had always attended this junior high.

One day, Ally announced that she was having a slumber birthday party. I was informed that I needed to bring my sleeping bag, a pillow and other stuff like makeup. My mom even let me buy a brand new pair of pajamas to wear at the party.

Finally, the momentous Friday evening arrived. I chattered

nonstop to my mom as she drove me over to Ally's house. When we arrived, I bounced out of our old car and, clutching my sleeping bag to my chest, I scrambled up the long walkway to ring the bell. This is sure going to be one great party, I thought, as I waited impatiently for the door to open.

Ally's mom, who always radiated perfection, opened the door. As usual, her dress was flawless and every blond hair was in place. At our school concert, when Ally had introduced me to her, her mom had smiled at me and even commented on my lovely voice. Tonight however, something was different. I was surprised by her lack of warmth and I saw that the smile on her lips did not quite reach her eyes. A sickening silence descended as her pinched smile faded and was replaced with a cold, questioning stare.

Then, she told me to go home. She said that I could come over and visit Allison tomorrow, but not tonight. I couldn't understand what she was talking about. Had I imagined Ally's friendship and the invitation? I started to cry. A queasy stomach followed my unstoppable tears.

"Mom, Mom, where are you?" Ally called from beyond the door. Before her mother could answer, Ally had rounded the corner and stood in the doorway. She had only to look at my tearful expression to see that there was a problem.

"Mom, what's wrong?" she asked. Ally's exasperated sigh and the gripping of her fists told me that this was not the first time that mother and daughter had had a run-in.

"Carmen is here to visit," Ally's mother explained. "I told her to come back tomorrow because you're having a party."

Ally's face flooded with crimson as she nervously glanced at me. "I invited Carmen to my party, Mom. She's my friend, and I want her here." Mortified, I stood quietly as the discussion continued.

"This is a sleepover," replied her mother in hushed tones. "I can't have a colored girl sleep in our home." I couldn't believe what I was hearing. A colored girl! I had never heard of such a term (except maybe in old movies) and certainly not in reference to me. And why would the color of my skin matter anyway?

In an act of ultimate defiance and unparalleled friendship, Ally firmly stood her ground. "Carmen is my friend. If she can't stay, no one stays. I won't have my party without her."

Was I hearing correctly? She was willing to cancel her birthday party on my behalf? A look of agitated confusion passed over her mother's face, and then I saw her face harden. "All right. If that's the way you want it, go tell the other girls they have to go home."

There are times when words are pointless. I was choking with gratitude at this display of friendship. Then, I became suddenly nervous that the blame for the catastrophic end to the party would fall on my fragile shoulders. One by one, the girls came out of the house and quietly assembled under the cold, moonless sky to wait for their parents to come and pick them up. As Ally and her mother argued inside their home, I sat alone, while the other girls spoke in whispers and glanced my way from time to time.

On Monday, the canceled birthday party was the main topic of conversation at our school. Some of my new so-called "friends" looked right through me, ignored me and generally acted as if I didn't exist—except for Ally.

Even with her support, the intense hurt took a long time to heal. As junior high ended and we went on to high school, Ally and I remained close—despite her mother. Ally's living example of true friendship exhibited a maturity far beyond her age and taught me, as probably nothing else ever could, the value of a friend.

I hope that I have learned my lesson well, that I have returned her friendship in kind, and that I have been the same kind of true friend to others. After all, wasn't it Emerson who said, "The only way to have a friend is to be one?"

~Carmen Leal
Chicken Soup for the Preteen Soul 2

64

My First Date

As a teenager you are at the last stage in your life when you
will be happy to hear that the phone is for you.
~Fran Lebowitz, *Social Studies*

Like most every girl, I wanted to be noticed by the opposite sex. I was more than ready to start dating. However, I was practically ignored, and this began to make me feel unwanted and inferior to all the other gorgeous, popular girls at my high school. Eventually, my self-confidence started to wither, and I even started to think there was something wrong with me. I had always wanted to date a religious guy, although most of the guys at my school weren't, so that cut back my options.

Then one Sunday, everything changed. I arrived at church, ready to teach a Sunday school class of perky five-year-olds, when I was greeted by Jeremy, a teenage helper like myself. Immediately, I could tell he had something on his mind. His eyes seemed to probe my face looking for any sign of emotion. Finally he inquired, "Did Brian ask you something?"

"Ask me what?" I replied.

"Oh... you'll see!" Jeremy said, with a slight twinkle in his eyes. As soon as he said it, I knew what he meant. Brian Jones, a shy, introverted senior, had liked me unceasingly for almost two years. Although aware of his crush, I hadn't been interested. I wanted to date someone with a more outgoing personality.

The rest of Sunday proceeded as usual. In the back of my mind,

I was waiting for Brian to ask me out; however, it came time to leave and nothing had happened. Puzzled and somewhat relieved, I hopped in my dad's van for the ride home. A few minutes after I got home, my mom walked through the door holding a delicate, pink rose accompanied by a note. When she left church, the flower had been sitting on the hood of her car, waiting for me. I had taken the wrong vehicle! Looking at the beautiful flower, I absolutely melted. If Brian asked me out, I would say yes! I figured a guy nice enough to give a girl a flower was someone special.

At that instant, the phone rang, and I became almost numb with excitement. My dad answered and knowingly handed it to me. My hands trembled with nerves, but I realize now that Brian must have been even more nervous talking with me. I thanked him for the flower, telling him that I adored roses and that pink was my favorite color. He said he had known this about me. Evidently, he went out of his way to find out and get my favorite flower. I was so touched by his thoughtfulness. Obviously nervous, Brian asked me everything from, "How was your day?" to "What did you do yesterday?" After posing almost every question in the book except the one he had called to ask, we said goodbye.

I understood the anxiety he was experiencing trying to ask me on a date, so I waited patiently for him to call me back. Within a few minutes, Brian called again and asked me out for coffee. Without hesitation I said yes, and we agreed that he would be pick me up at one thirty. I began tearing apart my wardrobe, searching for the perfect outfit to wear on my very first date. I wanted something attractive, but not flamboyant, and I decided on my pink blouse and tan shorts. I did my hair up in twists and, just as I finished, Brian arrived!

The ride there was mostly a blur; I was so nervous I could hardly focus. At one point, Brian awkwardly asked me if I was nervous and, in the most confident voice I could muster, I answered, "No... well, maybe a little." I realize now that hiding my feelings probably made him feel even more anxious.

We arrived at the coffee house and ordered our drinks. I had my own money, but Brian insisted on paying for me. We sat across from each other at a small corner table. At first, our conversation was awkward and seemed to struggle along. However, as we learned more about each other, we realized that we shared similar likes and dislikes, and our staggered conversation transformed into a lively discussion. With every new, intriguing piece of information I learned about Brian, the more attractive he became. We talked for two hours about any topic that arose, and I discovered that he was incredibly smart, pleasant and down-to-earth. My previous notion that I would only enjoy dating someone outgoing was totally incorrect.

After we were finished, he drove me back to my house, told me he had a wonderful time and said he'd like to do it again. I agreed and we said goodbye, both of us glowing with excitement. The next day he called and invited me to the beach with him later that week. I happily agreed. Our relationship was off to a wonderful beginning.

Brian and I have now been together for seven months and one week. Every day we grow closer, and because we bonded so quickly and solidly, we can even see marriage as a possibility in our future. What started as my first date has flourished into a beautiful relationship.

~Sarah Van Tine
Chicken Soup for the Teenage Soul IV

65

The Birthday Present

Envy is the art of counting the other fellow's blessings instead of your own.
~Harold Coffin

The minute Jenny and I got to the mall, I knew I shouldn't have come with her on this shopping expedition.

"My mom said she thought I'd have more fun shopping with you for my birthday present, so she gave me her credit card and told me to 'be reasonable,'" Jenny said, as we entered the clothing store.

I tried to smile at Jenny's remark, but I could tell my effort left something to be desired. I could feel my facial muscles tightening with forced cheerfulness as I imagined what "reasonable" meant. You'll probably only buy three new outfits instead of five, I thought, and each one complete with shoes and other accessories.

Before I could stop it, the green-eyed monster was rearing its ugly head.

Jenny and I had been best friends since the sixth grade. Over the years, we'd done everything together — got short haircuts that we hated, discovered guys and complained about school.

At first, it never bothered me that Jenny's family was much more well-off than mine. Now that we were in high school, though, I began noticing the things Jenny had that I didn't — a fabulous wardrobe, her own car, membership at a fitness club. It seemed the list could go on forever. More and more, I was envious of her lifestyle and the things she had.

I couldn't help comparing this shopping extravaganza with

birthdays in my family. We weren't poor, but four children in the family meant budgeting, even for birthdays. We had a good time, but my parents put a twenty dollar spending limit on presents.

I remembered my last birthday. In our family, it's a tradition that the one who's celebrating a birthday gets to pick the menu and invite one special person to the celebration. I invited Jenny, of course, and ordered my favorite meal complete with chocolate cake for dessert. It was fun, but nothing like this credit card shopping spree.

I was brought back to the present when Jenny held up a white sweater and matching skirt.

"Do you like this?" she asked.

"It is gorgeous," I said. Jenny nodded and continued looking while I moved from rack to rack, touching the beautiful clothes. "I'm going to try this on," Jenny headed for the dressing room. After a few minutes, she reappeared in the outfit she'd just shown me. She looked beautiful.

I sighed. While part of me wanted to tell her how good she looked, another part of me snatched the words back before they were uttered. Jenny was in such good shape that she'd look good in a potato sack. Sometimes, I doubted my judgment in choosing a best friend who was so pretty. Lord, why can't I be the one with the rich parents and the great looks?

"Well, Teresa, what do you think?" A question Jenny had asked me more than once. "Do you like it?"

The outfit looked great on her, but the green-eyed monster struck again. "Not really," I lied. "I think you need something with more color."

"You think so?" Jenny said doubtfully. "I don't know."

"Just trust me. We'll find something better," I told her pushing her back into the dressing room. "You just can't buy the first thing you see." I would have said anything to get Jenny out of the store and away from that outfit. As we left, Jenny gave the sweater one last look.

Just down the mall, we passed a frozen yogurt place. "My treat," Jenny said, pulling out her wallet. "The Taylors stayed out late Saturday night, so I've got a few dollars to spare."

I never could resist chocolate frozen yogurt, so we got our cones and sat down at a table. As Jenny chattered away about a million things, I thought about the feelings I'd had toward my best friend lately. Those feelings weren't very kind.

As I sat there, I began to see Jenny in a new light. I saw that Jenny was attractive not just because of her good looks, but more so because of her kindness. Treating me to yogurt was far from her only show of generosity. She took me to the fitness club she belonged to every chance she got. She also let me drive her car and borrow her clothes.

I also realized this wouldn't be a shopping extravaganza: Jenny only intended to buy one gift. I'd let envy take over my vision until it distorted the picture I had of my best friend. With that thought, the green-eyed monster seemed to shrink in size.

After we finished our cones, we headed for the next clothing store. "Look at that red sweater," Jenny said, as we passed the window. "It would be perfect for you, Teresa, with your dark hair. How are you doing saving your babysitting money? Soon maybe you'll have enough to buy something like that."

A few minutes ago, all I would have heard was the part about saving my babysitting money. I would have resented the fact that all Jenny had to do was ask her parents for the sweater, and they'd buy it for her. This time, though, I heard more. I heard my best friend complimenting me and saying how good I'd look. I heard the voice of someone who loved and cared for me for who I was. I needed to express the same to her.

"You know, Jen, I've been thinking," I said, linking arms with her and pulling her back to the first store, "that white skirt and sweater really was beautiful on you."

~Teresa Cleary
Chicken Soup for the Girlfriend's Soul

66

Lost Love

I don't know why I should tell you this. I'm nothing special, nothing out of the ordinary. Nothing has happened to me my whole life that hasn't happened to nearly everybody else on this planet.

Except that I met Rachel.

We met at school. We were locker neighbors, sharing that same smell of fresh notebook paper and molding tennis shoes, with clips of our favorite musicians taped inside our locker doors.

She was beautiful and had that self-assurance that told me she must be going with somebody. Somebody who was somebody in school. Me—I'm struggling, trying to stay on the track team and make good enough grades to get into the college my folks went to when they were my age.

The day I met Rachel, she smiled and said hello. After looking into her warm brown eyes, I just had to get out and run like it was the first and last run of my life. I ran ten miles that day and hardly got winded.

We spent that fall talking and joking about teachers, parents and life in general, and what we were going to do when we graduated. We were both seniors, and it was great to feel like a "top dog" for a while. It turns out she wasn't dating anybody—which was amazing. She'd broken up with somebody on the swim team over the summer and wasn't going out at all.

I never knew you could really talk to somebody—a girl, I mean—the way I talked with her.

So one day my car—it's an old beat-up car my dad bought me because it could never go very fast—wouldn't start. It was one of those gray, chilly fall days, and it looked like rain. Rachel drove up beside me in the school parking lot in her old man's turquoise convertible and asked if she could take me somewhere.

I got in. She was playing the new David Byrne CD and singing along to it. Her voice was pretty, a lot prettier than Byrne's—but then, he's a skinny dude, nothing like Rachel. "So where do you want to go?" she asked, and her eyes had a twinkle, as if she knew something about me I didn't.

"To the house, I guess," I said, then got up the guts to add, "unless you want to stop by Sonic first."

She didn't answer yes or no, but drove straight to the drive-in restaurant. I got her something to eat and we sat and talked some more. She looked at me with those brown eyes that seemed to see everything I felt and thought. I felt her fingers on my lips and knew I would never feel any more for a girl than I did right then.

We talked and she told me about how she'd come to live in this town, how her dad had been a diplomat in Washington and then retired and wanted her, all of a sudden, to grow up like a small-town girl, but it was too late. She was sophisticated and poised and always seemed to know what to say. Not like me. But she opened up something in me.

She liked me, and suddenly I liked myself.

She pointed to her windshield. "Look," she said, laughing. "We steamed up the windows." In the fading light of day, I suddenly remembered home, parents and my car.

She drove me home and dropped me off with a "See you tomorrow" and a wave. That was enough. I had met the girl of my dreams.

After that day, we started seeing each other, but I wouldn't call them dates. We'd get together to study and always ended up talking and laughing over the same things.

Our first kiss? I wouldn't tell the guys this, because they would think it was funny, but she kissed me first. We were in my house, in the kitchen. Nobody was home. The only thing I could hear was the ticking of the kitchen clock. Oh, yeah, and my heart pounding in my ears like it was going to explode.

It was soft and brief; then she looked deep in my eyes and kissed me again, and this time it wasn't so soft and not so brief, either. I could smell her and touch her hair, and right then I knew I could die and be happy about it.

"See you tomorrow," she said then, and started to walk out the door. I couldn't say anything. I just looked at her and smiled.

We graduated and spent the summer swimming and hiking and fishing and picking berries and listening to her music. She had everything from R&B to hard rock, and even the classics like Vivaldi and Rachmaninoff. I felt alive like I never had before. Everything I saw and smelled and touched was new.

We were lying on a blanket in the park one day, looking up at the clouds, the radio playing old jazz. "We have to leave each other," she said. "It's almost time for us to go to college." She rolled over on her belly and looked at me. "Will you miss me? Think of me, ever?" and for a nanosecond I thought I saw some doubt, something unlike her usual self-assurance, in her eyes.

I kissed her and closed my eyes so I could sense only her, the way she smelled and tasted and felt. Her hair blew against my cheek in the late summer breeze. "You are me," I said. "How can I miss myself?"

But inside, it was like my guts were being dissected. She was right; every day that passed meant we were that much closer to being apart.

We tried to hold on then, and act like nothing was going to happen to change our world. She didn't talk about shopping for new clothes to take with her; I didn't talk about the new car my dad had bought for me because that would be what I drove away in. We kept acting like summer was going to last forever, that nothing would change us or our love. And I know she loved me.

It's nearly spring now. I'll be a college sophomore soon.

Rachel never writes.

She said that we should leave it at that — whatever that meant.

And her folks bought a house in Virginia, so I know she's not coming back here.

I listen to music more now, and I always look twice when I see a turquoise convertible, and I notice more things, like the color of the sky and the breeze as it blows through the trees.

She is me, and I am her. Wherever she is, she knows that. I'm breathing her breath and dreaming her dreams, and when I run now, I run an extra mile for Rachel.

~Robby Smith as told to T. J. Lacey
Chicken Soup for the Teenage Soul II

67

Directory Assistance

They say that if you have one friend throughout your entire lifetime, you're lucky. That's not even close to true. Parents just say that to make their kids feel better when they get left out of something. You're going to make and lose a ton of friends throughout the course of your life, and if you don't, you've never lived or you smell or something. Sure, there will be one or two who stick with you through thick and thin, hard times and good, ugly haircuts and bad shirts. But friends like that are the exceptions. You want to make a friend? Some of the best people you'll ever meet are the ones you think the least about. Like your barber. Or your bus driver. Or, in my case, my local Directory Assistance operator.

We met on a Saturday night sometime in the middle of June when I was all by myself at home. I was feeling particularly lonely because, well, it was a Saturday night sometime in the middle of June, and I was all by myself at home. My regular friends were all out doing something enjoyable and, somehow, in the midst of all their fun, it had slipped their minds to invite me. No problem, I told myself. I grabbed the remote. The television has always been a friend. Not once have I ever seen it having a good time without me. I pressed the "On" button. Static. The cable guys were working down the street and must have cut a line. Awesome.

It was nine at night. My friends were out, I was alone, and the TV wasn't working. I didn't know what to do. Sleeping was out of the question—I wasn't tired, and it was too early anyway. Going out and finding my friends without having been invited would have made me look desperate. For a minute I considered getting my old action figures out of the attic. Then I saw the phone—a direct link to human contact. I picked it up without thinking and dialed the first number that came to mind: Directory Assistance.

It rang twice, and the computerized male voice asked me to state my city. I did. Then it asked me what number I needed. I didn't need anybody's number.

"Oh," I said, "I just wanted to talk to somebody." There was an awkward silence.

An operator picked up. "I'm sorry, sir, what was that?" Her voice was really southern. Sort of a cute southern sound, though, like the voice of that girl on *The Beverly Hillbillies* who used a rope as a belt. She sounded really nice.

"I just wanted someone to talk to, ma'am." When I realized how pathetic that must have sounded, it was too late.

"Someone to talk to?" she asked in that sweet voice of hers. She seemed amused.

"Yeah."

"Okay. What about?" That caught me off guard. I didn't expect anyone to actually want to talk to me. I thought they would have hung up. It was more of a prank call than anything. Then again, I didn't expect the operator to have such a nice voice, either. The whole phone call was somewhat of a shock. But hey, it beat loneliness. So we talked for a couple hours.

Her name was Alex, and she was twenty-nine and engaged. She had blond hair and blue eyes. Her fiancé was a thirty-something-year-old rich guy who was on a business trip in Japan and had been there for the past week. She missed him pretty badly. She said she felt really lonely at the moment. I told her I knew how she felt. She said it was surely nice having someone to talk to about it. I agreed. Her job stunk. She said it was really boring. She didn't even need the money anyway. She was marrying into money. Turns out we both loved popcorn shrimp, and when it came to movies, neither of us liked dramatic ones. She wanted to have three kids with her soon-to-be husband. I said three sounded like a good number to me. She asked me how old I was. I told her twenty-eight. She didn't believe me. So I told her the truth—fourteen. She told me that our phone call was probably costing my parents a lot of money by the minute. I said I didn't care. She laughed. She thought I was pretty funny. That made me feel good.

We got off the phone around eleven when my parents got home. The two hours that we talked to each other went by fast. When I hung up, I wasn't exactly sure what had just happened. But I knew I'd had a good Saturday night, thanks to her.

So a couple of days later, I called her back. We talked some more. Our phone calls became more and more frequent. Pretty soon, we were talking twice a day. My parents thought I had a new girlfriend and told me I should invite her over to the house. They were puzzled when I told them that her fiancé probably wouldn't like that. They understood when they got the phone bill at the end of the month.

I had to say goodbye to Alex. I miss her whenever I get lonely. But it's been two years, and she's probably moved somewhere with her fiancé by now. I hope he's good to her. It was a great friendship, even if it didn't last long. It's like I said—friends come in all shapes and sizes. And voices, I guess.

~Michael Wassmer
Chicken Soup for the Teenage Soul: The Real Deal Friends

68

Fugue

et's call her Monique. Her real name always seemed too common for her, too plain. She moved to south Texas during our senior year of high school. She had transferred from somewhere up north, maybe New York.

Just as she was too grand for her small name, she was too lovely, too classy for our high school. She liked yoga and Mozart, wrote poetry and preferred old movies to sitcoms. She couldn't pass a bookstore or antique shop without browsing for an hour. But her parents had money, gobs of it, so the clique of similarly wealthy, popular students sucked her in, claiming her as one of its own before she could do anything about it. These were cheerleaders and athletes, blond-haired and well-dressed, who drove convertibles and finagled beer kegs for the parties they threw when their parents went on ocean cruises.

I was never invited to the parties. Where Monique preferred books over beers, I preferred skateboarding to school spirit. My hair was long, and my clothes were baggy. While the popular kids didn't hate me—at times it seemed to be strangely "cool" to be seen talking to a skater or surfer—they certainly didn't embrace me. My parents could barely afford to pay our bills, let alone go on a cruise. I spent my nights tearing around parking lots on my board. Occasionally, I'd see a car full of athletes and cheerleaders buying provisions for their parties. All of them looked so beautiful, wearing pressed shirts and perfume I could smell from across the parking lot. Sometimes they'd wave to me, as if a dangerous river raged between us, one that would drown them if they came any closer.

Monique sat beside me in English class, and in the course of the school year we became friends. That is, that's what she said we were—friends—when I or anyone asked. And as we spent more and more time together, more and more people asked. We went to lunch together—she drove us for sushi or Indian food (I'd never had such meals before) in her white convertible VW Beetle. We studied for tests at the library, and spent days and even a couple of evenings at the beach. My nights skating in abandoned parking lots dwindled. Once we snuck into a club and listened to a live jazz band. I've always remembered it was called Fugue. Monique told me their name came from Bach's *Toccata and Fugue*, and that fugue basically meant different instruments or voices coming together, overlapping and finally harmonizing. We saw movies, and I noticed that when she was scared she chewed her thumbnail. Sometimes she held my hand or kissed my cheek good night. Sometimes we held each other's gaze for a second too long. I adored spending time with her, and when I stood near her, my nerves fluttered, and waves of joy and panic rolled in my stomach. Somewhere between English class and California rolls, I'd fallen in love with her.

And so, apparently, had Paul Williams, a beefy linebacker. When they started dating, she told me about him as if I should be thrilled. Fool that I was, I pretended to be. Monique and I still went for sushi—Paul didn't share our lunch period—and for a while she made an effort to study with me or go to movies, but our time together started to fade. When we talked, the word "friends" came up more than it had before, as if she were defining our boundaries, and I began to hate it. Less and less, she reached for my hand, and she stopped kissing my cheek good night. It felt as if those parts of my body had vanished or been amputated; if she no longer touched them, they no longer existed.

So I returned to the darkened parking lots. I began to see Monique in the overloaded cars making their beer runs—though she never drank, or hadn't when we spent time together—and always Paul Williams was attached to her. She started calling me less often, even when she'd promised to, and some nights I picked up the phone and listened for a dial tone, hoping the problem was beyond her control. The phone, though, functioned perfectly. The problem was Paul Williams. They walked arm in arm wherever they went and kissed each other before tardy bells at school.

One day after English class, I blew up at her. I told her she deserved more than the big oaf, that he didn't understand her and she should open her eyes. I said she was changing for the worst, becoming someone I no longer recognized, and if she wanted to be part of a group who cared more about partying than people, we couldn't be friends anymore. (I'd rehearsed the speech numerous times in the mirror and in the parking lots.) Her face crumpled and turned red, tears hung on her eyelashes, and just as I was building to the part about how much I loved her, she spun and ran away. I don't know where she went, but I've always imagined she ran straight into the arms of Paul Williams.

We stopped speaking. I heard that she went to the prom with Paul and that she'd been accepted to Yale for the fall. As our graduation neared, I tried to say hello to her, to ask how she was doing and eventually to apologize, but she never responded. It was as if I were talking to myself in the mirror.

So on the night her little white car pulled into the parking lot where I was skateboarding, I expected it to park near the store and for Paul Williams to jump out and run inside. But the VW steered away from the store and pulled up to where I was trying to learn a new trick. Monique was alone, and when she approached me I expected her to scream and slap me, then to speed away into the night. That's what I deserved.

But for a while she didn't say anything. She just stood beside her car with her arms crossed. She looked at her feet, occasionally biting her thumbnail.

"You were right," she said finally.

"I was?" I didn't know what I'd been right about. My stomach tightened.

"I've changed," she said.

"What do you mean?"

"We can't be friends anymore."

I didn't know what to say. I realized I'd always hoped she would prove me wrong on that point. I'd only said it so she would prove me wrong.

And just as I was about to respond—I didn't know what I was going to say; I hadn't rehearsed anything—she started toward me. "Here it comes," I thought, "the slap." She walked slowly, still looking at the ground more than me, and without realizing it, she crossed the river that had always separated me and the popular kids, the river that had, for the last few months, separated me and Monique. I braced myself and closed my eyes.

She kissed me. Her lips were soft and warm, but somehow they made me feel pleasantly cold. It took everything I had not to shiver. We kissed for a moment, and I didn't know what to do with my hands. I would learn. Before she left for college and we lost track of each other forever, Monique would spend the summer teaching me about love and friendship, showing me the strange and sad and occasionally beautiful ways the two complement each other or cancel one another out.

~Don Keys
Chicken Soup for the Teenage Soul on Love & Friendship

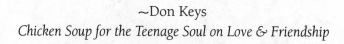

Teens Talk

Relationships

Putting Yourself Out There

If we listened to our intellect, we'd never have a love affair.
We'd never have a friendship. We'd never go into business, because
we'd be too cynical. Well, that's nonsense. You've got to jump off cliffs
all the time and build your wings on the way down.
~Annie Dillard

Losing an Enemy

ast year, my brothers were enrolled in Pioneer Clubs, a weekly kids program at our church. Daniel was nine, and Timothy was seven. My sister, my dad and I were all teachers at the same church program. At one point during the year, my brothers began to complain that a boy named John was picking on them.

John, an eleven-year-old foster boy, was in my dad's class. He was the type of kid who always seemed to be in trouble. Worse, he didn't consider that it was his behavior that was the problem, but instead decided my dad was picking on him. He often took it out on my brothers by knocking off their hats, calling them names, kicking them and running away. Even I received the occasional rude remark from John. We all thought he was a real pain.

When my mom heard about the problem, she came home from town a few days later with a bag of wrapped butterscotch candies.

"These are for John," she told Daniel and Timothy.

"For who?"

"For John." Mom went on to explain how an enemy could be conquered by kindness.

It was hard for any of us to imagine being kind to John; he was so annoying. But the next week the boys went to Pioneer Clubs with butterscotch candies in their pockets—one for themselves and one for John.

As I was heading to my class, I overheard Timothy saying, "Here

John, this is for you." When we got home, I asked Timothy what John's response had been.

Timothy shrugged. "He just looked surprised, then he said thank you and ate it."

The next week when John came running over, Tim held on to his hat and braced himself for an attack. But John didn't touch him. He only asked, "Hey, Tim, do you have any more candy?"

"Yep." A relieved Timothy reached into his pocket and handed John a candy. After that, John found him every week and asked for a candy, and most times Timothy remembered to bring them — one for himself, and one for John.

Meanwhile, I "conquered my enemy" in another way. One time as I passed John in the hall, I saw a sneer come over his face. He started to open his mouth, but I said, "Hi, John!" and gave him a big smile before he had a chance to speak.

Surprised, he shut his mouth, and I walked on. From then on, whenever I saw him I would greet him with a smile and say, "Hi, John!" before he had a chance to say anything rude. Instead, he started to simply return the greeting.

It's been a while since John picked on my brothers, and he's not rude to me anymore, either. Even my dad is impressed with the change in him. He's a nicer John now than he was a year ago — I guess because someone finally gave him a chance.

He wasn't the only one to change. My whole family learned what it meant to love an enemy. What's strange is that in the process, we lost that enemy — he was "conquered" by love.

Love: It never fails.

~Patty Anne Sluys
Chicken Soup for the Teenage Soul II

Crossing the Fence

Behold the turtle. He makes progress only when he sticks his neck out.
~James Bryant Conant

"Mommy, can I eat lunch with you in your car?"

A pained look fell on my mom's face, but only for a second, as she said, "Of course, dear." As I ate my sub sandwich and drank my juice, she must have looked at me with sorrow in her heart — nobody wants her child to be lonely. I didn't even know that she had seen me circling the field moments ago, squishing the grass by myself, the lone little black girl with beautiful braids coiled and dormant under her rain hat, cowering from the wind and from people.

Lunch recess in first grade was always sheer torture. To my shy, timid eyes, the children at the new school I had just moved to were leering at me, faces full of lechery. Scared and frightened and helplessly antisocial, I strayed away, pulled back from the curious and kind eyes, too afraid to speak up and out, too afraid of possible rejection from all the nice little white kids my own age. I was just over six years old, and my best friend was a fence.

The stick clanged as it bumped along the chain link fence surrounding the elementary school playground. Wood hit metal as I trailed the fenced perimeter of the field, stick in my right hand and hunger in my left. My mommy was going to drop off my lunch at school that day, and she hadn't come yet. So, clad in my orange raincoat, hat and big rubber boots, I kept my head down and roamed, friendless and sad.

The winds toyed with the tears in my eyes. "Even the air is popular," I thought. If only people liked me. If only I weren't so quiet and boring and stupid. If only I were pretty and longhaired like Amy. Maybe then I would have friends, I cried to myself. Suddenly, my fingers seemed very interesting to me, and, having nothing else to do, I studied them, noting the loops and swirls and hoops that God had imprinted on them. Then I noticed our family's huge maroon Aerostar van swooping in across the field in the parking lot. Mom was here. I ran with hunched shoulders, the wind at my back and water lurching up from under my rubbers. Breathless, I reached the car and slapped the front passenger door. Mom opened it.

"Hi, baby! How are you?"

"Good," I said, even though that was the farthest thing from the truth.

Mom handed me my lunch in a nice purple lunchbox as I leaned over the passenger seat talking to her. It stayed in her hand, floating in midair. Was I really going to take it and sit against the wall by myself eating, watching all the other kids play tag and ring-around-the-rosy? Self-conscious? Friendless? I looked at the purple lunchbox and then into my mom's eyes. I can only imagine what she saw in mine.

"Do you want to..." she said.

"Mommy, can I..." I said.

We both spoke at the same time.

"Go ahead, Meme," she said, letting me go first. I then asked her the question that summed up the sad fact of my social life.

"Can I eat lunch in the car?"

How to make friends was a lesson my own mother had to learn as well. Fortunately, I learned it by the age of eight. By then I had a whole band of friends. I guess I finally realized that to be a friend to someone else, I would have to be a friend to myself. There was no way a person would want to be friends with me when I was hiding from the world within a shroud of shyness. So I learned to throw off that shroud and let my inner self shine. I also learned that friendships are made only by communication, that the only way someone would know I wanted to be her friend was if I spoke up. "Hi!" and "Would you like to play with me?" became my new catch phrases. Finally, I wasn't alone anymore.

Now, at the age of fourteen, I look back on most of my friendships and realize that they are ones that I instigated. Considering my early childhood, it's ironic that now I am the one who reaches out to the people around me. I'm the one who warms another's day with a random act of kindness and watches a friendship bloom. I'm the one who chooses to open up and share some of myself, making a bond with someone else who opened up to me.

As I matured, I learned to cross the fence. I challenge everyone, whether shy or bold, to cross the fence from the side of shyness and pride or even hate, to the side of humility and warmth and love, to friendships that can last a long time. To cross the fence instead of trailing it.

~Omenka Uchendu
Chicken Soup for the Teenage Soul: The Real Deal Friends

71

Drowning in Somebody I'm Not

Always be a first-rate version of yourself,
instead of a second-rate version of somebody else.
~Judy Garland

There is nothing like being young and in love. Your body trembles all over, and you long for that special person. I was sixteen when it first happened. Her name was Mary; she was one grade ahead and the most beautiful girl in the entire school. I was smaller than the rest of the guys my age but had many friends. I would walk by her locker, act cool and do just about anything to gain her attention.

Nothing worked.

I often pondered to myself, "How would such a beautiful and amazing girl ever fall for a guy like me?" I constantly thought that if I were a "hip guy," she would eventually have to notice. Once, I "accidentally" dropped my letter jacket by her feet, just so she would note my varsity pins—and me.

She only laughed.

Then, at a weekend gathering one evening, she was there with all of her frightening friends. I decided that this had to be it; I couldn't live with myself one second more without at least trying to talk to her. I checked my ego at the door—and decided to be myself. She was alone outside for one moment, and all I can remember is that she was so incredibly beautiful it made me dizzy. I walked up to her and said,

"Hi, I'm Mark. You seem really nice; can we talk?" My belly rolled with butterflies while my head rushed with anxiety.

Time stood still for a moment.

She replied, "I know who you are; you're different when your friends aren't around." And then she smiled and said, "I'm walking up the street to meet a friend. Would you like to go?" I could hardly breathe: How could this beautiful girl ever talk to a guy like me? Needless to say, we walked and talked, and she was everything I thought she would ever be. We giggled about the world and how stupid our friends were.

Then, to my amazement, she gave me her phone number. That night, Mary revealed that dropping my letter jacket in front of her was a stupid thing to do. She didn't care about what sports guys lettered in, she only cherished wonderful people with substance. After I began being myself, we quickly fell for one another and became "high school loves."

We later went on to separate colleges and grew apart, but one thing that I learned from the experience has stuck with me my entire life. If you try to act like somebody you're not, any love or approval you gain won't mean anything.

It's best to just be yourself.

~Mark Whistler
Chicken Soup for the Teenage Soul IV

72

Experience Is a Teacher

I was shaking when I heard the car pull into the driveway. I blamed it on the chill in my house, although most likely it was because of my uncontrollable nerves. When I opened the door, Becca was standing on my porch with a smile plastered on her face.

"Hey," she said. As she stepped inside the doorway, the guys behind her became visible. "Oh, ya," she added. "This is Dan, Josh and Kevin."

"Hi," I said, and they replied the same in unison. They looked kind of like deer in headlights, standing outside the door, hands jammed in pockets, mouths half open. As Becca made her way into the house, the guys followed her, and I felt awkwardly lost, unsure of what to say. To avoid forced conversation, I took the opportunity to jot a note to my mom, explaining where I was going.

Eventually, we made it out of the house, and I found myself in the back seat of a navy blue truck, wedged between Josh and Kevin, two older guys from a different school. Becca was chattering away in the passenger seat, changing the radio station and singing along. My legs began to shake, a sure indicator of my nervousness, and I had to put my hands on my thighs to steady them. We soon reached the restaurant, and I was thankful for the chance to get out of the truck.

Dan was toying with the miniature coffee creamers at the end of the table. "I don't trust these," he announced. "They've probably been sitting here since 1982."

At the opposite end of the table, next to Kevin, I giggled, probably for the eighth time since we'd sat down. I wanted to smack myself. Between my legs shaking and my ridiculous giggling, my immature nervous habits were driving me crazy, and I prayed that nobody else noticed.

Suddenly, Becca stood up. "I have to call my mom. Dan, come with me."

"Um, I'll come, too," I said. Feeling the need to elaborate, I continued, "I have to call my mom, too." I felt stupid following Becca and Dan out to the lobby, like a girl in elementary school who can't go anywhere without her best friend.

As we waited while Becca called her mom, Dan nudged me and said, "So, what do you think of Josh and Kevin?"

"Josh is pretty cute," I said, figuring that honesty was the best way to go.

"Not Kevin?" Dan's eyes sparkled, and I knew what Becca had been talking about when she said how wonderful he was.

"No...." I looked out the window. "But don't tell him that I said that."

"I won't." Of course he wouldn't. What did I think this was, elementary school? I felt like a child in a world of adults, unsure how to act or what to say.

"Josh thinks you're really hot," Dan continued.

His statement immediately grabbed my attention. "Oh, really?" I was flattered.

Becca hung up the phone and caught the end of our conversation, saying excitedly, "You have to sit by him when we go back to the table!"

"No," I protested. "That'll look dumb."

"No it won't," she insisted, and Dan agreed.

"Yeah, we'll just move stuff around or whatever." It was obvious that this was an argument I was not going to win.

When we returned to the table and assumed our new seats, Josh didn't say anything. I wondered if he had figured out our juvenile plan, and then I wondered if he even cared. But I quickly tried to brush the thoughts out of my head and proceeded to giggle at everything Dan said.

Next we went to the movies. Without Becca next to me in the theater, I felt completely defenseless. I gripped my knees for support, angry at myself for being nervous. Why couldn't I have more self-confidence and be as charming as other girls are? I leaned my head back against the headrest, watching Dan and Becca out of the corner of my eye. No contact yet, I noted. I didn't know what to do with my hands, and it seemed like they took on a life of their own as they repetitiously roamed from my knees to my thighs and eventually gripped the edge of my purse.

I felt a nudge on my right arm. I looked over at Dan and watched as he mouthed the words, "Make a move." He then grinned at me and raised his eyebrows in Josh's direction.

"No!" I whispered emphatically.

"Why not?" he replied with a kind of urgency.

I half-shrugged my shoulders. "I don't know." How could I explain to him the way my mind works? I could never "make a move" on anyone; I didn't have the nerve. My fear of rejection was too intense. Out of the corner of my eye, I saw that Becca was leaning on Dan's shoulder, and his hand was resting on her knee. I sank farther into my seat.

On the way home from the movies, Becca asked Dan if he had a piece of paper. I knew immediately what she was doing and wanted to object, but couldn't. When she handed me Josh's number on a torn piece of paper, I didn't even look at it. I just played with it between my fingers, bending the edges and running it along the folds of my jeans. Josh's reaction to the piece of paper in his hand was similar.

We pulled into my driveway, and I thought that I was finally safe at home as I said goodbye to everyone and sauntered up to my porch. But as I turned around to give a final wave goodbye, I found Josh standing on the lawn.

"Hey," he said, in a way only older guys can. "When are you going to be home tomorrow?"

"Probably all day," I managed and immediately thought of how dumb I sounded.

"Okay, then. I'll, um, call you around one."

I flashed a slight smile. "Okay. Bye!" I stepped inside my house, allowing myself to breathe only when I had closed the door and was safe inside.

I washed my face, wondering if he would think that I was "really hot" without makeup. As I curled up in bed, the phrase "If only I had…" crossed my mind so many times that I became exhausted. But then I remembered that experience, even if awkward and uncomfortable, or in the form of a guy named Josh, is always a teacher. With that, I gradually fell asleep, knowing tomorrow was a new day, and I could rest assured there would be more lessons to learn.

~Julia Travis
Chicken Soup for the Teenage Soul III

The Funeral of My Rose

I turn on my high beams as I drive home from play rehearsal one night. The outside air is calm as it brushes my cheek through an open window. Hearing a good song, I turn the radio up a little louder. The song takes me to a different place. I begin daydreaming about my crush again. I notice a grocery store on my right, and, spontaneously, I swerve into the parking lot. Tonight is the night. I walk in through the automatic doors and head straight for my destination: the floral department. My choice is a single beautiful red rose. I wrap it in green tissue paper and head back to my car. My heart begins beating rapidly as I strategize. Tonight seems different, though. I've had enough planning, and I am now acting on impulse. It must be a sign.

After a fairly long drive, I turn into one of North Augusta's more classy subdivisions. I glance at my watch: 9:00 P.M. It seems like a good, solid time. My palms have begun to sweat, but I press on. I find myself parked in a driveway of an amazing house. I take a breath and pull myself out of the car. I leave the rose on the back seat, promising myself that I will return for it later. My footsteps are determined, and I swiftly walk to the front door. Ding, the doorbell rings as I nervously press it. The door opens.

"Hello, Derek," a familiar face greets me.

"Hi, Mrs. Johnson. Is Lauren home?" I sheepishly ask.

My cheeks burn as she turns and shouts for her daughter. It seems like an eternity, but soon enough I hear a door open. Lauren comes clumping down the stairs, and my heart jumps to my throat. One look into her big brown eyes, and I forget my own name. I have never had a problem communicating until I met this mythological siren disguised in Gap clothing. Her lips part to reveal white teeth, and her brilliant smile lights the dim room. She greets me with a look of confusion.

"Hey, Derek, what's up?" she asks, tilting her head to the side, perplexed. Her eyes examine me as if she is putting a puzzle together. I attempt to speak, but words don't seem to come.

"Can I speak to you out on the porch?" I finally spit out.

I open the door and let her pass. We take seats on the front stoop, and I turn to her. I try choosing my words carefully.

"So, are you going out with Kevin?" I blurt out abruptly and regrettably.

Taken by surprise, she waits a moment to let the question sink in.

"Umm... I think so," she slowly replies as she twirls a piece of her hair.

I had taken the time to investigate their relationship. I knew Kevin would eventually hurt her, and I knew what I had to do.

"He doesn't deserve you, Lauren," I tell her assertively.

"Why do you say that?" she asks, again looking confused.

"Because... look... umm..." I struggle and finally get back on track. "Because I like you, Lauren. I like you a lot."

I turn away. What have I done? Why did I say that? I look back in her eyes. They are more confused than ever now. They look hurt, and I so badly want to go over to her, take her in my arms and live happily ever after with her.

"Well... Kevin is funny, and sweet. He's not that bad."

My mind reels. What just happened? I proclaimed my love to her. I had just told the girl of my dreams that I liked her. Did she hear me? I look back in her eyes, the eyes of the girl I fell for as a little boy. The eyes of the girl my heart skips a beat for each time she passes me in the hall. Crushed, I know I have to leave. I have to get out of there. I have to escape. I have revealed something that has tormented me for days, and now my entire body feels like it is shriveling up in embarrassment. After saying goodbye, I get in my car and drive away from her house.

The next day I am in my car after a particularly wretched day at school. I sit there for a few moments letting my mind drift back to last night's activity. Suddenly I notice the rose I had left in the car. This beautiful, red rose has now transformed into a black, stiff, thorny twig. I hold it in my hands for a few moments, and a tear rolls down my cheek. It is time to move on. I realize I have done the right thing. Although I did not get the response I had hoped for, I have learned an invaluable lesson: You cannot make someone love you, you can only make yourself someone who can be loved.

~Derek Gamba
Chicken Soup for the Teenage Soul III

A Simple Hello

Sometimes someone says something really small,
and it just fits right into this empty place in your heart.
~From the television show My So-Called Life

I have always felt sympathy and compassion for the kids I see at school walking all alone, for the ones who sit in the back of the room while everyone snickers and makes fun of them. But I never did anything about it. I guess I figured that someone else would. I did not take the time to really think about the depth of their pain. Then one day I thought, "What if I did take a moment out of my busy schedule to simply say hello to someone without a friend or stop and chat with someone eating by herself?" And I did. It felt good to brighten up someone else's life. How did I know I did? Because I remembered the day a simple kind hello changed my life forever.

~Katie E. Houston
Chicken Soup for the Teenage Soul II

I Finally Did It

I've found that luck is quite predictable.
If you want more luck, take more chances.
~Brian Tracy

It was the last day of school of my sophomore year. I had just finished my English final, and everyone else in my class was exchanging their yearbooks to be signed. That's when he walked over—Jason, the six-foot-two, 175-pound, blond-haired, brown-eyed, mega-hottie varsity football player, whom I had been crushing on for four years. He came over to the girl I was sitting next to and asked her to sign his yearbook. He gave her his yearbook and went to the other side of the room to talk to some of his friends. When she finished writing, I asked her if I could have his yearbook. She agreed and handed it over. There I sat with Jason's yearbook. What was I going to write? Where would I even begin? I was shaking, and I could feel my face turning red. Whatever I was going to write, I had to do so quickly. I picked up my pen and started writing:

Dear Jason,

Another year has gone by. A chapter in our lives has come to an end and another one is about to begin. I guess now would be as good a time as any to tell you that I've had a crush on you since the seventh grade. I've been to almost all of your football games, and I've caught myself many times over the past few

years staring at you in the hallways and in class more than one
should. I think you are a wonderful person.

Love,

Katherine

Maybe it wasn't exactly that word-for-word, but it was pretty close. When Jason came back to get his yearbook, he had to ask who had it since the girl he left it with no longer did. This was my chance to talk to him and tell him I had it. When I did, he got this strange look on his face. I handed him his yearbook, and he went back to his desk. I watched him open the yearbook to where the girl sitting next to me had written. He read it then turned the page. My heart started pounding because I knew that was the page I had written on. He turned his yearbook to the side, and I knew then that he was reading my message. As he read his half-smile gave way to a full grin. I had no idea what to make of it. Was it good he was smiling? I think he was surprised that I had a crush on him, but I wasn't sure if he even cared. I guess I thought it was pretty obvious that I liked him.

Ever since middle school I would get all flustered and blush every time he was near me. In eighth grade during math class, he asked me once if he could borrow a pencil. When I got that pencil back, I treasured it and held on to it for a year or so, until I lost it. Then at eighth grade graduation, my friend was trying to get her camera to work and she accidentally took a picture. Coincidentally, when she got her film developed, it was Jason she had accidentally taken a picture of. I took it home and framed it. In ninth grade he borrowed my calculator and I know it's crazy, but he left a fingerprint on it, and I was extremely careful not to wipe it off. It stayed there for a good few months until I finally came to my senses and realized how insane I was acting.

Jason finally closed his yearbook, picked it up and went over to one of his friends. He said something to him, and then they both slipped out of the classroom with Jason's yearbook. I realized I should have written "for your eyes only" in big red letters in hopes he wouldn't share it with others. But that probably wouldn't have worked anyway. I had a feeling he was showing his friend. Was it all a big joke to him? Or could it have been that he was truly touched by my sincerity and flattered by my words?

Jason and his friend came back into the classroom but not to stay. He rounded up some other friends and went back outside with, yes, his yearbook. A few minutes later the bell rang. Jason and all of his friends returned to the classroom to get their things. I didn't talk to him after that, and he never said anything more to me. Honestly, though, I wasn't really expecting anything to happen between us. I had placed Jason on a pedestal in middle school and never took him down. To me, he was the type of guy a girl like me could only dream about. For the past four years I had wished on every star, birthday candle and wishing well that we would be high school sweethearts. I had laughed at his jokes and felt bad when he got hurt. But that day as I walked out of the classroom and shut the door behind me, I felt a sense of pride even after what had happened. I took a chance and told him how I felt. Even though it didn't turn out like a fairy tale—happily ever after—I was glad I did it. I felt closure, relief and satisfaction. I was able to put it behind me and move on. All of those years I had kept it inside, wondering "what if?" and being too scared to take a chance. I wasn't left wondering anymore. Now I knew.

~Katherine Rowe
Chicken Soup for the Teenage Soul on Love & Friendship

Teens Talk

Relationships

Growing Apart

*Hold a friend's hand through times of trial,
Let her find love through a hug and a smile;
But also know when it is time to let go—
For each and every one of us must learn to grow.*
~Sharon A. Heilbrunn

76

The Friend That You've Outgrown

Here's to the friend that you've outgrown,
The one whose name is left unknown.
The one who wiped away your tears,
And sought to hold your hand,
When others turned the other way,
No beginning, just an end.

She's the one you turned to,
The one that you called friend.
She laughed with you, she cried with you,
And felt it was her duty,
To remind you of your worth,
And all your inner beauty.

When others' eyes could only dwell,
Upon your exposed outer shell.
They saw a fat girl steeped in braces,
Not seeing you they turned their faces.
But she was there to whisper,
When others didn't care.

She held your secrets in her heart,
That friends like you could share.
You never had to be alone,
But now she is, 'cause you've outgrown
Her for those others whose laughs you share,
As you run carefree through the air.

Time has eased your form and face,
But she's the one who knew your grace
When those who you now call your friend
Saw no beginning... only end.

~C. S. Dweck
Chicken Soup for the Teenage Soul IV

77

I Know Exactly What You Mean

I was waiting anxiously by the phone when it rang, but still it startled me and I jumped. For a moment I was suddenly unable to move, and I stared at the phone as it rang again. Out of the corner of my eye I saw my little sister enter the room and stop to gawk at me. I guessed that I must have looked like an idiot, standing there staring at the phone as if I didn't know what to do with it when it made noise. As it rang again I broke from my trance and quickly snatched the receiver up from the cradle.

"Hello?"

"Hi," a shaking, choked voice said. "It's me." I wasn't used to hearing Annie's voice, but now it sounded as familiar as it had a couple of years ago.

Annie and I had been friends since we were little. All through elementary school we were the pair that everyone knew. Where one of us went, the other was sure to be right behind. But as we entered junior high, things began to change. Mainly, Annie began to change. Her social life became the most important thing to her, and being popular was what she strived for. She broke off from our circle of friends and joined a different, more popular crowd. I saw less and less of her, and when I did see her I felt uncomfortable and awkward, like we were strangers. Whether she tried to or not, Annie made me feel like I was inferior to her, not cool enough to hang around her, which hurt like nothing else I had known before.

I knew she didn't feel that way; she told me often how good a friend I was. And I knew she was going through a lot of confusion about herself, trying to find where she fit into the scheme of junior high. So I gave her some leeway and let her do some soul searching. Even though we were not as tight as we were when we were younger, we were still friends, even if I cared more about the relationship than she did at times. Often, though, I wished for the closeness, the sister-hood we had a couple of years ago. Things had been so simple then. They were easily defined: Annie and I were best friends, and we could talk to each other about anything. Now, everything was complicated. I was closer to other friends than I was to Annie, and there were things I told them that I never would tell her. It just wasn't like it had been when we were younger, and I wondered if we would even be able to achieve the kind of relationship we had before things started changing.

"Hi," I said again, unable to think of any other reply. It had been so long since I had actually talked to Annie, not counting the brief moment before school today when she told me with worry in her eyes, "I think he's going to dump me."

I hadn't had time to answer her then, or when she came to me during lunch and said, "I have to call you today." The buzz going around school was that Annie and her boyfriend Cory were having problems, and at first I didn't believe it. They had been together for almost eight months, and even at the last dance a couple of weeks ago I had seen them sneaking a kiss between songs. But then when she had said to me early that morning, her face taut with nervousness and sadness, that she was afraid Cory was going to break up with her, I knew that everything going around school was probably true.

I pulled myself from my thoughts as the silence grew longer, and I was trying to think of something intelligent to say when I realized that there was not silence from the end of the line but muffled sobs.

"Oh, God," I sighed, and I felt so horrible for not noticing at first that she was in pain. "How are you doing?"

"Not good, not good at all," Annie managed to reply, her voice thick with tears. "Cory just broke up with me."

I couldn't speak for a minute. I knew that it was coming, deep inside my subconscious had told me that it was inevitable, but it just seemed like Annie and Cory would somehow survive anything. They had been together so long, it was hard to imagine them apart.

Finally, my voice returned to me. "Oh Annie, I'm so sorry," I breathed, hoping my words sounded as sincere as they were meant to be. I didn't know what else to say, so I just kept repeating my apology.

"I know, I know," Annie mumbled, and I heard her blow her nose.

"You must be so upset. I know how much you liked him."

"No, I didn't like him," Annie coughed, and I was confused until she added in a low and unwavering voice, "I loved him."

I was overwhelmed into silence. Annie had spoken those last three words with such honesty and intensity that it had thrown me into shocked silence. I hadn't known she had such strong feelings for Cory. I knew that they went to the movies and talked on the phone and stuff like that, but I had never known just how much Cory had meant to Annie. She had really cared about him with a love that I had yet to truly experience myself. It made me sad to realize that the only time Annie had really talked to me about her relationship was to tell me it was over.

"I never knew you felt that way about him," I admitted. "I mean, I knew you liked him, but I never knew you loved him."

"I did," Annie cried, and I heard her wipe her nose. "I really did."

"So, why'd he break up with you?" I asked, hoping I wasn't treading on unstable ground. "Did he give you a reason?"

Now Annie's tone held more contempt than sorrow. "Well, he said, 'I'm getting bored. I need some variety in my life.' Can you believe him? He just got sick of me," she wailed, her voice her own again, and full of anguish. "What did I do wrong?"

"You didn't do anything," I made sure to tell her quickly and firmly. "It wasn't your fault. He's the one who broke up with you. It's his problem. This breakup doesn't mean that there's something wrong with you. You're perfectly lovable just the way you are." I was full of words of wisdom, and I hadn't been able to share that with Annie in a while.

"I guess you're right," Annie murmured, but I could tell she wasn't totally convinced. There was nothing I could do about that. I couldn't change how she felt about herself; all I could do was make sure to be there for her when she needed some encouraging words.

Through the phone I could hear Annie starting to cry again, and the sound made me hurt inside. It reminded me of the time when another boy Annie had liked dumped her, and I remember hugging her as she cried on my window seat. I had told her then that she would get through it, and she had, which meant that she could get over this, too. When I spoke, I made sure to keep my voice gentle and calm. "You two had such a long, wonderful time together, though, right?"

I thought maybe I detected a hint of a smile in Annie's voice when she replied. "Oh, yeah, definitely. The best."

"I never heard a lot about the relationship," I pointed out. "Tell me about it."

And suddenly she was talking to me. Serious, just-like-old-times talking. Remembering brought painful memories up to the surface, but also pleasant ones, and she started to laugh more often than she cried. As we talked, I could almost feel the gap of two years starting to close, and even though I knew it wouldn't stay closed long, I was just happy that we could regain our old friendship, even just for a little bit. Things felt back to normal again, almost perfect. But even though I tried to tell myself otherwise, I knew this wouldn't last. The next time Annie and a guy break up, we will have this conversation again, and things will feel normal. Yet, in between the start of a new relationship and the end of it, I will be second to Annie's new boyfriend, her new friends, her new clothes, her new schedule, her new personality. We will revert back to what we had been only last week—acquaintances. Distant friends.

I didn't care. I had other friends, other activities, other ideas to explore. Our lives would continue on separately, mine going one way, hers the other. I understood that. We were two different people now, with different views, attitudes, personalities, lives. We weren't as close as before, but we were still friends, and I wasn't the kind of person to drop old friends for new. Maybe Annie didn't care as much about our friendship as I did, maybe sometimes I was there for her more than she was there for me, and maybe sometimes I came second on Annie's list. I knew this, and I didn't care. I would always be there for Annie. We had been friends for so long, and I wasn't about to give that up.

"I have to go soon. I promised Bailey I'd call her tonight. But first, I want to thank you," Annie said, and her voice, I knew, was sincere. "You've always been such a good friend, Melinda. I know I must bore you to death with all this, but you still listen. Thanks." Annie knew what a good friend was; she just couldn't find it in herself to apply the knowledge. She was too confused, too unsure of herself, too caught up in the rush of teenage life. I understood that, too.

"I'm glad you're feeling better," I said sincerely. The conversation was coming to a close.

Annie thought for a minute. "It's going to take a long time to heal. I'm just going to miss him for a while." Annie grew more reflective, and her voice softer, more thoughtful, as she struggled to put her feelings into words. "We were so close.... It almost feels... It almost feels like a part of me has been taken away, a part I can't get back." She struggled for words. "Like... things feel different, like they won't ever be the same again." Annie sighed, frustrated. "Do you get what I'm trying to say?"

My voice was wobbly, and my cheeks were wet. "I know exactly what you mean," I told her. And I did understand — every word she said.

~Melinda Favreau
Chicken Soup for the Teenage Soul on Love & Friendship

78

Friends Forever

Some people come into our lives and quickly go.
Some stay for a while, leave footprints on our hearts,
and we are never, ever the same.
~Flavia Weedn, *Forever*

It seemed as if Chrissy and I had been friends forever. Ever since we'd met on the first day of fourth grade, we had been inseparable. We did almost everything together. We were so close that when it came time to pick partners, it was just assumed that we'd pick each other.

In ninth grade, however, things changed. We had been in the same classes for the last five years, but now we were going to different schools. At first we were as good friends as ever, but eventually we found we had no time for each other. Slowly but surely, we were drifting apart. Promises were broken and important get-togethers postponed. I think both of us knew we were breaking apart, but neither of us wanted to admit it.

Then one day, I finally faced the fact that Chrissy and I weren't close anymore. We'd both grown up, and didn't have much in common any longer. I still missed her, though. We had shared five incredible years together—years I will never forget. Years I don't want to forget.

One day, as I was thinking of our great times together, I wrote a poem about our friendship. It was about letting go and growing up, but never forgetting friends.

I still talk to Chrissy sometimes, though now it's hard because we both have such busy schedules.

To this day, I still think of Chrissy as one of my best friends... even though by some definitions we aren't. But when I'm asked to list my friends, I never hesitate to add her name. Because as she would always say: "Real friends are forever." When I gave her this poem we both cried, for it's changes like these that make growing up so difficult.

Changes

"Friends forever," you promised.
"Together till the end."
We did everything with each other.
You were my best friend.
When I was sad, you were by my side.
When I was scared, you felt my fear.
You were my best support —
If I needed you, you were there.
You were the greatest friend,
You always knew what to say:
You made everything seem better.
As long as we had each other,
Everything would be okay.
But somewhere along the line,
We slowly came apart.
I was here, you were there,
It tore a hole in my heart.
Things were changing,
Our cheerful music reversed its tune.
It was like having salt without pepper,
A sun without its moon.
Suddenly we were miles apart,
Two different people, with nothing the same.
It was as if we hadn't been friends;
Although we knew deep in our hearts

Neither one of us was to blame.
You had made many new friends
And luckily, so had I
But that didn't change the hurt—
The loss of our friendship made me cry.
As we grow older, things must change
But they don't always have to end.
Even though it is different, now,
You will always be my friend.

~Phyllis Lin
Chicken Soup for the Teenage Soul II

79

Behind the Scenes of Two Teen Queens

It takes courage to grow up and become who you really are.
~e.e. cummings

Bored with my life, irritated at who I was, and aching for change, I decided that middle school was the perfect time to introduce the "new me" to the world. My goal wasn't to become "popular." I was simply yearning for a new life. But as I began to morph from an awkward, frizzy-haired, acne-infested brace face to a smiling, straight-haired, lip-glossed teenybopper, that was what happened. My peers flocked to my side, and I was swept up into a whirlwind of parties and gossip, friends and boys, makeup and drama. Life in the fast lane. I loved it. I loved life in the "in crowd."

Amid my radical transformation, I met Laurie. We became best friends—we were inseparable. We spent the days together, with the air conditioner buzzing, the TV blasting and brand new glossy magazines strewn across her Winnie the Pooh bed sheets, sticking to our shaved, lotioned legs. We would point at the pictures of beauty: ladderlike stomachs, narrow calves, straight, blond, highlighted hair. Inspired by these images of perfection, we'd spend hours in the drugstore, searching for the perfect eyeliner, cover-up or lipstick, then rush home to recreate the sultry looks on our own pale, youthful faces.

Three times a week we would go to the gym. Passing mothers

and fathers, old people and teenage boys training for track, we'd run until we were the fastest, the most graceful, the most beautiful. We'd sit across from each other on the thigh machines, leaning forward, straining, counting breathlessly to 100. Or we'd be side-by-side on the ab machines, grunting in pain as we tried to rid ourselves of our "love handles" and baby fat. We would take breaks to sip at the water fountain and watch others work out. Envious of their dedication, we set weight goals for ourselves: 98 pounds, 95, 90.

After working out, we would slip into our colorful, tiny, two-piece bathing suits and ease into the hot bubbling fizz of the Jacuzzi. Our eyes closed, we would sit in the water, beaded with wetness, listening to the jets and feeling our bodies pulsing in the heat.

Our friendship seemed simple. We were the "teen queens," the coolest in the grade. With our trendy clothes, hair ironed straight, and faces painted, we strutted through the hallways, savoring the attention and basking in others' envy. We were smiling images of perfection, Polaroids of future prom queens. We looked so happy, confident, carefree.

But images often deceive. Sometimes, if you look close enough, you can see through goops of eyeliner and mascara and into the eyes. If you looked closely at either of us, you would see that we were simply living a façade. We knew it, and that was why we were best friends. Because together we could be insecure and imperfect, together it was okay to be ourselves.

Laurie and I no longer speak. It wasn't a devastating, heartbreaking fallout. Rather, it happened naturally, slowly, over time. Neither of us are the teen queens we once were. Without each other, the power was lost, the charisma gone, and each of us was left with only ourself.

I thought that I needed Laurie. I thought I needed her and our status as the "most popular" to be happy. Being with her, being part of the "in crowd" made me feel visible, like I was seen, and there was no need to question anything. I felt alive. I thrived in the spotlight and reveled in the attention. But as I have grown, my dependence on others to blossom has dissipated... I have realized that the "it" girl I once was wasn't really me. It was me simply playing the part. It was me, going through the motions of who I thought I was supposed to be.

~Jessica M. McCann
Chicken Soup for the Teenage Soul: The Real Deal School

Two Girls and a Friendship

We have been friends together
In sunshine and in shade.
~Caroline Sheridan Norton

Among the trinkets and decorative items in a fifteen-year-old girl's room, one stood out boldly—a bright blue clay vase with colorful painted flowers. Not a perfect or beautiful vase, this one is broken in several places. The owner of the vase has carefully mended it, but spiderlike cracks remain. If this vase could talk, it would tell the story of two girls and a friendship.

Amy and June met on an airplane on their way home from Bangkok where their fathers, who were business partners, were attending meetings. June sat behind Amy. Halfway toward home, Amy turned around hesitantly and gave June a bright blue vase made of clay. It was a small gesture, but a token of friendship and an introduction. June accepted, and they smiled shyly at each other. And on that day, a simple friendship between two four-year-olds was established.

Years flew by. Amy and June grew up together, played together, studied together and, naturally, became each other's closest confidante. June cried on Amy's shoulder when her little puppy died in a car accident. June was there for Amy when she fell during a gymnastic routine in the talent show and everyone had laughed at her. When June ran away at the age of ten after an argument with her mother, it was Amy who convinced her to go back home. And it was June who comforted Amy when Amy's favorite uncle passed away. June was part of Amy, as Amy was part of June.

Life is not, and never will be, a bed of roses. People change as they grow up, for better or for worse. Sometimes these changes are hard to accept. And even the most special friendships can be destroyed. When she was fourteen, Amy met a boy. A boy who, to fourteen-year-old Amy, was Heaven-sent. Amy started hanging out with this boy all the time, and she started to see less and less of June. And although June was hurt, she tried to be understanding. She was still there for Amy when Amy had arguments with her boyfriend and needed a shoulder to cry on. But Amy wasn't there when June needed her. June was going through a difficult period and found herself mildly depressed. But Amy still leaned on June for relationship support. Upset and depressed about the state of their friendship, June invited Amy to her house to talk. When June tried to bring up her difficulties and her problems, Amy brushed her off by saying, "Later." Instead, Amy asked June for ideas for what she should buy for her boyfriend on their half-year anniversary. June couldn't take it anymore. Anger, sadness, resentment, betrayal and disappointment washed over her. June exploded. She started crying and yelling at Amy.

"What am I to you, Amy? Your friend or just your little dog?" June cried. June was hoping for an apology and some support. Instead, Amy was defensive and yelled back at June. A friendship of ten years was disintegrating before their eyes. And there was nothing either of them could do about it.

"That's it, June! I hate you!" Amy yelled. There was no way of taking it back. June stared at Amy tearfully. Amy broke eye contact and spun around on her heel and stomped out of June's room, slamming the door hard behind her. A blue vase on the shelf jumped and fell onto the floor, smashing into several pieces. Unstoppable tears flowed freely as June knelt down on the floor and picked up the pieces. No more giggling, no more gossiping, no more endless sleepovers and no more long phone sessions with her best friend. Ten years of friendship... shattered like the vase, the vase that she had so preciously taken care of all these years, the vase that symbolized all that was wonderful about friendship.

The pain of losing a best friend, losing the one you trusted most, is worse than a thousand stabbing knives. Collapsing into a heap on the floor, June cried uncontrollably. This was not one of the stupid arguments she and Amy had sometimes. This was serious and possibly irreparable. A horrible emptiness filled her heart. She knew they had lost that special bond between them. She also knew there was no way of bringing it back. It was over.

At school, June and Amy were stiff and polite with one another. Not long after their argument, Amy broke up with her boyfriend. But both were stubborn, and remained icy and distant. Amy had not forgiven June for June's cruel words. And even June could not find a place in her heart where she could forgive Amy. Hurt and betrayal took time to heal. Sort of like the vase. The broken pieces lay unmended in June's dresser drawer. Even if it was put back together again, no matter how carefully, cracks would remain. A broken vase could never be perfect again.

One year passed. It was June's fifteenth birthday. Instead of feeling happy, June only felt gloom. She remembered her fourteenth birthday, one month before their big fight. It had been a great one, and they had been so happy. They had giggled over the silliest things and engaged in a food fight. They had vowed their friendship would last for an eternity. Bittersweet tears filled June's eyes. She could still remember an image of four-year-old Amy holding out the blue vase to her.

The doorbell rang. June hopped up and rushed to the door. She was expecting her cousin. The door swung open. June froze. Amy stood at the doorstep, holding a small package. "I just wanted to say, well, I…" The former best friends looked at each other, their emotions mirrored on each other's faces. "Hap... happy birthday, June," Amy finally stammered out. She shoved the gift into June's hand and ran down the pathway. June felt compelled to chase after her, but she didn't. Instead, she closed the door gently.

Going to her room, she sat down on her bed and opened the gift. It was a bracelet. Attached to it was a note that read, "Dear June, Happy Fifteenth Birthday, Amy." At the bottom was a small, "P. S. I'm sorry." Two words. Two simple words that filled June's heart with joy. She picked up the phone to call Amy. And made a mental note to mend her broken vase. Even though it would never be perfect, an imperfect vase was better than a shattered one.

~Pey Jung Yeong
Chicken Soup for the Teenage Soul on Love & Friendship

81

The Rift

Remember, we all stumble, every one of us.
That's why it's a comfort to go hand in hand.
~Emily Kimbrough

I sit perched on the edge of my bed, faint smiles drifting across my face, as I sift through all my old photographs. My sleeves pushed up over my elbows, I dig down into all the old memories. I hold each memory briefly in my hands before dropping it onto the pile in my lap and searching for the next happy moment to remember. Each picture evokes feelings long gone, but deep within me. I'm not exactly sure what has prompted this sudden trip to my past, but I feel like I need to stop and look back.

As I continue to relive the memories, I can't help but notice one photo in particular buried deep in the box. I pluck it from the sea of snapshots and hold it in my hands. The picture at first glance is lovely. The sun was shining with not a cloud to be seen in the bright blue canopy that hung high over my head. I was sitting with my arm around a happy looking girl, her arm rested casually on my shoulders. As I focus in on the person's face, the warm smile that covers my face is replaced by an agitated frown. It is Amy Soule, my now ex-best friend. A terrible pang of regret flashes through me, and I feel the familiar constriction in my throat.

I'm not sure exactly how, or when, our decline as friends started, but it started small. A simple crack that flourished in our awkward adolescence and shameful neglect. It began with simple differences in interest. She wanted to go to the mall and scout for guys, while I wanted to spend the evening watching old movies and talking about nonsense gossip. Suddenly, after school activities took up our usual time together and weekends were spent doing other things. Soon the only time I saw her was when we exchanged a hurried hello in the busy school halls between classes. A far cry from the whispered conversations behind my half-open locker at every spare moment. No more notes were passed behind the teacher's back, and my parent's phone bill became considerably cheaper. She found a new group of friends, and so did I. Before I had a chance to patch the crack between us, she moved away from me, turning the crack into an uncrossable rift.

I tried to make excuses for not keeping in touch. I couldn't visit; it was too far and I couldn't ask Mom to drive me all that way. I even tried to convince my nagging conscience with the notion that people change, and I matured. I knew that was not the answer, but I was too nervous to pick up the phone and call. The rift grew too large to bridge. Amy had left, and she had taken a huge chunk of my heart with her.

I stand up and stretch my cramping limbs. Pulling myself back into the now, I let the picture fall from my hand onto my cluttered desk. I glance up at my calendar and remember that Amy's birthday is around the corner. In fact, we were born in the same room, two days apart. It had always been a good-natured joke between us that she was two days older than I. We started so close, and ended up so far. This bittersweet memory causes me to smile despite my feelings of regret. I suddenly have an idea. I hastily drop to my knees and begin to rummage through my desk drawers. At last, I lay my hands on an old picture frame I have had around forever. I pick up the fallen photo of Amy and me and snap it into the frame. I quickly pen a note, and for lack of anything better to say, I simply write:

Happy Birthday Amy!

Erica

I stick the piece of white paper under the edge of the frame and search for Amy's address. I hold the frame tightly in my arms. I am not going to let this golden chance slip through my fingers. It's not much, but it is a beginning and the space between us has already gotten smaller. Maybe this time I will be strong enough to build a bridge.

~Erica Thoits
Chicken Soup for the Teenage Soul II

82

Friends Forever We'll Always Be

In a friend you find a second self.
~Isabelle Norton

We may not have been the most popular, most loved eighth graders at our middle school, but we didn't feel the need to be. Becky and I had each other, and we were inseparable. We did all of the same extracurricular activities and never really went anywhere without each other. We were more one person than two separate people. Other kids thought it was annoying that we were so inseparable, but I know that it made me feel more secure and confident. If Becky wasn't there, I wouldn't have made it through school each day, let alone be where I am today.

Although there were things that made us different—Becky was better at soccer than me, and I was student council president while Becky was just on the committee—we were also the same in many ways. We shared the same name (although she preferred Becky rather than Rebecca), we shared thoughts on many topics, and we shared the same outlook on life. After a while, we rubbed off on each other so much that we ended up sharing our style as well.

By eighth grade we had gone through three years of school together, and we were ready to face high school. We'd heard that many old friends were lost in high school, but Becky and I were best friends, and no matter what happened, we knew nothing would tear us apart. We had gone through too many rough times to let what other people said and did bring us down. Friends forever was what we would always be... or so we thought.

That summer was awesome. We had a blast spending almost every day together. Although I felt like I was changing on the inside, I knew Becky would be there for me no matter what. We got our schedules when school started and found out that we wouldn't share even one class together that year, but we still felt strong, spending every lunch hour together with our mutual friends and sharing a notebook, which helped keep us in touch with what was going on in our classes and at home.

Then, about halfway through first semester, we started spending less and less time hanging out together. It got to the point where I was listening to other people just to find out what was going on in Becky's life and what she was saying about me. Although we still spent every lunch hour with our mutual group of friends, Becky and I stopped talking. Fewer and fewer pictures of us together appeared in my photo albums. I had to listen to our other friends to find out if she was talking about me, and when they said she was, I believed them without confronting her.

I began to feel lost in our group. Even though I still talked with everyone except Becky, I started spending my lunch hours with new acquaintances. I knew that Becky was changing inside as well. We weren't the inseparable pair anymore — we had become separate people. She played soccer, and I played rugby. We saw less and less of each other. As the months went on, I continued to wonder about her and how she had changed. I couldn't believe I had lost touch with my best friend. How could I have let this happen? For some reason, I blamed myself. I broke down many nights just wondering where she was. I missed spending every day with her. I missed our adventures and our sleepovers. I missed just knowing she was there. I missed her family that I had become a part of.

We started to talk again, but it was actually more like fighting than talking. But then we both got sick of not understanding and blaming each other. We told each other how we really felt. I told her I cried myself to sleep many nights, and she told me she did the same. Although the half year we spent apart felt like a lifetime, we are slowly making up for it.

Today, we communicate and we trust each other. That's one thing I will never lose—her trust. I'll never understand why we let something come in and ruin our friendship, why we did the things we did and said the things we said. But we can't go back. High school is tough, but knowing Becky's still in my life and she doesn't hate me is making it easier. I will never forget the good times and bad with Becky, and I'll never lose her trust. I know that from now on, she's not going anywhere.

~Rebecca Ruiter
Chicken Soup for the Teenage Soul: The Real Deal Friends

Choices

The most important thing in communication is hearing what isn't being said.
~Author Unknown

When I first met Molly, she instantly became my best friend. We enjoyed the same things, laughed at the same jokes and even had the same love for sunflowers.

It seemed like we had found each other at the right time. Both of us had been in different groups of friends that didn't get along or we didn't feel comfortable in. We were thrilled to find each other.

Our friendship grew very strong. Our families became friends, and everyone knew that wherever you found Molly, you found me, and vice versa. In fifth grade, we were not in the same class, but at lunch we both sat in nearby assigned seats and turned around to talk to each other. The lunch ladies did not like this. We were always blocking the aisle, talking too loudly and not eating our lunches, but we didn't care. The teachers knew we were best friends, but we were also a disturbance. Our big mouths got us into trouble, and we were warned that we would never be in the same classes again if we kept this up.

That summer, Molly and her brother were at my house quite often. My mom took care of them while their mom worked. We went swimming, played outside and practiced playing our flutes. We bought best friend charms and made sure to wear them as often as possible.

Summer went by very quickly, and middle school began. As the teachers had warned us, we were not in the same classes. We still talked on the phone, went over to each other's houses, sang in choir and practiced our flutes together in band. Nothing could destroy this friendship.

Seventh grade started and again we were not in the same classes and could not sit near each other at lunch. It seemed as if we were being put to a test. We both made new friends. Molly started to hang out with a new group of people and was growing very popular.

We spent less time together, and we rarely talked on the phone. At school, I would try to talk to her, but she would just ignore me. When we did take a minute to talk, one of her more popular friends would come up and Molly would just walk away with her, leaving me in the dust. It hurt.

I was so confused. I'm sure she didn't know at the time how badly I felt, but how could I talk to her if she wouldn't listen? I began to hang around with my new friends, but it just wasn't the same. I met Erin, who was also a friend of Molly's. She was in the same situation I was with Molly. She and Molly had been close friends, and lately Molly had been treating Erin the same way as me. We decided to talk to her.

The phone call was not easy. Talking and saying how I felt was difficult. I was so afraid that I would hurt her feelings and make her angry. It was funny, though—when it was just the two of us talking on the phone, we were friends again. It was the old Molly.

I explained how I was feeling, and she did, too. I realized I was not the only one hurting. She was alone without me to talk to. What was she supposed to do, not make new friends? I didn't think about this before, but she was feeling left out by me and my new friends. There were times when I didn't even notice I was ignoring her. We must have talked for a long time, because once we were finished I had used a handful of tissues for my tears, and felt as if I had lifted a heavy weight off my heart. We both decided that we wanted to be with our new friends, but we would never forget the fun and friendship we had shared with each other.

Today, I look back on all of this and smile. Molly and I are finally in the same classes, and you know what? We still get in trouble for talking too loudly. Molly is not my best friend anymore, but more like my sister. We still enjoy the same things, laugh at the same jokes and share the same love for sunflowers. I will never forget her. Molly taught me something very important. She taught me that things change, people change, and it doesn't mean you forget the past or try to cover it up. It simply means that you move on, and treasure all the memories.

~Alicia M. Boxler
Chicken Soup for the Teenage Soul II

84

My Friend Andrea

I felt tears well up in my eyes as I heard my best friend's name called and watched her walk across the stage to receive her high school diploma. She shook hands with the school board president, had her tassel turned by the superintendent, and finally received her diploma from our principal. She stopped briefly to face the audience while they took pictures and applauded her. She was an honor student and first in her class. I felt a sense of pride and smiled to myself as flashback after flashback of our childhood paraded through my mind.

I remembered the winter that we decided to become bobsledders. We packed snow on the front steps of my house and let it set up overnight so we could sled down the icy strip on orange saucers at breathtaking speeds to the street that separated our houses. I relived the excitement of singing into our baking spoons about "rocking the town inside out" while sliding across the kitchen floor in our socked feet. One summer we both had Nickelodeon Moon Shoes. We would bounce all over Andrea's front yard and make music videos—without a video camera.

I had to suppress a laugh as I thought of the time that we lit a bonfire in our clubhouse that was located under my front steps. It was a normal summer day, and I was just hanging out in our clubhouse. As I looked around, I decided that we had too much garbage lying around and needed to dispose of it. Andrea came over in a flash and was more than willing to join the fun. We filled an ice cream pail with water in case something should happen, then out came the matches. We put the garbage in a pile and lit it up. It got a little out of hand and started climbing the wall. Fortunately, we had the bucket of water and put it out before anything of importance caught on fire. Yep, we got in trouble for that little episode. The front entryway of my house smelled like a chimney, and when my parents caught a whiff they herded us in for a lecture.

We took a stab at writing songs and hosting our own talk shows. We dealt with important issues like what kind of shoes we were wearing and what our moms were making for supper on that particular night. We also addressed the fact that Mr. Freeze popsicles were part of a balanced diet and should be included in one of the major food groups. Our friendship was full of slumber parties and now somewhat embarrassing escapades.

As she sat back down in her seat, one last memory came to mind. This one, however, was not quite a happy one. Even though Andrea is only two weeks older than me, she is a grade ahead. I was born two days after the cutoff to be part of her class. When Andrea started her freshman year in high school, we drifted apart. She made new friends, and we both got involved in our own activities and interests. Even though it bothered me a great deal, I kept it to myself. She didn't seem heartbroken, so I acted like I wasn't either. For two-and-a-half long years we went about our lives separately. Our friendship dwindled to a nod in the hallway at school or maybe a "hello" on rare occasions. I wanted to talk to her so badly. I would go to the phone to call her, but would hang up before the call went through. I was afraid that she wouldn't want to talk to me. The truth was, she wanted to call me, too, but would hang up for the exact same reason. We found out later that even though the other hadn't known it, we were both hurting and longing for the friendship we used to have.

I don't even know how it happened. I guess we finally realized that we had had too good of a friendship to ignore each other any longer. The months ahead held a lot of catching up. We found out that we were experiencing many of the same things and that we understood each other like no one else. We began what we later called cocoa talks. Even when the weather was warm, we would spend the evening sitting on Andrea's front steps, drinking hot cocoa with marshmallows and talking about everything that was going on in our lives. We laughed, and we cried. Sometimes we laughed so hard it made us cry. No matter what, we always left feeling better, feeling understood. It's been a bumpy road, but I wouldn't change any of it. In the nine years that she has lived across the street from me, we have formed an unbreakable bond of friendship that we both know is hard to come by. We are always asking each other how we got to be so lucky as to have our best friend living right across the street.

This next year holds uncertainty for both of us. Andrea will be starting college in the fall, and I will be left to survive my senior year alone. But one thing remains certain: Andrea and I have a friendship that will never graduate.

~Laura Loken
Chicken Soup for the Teenage Soul on Love & Friendship

85

The Five Flavors

The most beautiful discovery true friends make
is that they can grow separately without growing apart.
~Elisabeth Foley

In fourth grade I had four best friends. We were all as different as we could possibly be, yet we got along perfectly. One day we decided that we should be an official group. Since I love food, I thought we should be "The Five Flavors," kind of like Baskin Robbins's thirty-one flavors. We were all unique individuals, but together we were one sweet mix. We all came up with names for one another. I was Vanilla Bean, Samantha was Mix 'n' Match, Leah was Shaky Sherbet, Lily was Chilly Lily and Jessica topped it all off with Sweet Sorbet. And so The Five Flavors were born. We never really told anyone else about it. Just a little something we kept to ourselves.

That year Leah decided that she wanted to have The Five Flavors sleep over for her ninth birthday party. We slept outside in a huge tent. We had a blast staying up late, eating junk food and laughing at all the stupid things we did. It was that night that we decided this should be something we do at least once a year. We decided to call it "Tradition."

Between fourth and sixth grade, we had Tradition more than once a year. We were all so close and felt like nothing could ever tear us apart. We would joke about having Tradition when we would be eighty years old and how we would have to put our teeth in a cup rather than brush them. Tradition was a night where we could forget all of our troubles and just have a crazy time.

Then came seventh grade. We had managed to stick by each other through the first year of middle school, but we soon realized that we had all dramatically changed by seventh grade. We weren't the same Five Flavors that we had been three years before. We began hanging out with different groups. Despite our differences, we still had Tradition that year.

But by eighth grade, we were completely separate. We each had our own friends, opinions, teachers... everything. Lily's best friend was my worst enemy. Jessica's friends made fun of me. We all were our true selves, and we all liked it that way. However, surprisingly enough, we STILL had Tradition that year.

Next stop, high school. We were now each our own person with completely opposite personalities. We barely saw one another, and if we did, we wouldn't even say, "Hi." No one could have ever guessed that at one point we had been so close. The ninth grade school year was coming to an end, and we hadn't had Tradition yet. We had basically given up on the idea, but Leah insisted on having one. After multiple attempts to find one weekend that we were all free, Leah finally found one—the weekend of her fifteenth birthday. We all came, expecting it to be just like the first one we had had six years ago, and it was.

It was like we had never changed at all. We were all exactly the same. We all still laughed at the fact that Lily threw M&Ms in the tent, Jessica and I were still chasing each other around and fighting, Leah still yelled at us to stop screaming and Sam was still the sleeping doormat. The only thing that had changed was how little room we had in the once gigantic tent. That night you would have thought we were all still the best of friends. We were open about everything, as if nothing had changed between us. The past six years had altered the way we dressed, thought and talked, but we were still the original Five Flavors.

That night we all realized that no matter how far apart we grow, we would all have each others' back. I learned that nothing can replace good old friends; people who to this day can make you forget about all your problems and allow you to have nothing but fun. Sure enough, after our last Tradition, we went back to our own friends, our own ways, our own lives. But we all know that we'll be back in a year, laughing together as if we were still in fourth grade. And that's what's so great about a little thing we like to call Tradition.

~Roxanne Gowharrizi
Chicken Soup for the Girl's Soul

Chapter 12

Teens Talk

Relationships

Through Thick and Thin

*Lots of people want to ride with you in the limo,
but what you want is someone who will
take the bus with you when the limo breaks down.
~Oprah Winfrey*

A Fateful Friendship

Serendipity is one of my favorite words. It means "a fortunate accident." Fate, luck, destiny, whatever you call it—I find it exciting, and in a strange way comforting, to think that we might all be part of a "bigger plan," or at least play a role in some smaller, everyday miracles.

Two years ago, when my relationship with my then "best friends forever" (we even had BFF necklaces) took a sudden and unexpected turn for the worse, serendipity was the farthest thing from my mind. The breakup was an accident, surely. I spent weeks trying to figure out where I went wrong. But fortunate? My tears argued otherwise. I had always felt comfortable in my skin, but suddenly my BFFs were changing and trying to get me to change with them. We had always been able to tell each other everything, but suddenly I felt my friends weren't really listening, except when using my words to backstab me. We were once "the three amigas," but now it seemed like it was two against one, and I was always the one. I had always been a peacekeeper, but suddenly we were bickering constantly. Even though I wasn't a drama queen, I started crying myself to sleep at night. I was being sucked under in a whirlpool of turmoil, and one thing was certain—I had to get out.

Everyone talks about "broken hearts" in a romantic aspect, but nobody mentions how heartbreaking it is when friends split up. I had other acquaintances, friends from class, people to sit with at lunch, but it wasn't the same. Heather and Nadine had been the two sisters I never had. I missed them, even though I remembered how depressed I had been with them and how bad they were making me feel about myself. I had never lacked self-confidence, but now it was slipping away. Without my "two amigas," I felt miserable and utterly alone, like someone had changed the rules, and I didn't know how to play the game anymore.

Then one day, while I was feeling blue, Emma called me. Emma had been my best friend in middle school, and I still considered her one of my good friends, but we had grown apart the past few years. Even though we went to the same high school, we had different classes and different interests. Around the same time I met Heather and Nadine, Emma began to drift away, like a boat being pulled out to sea by a different current. I tried to keep up our friendship at first, but she was always too "busy" to hang out. My phone calls became less frequent and then almost nonexistent. Now, sitting in my bedroom listening to Emma's familiar voice on the other end of the phone, I realized how much I missed her.

"You've seemed sad lately," she said. "Are you okay?" Soon I found myself telling her everything, hiccupping with tears by the time I was done. Emma just listened. And then she said, "It's okay, Dallas. You'll always have me." I realized how selfish I had been to let Emma drift away in the first place, and how lucky I was that she had paddled back to me.

Instantly, it was like old times. In fact, before long Emma and I were closer than ever. I rediscovered what it was like to have a friend who accepted me for me, who really listened when I talked, who I felt safe confiding in. I was happier than I'd been in months. Emma seemed happy, too, yet something wasn't quite right. It seemed as if she was still holding something back from me.

One night, as we lay side by side in our sleeping bags after a late-night movie marathon—including, of course, the best chick flick ever, *Serendipity*—Emma turned on her side and looked at me, her face glistening with tears. "There's something I've been wanting to tell you for a really long time," she said, taking a deep breath. "My sister is... anorexic."

I sat there, holding my best friend's hand as she poured out everything she had buried inside for so long. Her sadness, her fear, her frustration and anger and loneliness. I felt like someone had flushed the toilet while I was in a steaming hot shower, suddenly shocking me with ice water. How could I not have known? How could I not have seen that something was wrong? All this time I had been so caught up in my own worries and troubles—things that didn't seem nearly so big anymore—that I hadn't even noticed Emma's world crumbling around her.

It started two years ago, she explained between hiccups, about the same time she started drifting away from me. Other than a few phone calls, I had barely made an effort to pull her back in. "I'm sorry, Emma," I whispered, crying now myself. "I'm so, so sorry."

"I'm sorry I didn't tell you sooner," she said. "I knew you would listen. I just... I didn't know how to get the words out. But now I feel so much better, like I've been carrying around a backpack full of textbooks and suddenly God's given me a locker."

A month later, Emma's sister left home to go to an eating disorder camp four hours away. Emma was beside herself with sadness, but at least this time she had me.

If you had told me two years ago that losing my BFF was an act of serendipity, I would have refused to listen. But the thing I've learned about fortunate accidents is that at first it's hard to get past the "accident" part. Oftentimes you have to look back through the lens of time to realize how fortunate you truly are. I see now that fate was smiling on me after all. My fallout with Heather and Nadine helped me find Emma again, and she showed me what a true friend is. Perhaps more important, losing my not-so-true friends allowed me to be there for Emma when she needed me the most.

Emma's sister is now doing much better, by the way. And our friendship is healthier than ever.

~Dallas Nicole Woodburn
Chicken Soup for the Teenage Soul: The Real Deal Friends

I Need You Now

My friend, I need you now—
Please take me by the hand.
Stand by me in my hour of need,
Take time to understand.
Take my hand, dear friend,
And lead me from this place.
Chase away my doubts and fears,
Wipe the tears from off my face.
Friend, I cannot stand alone.
I need your hand to hold,
The warmth of your gentle touch
In my world that's grown so cold.
Please be a friend to me
And hold me day by day.
Because with your loving hand in mine,
I know we'll find the way.

~Becky Tucker
Chicken Soup for the Teenage Soul II

Bobby, I'm Smiling

hen I was ten years old, my grade school closed, and I was transferred to a school in a nearby town. In each classroom, the teachers would seat my classmates and me alphabetically, thus seating me beside the same boy, time and time again. His name was Bobby, and he was as outgoing as I was shy. I didn't make friends easily, but Bobby managed to reach beyond my shyness, and eventually, we became friends.

As the years passed, Bobby and I shared all the normal school experiences—first loves, double dating, Friday night football games, parties and dances. He was my friend. My confidant. My devil's advocate. It didn't matter that we were so different—he the popular, handsome, self-assured football star who had a beautiful girlfriend; me the overweight, inhibited and insecure teenage girl. We were friends regardless.

One morning during the spring of our senior year, I opened my locker and, to my surprise, there was a beautiful flower. I looked around to see who might have left it for me, but no one stood by waiting to take credit.

I knew that Gerry, a guy in my history class, had a crush on me. Had he left it? As I stood wondering, my friend Tami walked by.

"Nice flower," she said.

"Yes, it is. It was left in my locker without a note, but I think I know who gave it to me," I said. "I'm just not interested in dating him, but how do I tell him without hurting his feelings?"

Tami said, "Well, if you're not interested in going out with him, tell him I will. He's awesome!"

"But Tami," I said, "you know that Gerry and I aren't anything alike. It would never work out."

At that, Tami laughed and said, "Gerry didn't give you that flower. Bobby did."

"Bobby? Bobby Matthews?"

Then Tami explained.

Earlier that morning, she had passed Bobby in the school's parking lot. Noticing the flower and unable to resist, she had asked him who it was for. His only reply had been that it was for someone special and meant to brighten their day.

I was touched by Tami's story but was certain that the flower had been intended to be given anonymously.

Later that morning, I carried the flower to class and set it on my desk. Bobby noticed it and said nonchalantly, "Nice flower."

I smiled and said, "Yes, it's beautiful."

Minutes later, while we stood to recite the Pledge of Allegiance, I leaned over to Bobby and whispered "Thank you," then proceeded to finish the pledge.

As we were retaking our seats, Bobby said, "For what?"

I smiled. "The flower."

At first, Bobby feigned ignorance, but then he realized I had discovered his secret. "But how did you know?"

I simply smiled and asked why he had given it to me.

He hesitated only briefly before answering. "I gave it to you, because I wanted you to know you're special."

In retrospect, as I look back over seventeen years of friendship, I don't believe that I ever loved Bobby more than I did at that moment. The flower itself paled in comparison with his unexpected and purely giving act of kindness. That kindness meant the world to me then—and still does.

As Bobby had hoped, I did feel special—not only on that day, but for many days to follow. To paraphrase Mark Twain, a person can live a month off a compliment. It's true. I've done it.

When my lovely flower finally wilted and died, I pressed it in a book.

In the years that followed, Bobby and I remained good friends, and although our lives took different paths, we kept in touch.

When Bobby was twenty-five, he was diagnosed with terminal cancer. Shortly before his twenty-seventh birthday, he died.

Since then, I've lost track of the times I have recalled that spring day so long ago. I still treasure my pretty pressed flower, and when I hear the old cliché, "Remember with a smile," I'm certain that it was coined by someone who understood the meaning of a friend's love, and the lasting impression of a kind gesture.

Bobby, I'm smiling.

~E. Keenan
Chicken Soup for the Teenage Soul II

89

"Friends with Benefits," Prom-Style

My knees shook inside my favorite pair of "skinny jeans." I took a deep breath, my courage fortified by a Mountain Dew sugar high. And then I did it. I walked right up to my high school crush and said five simple words: "Hey, wanna go to prom?"

Then the unthinkable happened. "Yeah," he said. "I'd love to."

Pause. Awkward smile. "But…"

Oh, no. Not but. Please, not but!

"…but I already promised to go with one of my friends."

Super duper dandy. My heart—and ego—deflated like a popped prom balloon. I mumbled something along the lines of, "Oh-yeah-that's-fine-totally-understand-just-thought-I'd-ask-you-know-ha-ha-okay-well-bye-now-I'm-gonna-move-to-a-convent-far-far-away-and-become-a-nun."

My friend gave me a "that's his loss" consolation speech. "Whatever," I said. "It probably worked out for the best. It's hard to dance in a habit, anyway." My friend laughed because she thought I was joking.

In all seriousness, though, I was angry at my crush's so-called "friend." I mean, everyone knows you don't go to prom with a friend. Prom is supposed to be a perfect romantic night. Doesn't she read teen magazines?

I'm a forgiving person, though. I forgave this friend, whoever she was, for her lack of prom know-how and mentally prepared myself for a Home Alone Prom Night Party of One. I compiled a list of chick flicks to rent, bought the ingredients for my mom's triple-chocolate fudge brownies and searched the Internet for nearby convents.

And then the unthinkable happened... again. One of my guy "friends" asked me to prom.

After mulling it over for about two-tenths of a second, I, of course, said, "Yes." Going to prom with a friend, I figured, was better than not going to prom at all. Besides, I don't like to bake, and I'd watched *How to Lose a Guy in Ten Days* fourteen times already. Plus, I still harbored a secret fantasy that once my crush saw me in my gorgeous dress with my perfect hair and flawless makeup, he would realize that I was the girl he was supposed to be with, and we would dance the night away in each other's arms....

Yeah, right.

(In case you're wondering, agreeing to go to prom with my friend does not make me a hypocrite. I specifically told my friend that if another girl asked him to go in a more-than-friends way, he had my blessing to go with her instead. I would understand—boy would I! But nobody asked him. So that was that.)

Surprisingly, I didn't spend the days leading up to prom worried and anxious that something would go terribly wrong, that I'd get a huge pimple on my nose, and that my date wouldn't have a good time. Even if disaster struck, I knew it wouldn't ruin the night. Whatever happened, I would have fun because I would be with my friends... and I always have fun with my friends.

My fellow girl prom-mates and I got together on the day of the big event and gave each other manicures and pedicures and help with hair and makeup. (In my opinion, getting ready for prom is one of the best parts of the night!) Then we met up with our guy friend "dates" at a backyard barbeque. We ate hamburgers and french fries, played charades and Twister, took tons of pictures, and even watched *Finding Nemo*. There was no forced small talk or awkward gaps of silence because I was with a big group of friends. And believe me, we never have a problem finding a topic to discuss. It was already turning out to be one of the most fun nights of my life... and the actual dance hadn't even begun yet!

When it comes to dancing, doing it with friends can have benefits—like not having to feel self-conscious. We waltzed; we jigged; we swing danced; we did the robot. A little wild, sure; a little immature, maybe. A lot of fun? Definitely! "When else," I thought, "will I get the chance to do the funky chicken in a formal dress? I'll have the rest of my life to act—and dance—like an adult. Why not take advantage of my youthful immaturity while I can get away with it?"

On the other hand, if I had gone to prom with my crush, I would have been one of those couples waiting around for someone else to kick up the party a notch, worried about making a fool of myself, worried about looking "stupid," worried about what others were thinking instead of what I should be worried about—having fun.

Instead of spending a fortune on expensive picture packages, my buddies and I took along disposable cameras and snapped pictures throughout the dance. Instead of stiff, formal portraits, we were left with rolls and rolls of fun, candid, wacky, real-life photos. Plus, friends generally have a much longer shelf life than crushes or boyfriends. I helped pass out prom pictures when they came in a few weeks after the dance. One girl stormed up, grabbed her $90 picture packet and promptly ripped it to pieces. I stood there in bewilderment until her friend explained, "Her boyfriend broke up with her a week ago." The dumpee looked over and said, "Yeah, I hate his guts." What wonderful prom memories she must have!

My friends and I, however, were left with priceless prom memories—even if they didn't include goodnight kisses on front stoops or confessions of undying love. Instead, we went out for ice cream, our boy friends went home, and my fellow girl prom-mites and I had a sleepover. It was the perfect PG ending to a wonderful night.

And, oh yeah, in case you're wondering whatever happened to my crush... I saw him briefly at the dance and said "hello." He seemed to be having fun with his "friend" as well, for which I was happy.

We ended up becoming good friends ourselves. In my yearbook he wrote, "I'm sorry I didn't go to prom with you." But the funny thing is, I'm not... sorry, that is. Looking back, I ended up having a much better time not going to prom with my crush than I probably would have if we had gone together.

I did the unthinkable. I went to prom with a friend. And, believe me, it had a lot of benefits.

~Dallas Nicole Woodburn
Chicken Soup for the Teenage Soul: The Real Deal Friends

90

My Perfect Friend

Sometimes people look at me like I'm strange. I catch them staring out of the corner of my eye and shudder. Their sideways glances pass through me, and I feel judged, unaccepted. My best friend, Mariah, never looks at me that way, though. Even though we are opposites—I spend my time in the world of books, escaping into other stories, while she spends hers in the world of boys and crushes—we have always gotten along perfectly. Somehow, our differences just seem to work well to create a relationship of comfort and acceptance.

On our first day of high school, Mariah and I walked into school together. It was intimidating, so I was glad that I had Mariah at my side. As we turned the corner toward our first class, we both saw him. He was beautiful. We giggled like little girls and followed him. When we lost sight of him, we both sighed with regret, wishing he had passed our way.

After school, Mariah and I waited at the bus stop together, discussing the day's events, eating whatever snack was left over from our lunch that day, and laughing. Mid-sentence, I looked over and there he was, standing right next to us! I threw my half-eaten banana to the side and fiddled nervously.

Although I'm painfully shy, Mariah doesn't have that problem. As I stood petrified by his looks, she walked boldly up to him and asked him his name. "Jonathan," he said, while he ran a hand through his hair, brushing it out of his pale blue eyes. That is when my infatuation began, even though I knew nothing about him. And for the first time in our whole lives, Mariah and I had the same crush.

"So, where are you from... Jonathan?" Mariah asked, emphasizing his name. As the bus pulled up and we boarded, I caught Mariah's eye. She winked, and I giggled. Jonathan sat across from me on the bus, and as he sat, he smiled. I awkwardly attempted to smile back.

That began the routine that I followed for about a week: seeing him in the hall, nervously sitting near him on the bus, and calling Mariah each night to reconstruct every detail. Our school had a dance planned, and the date was approaching. Mariah was determined to go with Jonathan, but she had a list of guys, just in case he didn't work out. I laughed. The chances of Jonathan asking me were slim to none, but it was fun to fantasize.

Then, one afternoon, we boarded the bus in the same fashion, hoping to sit as close to Jonathan as possible. But this afternoon was different. I didn't have to try to sit near him, for he sat right down beside me. I caught Mariah's eye and shot her a quizzical look. I thought to myself, "No one has liked me before. What is this guy doing?"

Then, my question was answered. He leaned over to me and whispered, "Hey, how about you let me take you to the dance on Friday?" It was more a statement than a question. I nearly choked on my gum.

I barely squeaked out my reply, "Yeah, sure, I guess... I mean, if you want to."

He smiled and said, "Cool."

Without words, Mariah motioned for me to get off at her stop. I quickly took inventory of the situation: the same guy who had been plaguing my thoughts just asked me out. I was on cloud nine. We remained calm until the bus was out of sight, and then, as the coast became clear, we grabbed onto each other and started jumping up and down. For once, I didn't feel so different. Mariah screeched, "Danielle, this is s-o-o-o-o-o cool!"

"I know. Was I shaking?" I replied.

She gave me a hug. "No. You were so calm, you did great." We split at the road and left it at that. I had done great.

The night of the dance, I was frantic. Desperately trying to apply my makeup in a hurry while talking to Mariah on the phone at the same time, I heard my mother yell that I was going to be late. Soon Mariah's parents dropped her off.

On our way to the dance, we met up with Mariah's date, Ben. When we reached the school, Jonathan wasn't there yet, so I waited outside and motioned for Mariah and Ben to go on ahead while I waited. I looked up and saw him. There he stood, with those pale blue eyes, that soft hair, that smooth skin and that sweet smile. There he stood, but... with another girl! He wasn't alone, and he definitely wasn't waiting for me.

I hid myself behind a tree. How could I have been so stupid? I should have known it was too good to be true. He was popular and I wasn't. I let myself feel ugly and undesirable. But worst of all, worse than the embarrassment and the shame, I felt heartbroken.

I made my way out from behind the tree, just in time to see their backs as they entered the dance together. I walked home and into my room, ignoring my mother's questions of why I had returned so early. Sitting alone on my bed, I was plagued by a voice in my head, the voice that told me I was ugly and unloved.

Later, my phone rang. It was Mariah. I knew she wasn't calling to torture me with the dance details, but, rather, to comfort me. This was my first time playing in her world, and I had been hurt. She knew that, and her soothing words helped mend my aching heart and silence that voice in my head that told me I wasn't good enough. Maybe Jonathan didn't think I was good enough, but who cared? Mariah reminded me that there would always be other guys. She told me I was beautiful, and most of all, that I was loved. The self-deprecating voice quickly faded. Mariah and I may be different, even worlds apart, but she accepts me for who I am, and she is my perfect friend.

~Danielle Eberschlag
Chicken Soup for the Teenage Soul III

91

Time Flies

Back in the 1960s, with six children ranging from toddler to teen, my parents' lives were already full. The house overflowed with lively voices. Dick needed his work shirt ironed. Virginia wanted her dolly. Walter needed help with his biology homework. I couldn't find my gym shoes. Tom and Ray waited for a bedtime story. There never seemed to be a quiet moment.

In the midst of these demands, Grandma Jessie moved in, with her deteriorating health, increasing confusion and never-ending fears.

During storms, Grandma panicked. "Mercy, look at the violence outside. I just know the roof is going to go!" Mom would quickly drop what she was doing to gently soothe Grandma's fears. "It's a good, strong roof, Mother. You know God will take care of us." Eventually, Grandma relaxed, at least for a little while.

At night, Grandma was afraid to go to sleep. "It's only nine o'clock, but if I go to bed now, I'll wake up in the night and won't be able to get back to sleep. Oh, mercy, what will I do?"

"Jessie, what was it like when you were a little girl?" Mom would ask to reroute Grandma's thoughts.

Days and nights overflowed with caregiving responsibilities. Mom dealt with Grandma all day long. After work, Dad joined the struggle.

Even as teenagers, my two brothers and I could see the toll that constant caregiving took on our parents. As their anniversary approached, we agreed it was time for action. After school one day, we huddled in the crisp air on the front steps and talked.

"Okay, I've been thinking," I said. "Mom likes to bowl, but Dad doesn't. Dad likes to fish, but it's December. Why don't we just send them to the movies?"

"Sounds all right, but are there any good movies around?" Walter wanted to know.

"Well, I can answer that," Dick exclaimed, and he ran inside to find the morning paper. Sinking back down onto the cold, concrete steps, he opened the paper and perused it. "Look. *Brigadoon* is playing downtown. That will work."

Walter agreed, "Okay. But how in the world are we going to get all the way into downtown Baltimore to pick up tickets without Mom and Dad finding out?"

"Simple," Dick said. "I'll bike over and get them at the local box office."

Soon, the tickets were bought, and we were ready.

The big day arrived. It was hard to contain our excitement. Mom and Dad would be so surprised! Everyone was gathered in the dining room for breakfast. I could hear the crackle of bacon even before the scent reached me.

I set the table and joined Mother in the kitchen.

"Hurry, Mom," I encouraged. I grabbed a big bowl of grits in one hand and a platter of eggs in the other.

Mom followed with a basket of steaming biscuits.

After the prayer, none of us touched our food. Dad and Mom looked around. "Is there a problem?" Mom asked. "Why aren't you eating?"

Dick began his succinct speech. "Mom, Dad, you're going out tonight for your anniversary. Here's two tickets for a movie date." He handed Dad a plain business envelope. "It starts at eight."

"How... my goodness, how did you do this?" Mother was amazed.

Then reality hit. "Oh, but, kids, we couldn't possibly go off and leave you with your grandmother. You can handle the younger children just fine. But taking care of Grandma Jessie would be way too hard."

Dad agreed. "Goodness knows your mother deserves a night out, but you know how Grandma is. And it's worse after dark."

Maybe it was knowing that we had spent our hard-earned dollars on nonrefundable tickets. Maybe it was our conviction that we could handle the situation. Whatever it was, Mom and Dad reluctantly agreed to give our plan a try.

So at seven that night, they walked out the door. Soon, we heard the diminishing roar of the car engine.

Our challenge began in earnest. It was simple enough to say we could handle anything. Now we were about to see if we actually could!

Our strategy was to "divide and conquer." While I doled out bedtime snacks to the little ones, Dick patiently listened to Grandmother's stories for the sixtieth time. Then Walter took over, calming Grandma Jessie's nighttime fears, while Dick made sure three little sets of teeth got brushed. While Walter read a bedtime story, I helped Grandmother look for the papers she imagined she had lost.

By nine o'clock, the younger children were settled in their beds and drifting off to sleep. But there was nothing "settled" about Grandma Jessie. Just as my parents predicted, she couldn't relax or rest.

"Oh my, are Bill and Frances going to be all right? What if they have an accident?" Grandma Jessie paced the floor. Pacing from her bedroom, through the living room, dining room and kitchen, and into her bedroom again, she walked in an endless circular pattern.

I soothed Grandma as best I could, while Walter and Dick snuck off down the hall and cooked up a plan.

"Dorothy, go sit with Grandma Jessie in her room for a while," Walter came and whispered in my ear. "Keep her there till we call you, okay?"

I took Grandma's hand. "Hey, Grandma, would you show me your crocheted teacup and saucer. How does the cup stand up like that?" I coaxed. Obligingly, Grandma led me into her room.

Within minutes, Dick beckoned me into the hallway. "Hurry, now, let me have your wristwatch." Quickly, he spun the hands on the small dial.

Time flew that night, as 9:15 became 11:15 in a matter of seconds. I looked around. Every clock had "magically" changed.

Grandma was soon wandering the house again, but we were ready for her. "Grandma, it's way past time for bed. Mother and Dad will be upset to come home and find us all still up," I reasoned.

She quietly studied the kitchen clock, then the living room clock, then my watch. "Oh, my, it's late!" she declared, and she shuffled off to bed.

Now we suddenly realized the three of us would have to turn out the lights and retire, too. We wouldn't have to be asleep, but we'd have to be as quiet as if we were!

The only other sound that night was the ringing of the telephone. I hurried to silence the bell. At the other end of the line, I heard Dad's strong voice. "It's intermission. How's your Grandmother? We can come on home now if you need us."

"Oh no, Dad," I whispered. "Everything's fine. We've all gone to bed. It's so late," I teased, quickly recounting our strategy.

"That's using your heads," Dad laughed. "I should've known you kids would figure out something. Your mother will be delighted."

I returned to my room. There was plenty of time to think before sleep overtook me. Come morning, things would still be the same. Children would fuss. Laundry would get dirty. Grandma would become distraught.

But for one night, my parents had a chance to be a newlywed couple again.

~Dorothy Palmer Young
Chicken Soup for the Caregiver's Soul

92

My Fairy Tale

The best way to mend a broken heart is time and girlfriends.
~Gwyneth Paltrow

He was the stuff fairy tales are made of—not unrealistically suave, but definitely charming. Tall and handsome, he was a prince by all conventional definitions and had the ability to steal unsuspecting young girls' hearts.

Our first kiss was perfect, and from that moment on, our relationship soared. Some days, he picked me up early for school so that we could eat breakfast together, and other days we sneaked away for snowball fights during study hall. On weekends, I watched him play soccer, and he came to all of my softball games. And then we'd end our week with the ritual of a Saturday night movie at his house. Without fail, we talked on the phone every night until we fell asleep. A few months into our relationship, I had no time for anyone but him. But at the time, I liked it that way. I was perfectly content to be with him every second, because I was, without a doubt, in love.

But sometime during our nine month walk in the clouds, the honeymoon stage ended, and our relationship lost its spontaneity and sparkle. Saturday nights spent together became routine, and phone calls and kisses became as natural and expected as breathing.

On one particularly cold June day, Chris broke up with me. He said that he woke up that morning and realized he didn't love me. He said our relationship consisted of nothing but the memories of our past. It was two days before our nine month anniversary. I felt empty inside, and the thought of being alone was uncomfortable and scary. Moreover, the person on whom I depended to pull me through hard times was the cause of my pain. My heart literally hurt.

Not knowing what else to do, I ran to a familiar place, Ashley's house. It was a place I hadn't visited often in the nine months before this afternoon. I stood at the door, and Ashley, seeing my tears, immediately understood what had happened. Within an hour, my three closest friends, the girls I had once spent so much time with, all arrived at Ashley's house. For the next two days, we camped out at Ashley's and analyzed every aspect of Chris's and my relationship, attempting to pinpoint where it went wrong.

Unable to form any meaningful conclusions, we agreed that we would never understand the male population, and so we moved on to bashing Prince Charming until he was reduced to a creature with the appeal of a toad. It felt good, and I even caught myself laughing for brief moments. Slowly, I began to reclaim my pre-boys, pre-broken-heart days with a little more wisdom and experience than I had before. I realized that life would go on, and I loved and appreciated my girlfriends for that invaluable realization.

Toward the end of our healing party, while we were laughing over ice cream sundaes, Erica looked at me and said, "We've missed you." The truth was, I had really missed them, too. I had unfairly neglected them in the midst of love's wake, and the past two days had shown me just how precious my friends were.

When love had removed its blindfold and all was said and done, I realized that maybe I hadn't had such a fairy tale boyfriend after all. What I had were fairy tale friendships. It took a heartbreak to realize the special gift I possessed all along: my girlfriends.

~Kathryn Vacca
Chicken Soup for the Teenage Soul III

93

Reality Check

He was perfect. The exact mix of bad boy and intellectual that I was looking for, and good looking, as well. He was six feet, three inches, with a medium build, dark brown hair and deep brown eyes I just wanted to gaze at for days. And probably did, when I got the chance. As much as I like to pretend that I'm above all those cheesy crush feelings, I'm not.

The best part of this particular crush was that, unlike so many of my others, he actually knew my name. He had my number stored in his cell phone and even used it! I swear I used to hear wedding bells when I saw his name on my Caller ID.

My friends were not his biggest advocates, to say the least, and you can bet they let me know it. I heard everything from "You can do so much better," to "He sucks, plain and simple." My logic remained unchanged. If I could do better, why wasn't I?

I couldn't understand why my girlfriends didn't like him. Okay, so maybe he used to show me his photo albums and point out all the girls he had dated. Yeah, he'd complain about the lack of an available hot girl in his life. But they didn't know him like I did. Isn't that always the case?

A few days before Valentine's Day, he sent me an instant message saying, "Red, pink, peach, white or yellow?" I immediately knew that he was asking me my preference in rose colors. I selected red, the most romantic kind. After the color, we debated between a dozen or a half-dozen. After that—to include a card or send them anonymously.

He had mentioned during the conversation that he simply wanted to "make some girl's day." I was convinced that I was "some girl." Three hours after we began chatting, we had chosen half a dozen red roses, to be sent anonymously. We had also, unfortunately, discussed all the possibilities among the girls he could surprise. When I playfully suggested that I be the recipient of the Valentine's Day bouquet, I was swiftly shut down. "Don't be greedy," was his reply.

After the incident, I immediately ran down the dorm hallway to relay the entire conversation to my friends. I was only partially upset about the outcome. I was more excited that he had just spent three hours asking me for advice. They rolled their eyes, knowing all they could do was wait it out, and eventually, I'd come to my senses.

Valentine's Day arrived, and since I had no date, I went about my business as I would any other day. When I returned to my dorm room after classes, I was shocked to find a vase of red roses on my dresser. I counted them—exactly six. I searched for a card and found none. Could it be? I knew it! He had gone through the pains of making me so sure I wasn't going to get those flowers just so I would be extra shocked when I found them. A few moments later, four of my closest friends bounded through the door. They handed me a small envelope. "It goes with the flowers," they said. I opened it, and it read:

> *Roses are red*
> *Violets are blue*
> *He doesn't love you*
> *But we sure do*

Yeah, I was disappointed, but only for a minute, because I realized at that moment how foolish I had been. I hugged my friends, and the unworthy boy was forgotten. My friendship with him has since faded, and frankly, I don't miss it. As for those four girls? They're keepers.

~Arielle Jacobs
Chicken Soup for the Teenage Soul IV

94

Missing the Dance

I couldn't believe he was asking me. My two best friends had gotten dates weeks ago, so I had given up hope of anyone asking me to the winter dance. Rick was the coolest guy in the senior class! And he wanted to go with me?

"Are you serious?"

"I've already taken care of the tickets, and my parents will let me use their car," he assured me.

My mouth worded, "Yes," as my heart leaped with joy. I had never been to a formal dance before, and now was my chance. This would be the best night of my life.

The moment I got home I told my mom about Rick's invitation. Immediately, she took me shopping to find the perfect dress. We decided on how to fix my hair and what color nail polish to wear.

Before I knew it, days had passed. I couldn't sleep at all. Butterflies fluttered in my stomach, and my head was throbbing. Friday morning I woke up, and the whole world seemed to spin. I tried to lift my head off the pillow, but I couldn't move.

"Honey, you're going to be late for school. Are you okay?" My mom came into the bedroom. Her hand went to my forehead. "Oh, no! You've got a fever."

I didn't feel hot; I felt cold, very cold.

My mother helped me dress and drove me to the doctor. I had been there only a few minutes before my doctor called an ambulance.

I couldn't understand what he was telling me. All I could hear was a muffled, "One-hundred-four degree fever."

The hospital looked so blindingly bright as a nurse stuck two IVs in my arm. I didn't remember seeing her come into my room, only the blanket being thrown on top of me. "Cold, very cold," I responded.

"It's filled with ice," she explained. "You have a bad infection. Your doctor ordered fluids and antibiotics for you. Just rest."

I closed my eyes.

It seemed only a few minutes later when I heard my doctor's voice. "Good morning. I'm glad you slept through the night. Luckily, we've brought your temperature down. You are one special girl. You have a very serious infection, but it seems we have it under control."

"Mom?" I gasped. "Dad?"

"We're right here." My mother grabbed my hand.

I looked up at them.

"Did I miss the dance?"

My mom smiled. "I called Rick. I got his number out of your address book and let him know that you were in the hospital."

"Oh, no," I cried.

"There will be other dances," said my doctor. "Be thankful you'll be alive to see them."

Days passed, and I got increasingly stronger and no longer had a fever. The medical staff discovered that I had developed a bad strep infection, which my doctor treated with antibiotics.

I hadn't heard from Rick at all. That bothered me. I worried that he was angry. Not only had I missed the dance, but I had let him down. Who could blame him if he never spoke to me again?

The same nurse who had given me my IVs came into my room holding a hospital robe. "Put this on," she said.

"Why? Aren't I going home today? I have a gown on already."

She just smiled and left, shutting the door behind her. I didn't feel like putting on the robe, but I did what she asked. Maybe there was another X-ray or test my doctor needed before I could be released.

Suddenly, the door swung open. Standing before me were my

parents holding balloons and a CD player, my two best friends in formals, and their dates and Rick in tuxedos.

"Would you care for a dance?" Rick asked. "Just because you missed the winter dance doesn't mean we can't have our own right here, right now."

Tears came to my eyes. "Sure," I stammered.

The nurse closed the curtains and left only the bathroom light on. My friends coupled together as Rick wrapped his arms around me and began to sway to the music.

"I'm so glad you're okay," he said. "I called your parents every night to check up on you."

"They didn't tell me." I pulled at my hair so it would look brushed.

"Don't worry," he smiled. "You look beautiful."

My friends and I danced for what seemed like hours.

We didn't mind the people watching from the hall or my parents dancing beside us. My hospital robe was less than formal, but I didn't care. When the CD was over, Rick helped me into a wheelchair and took me downstairs to his parents' car, which was waiting to take me home.

I will never forget that afternoon for as long as I live. I didn't have my hair done or a pretty dress on, but I felt truly beautiful and truly loved.

~Michele "Screech" Campanelli
Chicken Soup for the Christian Teenage Soul

Sketches

*I've always thought that a big laugh is a really loud noise
from the soul saying, "Ain't that the truth."*
~Quincy Jones

During fifth grade recess, my girlfriends and I wouldn't play kickball with the other kids. Instead, we stayed behind at the benches and made pencil sketches on blue-lined binder paper.

We sketched puppies, flowers, kittens, and my personal favorite—the future prom dress, with every detail, down to the long staircase (for the big entrance) and a crystal chandelier.

I was ten then; prom was seven years away. I was Chinese, so I didn't have a quinceañera, debutante ball or Bat Mitzvah. Prom was the one shot I had to live my Cinderella story. My only other opportunity to live the princess fantasy would be my wedding day—and I wasn't going to wait that long!

I needed prom. It was what high school was all about. Where even the most gawky of girls (me) could become a swan. It was puberty's heyday.

The dresses I sketched were fit for a night of being swept away by a prince. But I could never get a sketch quite right. All the other girls drew their dresses so evenly, earnestly and beautifully. I couldn't do it. All the while, I had a very picture-perfect vision of my prom even though it never translated well onto paper.

Years into my teenage life I still sketched these future moments.

Not with paper, but in my mind—sometimes down to the last syllable of imagined dialogue. Sometimes down to the most minute detail of weather or scenery. I sketched first kisses, weddings, relationships and big, important events that transform a life into a life.

Sometimes I think I've spent more time sketching than living.

Two days before the prom my boyfriend left me for someone else. He had a new girlfriend and a new date for the prom. I ended up going with my best friend, Danielle.

I wore a black slip dress. As Danielle and I danced, I tried not to look at my ex while he danced with and kissed his date. I tried not to cry about how wrong this whole scene was.

There was no romancing. No grand entrance. And it was expensive, the pictures especially, considering my eyes were closed and puffy. But I had Danielle, my best friend, to keep me from breaking down and crying through the night. I came home before midnight—not how I imagined my prom would turn out.

Danielle called me the other week while I was at work.

She said, "Remember the prom we went to? Can you believe it? That was a pretty funny night. And we are probably the only couple from that night who still talk to each other now!"

"Yeah, I guess that's true. I'm sure nobody is still as close to their prom date as we still are. Do you think it's too late to get a refund on those prom pictures? My eyes are closed in them!" Danielle started laughing, then I started laughing, and before we knew it, we were laughing hysterically on both ends of the phone as we relayed details back and forth from that night.

When we hung up, I realized it's the "little stuff" in life that's important, like a phone call from a friend and a good laugh.

~Kristina Wong
Chicken Soup for the Teenage Soul IV

Chapter 13

Teens Talk

Relationships

In Love

Love is everything it's cracked up to be.
It really is worth fighting for, being brave for, risking everything for.
And the trouble is, if you don't risk anything, you risk even more.
~Erica Jong

Two of Me

I never thought I'd find myself
the day that I found you.
Plans for only
one of me
are future plans for
two.
Soul mates in this universe
that make the world surreal.
For when I'd given up on dreams
you showed me love is real.
And now that all my love for you
will never cease to grow,
please take me in your loving arms
and never let me go.

~Anne G. Fegely
Chicken Soup for the Teenage Soul on Love & Friendship

My Knight on His White Horse

There is no surprise more magical than the surprise of being loved.
It is God's finger on man's shoulder.
~Charles Morgan

I expected to meet my first love in a magical way. Not necessarily "knight on white horse" magical, but I had a definite picture in my head—tall, blond, chiseled body, deep voice, designer clothes. He would be romantic, smart and very witty. He would be perfect. One day he did come along, my perfect love, although his perfection wasn't quite there—at first.

He was five years older than I and about five inches shorter. He had a high squeaky voice, considering he was nineteen at the time, and a scrawny little body. He wasn't what you would call "good looking."

We met at the beach. A mutual friend introduced us. He was annoying and kept cracking jokes and flirting with me. Somehow, he ended up giving my friends and me a ride home that night.

I rolled my eyes as the car pulled up to us. The brakes were shot, the door was broken, and he had to sit on a phone book to actually see over the dashboard. I could not help but laugh at the situation. "How embarrassing," I thought. But he was far from embarrassed. He kept cracking jokes about his "trusty steed" and had us all laughing to tears. We stopped off at his house on the way home, and I asked him if I could use his bathroom. He stopped, turned and said, "Yes, but... those who use my bathroom must give me their phone numbers." He was grinning.

"Whatever. Here." I jotted down my number and then sought out the bathroom.

I guess you could say that was where it all started. We became friends instantly. He would take me out to dinner and to the movies. He even brought me as his date to a Halloween party and stayed by my side the whole night. That Halloween was the night I realized that Chris was more to me than just a friend. We came to the party as "hitchhikers that escaped from prison" and won the prize for most creative costume.

His creativity and silliness was what did it. That's how he won my heart. I was in love with this beautiful friend.

Did I tell him? Oh, no way! I was very proud... and very stubborn. I had been hurt many times before meeting Chris, and needless to say, had learned that love confessions are dangerous. But this was different; it felt real. We had been friends for almost a year and knew each other inside out. I knew that he liked me. He told me so all the time. I was confused. I didn't want to ruin the amazing friendship we had.

I hid my feelings for him for another year. It drove me crazy. He gave up on me and got a girlfriend, and I dated off and on; thus, we grew apart. I was never happy with any other guy. I compared every date and hug and voice to his. It hurt inside, and I denied my own true feelings and hid them very well until one day....

He had just broken up with his girlfriend, and I called out of the blue. He asked if I wanted to come over and watch a movie, and I agreed.

"We have some catching up to do," he whispered, his voice giving me chills.

"Yeah, you're right. I've missed ya.... You haven't grown, have you?" I joked.

"Just come over," he laughed. So I did.

It felt good to be back. I threw my arms around him immediately as I walked through the door. Our eyes met awkwardly, and I pulled away.

We talked about our lives, each other and ourselves. We talked for hours about everything and anything, until silence interrupted our conversation.

I had always wondered how it would feel to kiss him—soft, sloppy, passionate?

And in that moment I decided that I needed to know. Our eyes met, and I leaned in and kissed him. His lips were soft, the kiss perfect. I was floating in his touch, his arms, his affection. It had been two years of flirting and friendship, and finally we were trapped in the moment, between our own true feelings.

I spilled to him the truth about my feelings. I told him how scared I was that I would lose him as a friend, but that he had become much more than that to me. I told him that I had never cared about someone this way. I told him that he was beautiful and that I was falling in love with him. I even began to cry.

He smiled and kissed me lightly on the cheek. "I love you, too," he whispered. "And I know how you feel. We go perfectly together, Becca."

"I know, Chris." At that moment he was the most beautiful person I had ever seen, every inch, up to his perfect ears. His voice was music, his touch tender. That was when our friendship became more. We were in love.

Months passed and our stability floundered. Love is a roller coaster, and I must admit sometimes all the turns and twists made me sick. But through everything we had an amazing and beautiful relationship. He taught me how to love and admired my passion for life. He instilled confidence in me and supported my individuality.

Love has a tendency to fade. Ours did. We had given each other a lot, including the confidence to grow into our own people, and, ultimately, to grow apart. One day, I just didn't see the love in his eyes any more. His kiss was different. We both felt the slow drift apart, yet neither of us really wanted to admit that our fire was blowing out.

We had been together for a year and a half and, secretly, I knew, no longer.

Although our relationship ended, our connection stayed strong. My friends had always warned me never to date your best friend; that you will ruin your friendship and it can never be the same again.

Three years later, he remains one of my best friends. We have changed and grown. I am involved with someone new and wonderful, and so is he. And yet we still remain major priorities in one another's lives.

The fantasy of my magical man has faded, and I no longer search for perfection. I know that it doesn't exist. What I do know is that love is mysterious, beautiful, and often very unexpected.

~Rebecca Woolf
Chicken Soup for the Teenage Soul III

98

Only a Matter of Time

The smoke billowed out of the second floor windows. I covered my face with my backpack and used my chemistry book as a battering ram to bust through the windowpane. Smashing through the apartment door with one hand, I grabbed the child with the other and ran to safety, coughing but alive. And there was Bethany, who happened to be passing by. "You're a hero!" she said as she flung her arms around me.

I had a rich fantasy life. It all revolved around the object of my obsession, Bethany Howe. Everyone called her B.H. Except for me. I loved to say the name "Bethany"—to myself, of course, because I rarely got within ten feet of B.H.

I first saw Bethany during our freshman year. I noticed her because she wasn't trying to be cool. I stood in silent solidarity with her on that front. I had given up trying to be cool in junior high. I learned my lesson after an unfortunate skateboarding incident. I won't go into too much detail, but it involved board shorts my mom constructed out of a pair of my dad's old Levis cotton Dockers—an attempt to make a fashion statement that failed miserably.

Not trying to be cool can be very liberating. It takes away a lot of pressure and stress. I didn't think Bethany had a skateboarding incident in her past. She was too cute for that. Her lack of coolness was just cool.

Two years went by and not much happened between B.H. and me. I would see her at lunch. Sometimes we had class together. The more I learned about her, the more I liked her. She had a part-time job at a daycare center after school. She liked to go to the beach. She had the most amazing smile.

I decided I would have to get her to notice me. I joined the track team for Bethany. I spent two hours hitting tennis balls off the backboard every day so I could make the tennis team — for Bethany. I read the newspaper every morning so I'd have something interesting to say in case Bethany decided to talk to me. Bethany was a good influence on me, even though we never spoke. I made new friends, became more talkative and outgoing, and got into pretty good shape. Now if I could only meet her.

One day, I was asked by one of my teachers, Mr. Houston, to go to the office to get some paper and videos. As I walked down the hall, I was lost in thought, having another Bethany fantasy. I loaded up on the paper for Mr. Houston and went to the A.V. room to get the videos. I was arranging the paper, thinking about Bethany. And then I heard a voice. "This tape is checked out."

"Huh?"

"Excuse me, but the tape you want is checked out."

I looked up. It was Bethany. She worked in the A.V. center.

"Hey, I know you," she said. "You're in my history class."

I stammered something, inaudibly.

Then she stammered something, inaudibly.

Then we both tried to speak at once.

I was flustered. I wasn't prepared. Our first meeting wasn't supposed to happen like this — it wasn't even a good hair day, for me. I started to leave, then turned back and muttered, "See ya, Bethany."

"What did you call me?"

"Bethany. Isn't that your name?"

"Yeah, but everyone calls me B.H."

"But Bethany is such a pretty name."

"Really?" She laughed nervously.

"Yeah."

I couldn't believe it. We were actually having a conversation.

"Aren't you on the tennis team? I go to the matches sometimes."

"Tennis?" I couldn't remember what that was. Something about a racket and a court was all I could remember as she spoke to me. Then I remembered I had a match that afternoon and before I could talk myself out of it, I invited her.

The bell rang before she could answer and I realized Mr. Houston was waiting for his supplies. After school, I suited up for my match. I scanned the stands for Bethany but didn't see her. I can't remember the score but I won. I hoped she saw when I made an especially good volley or an ace.

After the match, I still didn't see her. I started walking toward the locker room when I heard my name being called. I didn't even know she knew it. I'd always hated my name but it sounded like an angelic ballad when she said it.

That afternoon at the entrance to the guy's locker room I asked Bethany out. She told me she'd had her eye on me since freshman year too, but our paths never seemed to cross. I'm kind of glad it took so long for us to get together. The day Bethany and I met, even though my hair was messed up and I wasn't wearing my favorite shirt, I was ready to meet her. And I didn't even have to brave a burning building.

~Tal Vigderson
Chicken Soup for the Teenage Soul IV

99

Nineteen

Happiness is like a kiss—it feels best when you give it to someone else.
~Author Unknown

There he was, standing out in the crowd at the mixer that the student council puts on every year at the beginning of school. He had grown well over six feet, gotten contacts, developed a tanned and chiseled face, and let his dark brown hair grow enough to curl adorably. It was the first time in two years that I'd seen him—Michael, my ex-boyfriend from back in middle school. He was the first boy I'd ever gone out with.

To get a better look at him, I gathered up the courage to ask him to dance, and he didn't run away screaming. We slow danced.

After the mixer, I couldn't stop thinking about him. I realized that the old crush I had had on him was reviving itself, and I wanted to see him again. Considering our history, I should have beaten my head with a board until I fell unconscious. Two years before, we had dated for a month and then he told me that he loved me. I dumped him because of it. A week later, when I told him what happened, we got back together. His friends took it upon themselves to disapprove. They kept telling me that I wasn't good enough for him, that I was going to break his heart. They told him the same thing. I guess they got the best of him, because he dumped me a few weeks later over the phone.

None of that mattered to me anymore. I wanted to get to know this ex-boyfriend again—this intriguing stranger.

I decided to take a walk and "just happened to pass by" Michael's house, which was a mile down the road from mine. I walked by it... passed it... turned around to pass it again... and again. I wanted so badly to go up and knock on the door, but I was scared. What if he thought I was a freak or a stalker?

I gathered some courage, headed up the walkway and banged on the door. I could hear his dogs going crazy inside the house, and soon Michael was standing at the front door, staring at me like I was some sort of mutant.

"Hey," his deep voice boomed.

"Hey," I managed to squeak. "I was just taking a walk and... ummm... I know this is weird... but do you want to... ummm... come for a walk with me?" I was so articulate and intelligent sounding—NOT!

"Uh... sure." To my amazement, he went to get his shoes, and before I realized that the sky hadn't fallen, we were on our way, in the direction of my house.

We walked along and talked about what had happened in our lives while we were apart. Michael used to be unbearably shy, but he didn't seem afraid to talk to me anymore. We chatted about ice hockey, school, my year at private school and everything else that we could manage. We wound up in a park near my house. I stopped and turned to face him when I reached the jungle gym. I curled one hand over the cool metal, leaning on it.

"You know, I still have all the notes you used to write me in eighth grade," I said, teasing him.

"Really?" He smiled as his entire face lit up at the thought. "I have all of yours, too."

"Are you serious?" I couldn't believe that he'd actually cared enough to keep them. I had thought myself sentimental, maybe even a little weird for doing the exact same thing.

That's when I felt his hand close over mine. I lowered my gaze to stare at it. His other hand wound around my waist. I glanced up into his eyes for a brief second, totally bewildered, and then, he kissed me.

Now, I've been kissed before, but I can still feel his gentle lips pressing down on mine. It had to be the most impulsive thing that he'd ever done. We just stood there kissing, until I realized what was going on.

As I pulled away, I whispered, "Nineteen more."

While we were together in junior high, Michael had given me a little certificate that was good for twenty kisses. We never used it. I think maybe he was afraid of me or of kissing. Or both.

Michael didn't need me to explain it. He just smiled and leaned forward to kiss me again.

~Kathleen Benefiel
Chicken Soup for the Girl's Soul

Prince Charming

When I was a little girl, I used to read about love in all my favorite fairy tales. However, it wasn't until I experienced love myself that I really understood what it meant and how truly remarkable it could make me feel....

We had been friends for a while, and he knew almost everything about me. If I was upset or angry, excited or scared he could always tell and knew exactly what to say to make the moment that much better. Whenever I had a bad day and just needed to cry, he always had a joke to cheer me up and make me smile. When something exciting happened, he'd be there to share in my happy tears and laughter. He knew me for who I was and I loved him just for being my friend.

As I entered my last year of high school, I had yet to find Mr. Perfect. My friends kept telling me that I was looking too hard, and that when I least expected it, Prince Charming would sweep me off my feet. It seemed to me as though everyone around me was finding his or her high school sweetheart, and there I was, left behind with nobody. Prom was approaching, and everyone's biggest fear was going to his or her high school prom dateless. I knew that I was no exception and realized that I had to start looking again. I went out on dates with countless guys, but none of them seemed right. None of them were what I was looking for.

One night as I lay trying to fall asleep, something hit me which scared me more than anything had before. I loved him. My best friend... I loved him. I didn't know what to do, I didn't know what to think or feel or say. My heart was racing as I looked through pictures of us laughing and having fun together. The one person who I had never expected to feel this way about, yet here I was, so sure that I loved him. I cannot even explain the feeling I felt that night. It was if my heart had found its other half. Should I tell him? Should I leave it be? Not knowing if I'd have the courage to give it to him, I grabbed a piece of paper and wrote him a letter that will forever remain in my mind and heart:

Dear Jo,

As the time comes for us to almost graduate, it seems as though the past year has flown by. I knew from the moment we met that we would be forever friends. You have been there for me through the good times and the bad, and you have never let me down. Yet here I am writing to tell you something that I never thought I would. Telling you something that I never thought I could. You know how sometimes we talk about love, and I always tell you that I've never been in love before. That the only love I know is that of which my mother read me when I was a little girl. I was wrong. As I lay in my bed tonight I realized something that until now has been so unclear. You've been my best friend for so long that I was too scared to let myself love you... but I do. I do love you. I know it, because you are all I ever think about. Your happiness at times means more to me than my own. My binder is filled with doodles, all of which say your name. I circle your name, because we both know that hearts can break but circles go on forever. I know that I love you, because when I'm upset, the mere thought of you makes me feel a little better. I know that I love you, because when you are with any other girl... I'm jealous. I don't know what else to say, but I know that my heart never lies, and it is telling me that each ounce of my being... loves you.

Love always and forever

Your best friend,

Casey

The next day at school I slipped my letter into his locker, fearing what would happen. Would I lose the love of my best friend? Or would I gain the love of the person who I had loved for so long? The day seemed never ending. It dragged on for so long that the minutes turned into hours, and the hours into what felt like weeks. As the final bell rang, my heart began to pound. As I approached my locker, I noticed that there was a little piece of paper sticking out through the vent. I ran over, and grabbed the piece of paper. The few words written filled my heart with a love greater than I thought possible:

Dear Casey,

I never thought someone could put into words what I was feeling.

How did you know how much I loved you?

Love always,

Jo

I shoved the note in my pocket, and with a tear in my eye I took a nice long walk home. For the first time in my seventeen years I was overcome with a love that was greater than those found in the fairy tales. It was a love that filled my heart with this indescribable amount of happiness, and for the first time in my life... I had my very own Prince Charming.

~Michele Davis
Chicken Soup for the Romantic Soul

The Sound of Silence

There comes a time in a relationship when someone will "drop the L-word bomb," as they say, and in our five month relationship, it was Micah who did the duty. "I love you," he said. "I love you, too," I answered back. The words fell like paint out of my mouth. They were unnatural and tasted funny: so easy to say, and yet they were like a tough steak and I was a vegetarian.

It was my senior year in high school. I was eager to break out of the silly little life I had awkwardly outgrown, and Micah was the sailor who could rescue me from my desert island of high school kookiness. He did, I suppose, but it was more than that. He was like no one I had ever met. He treated me like I was the only girl in the world. If Cameron Diaz walked by, he wouldn't turn his head. I was all he needed and all he wanted. Everyone else was out of focus in his eyes while I was crystal clear. No one had ever loved me the way Micah had. No one else could convince me that, even after a wisdom tooth operation, I was beautiful, and that I had a "lovely" voice as I belted out Guns and Roses' "Sweet Child of Mine."

When Micah first told me that he loved me, I froze. We were lying side-by-side under the stars on the sand of Moonlight Beach when it happened. I had been told "I love you" before, but Micah was the first person who really meant it with every strand of his being. I had heard of out-of-body experiences, but had never really understood how they could happen. At that moment, though, I could actually see myself stiffen and visualize my words tumbling out of my mouth. He smiled at me, and we kissed. That moment stayed with me for weeks; in fact, it's still with me in the archives of my memory. We exchanged "I love yous" like baseball cards. And within a couple of weeks, "I love you" became our universal language. "I love you" meant hello, goodbye, I'm sorry, I'm happy, kiss me and thanks for lunch. Those three little words, those eight little letters, could sum up just about anything. I said them without thinking or feeling. I forgot that there was actually supposed to be meaning behind them. And then one day I realized that, even though I loved Micah and knew that I could fall in love with him, I was not "in love" with him, not yet. I had to tell him. I had to stop the hollow words that became the bookends to our verbal communication.

We sat in the silence of his truck for what seemed like hours.

"I love you," he said.

Silence.

"Babe? I love you." His voice rose, and his eyes became question marks. The sound of silence filled the interior and slowly rose like smoke out the window.

"Listen, Micah," I said. "Don't say that. Please. I'm not ready. I can't say it back right now. I mean, I love you, I do, but I'm not in love with you. Please give me time. I want to mean it, I want to mean it with my whole heart, and right now—I don't. I'm sorry." I looked up at him, into those glass eyes, waiting for them to break.

He smiled softly and nodded.

"Okay," he said. "You're right. I know how I feel. I am in love with you, Becca, but you need to find out for yourself. You need to tell me without my saying it first." He reached over and kissed me on the forehead.

"No more hollow 'I love yous,'" he said. "No more reciprocation. This isn't 'monkey see, monkey do!'"

I agreed, thanking him for understanding, and we went on, acting more and saying less.

Three weeks later, we were at the movies when it happened. Suddenly, with great force, my heart was flattened against my chest like wallpaper. I looked over at him and I knew. He was the most beautiful thing I had ever seen. He was glowing. All those times he had looked at me as if I was the world, and now I sat overcome by his presence and the tingles that filled my body. He was alive, the enigma of all that was heartfelt, and at that moment I was in love with him.

I lifted my chin and slowly moved my lips against his ear.

"I love you," I said, and this time my words were soft like cotton. I could feel my heart echo as the words fell out into the darkness.

He turned, slowly, and with a tear in his eye answered back.

"I love you, too," he said, kissing me.

And for a long time, even if Brad Pitt walked by, I wouldn't turn my head.

~Rebecca Woolf
Chicken Soup for the Teenage Soul on Love & Friendship

More

Chicken Soup for the Soul®

...

Chicken Soup for the Soul

Share with Us

We would like to how these stories affected you and which ones were your favorite. Please write to us and let us know.

We also would like to share your stories with future readers. You may be able to help another teenager, and become a published author at the same time. Please send us your own stories and poems for our future books. Some of our past contributors have launched writing and speaking careers from the publication of their stories in our books!

The best way to submit your stories is through our web site, at

www.chickensoup.com

If you do not have access to the Internet, you may submit your stories by mail or by facsimile.

Chicken Soup for the Soul
P.O. Box 700
Cos Cob, CT 06807-0700
Fax 1-203-861-7194

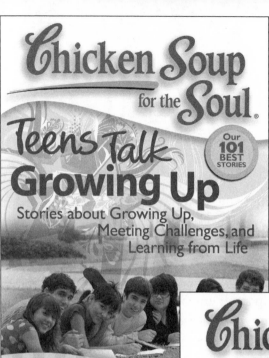

Teens Talk Growing Up

You have lots of friends in the Chicken Soup family, sharing their stories with you about growing up, meeting challenges, and learning from life. This book contains the best stories from Chicken Soup's library on the ups and downs that you and your friends experience every day.

Jack Canfield
& Mark Victor Han
edited by Amy New

Teens Talk Tough Times

Being a teenager is difficult. This book contains the best stories from Chicken Soup's library on tough challenges and issues that you and your friends face. Think of it as a support group that you can carry in your hand!

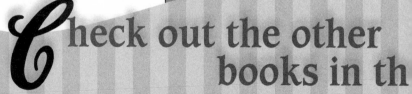

Check out the other
books in th

And for Younger Family Members...

Preteens Talk

Being a preteen is harder than it looks. School is more challenging, bodies are changing, relationships with parents are different, and new issues arise with friends. This book supports and inspires preteens and reminds them they are not alone, as they read stories written by other preteens just like them, about the problems and issues they face every day. This book contains Chicken Soup's 101 best stories and poems for preteens from its 15-year history. Stories cover friends, family, love, school, sports, challenges, embarrassing moments, and overcoming obstacles.

More books for *Teens!*

Chicken Soup for the Preteen Soul

Chicken Soup for the Preteen Soul 2

Chicken Soup for the Girl's Soul

Chicken Soup for the Teenage Soul

Chicken Soup for the Teenage Soul II

Chicken Soup for the Teenage Soul III

Chicken Soup for the Teenage Soul IV

Chicken Soup for the Teenage Soul on Tough Stuff

Chicken Soup for the Teenage Soul Teen Letters

Chicken Soup for the Christian Teenage Soul

Chicken Soup for the Teenage Soul Journal

Chicken Soup for the Soul: The Real Deal School

Chicken Soup for the Soul: The Real Deal Friends

Chicken Soup for the Soul: The Real Deal Challenges

Chicken Soup for the Teen Soul: Real-Life Stories by Real Teens

Chicken Soup for the Soul for the Teenage Soul on
Love & Friendship

More of for
Teens & Preteens!

Chicken Soup for the Soul: Christian Teen Talk
Christian Teens Share Their Stories of Support, Inspiration and Growing Up
"Our 101 Best Stories" series
978-1-935096-12-2

Upcoming for
Teens & Preteens!

Chicken Soup for the Soul: Teens Talk High School
101 Stories of Life, Love, and Learning for Older Teens
978-1-935096-25-2

Chicken Soup for the Soul: Teens Talk Middle School
101 Stories of Life, Love, and Learning for Younger Teens
978-1-935096-26-9

Chicken Soup for the Soul: Teens Talk Getting In...to College
101 Stories of Support from Kids Who Have Lived Through It
978-1-935096-27-6

About the

Chicken Soup for the Soul.

Authors

Chicken Soup for the Soul

Who Is
Jack Canfield?

Jack Canfield is the co-creator and editor of the *Chicken Soup for the Soul* series, which *Time* magazine has called "the publishing phenomenon of the decade." Jack is also the co-author of eight other bestselling books including *The Success Principles™: How to Get from Where You Are to Where You Want to Be*, *Dare to Win*, *The Aladdin Factor*, *You've Got to Read This Book*, and *The Power of Focus: How to Hit Your Business and Personal and Financial Targets with Absolute Certainty*.

Jack has recently developed a telephone coaching program and an online coaching program based on his most recent book *The Success Principles*. He also offers a seven-day *Breakthrough to Success* seminar every summer, which attracts 400 people from fifteen countries around the world.

Jack is the CEO of the Canfield Training Group in Santa Barbara, California, and founder of the Foundation for Self-Esteem in Culver City, California. He has conducted intensive personal and professional development seminars on the principles of success for over a million people in twenty-three countries. Jack is a dynamic keynote speaker and he has spoken to hundreds of thousands of others at more than 1,000 corporations, universities, professional conferences and conventions, and has been seen by millions more on national television shows such as *The Today Show*, *Fox and Friends*, *Inside Edition*, *Hard Copy*, *CNN's Talk Back Live*, *20/20*, *Eye to Eye*, and the *NBC Nightly News* and the *CBS Evening News*.

Jack is the recipient of many awards and honors, including three honorary doctorates and a *Guinness World Records Certificate* for having seven books from the *Chicken Soup for the Soul* series appearing on the *New York Times* bestseller list on May 24, 1998.

To write to Jack or for inquiries about Jack as a speaker, his coaching programs, trainings or seminars, use the following contact information:

Jack Canfield
The Canfield Companies
P.O. Box 30880 • Santa Barbara, CA 93130
phone: 805-563-2935 • fax: 805-563-2945
E-mail: info@jackcanfield.com
www.jackcanfield.com

Chicken Soup for the Soul

Who Is
Mark Victor Hansen?

Mark Victor Hansen is the co-founder of *Chicken Soup for the Soul*, along with Jack Canfield. He is also a sought-after keynote speaker, bestselling author, and marketing maven.

For more than thirty years, Mark has focused solely on helping people from all walks of life reshape their personal vision of what's possible. His powerful messages of possibility, opportunity, and action have created powerful change in thousands of organizations and millions of individuals worldwide.

Mark's credentials include a lifetime of entrepreneurial success. He is a prolific writer with many bestselling books, such as *The One Minute Millionaire*, *Cracking the Millionaire Code*, *How to Make the Rest of Your Life the Best of Your Life*, *The Power of Focus*, *The Aladdin Factor*, and *Dare to Win*, in addition to the *Chicken Soup for the Soul* series. Mark has had a profound influence in the field of human potential through his library of audios, videos, and articles in the areas of big thinking, sales achievement, wealth building, publishing success, and personal and professional development.

Mark is the founder of the *MEGA Seminar Series*. *MEGA Book Marketing University* and *Building Your MEGA Speaking Empire* are annual conferences where Mark coaches and teaches new and aspiring authors, speakers, and experts on building lucrative publishing and speaking careers. Other MEGA events include *MEGA Info-Marketing* and *My MEGA Life*.

He has appeared on *Oprah*, *CNN*, and *The Today Show*. He has been quoted in *Time*, *U.S. News & World Report*, *USA Today*, *New York Times*, and *Entrepreneur* and has had countless radio interviews, assuring our planet's people that "You can easily create the life you deserve."

As a philanthropist and humanitarian, Mark works tirelessly for organizations such as Habitat for Humanity, American Red Cross, March of Dimes, Childhelp USA, and many others. He is the recipient of numerous awards that honor his entrepreneurial spirit, philanthropic heart, and business acumen. He is a lifetime member of the Horatio Alger Association of Distinguished Americans, an organization that honored Mark with the prestigious Horatio Alger Award for his extraordinary life achievements.

Mark Victor Hansen is an enthusiastic crusader of what's possible and is driven to make the world a better place.

Mark Victor Hansen & Associates, Inc.
P.O. Box 7665 • Newport Beach, CA 92658
phone: 949-764-2640 • fax: 949-722-6912
www.markvictorhansen.com

Chicken Soup for the Soul

Who Is
Amy Newmark?

Amy Newmark was recently named publisher of Chicken Soup for the Soul, after a thirty-year career as a writer, speaker, financial analyst, and business executive in the worlds of finance and telecommunications.

Amy is a graduate of Harvard College, where she majored in Portuguese, minored in French, and traveled extensively. She is also the mother of two children in college and has two grown stepchildren.

After a long career writing books on telecommunications, voluminous financial reports, business plans, and corporate press releases, Chicken Soup for the Soul is a breath of fresh air for Amy. She has fallen in love with Chicken Soup for the Soul and its life-changing books, and found it a true pleasure to conceptualize, compile, and edit the "101 Best Stories" books for our readers.

The best way to contact Chicken Soup for the Soul is through our web site, at www.chickensoup.com. This will always get the fastest attention.

If you do not have access to the Internet, please contact us by mail or by facsimile.

Chicken Soup for the Soul
P.O. Box 700
Cos Cob, CT 06807-0700
Fax 203-861-7194

Chicken Soup for the Soul.

Acknowledgments

Chicken Soup
for the Soul

Thank You!

O Our first thanks go to our loyal readers who have inspired the entire Chicken Soup team for the past fifteen years. Your appreciative letters and emails have reminded us why we work so hard on these books.

We owe huge thanks to all of our contributors as well. We know that you pour your hearts and souls into the stories and poems that you share with us, and ultimately with each other. We appreciate your willingness to open up your lives to other Chicken Soup readers.

We can only publish a small percentage of the stories that are submitted, but we read every single one and even the ones that do not appear in a book have an influence on us and on the final manuscripts.

As always, we would like to thank the entire staff of Chicken Soup for the Soul for their help on this project and the 101 Best series in general.

Among our California staff, we would especially like to single out the following people:

D'ette Corona, who is the heart and soul of the Chicken Soup publishing operation, and who put together the first draft of this manuscript

Barbara LoMonaco for invaluable assistance in obtaining the fabulous quotations that add depth and meaning to this book

Patty Hansen for her extra special help with the permissions for these fabulous stories and for her amazing knowledge of the Chicken Soup library and Patti Clement for her help with permissions and other organizational matters.

In our Connecticut office, we would like to thank our able editorial assistants, Valerie Howlett and Madeline Clapps, for their assistance in setting up our new offices, editing, and helping us put together the best possible books.

We would also like to thank our master of design, Creative Director and book producer Brian Taylor at Pneuma Books, LLC, for his brilliant vision for our covers and interiors.

Finally, none of this would be possible without the business and creative leadership of our CEO, Bill Rouhana, and our president, Bob Jacobs.

Chicken Soup
for the Soul

www.chickensoup.com